A

BOOK

The Philip E. Lilienthal imprint
honors special books
in commemoration of a man whose work
at University of California Press from 1954 to 1979
was marked by dedication to young authors
and to high standards in the field of Asian Studies.
Friends, family, authors, and foundations have together
endowed the Lilienthal Fund, which enables UC Press
to publish under this imprint selected books
in a way that reflects the taste and judgment
of a great and beloved editor.

The publisher and the University of California Press Foundation gratefully acknowledge the generous support of the Philip E. Lilienthal Imprint in Asian Studies, established by a major gift from Sally Lilienthal.

Public Goods Provision in the Early Modern Economy

Luminos is the Open Access monograph publishing program from UC Press. Luminos provides a framework for preserving and reinvigorating monograph publishing for the future and increases the reach and visibility of important scholarly work. Titles published in the UC Press Luminos model are published with the same high standards for selection, peer review, production, and marketing as those in our traditional program. www.luminosoa.org

Public Goods Provision in the Early Modern Economy

Comparative Perspectives from Japan, China, and Europe

Edited by

Masayuki Tanimoto & R. Bin Wong

UNIVERSITY OF CALIFORNIA PRESS

University of California Press, one of the most distinguished university presses in the United States, enriches lives around the world by advancing scholarship in the humanities, social sciences, and natural sciences. Its activities are supported by the UC Press Foundation and by philanthropic contributions from individuals and institutions. For more information, visit www.ucpress.edu.

University of California Press
Oakland, California

© 2019 by Masayuki Tanimoto and R. Bin Wong

Suggested citation: Tanimoto, M. and Wong, R. B. *Public Goods Provision in the Early Modern Economy: Comparative Perspectives from Japan, China, and Europe*. Oakland: University of California Press, 2019. DOI: https://doi.org/10.1525/luminos.63

This work is licensed under a Creative Commons CC-BY license. To view a copy of the license, visit http://creativecommons.org/licenses.

Library of Congress Cataloging-in-Publication Data

Names: Tanimoto, Masayuki, 1959- editor. | Wong, Roy Bin, editor.
Title: Public goods provision in the early modern economy : comparative
    perspectives from Japan, China, and Europe / Edited by Masayuki Tanimoto
    and R. Bin Wong.
Description: Oakland, California : University of California Press, [2019] |
    Includes bibliographical references and index. | This work is licensed
    under a Creative Commons CC-BY license. To view a copy of the license,
    visit http://creativecommons.org/licenses. |
Identifiers: LCCN 2018038420 (print) | LCCN 2018042484 (ebook) | ISBN
    9780520972797 (Epub) | ISBN 9780520303652 (pbk. : alk. paper)
Subjects: LCSH: Public goods—History. | Japan—Economic
    conditions—1600–1868. | Prussia (Germany)—Economic conditions. |
    China—Economic conditions—1644–1912.
Classification: LCC HB846.5 (ebook) | LCC HB846.5 .P833 2019 (print) | DDC
    330.9/03—dc23
LC record available at https://lccn.loc.gov/2018038420

28   27   26   25   24   23   22   21   20   19
10   9   8   7   6   5   4   3   2   1

CONTENTS

PART IV: MANAGING THE FOREST

ILLUSTRATIONS

FIGURES

MAPS

TABLES

Many of our expectations regarding patterns of historical change in global history continue to be based upon understandings of the significance of what William McNeill called "The Rise of the West" in the title of a seminal work he first published in 1963. Marx and Weber are the nineteenth- and early-twentieth-century intellectual ancestors of this basic approach to human history. For many social scientists who provide us contemporary approaches to economic development and state building, the readings of history that inform their approaches to contemporary political priorities and economic possibilities continue to be based on a tradition of grand social theories. The metrics they employ for evaluating times and places beyond early modern Europe and the modern West remain anchored in European history and its connections to modern historical transformations of the nineteenth and twentieth centuries, however irrelevant those intellectual foundations appear to them.

Anxieties over the extreme simplifications that considerable numbers of scholars writing between the late 1960s and early 1980s utilized in their approaches to economic development and political change led a generation of scholars across the humanities and social sciences to question the limitations of metrics for historical change predicated on traits found in European societies and their white settler society offspring in other world regions. But as our empirical knowledge has subsequently expanded dramatically regarding other world regions we have done surprisingly little to begin the formulation of reworked metrics of evaluation that seek to retain elements of earlier understandings that appear applicable in other world regions at the same time as we formulate new measures of understanding the significance of practices not seen or underappreciated in early modern Europe and the modern West.

Scholars continue to be attracted to intellectually opposite poles of perception. There are those who persist in stressing the similarities and commonalities to any processes of change they deem desirable and positive. There are others who proclaim the significance of differences, as often cognitive as material, that signal distinctive and even incommensurate practices that separate the modern West from the experiences of many people in other world regions. These competing conceptual or even theoretical centers of gravity hinder the development of methodologies for navigating the force fields these ideas have created.

This book seeks to formulate elements of a methodology sensitive to these problems of similarities and differences in early modern Eurasia for the specific topic of public goods, especially those significant to economic performance. The challenge of confronting both similarities among and differences between places is a more general one that concerns many humanists and social scientists toiling in very diverse fields of inquiry and often deploying different tools for research. We will argue for an expanded definition of "public goods" to include all those created through nonmarket processes. In the modern era it was easy to see most such goods to be provided by government. But neither in contemporary times nor in the early modern era was this the case. Understanding our contemporary choices regarding public and private goods and the variety of "public-private partnerships" created to bridge the divide between them might well benefit from an awareness of early modern practices.

Since our expectations about how both markets develop and government provision of public goods expands are derived from European historical experiences, we are unlikely to look for practices in other world regions absent in Europe. In contrast, in this volume we will begin from an alternative empirical frame of reference, early modern Japan. We will propose the subject of an expanded definition of public goods to include those non-market-produced goods not limited to people with strong personal connections, which we find in early modern Japan. We believe the intellectual payoff can reach scholars with interests well beyond early modern Japanese history and generally will concern those with curiosity about the larger patterns of historical change that created possibilities in the modern era at least in part from the practices of early modern ancestors, both one's own and those of others.

The organization of the book, explained in more detail in chapter 1, invites the reader to first learn some basic practices responsible for public goods provision in early modern Japan and then takes us through three substantive areas of activity—poor relief and famine relief, infrastructure building, and forestry management—typically leading with Japanese examples and then adding both European and Chinese examples, which the reader can then compare. For European cases we deliberately choose Prussian cases (to be precise, cases that fall within the eighteenth-century boundaries of Prussia even if the practices themselves include those of earlier centuries) in all three case studies and offer far more limited evidence for the paradigmatic Western European case of England, providing a full case study only for poor relief. The addition of China allows multiple forms of comparison between Japan and both European cases and Chinese cases. From these comparisons can emerge multiple dimensions of variation and difference as well as an appreciation for what kinds of issues were conceived in similar ways even if addressed with somewhat different practices. These exercises can become elements of a methodology of analysis that aims to build a common framework for understanding public goods formulation and provision that doesn't depend solely on understandings derived from a selection of European practices made according to what was a crucial dynamic of state formation in that world region, namely, war making, that neither was uniformly important across Europe nor played the same crucial role in other world regions. Those possibilities will be further explored in chapter 16, the concluding chapter of this book. We hope potential readers of the studies to follow will have enough curiosity to make their way through a time and place foreign to most of us in order to discover guidance toward problems that should be of concern to all of us.

Many of the papers contained in this volume were presented at the conference held at the Graduate School of Economics, the University of Tokyo, in March 2015. We are grateful to Fabian Drixler, Koji Yamamoto, and Toyo'o Yoshimura for their inspiring presentations, and Eisaku Ide, Linda Grove, Kojiro Taguchi, and Osamu Saito for their constructive comments. The overall result at this conference was presented at the session in World Economic History Congress 2015, held in Kyoto, August 2015, in which we also received stimulating feedback from participants. In improving the contents for publication, we are greatly indebted to two reviewers of this project for their invaluable suggestions. We also would like to thank Linda Grove for her superb English editing work.

This research project was supported financially by Japan Society for the Promotion of Science (JSPS), KAKENHI Grant Number 25285104 and 17H02548. Papers in part 4 were financed by MEXT-Supported Program for the Strategic Research Foundation at Private Universities 2014–2018 as well. We are most grateful for their generous support.

June 2018

M. Tanimoto and R. B. Wong

Toward the Public Goods Provision in the Early Modern Economy

Masayuki Tanimoto

WHY "PUBLIC GOODS"?

Historically, to sustain and reproduce their economic lives, people have obtained goods and services in various ways. Although market transactions have taken a central position in the present economy and historical research has tended to stress this feature of economies due to an interest in economic growth, we must consider the possibly significant roles of nonmarket activities in the economy in order to grasp the entire picture of people's lives in history as well as the present world. How did people tackle issues that the market did not handle well? To what extent did their approach to finding solutions to their economic challenges reflect their political and social institutions as well as the structure of their economy? The present volume explores these questions by investigating efforts made for the provision of "public goods" in early modern economies from the perspective of comparative socioeconomic history.

The concept of "public" in this volume denotes the sphere in which people obtain goods and services for their lives through neither market transaction nor direct provision based on "personal" relationships. The latter, "personal" relationships, includes the relationships between a lord and his subject as well as family or kinship ties. Thus, this concept of publicness is defined in contraposition to "market" as well as "personal"[1] relationships, not in relation with the specific characteristics of providers such as government or state. The reason why we introduce the term "public goods," which originated in economics, is owing to the fact that this concept is useful in identifying our intention to use "public" in this manner. Economists conventionally define "public goods" according to their attribute of exhibiting nonrivalry and nonexcludability, traits that hinder proper provision through the market since providers are unable to obtain appropriate rewards due to free riders who enjoy benefits without incurring costs. As we discuss later, many of the cases we address in the present volume fail to fulfill fully the requirement of this definition, showing the attributes more of, in economics vocabulary, "club goods" (nonrivalry but excludable), "common pool goods" (nonexcludable but rivalry), or goods with positive externalities. Such expressions are cumbersome to use frequently and they share with the economist's definition of "public goods" the trait of being ill suited to market transactions, thus deserving to be regarded as "quasi-public goods" in the economist's array of more conventional concepts. The aim of this volume is to investigate how and to what extent "public goods" (hereafter without quotation mark and including "quasi-public goods") were provided to satisfy the needs for people's ordinary lives and reproduction. They are public in the sense that they are produced and distributed neither by market mechanisms nor through personal relationships, but in a political-social space including government actors and other social entities. The early modern period is suitable for considering this subject since these three components, markets, personal relationships, and a political-social space in which we find public goods (hereafter "public social space"), were sufficiently active to identify their functions in the economy, in addition to being sufficiently diverse in terms of the ways each component was weighed. The volume tries to disentangle the functions of these three components in order to identify the diversity of public goods provision across different early modern societies.

To clarify our approach in distinction to the existing literature, we first explain how we modify the concept of public goods, of the state, and of the demarcation of market and nonmarket to address features of the early modern economy. The discussions on economic development in history, specifically those linked to industrialization or modern economic growth, have paid great attention to the formation and development of the market economy as a set of institutions able to augment people's welfare, in theory by realizing the optimal resource allocation of the society. The literature that has been concerned with development in the early modern period, such as the proto-industrialization thesis[2] or the Smithian growth argument,[3] has revealed that actually market activities were spreading across both urban and rural sectors of the economy. The role of specific nonmarket practices for promoting the economic development and welfare has been a distinct concern, typically involving the discussion of the state's economic policies. In fact, there has been a long-standing debate regarding the role of mercantilism in early modern Europe, with recent literature reviving and even enlarging concerns about the state's roles in economic development in light of institutions and political economy (North and Weingast 1989, Acemoglu and Robinson 2012). In addition, the role of the state for augmenting the well-being of the subjects has been newly discussed in the early modern history and the fiscal state argument, apart from the viewpoint of mercantilism (Rosenthal and Wong 2011, Yun-Casalilla and O'Brien 2012, He

2013, Sng and Moriguchi 2014, Vries 2015). In much of this discussion, early modern states are expected to be the main provider of public goods, which, in light of the economic theory of "market failure," were undersupplied through the market transactions. In short, the good workings of the market in the early modern economies were complemented by the contribution of the state providing public goods.

This volume looks at nonmarketed goods that only involved the government as one of several actors. Quite a few goods and services were supplied in early modern societies by various kin groups, communities, lords, and governments to sustain and reproduce the economic lives of ordinary people. It is impractical to confine our focus to the activities directly related to the state in paying attention to the role of nonmarket activities in economic life. By taking the following three fields up, all of which were apparently essential for sustaining people's lives and reproductions in the early modern economy, this volume relativizes the role of states and the market/state dichotomy present in the available literature discussing the state formation and public goods provision.

In part 3, the chapters deal with infrastructure projects such as dikes, roads, and water control facilities. If we take a dike as an example, it appears to qualify as a public good since inhabitants near the dike are to be protected equally against a flood (nonrivalrous), without excluding neighboring inhabitants (nonexcludable). Strictly speaking, however, nonexcludability is unclear, as the expected benefits from the dike are confined to the inhabitants within a specific geographical area. The smaller the area, the larger the excludability of goods provision is. Therefore, we should recognize that nonexcludability has been rather weak in most of the dike cases, and this attribute is applicable to other physical infrastructures such as roads and water control facilities, which deserve to be defined as "club goods." In contrast, part 4 deals with cases that lacked the attribute of nonrivalry. Each chapter tackles the benefits obtained from the forest where the concept of "common lands" is often applied. The common lands are open to users (nonexcludable) and are zero-sum in terms of benefits (rivalrous), fitting the criteria of what Nobel laureate Elinor Ostrom labeled "common pool goods." Furthermore, goods and services with "external effects" are not provided optimally through market mechanisms despite the fact that they are excludable and rivalrous, since the benefits and/or costs are not properly paid for by the beneficiaries or imposed on the providers. The former case may result in an undersupply and the latter an oversupply of a good. For our discussion, the positive externalities are significant because the provision of non-market-produced goods can supplement the undersupply of goods in ways that may benefit people through their external effects. Poor relief, on which chapters in part 2 focus, can be discussed from this point of view, since it is beneficial for social order and peace at the same time as it enhances individual recipients' well-being.

Thus, the attributes of goods and services discussed in the three main subjects of this book, namely, welfare policies for the poor, infrastructure construction and maintenance, and forest management, can be recognized under the name of public goods in a theoretically relaxed sense, requiring provision outside the market to avoid undersupply. This recognition not only allows us to weave together three subjects having their own distinct strands of literature into a common fabric of discussion, but also enables us to contextualize the role of "state" as a provider of public goods. There is a good reason that certain public goods, for example, dikes, were provided by a local governing body, not by the state, because the excludable nature of the goods could limit beneficiaries geographically. In contrast, military capabilities, a representative example of pure public goods in economics textbooks, are provided almost exclusively by states of one kind or another in the early modern period. In fact, the fiscal state argument, coined by John Brewer for England and applied by scholars to other early modern European countries, evaluates the capacity of the state mainly through its fiscal capacities to absorb major military expenses (Brewer 1989, Glete 2002, Storrs 2009). To understand more fully the role of public goods in early modern economies, it is therefore necessary to go beyond the specific subject of the state's military expenditures in order to identify the goods and services affecting the economic lives of ordinary people.

This observation leads us to consider more carefully the nature of early modern states that are understood to be both centralizing their rule by growing their capacities and exhibiting features of what the social theorist Max Weber called "patrimonial states." The evolution of absolutism in Europe, the transition from the declining Ming to the rising Qing dynasty in China, and the establishment of the Tokugawa regime in Japan all occur during the sixteenth and seventeenth centuries. In many parts of Europe, as well as in China and Japan, central governments emerged that acquired wider governing ability over their territories and provided the geographical foundations of subsequent modern national states. On the other hand, it is also apparent that a specific ruling family whose household economy was closely related to its public finance dominated the "state" in this period. Inevitably, the government's behavior tended to be influenced by the ruler's arbitrary motivations, which might be different from that of the modern fiscal or tax state, as Joseph Schumpeter argued a century ago (Schumpeter 1918/1991). For Schumpeter, the relationship between a ruler and the subject in the case of a "patrimonial state" was a personal relationship between kings or lords and ordinary people, most often farmers. If people were provided with any goods or services based on their mutual personal relationship, it is hard to apply the concept of public goods to this "transaction" even though they were provided by a patrimonial state. Thus, this influential characterization of the historical nature of the state in the early modern period prevents us from conceiving naively the state as a main provider of the public goods specifically other than military affairs.[4]

To open up our abilities to understand public goods provision in early modern times, we can consider how the demand side for public goods to sustain and enhance people's economic lives can be met within the social and political space beyond familial and personal relationships. In fact, there were diverse ways of providing for the poor, from the use of lineage ties in China to the promulgation of the Poor Law in England, that is, from the usage of personal relationship to creating space for public goods provision. Even though poverty has been a universal phenomenon throughout history, demand for public goods was triggered under specific conditions in which the poverty emerged as a problem to which social responses were deemed possible and desirable. Similar aspects can be observed in terms of the existence of common lands, as they could alternatively be enclosed to form a self-sufficient economy such as lords' landed estates or thrown into the market by establishing exclusive private property rights on each plot. Thus, it is important to notice that the magnitude of the need for public goods depends heavily on the historical context determining the width and depth of nonmarket activities organized outside of self-sufficient entities. With a consciousness of the theoretical sense of publicness, the role of public goods provision in early modern economy should be explored by identifying specific historical and sociopolitical contexts in which they emerge.

COMPARATIVE APPROACH SETTING JAPAN
AS A BENCHMARK

The present volume explores the public goods provision and their diverse providers by comparing the cases in East Asia and Europe. In doing so, we have selected Japan, Germany (using early modern Prussia as a key ancestor of the late-nineteenth-century German state), and China to show three kinds of public goods provision quite different from Britain, which is conventionally understood as the paradigmatic case. This is an approach different from the major family of approaches to early modern global history that extends the tradition of comparing European historical practices to those of other world regions found in Marx and Weber and in much early modern economic history, the field in which this volume is most centrally located. In this approach to the early modern era, there are competing clusters of causal mechanisms intended to explain how Europeans came to achieve their political dominance and economic leadership in the nineteenth-century world, a situation that moved into a twentieth-century era of American political and economic prominence and created a longer modern era dominated by Western power and wealth. Within these accounts of economic and political change the subject of public goods provision doesn't occupy a very salient position. The subject is brought up both implicitly and explicitly in the fiscal state literature by historians recounting what European states spent their revenues on, but the subject is only sometimes connected to how these expenditures affected the economy. Because Great Britain was the first industrial economy and its fiscal state focused so heavily on building an eighteenth-century navy, which was the foundation of its global reach politically and supported its economic ventures into other world regions, the analysis of other public goods has not seemed so important to economic change of the early modern period.

In order to relativize this influential approach, we take advantage of the rich scholarship on the Tokugawa era (1603–1868) to take Japanese public goods provision as our benchmark case. We devote part 1 of the book to a concentrated introduction to Japanese practices to form the frame of reference to consider poor relief, infrastructure, and forest management in parts 2 through 4. Under the Pax Manchurea (the peace under the Qing dynasty) and the Pax Tokugawa regime, early modern East Asia showed sharp contrast with contemporary Europe in terms of their respective military affairs. Therefore, it is true to state that the case of Japan is well suited for a focus on nonmilitary public goods provision. Moreover, our choice is made more attractive for the following reasons. Although the fine-grained local and regional histories that are available for Japan are lesser known than their counterparts for countries in Europe, there exists a considerable literature in Japanese that supplies the foundation on which we build our framework that takes Japan as the benchmark case. The archival sources that make this possible include village documents, which originally remained in the house of the village head's descendant, as well as the official documents kept in the rulers' archives. They provide us with rich information on the economic and social situation of ordinary people, and reveal the relationship between public goods provision and the reproduction of people's lives. We think that the literature on Japanese rural history that is established on the solid archival foundation is one of the valuable resources for exploring early modern economy and deserves to be a benchmark that comparative discussion would rely on.

Regarding the village level documents, it is worthwhile emphasizing that they comprise basic administrative information such as "taxation" and the registration of residents and lands. Although no village was large in terms of area and population, comprising, very roughly, around one hundred households and five hundred individuals on average, the village was more the public governing body rather than just a private community, whose entitlement was delegated originally from the Tokugawa shogunate or *daimyō*s, rulers of the Tokugawa regime. It means the validity of the literature on early modern Japan is not just based on the archival advantage. Rather, it is the function of the rural village that deserves closer attention in considering providers of public goods in the early modern economies and that is most significant.

Interestingly, the autonomy of the village in terms of being the governing body evolved under the Tokugawa regime.[5] Because of the deterioration of its financial situation, the Tokugawa shogunate as well as other *daimyō* (domain) governments reduced outlays on social welfare and infrastructure maintenance in the latter half of the Tokugawa period. On the other hand, the village, which had been authorized as the basic unit for controlling peasants by "feudal" authorities, achieved a considerable level of autonomy in administration, accompanied by the formation of village-level "public finance." Although historians have conventionally used "public" to refer to certain activities of the warrior classes, we distinguish our focus on the economy from their focus on issues of social order involving the shogunate, *daimyōs*, and their warrior vassals. The Japanese publicness developed among villagers as relations within a social space that made possible collective decisions to respond to demands emerging among themselves, as well as to those placed on them by the warrior class that ruled them.

Furthermore, the cooperative unit of villages emerged and even evolved to form a public social space beyond the administrative unit of the village. It was a loosely integrated area called *Gunchū*, or other name, substantialized by the development of the rural economy based on market-oriented agriculture and proto-industry. The wealthy peasant-farmers led this development and behaved as "local notables," complementing or even substituting the task of public goods provision. The recent scholarship discusses this by using the term "regional society" defined in this historical context.[6] We think this recently revealed trajectory is distinct in emphasizing the role of "regional society" for public goods provision, and is expected to work as a catalyst that may clarify the focal point necessary for the comparative approach to be fruitful.

Based on this observation for the Japanese case, we can identify in Prussia people's dependence upon relationships between lords and subjects in which ordinary people had "personal" contracts with lords regarding the provision of necessities not provided through market transactions or their self-sufficient activities. The public social space emerged outside of this relationship. Here, the role of the Prussian state or its prototype in the Brandenburg Electorate mattered in the absence of a strong self-governing body such as the village present in the Japanese case. The Prussian generation of "common goods" from the ruler's side, discussed in a chapter of part 3, can be recognized in this context. The public social space in this sense enlarged as population increased between the eighteenth and nineteenth centuries, reaching an even-higher level of abstraction and generality after German unification in 1871.

The early modern Chinese state is similar to Prussia in terms of lacking any formal and relatively independent local or regional governing bodies. In fact, the chapters dealing with Chinese cases of poverty and famine relief, water control, and forest management commonly focus on the roles of the emperor and bureaucrats, addressing their policy practices and in some instances addressing the ideas underlying their behavior. On the other hand, the market transactions were much more prevalent in China even in the rural level, distinguishing it from the case of Prussia, and perhaps from Japan. Perhaps unexpectedly, the Chinese case offers a kind of early modern public goods more similar to modern meanings of public goods. The eighteenth-century Chinese state organized and funded goods outside market channels, incorporating in varied ways the efforts of lower-level bureaucrats and local elites to achieve public goods provision, in some ways anticipating some features of public goods provision more generally present in the modern era.

Thus, our comparative approach using Japan's case as the most common reference point highlights the diverse approaches to public goods provision across societies without invoking an "advanced" Western Europe as the standard of excellence against which other societies are typically found wanting. Even in the case of England, the chapter in part 2 discussing the workings of the English Poor Law in the local settings suggests the decentralized and regional nature of this nationally operating institution similar in some ways to regionally based public goods provision in Japan.

Together, our three main sites for what we consider three topics important to the economy give us alternative viewpoints from which to view the emergence of modern-era public goods. Choosing Japan as our primary reference point enables us to consider alternative ways in which early modern public goods provision was organized and how those practices became the background for modern-era developments. Our method seeks to identify the kinds of problems and opportunities to which elites and common people responded in early modern times by producing what we consider to be public goods. Furthermore, in general, to understand the varied constellations of practices occurring in different countries in the modern era, a look back at their early modern practices is useful. When we recall the typology of distinct kinds of modern welfare states noted by many scholars such as Gosta Esping-Andersen, who has written about "the three worlds of welfare capitalism," it seems inappropriate to assume naively the convergent path of public goods provision from the nineteenth century onward (Esping-Andersen 1990). Our expectation is not that modern practices remain closely similar to those of the early modern era but that modern-era features in each case can at times be seen as transformations of earlier practices, the absence of which would have made the subsequent practices less likely in one or more ways. Such an understanding supplements our conventional ways of understanding modern state formation and the place of public goods provision in that process. Certainly, it is worthwhile asking how, and to what extent, the structure of public goods provision in the early modern economy affected the diversity in public goods provision by the modern state. We will take up this subject further in our concluding chapter. The main work of the book, however, is to construct the beginnings of an early modern basis for forecasting the future into the modern and contemporary periods.

NOTES

1. Note that the term "personal relationship" in this volume does not exclude relationships based on "impersonal" foundations such as legal contracts based on the contemporary law system. The lords-subjects relationship in Prussia discussed in the following chapters exemplifies this aspect.

2. For the survey of literature, see Ogilvie and Cerman 1996/2010.

3. Mokyr 1990. For Japanese case, see an overview by Saito 2013.

4. In considering the military action carried out by the arbitrary motivation of the state owner of kings or lords, wars and military affairs might also have been done in the "personal sphere."

5. For the details of this discussion, see the chapter 2 of this volume.

6. For overviewing this discussion, see Sawai and Tanimoto 2016, chap. 2.

REFERENCES

Acemoglu, Daron, and James A. Robinson (2012). *Why Nations Fail: The Origins of Power, Prosperity, and Poverty*. New York, Crown Business.

Brewer, John (1989). *The Sinews of Power: War, Money, and the English State, 1688–1783*. London, Unwin Hyman.

Esping-Andersen, Gøsta (1990). *The Three Worlds of Welfare Capitalism*. Cambridge, Polity.

Glete, Jan (2002). *War and the State in Early Modern Europe: Spain, the Dutch Republic and Sweden as Fiscal-Military States, 1500–1660*. London, Routledge.

He, Wenkai (2013). *Paths toward the Modern Fiscal State: England, Japan, and China*. Cambridge, MA, Harvard University Press.

Mokyr, Joel (1990). *The Lever of Riches: Technological Creativity and Economic Progress*. New York, Oxford University Press.

North, Douglass C., and Barry R. Weingast (1989). "Costitutions and Commitment: The Evolutions of Institutions Governing Public Choice in Seventeenth-Century England." *Journal of Economic History* 49 (4).

Ogilvie, Sheilagh C., and Markus Cerman (1996/2010). *European Proto-Industrialization: An Introductory Handbook. Rev. ed.* Cambridge, Cambridge University Press.

Rosenthal, Jean-Laurent, and R. Bin Wong (2011). *Before and beyond Divergence: The Politics of Economic Change in China and Europe*. Cambridge, MA, Harvard University Press.

Saito, Osamu (2013). "Proto-Industrialization and Labour-Intensive Industrialization: Reflections on Smithian Growth and the Role of Skill Intensity." In *Labour-Intensive Industrialization in Global History*, edited by Gareth Austin and Kaoru Sugihara. London, Routledge.

Sawai, Minoru, and Masayuki Tanimoto (2016). *Nihon Keizaishi: Kinsei kara Kindai made* (Economic History of Japan: From the Early Modern Era to the Present). Tokyo, Yūhikaku.

Schumpeter, Joseph A. (1918/1991). *The Crisis of the Tax State*. In *Joseph A. Schumpeter: The Economics and Sociology of Capitalism*, edited by Richard Swedberg. Princeton, Princeton University Press.

Sng, Tuan-Hwee, and Chiaki Moriguchi (2014). "Asia's Little Divergence: State Capacity in China and Japan before 1850." *Journal of Economic Growth* 19 (4).

Storrs, Christopher, ed. (2009). *The Fiscal-Military State in Eighteenth-Century Europe*. Farnham, UK, Ashgate.

Vries, Peer (2015). *State, Economy and the Great Divergence: Great Britain and China, 1680s–1850s*. London and New York, Bloomsbury Academic.

Yun-Casalilla, Bartolomé, and Patrick K. O'Brien, eds. (2012). *The Rise of Fiscal States: A Global History, 1500–1914*. New York, Cambridge University Press.

PART ONE

Public Finance and Regional Society in Early Modern Japan

AS STATED IN CHAPTER 1, the present volume takes the Japanese case as the benchmark case for a comparative analysis of public goods provision in early modern times. In fact, parts 2, 3, and 4, dealing with poor relief, infrastructure, and forests, respectively, include at least one chapter on the Japanese case. (For a view of the Japanese Archipelago, see map 1.) Before delving into the individual issues, however, we devote this first part to a formulation of the frame of reference by investigating the structure of "public finance" in early modern Japan; we expect that this structure will generally reflect rulers' behavior toward public goods provision.

In this volume, we regard the Tokugawa regime (1603–1868) as the early modern period in Japan. During the Age of Civil Wars in the sixteenth century, there emerged prominent local lords with superior economic, as well as military, power. After winning the decisive battle at Sekigahara in 1600, the Tokugawa family acquired the power to rule over the entire Japanese archipelago and established a government called the Tokugawa shogunate in 1603. Their rule, which lasted for more than 250 years, came to an end in 1868. Although theoretically the Tokugawas were one among the many "feudal" lords, the Tokugawa shogunate behaved as a central government that monopolized diplomacy, coinage of specie, foreign trade,[1] and the authority to guarantee feudal lords (*daimyō*) the right to rule over a particular domain. It not only ruled the largest domain, worth six million *koku*,[2] and thus occupied one-fifth of the entire Japanese territory, but also benefited from monopolizing those aspects of power that fostered the rule of the shogunate. Under the shogunate reign, around 250 lords ruled domains, whose sizes varied from one million to ten thousand *koku*; there were also a certain number of direct vassals of the shogunate, the *hatamoto*, who ruled territories less than ten thousand *koku*.[3]

MAP 1. Japanese Archipelago

These lords and vassals had exclusive rights to impose levies on the lands they ruled, and maintained the autonomy to manage their revenue and expenditure, that is, "public" finance, as well as the jurisdictional power over residents in their domains. In return, each feudal lord was obliged to render "military duty" to the Tokugawa shogunate and had to stay at Edo (the capital, where the *shogun*—the head president of the shogunate—resided) every other year.[4]

There were two dimensions to the ruler-subordinate relationship in the Tokugawa regime. The first one was among the rulers, shogunate, and lords; the other was between the rulers and ordinary people. The ruling class comprised the lords and their vassals—the *samurai* (warriors)—who were based at the capital of each of the domains; the capitals were called castle towns (*jōka-machi*). This resulted in an urban concentration of the warrior class (*samurai*) and their families in the castle towns; further, they made up a remarkable 6% to 7% of the population. In addition, the merchants and craftsmen, who were originally supposed to serve the warrior class, also moved to the castle towns. Edo, with a population of around one million in 1700, was the largest castle town in Japan; it was followed by Osaka, a distribution center providing merchandise to Edo and other towns, and Kyoto, an agglomeration of traditional craftsman.

In contrast, the ordinary people classified as peasants (*hyakushō*) constituted around 80% of the population and resided in the villages (*mura*) in the countryside. Peasants usually paid the land levy in kind (rice) to the office of each domain through the village, the formal unit responsible for transferring the land levy to lords. A certain percentage of the domains' revenue was distributed to vassals according to their ranks. It is noteworthy that the village had to assume responsibility for paying in full the levy imposed on the lands within its territory, even though the levy was officially imposed on an individual household basis. This administration method, known as *muraukesei*, worked as a significant factor in establishing the village as the formal governing body. Thus, in theory, the residential place of rulers and ordinary people (except that of merchants and craftsmen) was geographically remote. It is also worth noting that the local notables discussed in part 1 did not belong to the ruling warrior class; they were drawn from the ordinary people, mostly of *hyakushō* (peasant) status, residing outside the castle towns.

Overall, the Tokugawa regime was organized as an agricultural economy that was mainly based on rice cropping in the paddy fields equipped with an irrigation system. The peasant households comprising stem-family members with a single inheritance system played the central role in the agricultural production, which used family labour and labour-intensive technology. On the other hand, market transactions were intrinsically integrated within the Tokugawa system because the rulers sold the land levy, which was, in principle, paid in kind, to purchase necessities, as well as luxuries, for coins minted by the shogunate. The development of the market economy and the growth of commercial sectors and nonagrarian production in the latter half of the Tokugawa regime were remarkable developments; this led to an increase in their contribution to the entire economy. We should also keep this trend in mind when we consider the changing patterns in "public" finance of the shogunate and lords.

The first chapter by Masayuki Tanimoto (chapter 2) examines the relative size of the Tokugawa shogunate's as well as domains' public finance to evaluate the changing role of rulers in the latter half of Tokugawa era. The chapter goes on to discuss the role of the regional society in public goods provision and as an incubator of industrial development by focusing on the activities of local notables comprising wealthy farmers, land owners, brewers, and local merchants. Overall, the chapter evaluates the substitutable and complementary roles of "regional society" as a provider of "public goods" in early modern and modern Japan.

The next two chapters deal with the details of public finance, concentrating on the relationship between the rulers and the villages or local notables under them. The second chapter by Kenichiro Aratake (chapter 3) focuses on rulers, investigating the various data derived from several individual domains, such as Hiroshima, Okayama, and Sendai. The chapter looks into the composition of the administrative organization run by the lords' vassal band. The author also observes and evaluates the actual workings of the individual vassals in terms of governing ability. Based on these observations, the chapter emphasizes the limited role of lords and vassals in administering villages and providing public goods for regional society.

The third chapter by Kazuho Sakai (chapter 4) discusses the same issue from another angle. Focusing on a case in which a lord outsourced the fiscal management activities to local notables, the chapter reveals that the local notables reduced the lord's household expenses and created a fiscal surplus. This surplus was used not only to repay the debt to intradomain creditors, but also to create a fund that they expected to spend on civil engineering, building, or relief projects for the domain's inhabitants. In other words, the local notables diverted the lord's finances to establish a financial basis for providing public goods to local inhabitants. This diversion can be recognized as a contribution to the formation of local public finance that played a significant role in public goods provision, well into early-twentieth-century Japan.

Through these chapters, part 1 reveals that the formation of the centralized power of the Tokugawa shogunate did not necessarily entail an increase in the public goods provision by rulers. Further, it emphasizes the role of villages and regional societies as the entities creating the public social space for public goods provision, with local notables, who had emerged from *hyakushō* (peasant) status, as the leaders.

Masayuki Tanimoto

NOTES

1. The profit from the monopolization of foreign trade began to decline from the latter half of the seventeenth century, owing partly to the so-called seclusion policy that began in the 1640s and limited trade by Japanese traders to only their Dutch and Chinese counterparts, mainly because of the depletion of silver mines in the Japanese archipelago.

2. During the Tokugawa regime, the size of territories was expressed in terms of the formal estimate of the annual production of rice by volume. *Koku* is the unit of volume used to measure rice and one *koku* is equivalent to 180.39 liters.

3. Of the six million koku ruled by the shogunate, two million were delegated to *hatamotos*.

4. Among the lords, there were variations in the duration of stay at Edo. For example, the lords in the Kanto area, which was the hinterland of Edo, stayed for around six months in Edo every year. The lord's family, wife, and underage children had to live in Edo all the time.

From "Feudal" Lords to Local Notables

The Role of Regional Society in Public Goods Provision from Early Modern to Modern Japan

Masayuki Tanimoto

This chapter reviews the workings of public finance in early modern Japan, that is, those of the shogunate and domains (*daimyōs*) and describes the changing patterns of public goods provision toward the nineteenth century—the period covering the transition from the Tokugawa to the Meiji era. The first section of this chapter examines the relative size of public finance of the Tokugawa shogunate and domains, with the purpose of evaluating the changing role of rulers in the latter half of the Tokugawa era. We go on to discuss the role of the regional society in terms of public goods provision by focusing on the activities of local notables, comprising wealthy farmers, landowners, brewers, and local merchants. The second section extends the scope of the discussion to the Meiji era. After pointing out the significant role of local public finance, which was institutionalized under the centralized Meiji government, the diverse activities of local notables, ranging from industrial investments in local enterprises to being the leader of local entities, are discussed in search of the driving force for public goods provision in the regional society.

THE CHANGING FACE OF "PUBLIC FINANCE" UNDER THE TOKUGAWA REGIME

The "Annual Tribute" as the Financial Basis of Rulers

We describe the financial situation of the rulers by examining their revenue and expenditure, and discuss the changing behavior of rulers in terms of public goods provision. Throughout the Tokugawa regime, the levy (*nengu*, in Japanese) imposed on lands and paid in kind (i.e., generally in the form of rice) constituted the major part of the revenue earned by the shogunate, as well as domains.

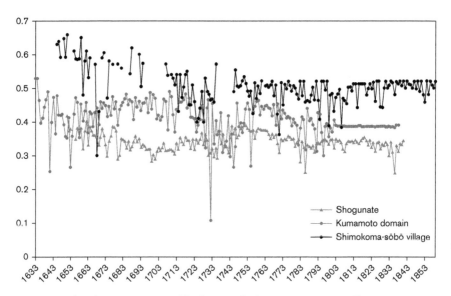

FIGURE 1. The Changing Patterns of "Tribute Rate": Shogunate, Domain, Village
Source: Sawai and Tanimoto 2016, figure 1.2, Tanimoto 2018, figure 2.

Hereafter, we use the term "annual tribute" for this levy, as literally implied by the Japanese term *nengu*. The amount of revenue collected by each domain was influenced largely by the volume of the annual tribute.

Then, how were the volumes of annual tribute determined? The rulers executed a cadastral survey to set the official estimation of yearly rice production per land area during an early stage of their reign, and a certain proportion of this official estimation was imposed on each landowner (usually a peasant household) as annual tribute. Figure 1 shows the long-term fluctuation of this proportion in each territory, that is, the imposed volume of the annual tribute divided by the formal estimation of production (hereafter, "tribute rate"). Figure 1 shows the tribute rates of three different areas. The grey line with triangle markers and gray line with circle markers express the weighted average of tribute rates among villages in the domains of the Tokugawa shogunate and the Hosokawa family (Kumamoto domain), respectively.[1] The remaining solid black line with circle markers shows the tribute rate of Shimokoma-sōbō village in the Yamashiro province, located in the western part of Honshū, the "Main Island" of Japan.

First, it is worth pointing out that the tribute rates in these figures stagnated or even declined over time. In fact, all the tribute rates remained stagnant after the latter half of the eighteenth century. Furthermore, we notice the relatively high tribute rate in the seventeenth century. This is particularly distinct in Shimokoma-sōbō village, where the tribute rate from the 1640s to the 1670s exceeded that from the late eighteenth century onward by more than ten percentage points. Even in the domains of the Tokugawa shogunate and the Hosokawa family, the relatively high rate in the mid-seventeenth century cannot be denied.

Second, we have to pay attention to the fact that the tribute rates indicated in these figures should be taken as a "nominal" index for measuring the distribution of the economic value between rulers and peasants. It was often the case that the official estimate of production per land remained at the level fixed during the seventeenth century, when the rulers had executed cadastral surveys, even in the subsequent centuries. Indeed, *muradaka*, the values of villages expressed in *koku*, were recorded as fixed numbers from the mid-seventeenth to the mid-nineteenth century in Shimokoma-sōbō village.

In contrast, there are several pieces of evidence that indicate the continuous increase in land productivities. The estimation of average land productivity of whole domains from the seventeenth to the nineteenth century suggests that rice yield per acre increased from 0.98 *koku* in 1650 to 1.30 *koku* in 1850 (Miyamoto 2004, 38), and the similar trends were exemplified by several villages in western Japan by aggregating the records from primary sources.[2] Considering the fact that a cadastral survey was rarely carried out after the eighteenth century, it is not unrealistic to conclude that the "substantial tribute rate" that accurately reflects the distribution of economic value to the ruling class was much lower than the level shown in the figures mentioned earlier. In fact, the estimation based on the industrial census in the Kumamoto domain carried out in 1842 revealed that the proportion of the total annual tribute to the aggregate value of production was not more than approximately 23% (Yoshimura 2013, 196–200). In other words, the weight of the public finance of rulers relative to the whole economy tended to deteriorate, at least during the latter half of the Tokugawa period. We have to bear this long-term trend in mind during the following discussion on expenditure.

The Changing Pattern of Rulers' Expenditure

Owing to the loss and destruction of the official documents, data sources for the analysis of the comprehensive financial expenditure of the Tokugawa shogunate are scarce. Table 1 compiles the extant data from three different years of the eighteenth and nineteenth centuries to show the breakdown of the entire annual expenditure. As is shown in the table, the payment for vassals constituted the largest portion in 1730, followed by the expense of satisfying the needs of the Tokugawa family, and these were the largest two in the nineteenth century as well. If we add the expense in kind (rice) for vassals that were managed through another account, the proportion of the two items mentioned earlier increases to more than 60%. On the other hand, the direct expenses, which can be regarded as those incurred to provide public goods, such as the maintenance of infrastructure, seem to have represented a rather small part of expenditure in these years. The significance of the expenditure incurred because of the needs of the lord's family and the vassals

TABLE 1. Breakdown of the Expenditure of Tokugawa
Shogunate (Excluding Temporal Expenses)

	(%)		
	1730	1814	1844
Vassals	40.7	29.4	28.0
Tokugawa family	21.3	32.7	30.8
Administrative expense	16.8	7.8	10.9
Providing loans	6.4	11.5	18.9
Others	14.8	18.6	11.3
Total	100	100	100

SOURCE: Calculated from the data shown in Ōguchi 1984, 1989.

was also seen in the case of the domains. For example, the financial data of the Saga domain around 1650 showed that 64% of the expenditure on rice, which accounted for 38% of the total expenditure, was allocated as stipends of vassals, and around 50% of the entire expenditure was spent outside the domain, mainly in Edo,[3] the capital of the Tokugawa regime (renamed Tokyo in 1868). Since the needs of the lord and his family are likely to have occurred at their place of residence, the Edo expenditure should largely be classified as consumption-related expenditure, mainly for the lord's family and his vassals.

However, considering the irregularity of expenses on construction or famine relief, table 1 is not sufficient for the evaluation of the role of public goods provision by the Tokugawa shogunate or other domains. In fact, many extant individual records show that the participation of rulers in construction and civil engineering projects or famine relief. Table 2 lists the various projects run by the Tokugawa shogunate with the help of *daimyōs (otetsudai-fushin)*. From the table, we can identify that the seventeenth century was the age of construction. A number of construction projects, comprising the building as well as repairing of castles, temples, and shrines, were executed under this scheme. For example, the Tokugawa shogunate started the expansion work to Edo castle in 1606, and it lasted more than thirty years. After the Siege of Osaka in 1614–1615, whereby the Tokugawa shogunate overthrew the former ruler of the Toyotomi family, the shogunate reconstructed the Osaka castle as a symbol of Tokugawa's reign over the western part of the Japanese archipelago from 1620 onward. As the castle construction projects included a wider range of works, these projects should be recognized as contributing not only to the construction of the place of residence of the Tokugawa family, but also to the creation of the capital (Edo) or the core city in western Japan (Osaka). In fact, the construction works that began in 1603 reclaimed a part of Edo bay by leveling a nearby hill, thereby creating an urban area where the warrior class and others could gather; this realized the policy of residential demarcation between the ruling class of warriors and their peasant subjects.

TABLE 2. Number of Project under the Scheme of *otetsudai-fushin* (Construction Helped by Domain Lords)

	1601–1650	1651–1700	1701–1750	1751–1800	1801–1850	1851–	Total
Number of projects							
Castle building	2						2
Castle repairing	46	13	10	4	4	1	78
City/town building	11	8	5	1			25
Temple and shrine building and repairing	13	55	35	24	18	4	149
Imperial Palace repairing	2	3	2	2	1	1	11
River repairing			14	24	21	1	60
Total	74	79	66	55	44	7	325
Average number of helping domain lords per project (Available cases, 311 out of 325)							
Castle building	13.0*						
Castle repairing	9.4*	4.2	5.1	3.0	5.0*		
City/town building	9.5*	1.1	1.8	1.0			
Temple and shrine building and repairing	3.9	1.3	1.3	1.8	3.4	3.5	
Imperial Palace repairing	250.0	8.5*	7.5	4.0	3.0	13.0	
River repairing			3.9	4.0	5.0	7.0	

SOURCE: Made out of the data set compiled in Yoshizumi 1968.
NOTE: * Denotes that the number is underestimated due to the constraint of the data.

On the other hand, the number of projects categorized as civil engineering works on river control in table 2 requires additional information for an appropriate interpretation. Their appearance from the early eighteenth century onward did not mean that the shogunate or domains had not been engaged in this field before. While we have not had a comprehensive data set yet, many records indicate that the shogunate as well as the domains directly managed the civil engineering works during the seventeenth century; these included river improvement, harbor constructions, building of irrigation ponds, and land reclamations (Furushima 1956). Most of these large projects, which were organized directly by the shogunate or domains in terms of finance and management, were called *go-fushin,* which literally means "construction by rulers," in the Japanese of that period. Thus, the seventeenth century can largely be seen as the age of construction by rulers.

Considering these facts, we could derive two intriguing implications from table 2. The first is that the large works of castle and town construction almost ceased before the turn of the eighteenth century. Specifically, the number of construction works related to castles decreased significantly in the latter half of the seventeenth century. This was a direct reflection of the relaxation of the military tension between the Tokugawa shogunate and the domain lords. In fact, the number of events related to military affairs—such as the military parade to the Nikkō Tōshōgū, a formal pilgrimage to the sacred shrine dedicated to the founder of the Tokugawa shogunate—decreased drastically from the latter half of the seventeenth century onward (Tanimoto 2015). This marked the substantial start of "peace" under the Tokugawa regime, which might have changed the rulers' financial needs.

While military issues lost their significance, the influence of diplomatic manipulation increased, especially in the political arena in Edo. This required expenditure for facilitating social contact among rulers, which was reflected in the rising expenses of rulers' "public finance" in Edo, and also in the rulers' hometown.

Establishing a domain-ran kiln in the Saga domain distinctively exemplified the efforts that the domains made for pursing diplomatic success. Based on the transplanted technology via Korean craftsman around the turn of the seventeenth century, the Saga domain built its own kiln in the middle of the seventeenth century; it would specialize in producing uniquely designed and sophisticated porcelains. They were given to the shogun or other prominent *daimyōs* as gifts, facilitating social contact with politically influential entities for sustaining, or in some cases acquiring, a favorable position among the ruling class (Ōhashi 2007). In addition, because of the concentration of the warrior class in an urban agglomeration, the standard level of consumption among lords and vassals must have increased in the capital city of Edo or in the castle towns. In short, the stress given to the rulers' expenditure moved from "investment" to "consumption," in accordance with the start of the so-called Pax Tokugawa era.

The second point is that the shogunate added the civil engineering works for controlling river waters into the *otetsudai-fushin* scheme from the beginning of the eighteenth century. Given that rulers, including the Tokugawa shogunate, had been reducing their investment in construction, it is not unrealistic to assume that this was derived from the motivation of the shogunate to reduce its financial expenditure by utilizing the domains' resources for shogunate-run projects on river control (Yoshizumi 1967).

A similar motivation can be observed in the shogunate establishing a new scheme called *kuniyaku-fushin* (which literally means "province's construction duties") in 1720, under which the shogunate bore 10% of the total cost, whereas the domain lord and the village whose territory was located within the area of the province *(kuni)* concerned bore the rest (Kasaya 1976). The significance of these schemes for the Tokugawa shogunate can be seen through the available data (which is rather fragmented) on the finance of the Tokugawa shogunate between 1789 and 1815. According to this, the average annual additional revenue and expenditure reached approximately 10% to 15% of the normal revenue and expenses. An extra expenditure of 3.5 million *ryō*[4] included 1.3 million *ryō* on riparian works, which were largely financed by the *otetsudai-fushin* and *kuniyaku-fushin* schemes mentioned earlier. Here, we notice signs of the changing behavior of the Tokugawa shogunate in terms of building and maintaining infrastructure to control water.

A similar change can be seen in the areas of famine and poverty relief. Though the shogunate was accustomed to providing loans to impoverished domains affected by a bad harvest, it turns out that these loans were apparently reduced during the 1780s when the great famine of Tenmei occurred. Concerning the method of poverty relief, the shogunate indeed established a loan system for the poor, and ordered villages to ensure adequate stock in granaries to counter the impact of a bad harvest, as part of the political reform of the late eighteenth century by the Tokugawa shogunate, known as the Kansei Reforms.[5] However, even in these projects, the shogunate tried to control its expenses by introducing external monetary resources. For example, the financial basis for the loans provided to the needy and destitute by the shogunate was the interest income earned by a scheme of lending official money to merchants and wealthy farmers. Official granaries in the village were also filled with rice or other grains that were mainly delivered by the villagers, rather than rulers. Thus, each scheme was usually planned in such a way that its financial basis was the introduction of money or in-kind delivery from wealthy peasants or landowners (Takeuchi 2009, Matsuzawa 2009). In sum, the expenditure on infrastructure or poverty relief by the Tokugawa shogunate, which can be categorized as public goods in this volume, was dependent on the external introduction of extra money and resources, apart from the "annual tribute" that was the economic foundation of rulers under the Tokugawa regime.

Structural Change

We assume that the structural change in public finance was responsible for the change in behavior of the Tokugawa shogunate, as was the case in other domains toward public goods provision during the course of its regime. In the seventeenth century, specifically the first half, the projects run by the shogunate and *daimyōs* were more or less related to the "military" issues. Not only organizing military parades but also the outlay for construction and repair of castles and castle towns were recognized as "military" expenditure in preparation for conflicts among rulers.

In contrast, active expenditure on public engineering works for water control and transportation facilities might be seen, prima facie, as a kind of infrastructure development that resembled the so-called public investments by modern governments. However, the motivations for this investment were largely derived from the rulers' interest in enhancing the basis of imposing land levy, or settling the ways to sell their annual tribute in a more profitable manner. Insofar as they are recognized as methods to strengthen the fiscal and military ability of rulers, they shared an objective that was similar to that of the military-related expenses mentioned earlier.

Therefore, it seems far-fetched to assume any kind of benevolent ideas behind this "public" expenditure during the Tokugawa regime, at least through the seventeenth century. In fact, the Confucian idea of benevolent rule was not prevalent among the warrior class in this period, and only a few *daimyōs* showed interest in these rather new ideas that originated in China or Korea and were later introduced into the archipelago. The rulers' main concern was the formation of a social and political order among the ruling warrior class, which was originally based on its military powers, as well as economic abilities. The subjects were considered to be governed because of the power and authority of the rulers (Watanabe 2010). From the rulers' point of view, the public social spaces for public goods provision were nonexistent.

However, for ordinary people, the need to be protected from the external military threat might have been pressing because of the simmering tension among members of the ruling class in the first half of the seventeenth century, not long after the Age of Civil Wars. In this context, the rulers' military expenses could possibly be justified as the unavoidable costs incurred from self-defense. As per this line of thinking, establishing and maintaining sociopolitical order among the rulers were also deemed efforts at keeping "peace." Considering the fact that national defense exemplifies the attribute of a "pure" public good in textbooks of economics, rulers' expenses related to military issues in a broad sense might have been situated in public social space by peasant subjects in light of people's ordinary lives.

Regarding the civil engineering works for infrastructure, the economic interests of the people and rulers were likely to overlap more. The Owari domain, for instance, expended its resources on the river-controlling project in response to the peasants' request during the land reclamations around 1650 (Nishida 1984). If "peace" and infrastructure construction were demanded by the people, they deserved to be defined as public goods, regardless of the intention of the providers, that is, the shogunate and *daimyō*s. It is noteworthy that the cost of these projects could be covered by the relatively high tribute rate in the seventeenth century. From our point of view, the high tribute rate in this period seems to be balanced, thereby allowing the expenditure on these projects. In other words, public goods such as "peace" that were potentially seen as expensive by peasants subjects deserved to be acquired at the cost of a heavy levy imposed on their lands, or at least recognized as in the tolerable range of balancing the costs and benefits.

However, the relaxation of the tension among rulers (specifically between the shogunate and the lords) in the late seventeenth century changed the requirement for public finance. In fact, temples built for the use of the families of the Tokugawa or other lords became a major component of the expenditure on urban construction. While military issues lost significance, the expenditure on social contact among rulers increased; this is because the issue of maintaining sociopolitical order was intrinsically a matter among the ruling class. In a broad sense, the expenditure tended toward consumption instead of investment.

The financial deficit of the shogunate, as well as many other domains, around 1700 can be regarded as a consequence of this structural change. In theory, the deficit in public finance can be tackled by increasing revenue, and specifically by raising the annual tribute rate. In fact, as shown in figure 1, the shogunate was at least nominally successful in regaining during the mid-eighteenth century the rate prevalent earlier. However, even the shogunate could not let the tribute rate exceed the nominal seventeenth-century level; therefore, it began to decline from the latter half of the eighteenth century onward.

As can be seen in figure 1, the tribute rate in other areas remained stagnant or even decreased over time. It is noteworthy that there was a decline in the annual tribute rate not only relative to production growth, which has been widely mentioned in the existing literature, but also in absolute terms when compared with the rate during the seventeenth century. The persistent imbalance, that is, the increase in consumption-related expenditure and the stagnation in revenue, seems to be, at least partially, a reflection of the mismatch between the expectation of the defrayers of the annual tribute and the rulers' behavior. It is not incorrect to believe that the "publicness" of the expenditure of the shogunate and domains weakened as military issues lost their social significance, and that the rising expense on rulers' consumption could not obtain the recognition that accommodates the need to provide public goods that might raise welfare.

How did the rulers cope with the persistent financial deficits? On the revenue side, studies exist that discuss the loans from merchants, the role of recoinage and issuance of paper money, and the industry-promoting policy executed by the domains. From our point of view, however, the expenditure side should be significant. As we have seen in table 1, several studies insist that the number of redundant vassals could not be effectively curtailed (Ōguchi 1989, Morishita 2012). In fact, as the chapter by Kenichiro Aratake in part 1 suggests, only a small number of them could be regarded as officials engaged in civil administration. The recognition of legitimacy of ruling people and maintaining political and social order with the ruling warrior class had still depended on fulfilling the military responsibilities. Under these conditions, if thrift ordinances could not drastically reduce the consumption level, the persistent financial problems affected the provision of public goods; this was the case for the shogunate, as well as most of the domains. The above-mentioned schemes, executed by the shogunate to introduce external monetary resources, were among the ways devised to cope with these issues, thereby avoiding a significant retreat from public goods provision. However, considering the ruling class as a whole, some schemes, such as *otetsudai-fushin* (domains' help), which transferred a certain amount of funds from domains to the shogunate and might have resulted in curtailing the expenditure for the domain's own purpose, were insufficient to meet the needs.

In that sense, the introduction of external monetary and other resources, that is, from merchants or wealthy farmers, was an essential source for public goods provision, besides the annual tribute to the rulers. From the rulers' point of view, these might be recognized as intentional outsourcing of public goods provision because of the shortage of revenue. In fact, it is said that the idea of benevolent policy toward the ruled, *osukui* (literally "help" in Japanese), existed widely among rulers from the eighteenth century onward (Fukaya 1993). In contrast, it was also in this century that the public finance capacity of the rulers weakened so much that they could not even collect sufficient annual tribute to meet their financial demands. Therefore, it does not follow that there were potential agreements between the rulers and the ruled about public goods provision, which we supposed earlier to exist in the seventeenth century, though in a different manner, even if we recognize the prevalence of the idea of benevolent policy in this period. It could potentially be interpreted as the emergence, at least from a financial perspective, of new providers of public goods who were not from the ruling warrior class. Examples of direct commitment to public goods provision by the nonruling class are discussed in the following section.

Infrastructure Development in the Regions

Shifting our focus from rulers' activities to a regional level, we can easily find examples of public goods provision (specifically from late eighteenth century) in which ordinary people from outside the ruling warrior class had a significant participation.

The construction of an irrigation pond in Izawa village, located in Ise province (the present-day Mie prefecture) in the central part of Honshū, was one of these cases.[6] In 1836, three prominent members of this village—all of whom had made their fortunes by being engaged in businesses other than cultivation or landholding—planned a project of building an irrigation pond to solve the water-shortage problem faced by farmers of the village. They had already contributed to the village by taking over its debt of two thousand *ryō* in 1833. According to a diary written by Hikosaburō Takekawa, the leader of this irrigation project, the plan aimed to rebuild the livelihood of villagers who were grievously affected by an extremely poor harvest in 1836; this was known as the Great Famine of Tenpō period. Three families shared the total expenses of thirty-five hundred *ryō*;[7] the project, which was completed in 1838, started to provide water to twenty-six hectares of paddy lands.

Thus, this construction work depended entirely on villagers' finance under the "authorization" of the ruler of the village, that is, of the Toba domain. We use the term "authorization" instead of "permission" because we assume that the ruler had a role during arbitration proceedings in the case of disputes such as irrigation works that might potentially affect the water supply to neighboring villages. In this sense, the works were carried out under the jurisdiction of the Toba domain. However, the execution and management of the works were delegated entirely to Takekawa and other prominent villagers. At first, they made contact with engineers through their acquaintances in the neighboring village. It is noteworthy that these two engineers, Saisuke Otobe and his subordinate, were skilled engineers of the warrior class who were in the service of the prominent Kishū domain, which was adjacent to the Toba domain. They made a concrete plan by measuring the area, and gave advice in their spare time to Takekawa during the construction works. In short, they were "hired" by villagers on a private basis, and this responsibility was in addition to that arising from their official assignments for the Kishū domain.

Though the labor force was mainly provided by villagers, they were hired by daily wage, apart from the conventional villager's duty imposed by the rulers. In fact, the use of the latter form of labor mobilization had diminished from the mid-seventeenth century onward. The group of skilled workers in the civil engineering works, called *kurokuwamono* (literally "man with black hoe"), was also hired to deal with relatively high-skilled tasks. There even existed some claims from villagers that the employment of skilled workers from outside would reduce employment opportunities for the villagers. These claims clearly imply that the construction works additionally aimed to be a form of job creation for the destitute—an intention that was also mentioned in Takekawa's diary. In fact, although Takekawa estimated that the productivity of *kurokuwamono* exceeded that of the villagers by thirty percentage points, he continued to hire villagers. In sum, this case shows that the irrigation pond and the employment, that is, the infrastructure and poverty relief, were provided by village-based activities that were not dependent on rulers in terms of finance, technology, and workforce.

The Hamaguchi family's contribution to the construction of protection facilities against natural disasters was another distinct example. When a great tsunami hit Hiro village—located in Kishū province (the present-day Wakayama prefecture) in 1856, the seventh Gihei Hamaguchi organized construction work to build an embankment, and supplied fifteen hundred *ryō* over a period of three years. During this time, his soy sauce brewing business was completely entrusted to a manager who, it was said, had to restrain Gihei's demands for money (Tanimoto 1990 and 2006).

Besides these purely civil and voluntary activities, the wealthy and influential families in the region, referred to as "local notables" in this chapter, contributed financially to the projects planned by rulers. Half of the construction of bridges and watercourses in the Kumamoto domain during the first half of the nineteenth century was financed from the reserve fund of annual tribute in the district, and the rest by donations and loans from wealthy farmers (Yoshimura 2013).[8] Although the establishment of a village-level granary from the late eighteenth century onward was based on a policy ordered by the shogunate, it was managed and financed by village people, as mentioned in the previous section.

Village Community and the Formation of a Regional Society

We assume that these activities were driven not only by a personal and individual motive, but also by the sense of responsibility for the regional society felt by the notables; this sense was derived from the notion of the village as a kind of official entity. The institutional basis that substantialized the notion of the regional society seems to have emerged in the latter half of the Tokugawa regime.

The appearance of quasi-public finance at the village level can be seen as a part thereof. Several empirical studies revealed cases in which the head of the village collected levies from land-owning villagers, in addition to the annual tribute to rulers, in order to fund the village's own expenses. Although rulers tended to dislike the emergence of this budget for fear of it affecting the collection of annual tributes, it did, on occasion, amount to 30% to 40% of the annual tribute.[9] Villages' own expenditure ranged from expenses for maintaining facilities to sponsorship of village festivals, adding the expenses by *gunchū*, which literally means "among the district," the amount of which was allotted to each village (Fukuyama 1975, Sugahara 1979, Yazawa 1985, Kurushima 1993).

This last expense reveals the formation of a public social space beyond the village, which is called *gunchū*, that is, a cooperative unit of villages. The village heads held meetings, laid down some kind of a protocol that was called *gunchū gijō*, and carried out the tasks that could not be performed by a village on its own. A well-known case in the literature was a petition to the shogunate's office jointly made by the cooperatives of around one thousand villages located in three provinces surrounding Osaka in the 1820s (Tsuda 1961). Their purpose was to break the coalition of the monopolistic merchants of Osaka in order to defend their economic interest in producing and dealing in cotton products. Moreover, a later study revealed that the cooperatives' tasks were not only to organize these temporary movements, but also to manage daily problems, such as responding to the poor people wandering about in the countryside (Yabuta 1992).

Thus, the geographical unit that covered a much wider area than a single village emerged at least in the early nineteenth century. In fact, the basic idea of the term "regional society" in this chapter is derived from this observation. Founded on the basic and tightly knit institutional body of the village, the regional society extended its coverage beyond this by forming the institution of cooperative villages, which was relatively weak but still quite substantial. In addition, it is important to notice that economic factors might have contributed to substantialize the area. As we have already seen in the case of the petition by villages in the Osaka region, the development of cotton-related businesses communized the economic interest among traders beyond the village, serving as a foundation for collective actions. Therefore, considering that the market-oriented farming and proto-industry characterized the economic development of nineteenth-century Japan, it does not seem unrealistic to assume that economic forces worked as important drivers in the formation of a regional society (Hayami, Saitō, and Toby 2004).

The question is whether the emerging, economically powerful agents, such as the wealthy farmers, brewers, local merchants, and manufacturers, behaved in a manner that substantialized the region. In fact, we have some examples of the wealthy, who were solely pursuing their private profits as economic agents; this invited criticism from other residents (Watanabe 1998). However, it is important to point out that a number of rural wealthy families behaved as notables by pursuing social reputation as well as economic profits; they did so by responding to the expectations of the residents or fulfilling responsibilities toward them. If the social relationships generated by their economic activities extended beyond the village, the residents concerned could not be limited to the villagers. In that sense, economic factors worked as a driving force to substantialize the regional society, which provided many actors who complemented the public goods provision by the rulers. In the next section, we will see how and to what extent this structural change succeeded in the Meiji regime, which heralded the age of centralization.

BEYOND THE CENTRALIZATION OF MEIJI STATE

The Role of Local Public Finances

In 1868, the Tokugawa shogunate was abolished and the Meiji state's reign began. By abolishing the domain system and executing land reform in the 1870s, the Meiji government established a centralized system of public finance, under which the entire amount of land tax, almost equivalent to the total annual tribute under the Tokugawa regime, was collected as the revenue of the central government.

The proportion of government expenditure to GDP remained stagnant or even declined to 10% during the first stage in the 1880s and early 1890s.[10] The trend reversed with the outbreak of the Sino-Japanese war in 1894, and there were stepwise rises by way of two wars that were the Sino-Japanese war in 1894–1895 and the Russo-Japanese war in 1904–1905. Note that this figure implies the expenditure by the central as well as the local governments; these correspond to two levels—at prefecture and city/town/village. Regarding the relative size of each government, central and local, we recognize from the statistics that the share of central government remained around 70% or above.

Studying the breakdown, however, we find that more than half of the expense of the central government comprised the sum of the military expenditure, and the cost of national debt consisted of interest payment and the redeeming of national bonds. In other words, the amount of expenditure of the local governments was almost equal to the nonmilitary expenditure of the central government. Therefore, if we limit our focus to the expenditure related to the people's livelihood, that is, the provision of public goods for public welfare in a broad sense, the public finance of the local governments carried significant weight.

Specifically in the field of civil engineering and education, the decisive role of local public finance was apparent. Figure 2 shows that the main providers of civil engineering works were the prefecture governments, followed by those of the city/town/village. In fact, this figure indicates that their expenditure occupied around three-quarters of the entire expense on civil engineering works in almost all years. Even though the prefectural governor—usually the senior officer of the Ministry of Home Affairs—was appointed by the central government in those years, the prefectural government was rather independent in financial terms because the prefectural taxes were distinct from national taxes (Kanazawa 2010).

In terms of education, the introduction of the public primary schooling system in 1872 was an epochal moment in institutional change. It was based on the promulgation of the "education system order" by the central government, which ordered the start of primary schooling in each of the local entities—village and town—that were reorganized through the institutional reformation processes in the early Meiji period. However, there was only a small expenditure on education by the governments up to 1878. Even though the expenditure increased significantly in 1879, the primary school system that was launched depended mainly on donations from the regional society, as the central government solely focused on higher education (at least up to the early twentieth century). The local governments, especially those of the city/town/village, incurred education expenditure from 1879. The expenditure first rose at the turn of the century, and then, after 1907, with the extension of the primary school period from four to six years, taking up nearly half of the total expenditure of the city/town/village governments. Among the entire expenditure on education by the governments, the share of the central government did not exceed 20% up to the 1910s.

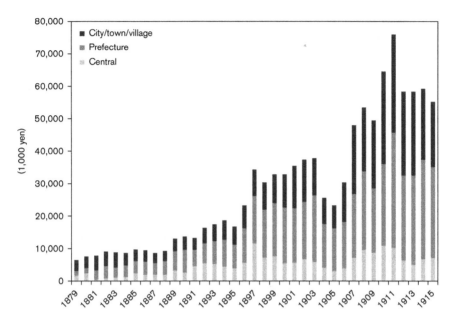

FIGURE 2. Expenditure for Civil Engineering Work by Public Finance (Estimated by Source of Revenue)

Source: Naikaku Tōkeikyoku, ed., *Nihon Teikoku Tōkeinenkan* (Japan's Annual Statistical Book).

Thus, the local public finances in the Meiji period carried the burden of providing public goods in critical areas, such as public engineering works and public education. One may regard it as a significant change by emphasizing the formalization of the local public finance system through institutional trial and error during the early Meiji period. However, we notice the substantial continuity of the revenue of local governments. This was heavily dependent on wealthy farmers, landowners, or local wealthy people paying local taxes, in addition to national taxes, such as the reformed "land tax." The central government was further dependent on increasing indirect taxes, comprising brewery tax and consumption tax.

The system of imposing household tax (*kosūwari*, literally meaning "dividing among households") provided prefectures around 20% of their tax revenue; the corresponding figure for city/town/village governments was 50% to 70%. Since the taxation was determined by the assembly of each local government, according to the estimation of income and asset holdings of each household, wealthy households tended to have a heavier tax burden. This resulted in a distribution of the tax burden that was rather similar to that during the late Tokugawa period, in spite of the formalization of local public finance.

Hoping to retain their social reputation, the wealthy still behaved as notables, responding to the expectations of the regional society. What was new in the Meiji era seems to have been the extension of the fields to which notables were required to respond. Contribution to the public education system was an important one, but the field of regional business-based activities also rose to prominence. The following cases vividly show the diverse activities undertaken by local notables, along with the political centralization of the Meiji government.

Region as a Motive for Activity

The case of the Hamaguchi family, to which we have referred already as making a notable contribution to the construction of an embankment to protect against tsunamis, exemplifies the inclination toward regional business activities. The Hamaguchi family invested about half of its assets in enterprises other than its traditional family business of soy sauce brewing. Besides supporting a local shipping firm, Kisaka-Hikifunegumi, the Hamaguchi family moved its investment from relatively secure assets, such as national bonds and the stocks of already established national companies—Nihon Tetsudō (railroad) and Kanegafuchi Bōseki (cotton spinning)—to businesses that were connected with the Wakayama or Chiba prefecture, the home bases of the Hamaguchi family.[11] Out of their seventy-thousand-yen stock investment balance in 1900, close to half was invested in local enterprises, such as local banks (Arita Kigyō Bank and Busō Bank) and a steamship transportation firm (Chōshi Kisen).

This regionally inclined investment behavior can be generalized to some extent by considering cases from a database comprising 251 shareholders in the Niigata prefecture in 1901. By analyzing their shareholding, we distinguished two types of investors: the first type inclined to invest in established nationwide corporations, and the other investing in newly established and Niigata-based corporations with a relatively uncertain future. A wide range was observed in both types. Combining this with the information of shareholding patterns, we identify a specific type of shareholder who concentrated investment on Niigata corporations but did not participate in their management. This type of investor can be characterized as a "sponsor" type, in contrast to the entrepreneur or rentier types; they comprise almost 60% of shareholders and 30% of the investment portfolio (Tanimoto 1998). By combining this "sponsor" type behavior with the Hamaguchis' investment activities, we can infer that investment in private firms were not solely a profit-pursuing activity for a certain number of the wealthy in those years.

Recalling that public goods were intrinsically undersupplied through market transactions due to their particular attributes, we can identify that the investment in these recently established enterprises shared characteristics with public goods in terms of being undersupplied through the existing capital market owing to the large uncertainty in expectation of profits because of their newness. Under these conditions, investing in local corporations was a new activity that was driven by a motivation similar to that behind the provision of public goods during the late Tokugawa period by the notables.

The diverse activities of Hachibei, the head of the Sekiguchi family, in the 1890s, who made his fortune with soy source brewing from the mid-Tokugawa era, exemplify the motivation of these local investors.[12] Besides starting new business activities, such as beer brewing, Worcestershire sauce production, brick manufacturing, and a water transportation company to conduct a billing and shipping business on the nearby Kasumigaura Lake, in the vicinity of the residential area of Edosaki (Hitachi province), the Sekiguchi family was involved in social and political activities. Hachibei became a chief of the league of villages in 1881, besides being a member of the committee for educational affairs of these villages. In 1883, he donated over one tan (approximately 0.1 hectare) of land and five hundred yen for the construction of a primary school in his area of operation. Moreover, Hachibei joined the Rikken Kaishintō (Constitutional Reform Party)—one of the major parties of the people's rights movement in the early Meiji period—and financially supported a party-affiliated magazine called Jōsō Zasshi (Jōsō Magazine) that was published in the Edosaki area. He himself wrote two short essays on social systems and customs in this magazine. Finally, Sekiguchi Hachibei was a candidate in the first House of Representative election of 1890 and was elected as the only representative from the sixth constituency of the Ibaragi prefecture.

It is, of course, quite normal for those involved in politics to be property owners. Max Weber, who argued the administration by notables as a type of legitimate domination, defined a notable as "the individual" who is able to "count on a certain level of provision from private sources" and is "free for political activity" (Weber 1968, 290). For Weber, business activities are seen as the economic foundation that enables people to behave as notables. However, in the case of the Sekiguchi family, both business and sociopolitical activities took off at the same time. Wealthy property holders in the early Meiji era did not seem to consider these two apparently different spheres of activities as strictly separate. If this is true, one can assume a common ground for their activities spanning both spheres.

Recalling the achievement of the Tokugawa regime in terms of the formation of regional society, we assume that acquiring a reputation as a notable in a regional society is a common motive for property owners, namely, notables. This assumption tallies with the fact that numerous examples exist of notables who were financially, as well as politically, committed to the introduction of railways to the region, or to the establishment of the branch of a government-run post office or telegraph station in the village or town during the late nineteenth century (Fujii 2005). Even if they were run on a business basis, which was more likely in the case of a private railroad corporation, they certainly provided critical infrastructure that connected their regional society to the nationwide transport and information system. Thus, the significant role of the regional society in public goods provision was based on the activities of notables acting in a wide range of social roles, such as that of a donor, taxpayer, entrepreneur, investor, and politician. In other words, the social order based on propertied persons characterized the nineteenth-century transformation of the political structure, from the Tokugawa regime to the Meiji society; this social order accomplished the task of providing public goods in rural Japan.

For the sustainability and reproduction of their economic lives, ordinary people depend not only on goods and on services obtained through market activities, but also on public goods in a broad sense. When the rulers under the Tokugawa regime largely withdrew from the provision of public goods, the regional society that developed with the emergence of local notables complemented or even substituted the task. Although a modern fiscal state was established through the Meiji Restoration, the regional society that maintained its structure throughout the political reform process played significant roles in providing public goods, especially in the field of public welfare. They did so by way of institutionalizing the support of local public finance through taxation on property owners, that is, notables.

Moreover, the establishment of modern enterprises, as well as the infrastructure for transport and information, was supported financially, at least in part, by the wealthy, who dared to invest their monetary accumulation in the risky local corporations or nonprofit organizations as "sponsors." In other words, these projects were undersupplied with necessary funds if they depended only on ordinary capital markets. Considering that public goods were also undersupplied through market transactions, it is not incorrect to say that investing in profit-making projects was similar to the provision of public goods in a specific historical context. Thus, the regional society itself functioned as a motive for the local notables, who played a significant role in providing public goods from the eighteenth century to the early twentieth century, that is, during the eras that saw the emergence of early modern and modern Japan.

We assume that a sense of responsibility toward the regional society led to this phenomenon. This sense would be rooted in the rather strong adherence of inhabitants, specifically the peasant households that constituted the largest proportion of the population, to the place where they managed their family farms. This particular behavior originated in the establishment of the *ie* system among peasant households around the turn of the eighteenth century; it represented the end of the age of reclamation that spanned the seventeenth century. According to Kizaemon Aruga, a leading sociologist in this field, the Japanese peasant family can be characterized as a stem-family with the custom of single inheritance of lineal male descendants. *Ie* was a family system well suited to a system that placed a high value on the succession of the *ie* as an independent unit (Aruga 1972). If the *ie*—rather than the individual or the nuclear family unit—became established as the subject of inheritance, a choice to sell land and to abandon farming could not be made by a single generation. As a result, the household gave first priority to farming, suggesting strong adherence to the inherited land.[13] This argument can also be applied to landless tenants, if we recall the long-term stability of the relationship between landowners and tenants in modern Japan (Sakane 2011).

Thus, the *ie* system resulted in a geographically low mobile society in which people formed rather long-term and coherent relationships under the regional bond. A sense of loyalty to the region where most people would spend their entire lives would be fostered under these circumstances. The wealthy were prepared to make any contribution to the region in order to fulfill their responsibilities, and consistent "good" behavior on their part would result in a good reputation; this might represent an indispensable nonmonetary reward, namely, to be regarded as "notables" in a long-standing regional society whose composition remained more or less fixed. The adherence to their place of residence was a basic social condition underlying the workings of a regional society that undertook the public goods provision discussed in this chapter.

NOTES

1. The range of the territory of the Tokugawa shogunate extended from the northeast to the southwest of the Japanese archipelago. The Hosokawa family ruled a territory named Higo (Kumamoto) region, which was worth three hundred thousand koku of rice and occupied most of the central Kyūshū Island, located in southwestern Japan.

2. See Tanimoto 2015 for the details.

3. Calculated by the financial data in Nagano 1980, 203–205.

4. *Ryō* was the unit of currency used in the Tokugawa period. Its value in the eighteenth century was approximately equal to one *koku* (unit of volume equivalent to 180 liters) of rice, except during years of bad harvest.

5. Kansei is the name of era that lasted from 1789 to 1801.

6. Information on construction of irrigation ponds is obtained from Yamazaki and Kitano 1955, 196–240.

7. The value was approximately equivalent to the price paid in 1830 by consumers in Edo for 2,500 koku (450 kiloliters) of polished rice.

8. In the Kumamoto domain, the head of a village union that comprised several villages played a significant role in activating civil engineering and construction works in the first half of the nineteenth century. Called *Sōjōya*, these heads had *hyakushō* (peasant) status and worked as civil engineers, as well as governors of regions.

9. Tanimoto (2018) gives a case study of Nishihokkeno village in the early nineteenth century. Although this calculation of proportion was based only on fragmented village level data, the representativeness of these results can be verified by the official estimation of land reform, carried out by Meiji government in the 1870s. This estimation set the village-level tax at one-third of the land tax when it calculated the official price of each plot of land through the capitalization method.

10. See Sawai and Tanimoto (2016), figure 3.9, for the details.

11. Hamaguchi's head family resided in Hiro Village in the Wakayama prefecture, and the family's soy sauce brewery business operated in Chōshi, a town in the Chiba prefecture (Shimosa province).

12. Historical facts concerning the Sekiguchi family are taken from Tanimoto 1996.

13. The fact that the number of farming households remained almost constant at around 5.5 million from the 1890s to the 1930s suggests that the assumption is valid (Namiki 1955).

REFERENCES

Aruga, Kizaemon (1972). *Ie* (The Family).Tokyo, Shibundō.

Fujii, Nobuyuki (2005). *Tsūshin to Chiiki Shakai* (Communication and the Regional Society). Tokyo, Nihonkeizai Hyōronsha.

Fukaya, Katsumi (1993). *Hyakushō-naritachi* (Peasants and Lords in Early Modern Japan). Tokyo, Hanawa Shobō.

Fukuyama, Akira (1975). *Kinsei Nōson Kinyū no Kōzō* (The Structure of Finance in Farming Village during Early Modern Japan). Tokyo, Yūzankaku Shuppan.

Furushima, Toshio (1956). *Nihon Nōgyō-shi* (Agricultural History of Japan). Tokyo, Iwanami Shoten.

Hayami, Akira, Osamu Saitō, and Ronald Toby, eds. (2004). *Emergence of Economic Society in Japan, 1600–1900*. Oxford, Oxford University Press.

Kanazawa, Fumio (2010). *Jichi to Bunken no Rekishiteki Bunmyaku* (Historical Context of Self-Government and Decentralization). Tokyo, Aoki Shoten.

Kasaya, Kazuhiko (1976). "Kinsei Kuniyaku-fushin no Seijishitekiichi" (Kuniyaku-fushin in Political History of Early Modern Japan). *Shirin* 59 (4).

Kurushima, Hiroshi (1993). "Chihōzei no Rekishiteki Zentei" (The Historical Background of Local Taxes). *Rekishigakukenkyū* 652.

Matsuzawa, Yūsaku (2009). *Meiji Chihōjichitaisei no Kigen* (The Origin of the System of Local Government in Meiji Era). Tokyo, Tokyo Daigaku Shuppankai.

Miyamoto, Matao (2004). "Quantitative Aspects of Tokugawa Economy." In *Economic History of Modern Japan*, vol. 1, *Emergence of Economic Society,* edited by Akira Hayami, Osamu Saitō, and Ronald Toby. Oxford, Oxford University Press.

Morishita, Tōru (2012). *Bushi toiu Mibun* (The Warriors as Social Status). Tokyo, Yoshikawakōbunkan.

Nagano, Susumu (1980). *Bakuhansei Shakai no Zaisei Kōzō* (The Fiscal Structure of the Society of Shogunate-Domain System). Tokyo, Ōhara Shinseisha.

Namiki, Shōkichi (1955). "Nōka-Jinkō no Sengo 10-nen" (Population of Farming Households during Ten Years after the Second World War). *Nōgyōsōgōkenkyū* 9 (4).

Nishida, Masaki (1984). "Kawayoke to Kuniyaku-fushin" (River Controlling and Kuniyaku-fushin). In *Doboku,* edited by Keiji Nagahara and Keiji Yamaguchi (Kōza Nihon Gijyutsu no Shakaishi). Tokyo, Nihon Hyōronsha.

Ōguchi, Yūjirō (1984). "Kansei-Bunka ki no Bakufu Zaisei: Matsudaira Nobuaki Seiken no Seikaku" (The Shogunate Public Finance during the Period of Kansei-Bunka: The Characteristics of the Reign of Matsudaira, Nobuaki). In *Nihon Kinseishi Ronsō, Gekan,* edited by Bitō Masahide Sensei Kanrekikinenkai. Tokyo, Yoshikawakōbunkan.

——— (1989). "Bakufu no Zaisei" (Public Finance of the Shogunate). In *Nihonkeizaishi 2 Kindaiseichō no Taidō,* edited by Hiroshi Shinbo and Osamu Saitō. Tokyo, Iwanami Shoten.

Ōhashi, Kōji (2007). *Shōgun to Nabeshima, Kakiemon* (The Shōgun and Nabeshima, Kakiemon). Tokyo, Yūzankaku Shuppan.

Sakane, Yoshihiro (2011). *Ie to Mura: Nihon Dentō Shakai to Keizai Hatten* (Family System and Village: Economic Development and Japanese Traditional Society). Tokyo, Nōsangyoson Bunkakyōkai.

Sawai, Minoru, and Masayuki Tanimoto (2016). *Nihon Keizaishi: Kinsei kara Gendai made* (The Economic History of Japan: From the Early Modern Era to the Present). Tokyo, Yūhikaku.

Sugahara, Kenji (1979). "Kinsei Sonraku to Muranyūyō" (Village and Its Expenditure in Early Modern Japan). *Nihonshikenkyū* 199.

Takeuchi, Makoto (2009). *Kanseikaikaku no Kenkyū* (The Study of Kansei Reform). Tokyo, Yoshikawakōbunkan.

Tanimoto, Masayuki (1990). "Chōshi Shōyu Jōzōgyō no Keieikōzō" (The Business Structure of Chōshi Soy Sauce Brewing). In *Shōyu Jōzōgyō-shi no Kenkyū*, edited by Reiko Hayashi. Tokyo, Yoshikawakōbunkan.

——— (1996). "Sekiguchi Hachibei/Naotarō: Shōyu Jōzōgyō to Chihō Kigyōka, Meibōka" (Soy-Sauce Industry and the Local Entrepreneur/Notable). In *Nihon niokeru Kigyōka no Shokeifu*, edited by Johzen Takeuchi, Takeshi Abe, and Minoru Sawai. Osaka, Osaka Daigaku Shuppankai.

——— (1998). "Nihon niokeru Chiikikōgyōka to Tōshikōdō: Kigyōbokkōki, Chihōshisanka no Kōdō wo Megutte" (Investment Activities in Regional Industrialization in Japan: The Activities of Men of Property in Local Areas). *Shakai-keizai-shigaku* 64 (1).

——— (2006). "Capital Accumulation and the Local Economy: Brewers and Local Notables." In *The Role of Tradition in Japan's Industrialization*, edited by Masayuki Tanimoto. Oxford, Oxford University Press.

——— (2015). "Zairaikeizai, Sangyō no Hatten" (The Development of Indigenous Industry and Economy). In *Iwanami Kōza Nihon Rekishi Kinsei* 5, edited by Tōru Ohtsu et al. Tokyo, Iwanami Shoten.

——— (2018). "Kinsei Minami Yamashiro niokeru Nengu Futan to Murazaisei" (The Burden of Annual Tribute and Public Finance of Village in South Yamashiro Province). In *Gōnō tachi no Kinsei, Kindai*, edited by Shigehiko Ioku and Masayuki Tanimoto. Tokyo, Tokyo Daigaku Shuppankai.

Tsuda, Hideo (1961). *Houken Keizaiseisaku no Tenkai to Shijōkōzō* (Market Structure under the Deployment of Feudal Economic Policy). Tokyo, Ochanomizu Shobō.

Watanabe, Hiroshi (2010). *Nihon Seiji Shisōshi: 17th to 19th Century* (The History of Japanese Political Thoughts). Tokyo, Tokyo Daigaku Shuppankai.

Watanabe, Takashi (1998). *Kinsei Sonraku no Tokushitsu to Tenkai* (The Feature and Deployment of Villages in the Early Modern Period). Tokyo, Azekura Shobō.

Weber, Max (1968). *Economy and Society: An Outline of Interpretive Sociology*, vol. 1. Edited by Guenther Roch and Claus Wittich. New York, Bedminster Press.

Yabuta, Yutaka (1992). *Kokuso to Hyakushō-ikki no Kenkyū* (The Study on Provincial Petition and Peasant Uprising). Tokyo, Azekura Shobō.

Yamazaki, Ujihiko, and Shigeo Kitano (1955). *Izawabunkashi* (The Cultural History of Izawa). Izawamura, Mie prefecture, Izawamura Kyouikuiinkai.

Yazawa, Yōko (1985). "Kinsei Sonraku to Mura Zaisei" (Public Finance of Village in Early Modern Japan). *Shigakuzasshi* 94 (10).

Yoshimura, Toyo'o (2013). *Nihonkinsei no Gyōsei to Chiikishakai* (Civil Administration and Regional Society in Early Modern Japan). Tokyo, Azekura Shobō.

Yoshizumi, Mieko (1967). "Tetsudai-fushin Nitsuite" (On Tetsudai-fushin). In *Bungakubu Kenkyū Nenpō* (Gakushūin University) 14.

——— (1968). "Tetsudai-fushin Ichiranhyō" (The List of Tetsudai-fushin Projects). In *Bungakubu Kenkyū Nenpō* (Gakushūin University) 15.

Samurai and Peasants in the Civil Administration of Early Modern Japan

Kenichiro Aratake

What role did samurai play in the functioning of civil administration in early modern Japan, and how did they interact with peasants in the areas they were charged with supervising? Did the administrative organizations under the feudal lords (the shogunate and domains) employ a large number of samurai, and what did they contribute to the governing of rural areas? The answers to these questions are important for thinking holistically about the provision of public goods by the feudal lords, as well as for gaining a more concrete understanding of the allocation of human resources.

In early modern Japan, the shogunate and domains collected land levy called *nengu* (annual tributes)[1] from commoners, out of which the samurai's salaries were paid. This system of public finance gave rise to two obligations in the relationship between feudal lords, retainers (samurai), and commoners (Ravina 1999). The first obligation is that, in order to pay retainers' salaries, feudal lords levied tributes on commoners; the second is ethical in nature: feudal lords were to act with mercy toward commoners. This is the starting point for understanding the civil administration and society of early modern Japan and the relationship between feudal lords and subjects. The topic we expand is the ways samurai and peasants were involved in tribute collection and in the governance of the domain. Collection of the annual tribute was based on a cooperative effort between samurai and the peasants who were delegated to represent their village communities.

Let us begin with an examination of who was appointed to the civil administration and what roles they played. Did the samurai play a leading role in the departments of civil administration, which were created to facilitate the domain's rule of rural areas, or did the representatives of the peasants take the lead? One of the key steps in administration was the cadastral survey, which registered land holdings, which were the basis for assessment of annual tribute. Though it would not have been strange for the samurai to assume all roles in conducting the surveys, as the surveys primarily served the interests of the lords, peasants were actively involved as well. A second question involves the domain's attitude toward civil administration as reflected in its staffing, the proportion of samurai in the domain's vassal band involved in the civil administration. Finally, the answers to these questions tell us about the relationship between the nature of the participation of samurai in the civil administration and the regions they ruled.

RULER AND SUBJECT: THE RELATIONSHIP BETWEEN SAMURAI AND PEASANTS

Under the rule of the Tokugawa shogunate, which lasted from the seventeenth century to the second half of the nineteenth century, Japan was divided among about 250 domains. Although each domain, in principle, had autonomy over the management of its revenue and expenditure, the organization and rules that applied to the villages were similar to the structure employed in the territories under the direct rule of the Tokugawa shogunate. All domains had a local intendant's office, to which the samurai belonged, and this office appointed a group of village officials, which mostly comprised local villagers. The structure by which domains ruled villages, therefore, involved the participation of both samurai and peasants, and in nearly all domains, interaction in administration created relationships between samurai and peasants. The samurai and peasants composing the group of village officials were responsible for collecting tributes and maintaining the public order. The Okayama domain can serve as an example of how samurai and peasants were organized within the civil administration (Taniguchi 1964).

In the "Samurai" structure of Okayama domain, the county director (*gundai*, referring to a director general) was at the top of a village's judicial system; there were a maximum of two director generals. This post, which was created by the rural administrative reforms of 1682,[2] was filled by what at first were called "experts in village administration" *(jikatakōsha)*. Appointed under the county director were officials called county magistrates *(kōribugyō)*. It is unknown when this post was established, but it existed before the creation of the county director. Originally, there were four magistrates, and they lived in the castle town district *(Jōka-machi)*, but in 1654 their number was increased to eleven and they were moved to the counties they were to administer. The reforms of 1682 reduced their number once again to four. From then until the end of domain rule in 1871, the county magistrates lived at their residences in Minamigatamura, on the outskirts of the *Jōka-machi* of Okayama Castle, and commuted to the county office, which was in the *Jōka-machi*. Under this system of village administration, the county director was something of a figurehead position, with the real power being held by county magistrates.

The chief duty of the county magistrates was the oversight of all aspects of rural governance; their specific duties were (a) determining annual tribute amounts, (b) conducting twice-yearly village inspections,[3] (c) appointing village officials,[4] and (d) informing villages of laws promulgated by the Tokugawa shogunate and by the domains, among other things. The post of county inspector (kōrimetsuke) was also established in 1682, to be filled by five people. In the beginning, each inspector was assigned to his respective area; however, after 1789, all five inspectors shared jurisdiction over the entire domain. The job of county inspector was to monitor everyone, from the samurai under the county magistrates to peasants in the most far-flung villages. According to the regulations established by the domain, the county inspectors were responsible for examining the working conditions of county magistrates and the local administrator (muradaikan) and the farming and living conditions of the peasants. While it may have been possible for them to monitor the small number of samurai engaged in village administration, it would have been very difficult in practice for five officials to survey and monitor the approximately 350,000 peasants in the more than seven hundred villages under their jurisdiction.[5] The local administrators were the samurai who were closest in position to the subjects of the domain. Their numbers decreased over time from fifty-four in 1654 to thirty-four in 1676, and finally to twenty-six in 1682. They took orders from the county magistrates and were originally responsible for communicating a wide range of messages to the villages, but a decree in 1682 limited their role to carrying out the religious inquisition[6] and to duties related to the annual tribute. These annual tribute duties, however, consisted of drafting measures to boost agricultural production, which had been waning since the latter half of the eighteenth century, and do not necessarily signify their actual involvement in the collection of annual tributes.[7]

This concludes the description of the organization of the samurai in village administration and the changes in their posts, appointments, and official duties. Aside from the fact that the positions of county director and county inspector were newly created in 1682, there was a clear decrease in the overall number of samurai assigned to all of the official positions from county director through local administrator. From the end of the seventeenth century until the end of domain rule in 1871, no more than forty or so samurai ruled Okayama domain's 350,000 peasants and, although village management was ostensibly their primary duty, the number of samurai who actually visited villages was fewer still. It is difficult to imagine that they managed to fulfill the monitoring and surveying responsibilities stipulated in the feudal decrees. However, before it can be concluded that there were not enough samurai in village administration, it is necessary to consider how their subjects, the peasants, were organized.

The administrative unit of rural areas in early modern Japan was the village, and the "Big Three" village officials (murakata sanyaku), consisting of village headman (shōya, nanushi), vice headman (toshiyori, kumigashira), and peasants' representative(*goningumi-gashira, hangashira*), played leading roles in the administration. In the Okayama domain, when the rule of the Tokugawa shogunate was established in 1603, the Big Three were called *shōya* (village headman), *toshiyori* (vice headman), and *goningumi-gashira* (peasants' representative). In 1689 these titles were changed to *nanushi, kumi-gashira,* and *han-gashira*.[8] The typical procedure was for each village to choose its officials and subsequently obtain the county magistrate's approval for their appointment.

Among the Big Three, the most important role belonged to the village headman, who either inherited the post or was voted in by peasants in an election *(irefuda)*.[9] Most villages had one village headman, but some large villages of one thousand *koku*[10] or more appointed two. In contrast, some village headman served double duty for two smaller villages (five hundred *koku* or less). The Okayama domain encompassed approximately seven hundred villages, so we can estimate that there were roughly 750 village headman, based on the proportion of large and small villages. The duties the village headman fulfilled during the Edo period are enumerated in historical records compiled in Okayama during the Meiji period. They were (a) to gather the annual tributes collected from individual peasants, (b) to create records about the villages, and (c) to oversee general affairs in the villages. The role of vice headman was to assist with these duties. There were usually two vice headmen appointed to a village so we can estimate that the number of vice headmen was approximately fifteen hundred across the entire Okayama domain. Finally, villages did not have a fixed number of peasants' representatives; rather, it was stipulated that there should be one peasants' representative for dozens of households, to be determined by an election within the village. The fact that they were elected as peasants' representatives meant that they served as village inspectors in addition to participating in village administration under the headman and vice headman.

One of the important duties of these village officials was to collect the annual tributes levied on peasants in the village and deliver them to the domain. If a peasant could not pay the annual tribute, it was stipulated that the village would be held collectively responsible for payment (Shirakawabe 2010). Evidence for the important role that the village officials played in paying these annual tributes to the domain is contained in the records they kept. Previous research shows that the village officials had to become proficient in the creation of "administrative documents," which gave them a strong sense of responsibility toward village administration (Kurushima 1995). Certainly the historical materials that were passed down from the houses of village headmen include many documents about annual tributes and substantiate the claim that village officials took the initiative in performing this role. Furthermore, Miyaoi Yasuo, an author who had firsthand experience as a village headman in the early nineteenth century, wrote in one of his books that "village headmen selflessly devote themselves to village administration, for which not only the precise calculation of annual tributes, but also the careful maintenance of village records" is of utmost importance (Watanabe 1989).

Above the village officials were the *ojōya*[11] (representative of the village head-man); five to fifteen *ojōya* were chosen to represent multiple villages.[12] In the Okayama domain, sixty-three *ojōya* were appointed in 1701, with roughly similar numbers being appointed after that. Their main duty was to represent their vil-lages in direct negotiations with samurai; this, in effect, connected villages to the administration of the domain.

From this description we can see that some forty or fifty samurai were appointed to posts in village administration and that 3,750 village officials[13] composed the peasants' side of the administration. These numbers also seem to indicate a declin-ing trend in the numbers of samurai in charge of civil administration from the seventeenth to the eighteenth centuries. The domain's acceptance of fewer samurai in village administration is surely due, at least in part, to the growth of village organizations made up of peasants.

The heavy burden assumed by the village headmen and others and the limited involvement of the samurai suggest that the samurai could not fully grasp the local areas' administrative issues. The next question that arises is how this impacted the collection of annual tribute and the roles of samurai and the peasants in collection.

CADASTRAL SURVEYS AND LOCAL INSPECTIONS BY SAMURAI

The annual tributes collected from peasants, compiled by village officers, and paid to feudal lords (the shogunate or domains) were calculated according to data col-lected in cadastral surveys conducted by the rulers. What roles did the samurai and peasants play in carrying out these cadastral surveys?

Land surveys were conducted in many villages under the command of rulers, and in the second half of the sixteenth century they were used to calculate annual tributes. These surveys began with the Taikō survey, which was actively pursued under Hideyoshi Toyotomi's rule. This was followed by the Tokugawa shogunate's Keichō survey in the first decade of the 1600s, which was nationwide in scale; the Kan'ei-Keian survey during the 1630s and 1640s; and the Kanbun-Enpō survey[14] during the 1660s and 1670s, which focused on the shogunate's territory in Kanto and Kinai, to name just a few. In contrast to these surveys, which were carried out by the shogunate, domains sometimes conducted surveys themselves within their own territories. However, from the end of the seventeenth century until the Meiji Restoration, hardly any large-scale surveys were conducted by the shogunate or domains.

The process of conducting a survey was as follows: (1) determine the bound-aries of the village, (2) measure the area of the village's land according to zones defined by usage (e.g., rice field, vegetable field, housing, and so on), (3) assess the agricultural yield of each zone based on the fertility of its soil,[15] and finally (4) identify the owners of the plots of land thus measured and assessed. The names of these individual landowners from whom annual tributes were collected, along with the agricultural output assessments, were then documented in a cadaster[16] for that village. Analyses of land surveys in many historical studies have been based on these results, with the assumption that the villages were surveyed by the ruler's vassals (Watanabe 2004). However, surveying all the farmland in Japan required extensive manpower and was very expensive; thus, many surveys could be conducted only once. Furthermore, while the domain did send samurai to villages to conduct surveys, the work could not have been completed without the help of the village headmen, who were familiar with the villages (Watanabe 2008).

From 1640 to 1643, a "General Survey" was carried out across all rural areas in the Sendai domain in the Tohoku region[17] (Sendai-shi 2001). The survey was prompted by, among other factors, the loss of the previous survey books in a fire in 1636 in the office where the domain's administrative records were kept, and heavy damage incurred to rural areas by major flooding throughout the domain in 1637. The Sendai domain sent 160 samurai in thirty-five groups[18] from the castle town to villages. Armed with specialized techniques for land measurement and assessment, these samurai were tasked with conducting the survey and recording their findings. To do so effectively, however, would have required the guidance of the village officials, who were knowledgeable about village affairs, as well as the participation of peasants, who could help with small tasks. The precise number of peasants mobilized for the Kan'ei-era survey is unclear, but their cooperation was surely indispensable for a mere 160 samurai to survey one thousand villages (Watanabe 1983).

Moreover, the Tokugawa shogunate's Kanbun-Enpō survey conducted around Osaka can serve as a reference for estimating the proportion of samurai and peasants participating in cadastral surveys (Mori 1970). The neighboring domains of the shogunate's territory, who were in charge of the task instead of the shogunate's officials, sent their vassals to the villages targeted for the survey, and for each ten samurai the village enlisted the participation of twenty people, including village officials. Conducting cadastral surveys was important not only for the rulers (shogunate and domains) to collect annual tributes, but also as recognition of the domain's authority in the villages. In addition, because surveys could not be conducted frequently, they were a rare opportunity for samurai to set foot on peasants' lands. However, in practice, very few samurai were actually dispatched, and thus they needed the help of the peasants as a matter of course.

While the collection of annual tributes was based on large-scale cadastral surveys conducted by the shogunate and domains that focused on existing fields, there was also an established rule throughout the country stipulating that agricultural land that had been expanded through the development of new fields was also to be registered in the cadasters, in a system called *takaire*. The Hiroshima domain in the mid-eighteenth century provides evidence for considering the relationship between samurai and peasants in the basic *takaire* system (Hiroshima-ken 1973).

Once a newly developed field in a rural area became capable of sustaining production that was equally as stable as existing fields,[19] the village headman recorded its land area and projected yield in what was called a "preliminary inspection book" and submitted it to the county magistrate.[20] Upon receiving the document, the county magistrate would check to see if it followed the correct format, without going to inspect the field directly. If he deemed it correct, the county magistrate approved the *takaire* registration of the new field and issued a directive to the village headman to pay annual tribute of 50% of its projected yield for the next five years. Since the figures written in the preliminary inspection book were, above all, estimated yields, the actual yields over its initial five-year tribute-exempt period were checked,[21] and their average was registered as the official number in tribute-related documents such as the cadastral. That is the process by which new agricultural land in the Hiroshima domain was registered as official territory: the village headman undertook land inspection and documentation from the very beginning, whereas the county magistrate (responsible on the domain's side) merely received the document and made decisions based on it without verifying it.

However, the county magistrate and his subordinate samurai did tour the area under their jurisdiction every year under a system called *junken,* which, in the Hiroshima domain, was defined as follows. First, every March, the county magistrate was to visit the villages under his jurisdiction to verify village affairs firsthand. March was chosen (a) to ensure that the peasants were preparing for the upcoming rice planting season and (b) to motivate peasants to work hard at farming. The magistrate's subordinate administrators[22] were also to conduct village inspections at least twice in total over the spring and summer every year. The purpose of the administrators' inspections was to ensure that crops were growing normally. If a crop failure was forecasted due to the weather, measures such as tribute abatement needed to be taken to adjust for the poor rice harvest in the fall. It was this predictive ability that was sought in an administrator. All together, there were to be three inspections per year in the Hiroshima domain, conducted by samurai in the civil administration, and it is probable that other domains generally had a similar rule. But did samurai in the Hiroshima domain actually make the rounds they were supposed to? Excluding years when there were major natural disasters such as droughts and floods, samurai did not visit villages more than once a year or so. Rather than inspecting villages themselves, it became the norm for the country magistrate and administrators to implement laws relating to the village based on reports submitted by village headmen. Even in the case of annual tributes, which are of utmost importance in feudal rule, village headmen and other officials collected grain from individual peasants and delivered it to the domain office. The county magistrate thus came to depend on the peasants for his work.

From the perspective of cadastral surveys and annual tribute collection, which are central issues in rural administration, the preceding analysis of the samurai's and peasants' roles shows that the role of the samurai was even smaller than previously thought, which leads to the conclusion that their duties were proactively handled by the village headmen and other peasants. How, then, did civil administration in rural areas come to be dependent on the peasants? The self-reliance of villagers who performed all of the basic work involved in administration has been cited as one reason (Kurushima 1995, Watanabe 2010). Village headmen and village officials accumulated knowledge about village management, increased efficiency, particularly in duties that had become routine work, and worked toward maintaining good relations with the feudal rulers.[23] Taking into account the structure of organizations in the Okayama domain along with the distribution of work between the samurai and peasants as described for the Hiroshima domain here, it is apparent that the rulers did not need to appoint a great number of people from their side. This leads to the next question, what proportion of samurai were involved in civil administration?

THE POSITION OF THE CIVIL ADMINISTRATION IN VASSAL BANDS

The Organizational Structure of the Vassal Band in the Hiroshima Domain

The average percentage of the population holding the rank of samurai is estimated at about 6% nationwide, though there were domains with higher percentages, such as Sendai with 23% (Morris 2009). In the Hiroshima domain, there was a total population of approximately 910,000 in 1869 as the domain system was approaching its end, just over fifty-six thousand were samurai.[24] That puts the percentage of samurai in the total population at 6.2%, roughly on par with the national average (Hiroshima-ken 1984). Though these numbers cannot be precisely verified because of the nature of available statistics, there was a vassal band in the second half of the eighteenth century predominantly comprising about four thousand close attendants[25] to the ruler.

The organizational structure of the vassal band in the Hiroshima domain is shown in figure 3, along with the respective numbers of samurai who held each post in 1753 and 1862. These numbers should be understood to represent the upper echelon,[26] those who were superior in rank to the ruler's aforementioned four thousand close attendants. At the very top was the ruler *(daimyō)*, and directly under him were the chief vassals: elders *(karō)*, chief directors *(toshiyori)*, and chief inspectors *(ōmetsuke)*, in that order. Second in command to the ruler, the elders oversaw the domain administration and vassal band. Next in line, the chief directors' role was to take directives from the elders and issue instructions accordingly to the specialized departments, whose roles are described later. Finally, the chief inspectors, despite their title, composed the remainder of the core of the domain administration along with the elders and chief directors. There were no great changes in the numbers of these chief vassals between 1753 and 1862 except for the chief inspectors, whose numbers increased.

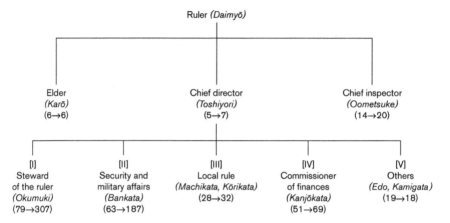

FIGURE 3. Hiroshima Organizational Formation of 1753 and 1862
Source: Hiroshima-ken 1984.
Note: Numbers in parentheses denote the change from 1753 to 1862.

Under the chief vassals were five specialized departments: (1) "steward of the ruler," which dealt with various tasks on behalf of the ruler; (2) "security and military affairs," the department that defended the castle and the territory; (3) "local rule," the samurai engaged in the work of governing towns and villages as government officials; (4) "commissioner of finance," the department that dealt with fiscal issues, comparable to present-day financial departments; and finally (5) "others," including samurai who lived in Edo, Kyoto, and Osaka permanently as government officials.[27]

The numbers under each section denote the numbers of samurai included therein. Let us consider the changing pattern of these numbers. In 1753, 304 out of four thousand samurai held posts of elder or below. Then in 1862 the number of samurai holding official posts, which had remained steady at around three hundred for over a century, skyrocketed. This was because, during the nineteenth century, each domain attempted to expand its army to face the international crisis in Japan. As table 3 indicates, this entailed the near-quadrupling of those attached to the Office of the Ruler and a threefold increase in the section charged with security and military affairs. However, the numbers of samurai in the other three departments remained the same, suggesting that the ruler was actively looking to strengthen the military and augment his staff of close attendants.

An analysis of the "public office work" conducted in 1862 found that a total of 268 people were employed as close attendants, forty-five worked for the commissioner of finance, and thirty-two were in civil administration. These close attendants served the domain ruler and his family, and performed everyday chores. They also included doctors who provided medical treatment to the ruler. The commissioner of finance's office managed the domain's finances and oversaw the production of wood, paper, iron, and salt. It also managed finances for merchants and peasants. Civil administrators assessed annual tribute collections and implemented related laws in the villages.

What can be inferred from these numbers? First, the domain ruler had an overwhelming number of close attendants, whereas there were only a small number of employees in the offices of commissioner of finance and local rule. In addition, because of the *sankin-kōtai* system, it had become the ruler's duty to live in his Hiroshima castle and the Edo capital each for two years at a time. Therefore, there must have also been a large number of people accompanying the ruler who also had to go back and forth between Hiroshima and Edo. The retirement of a ruler presents another point to consider. When passing the position of ruler down to a successor, the retiring ruler typically built himself a retirement mansion. However, after the mansion had been built, close attendants would be employed to serve the retired ruler, creating a situation where there were effectively not only "two rulers" but also a dual structure in personnel and funding.

This concludes the discussion of the characteristics of the vassal band in the Hiroshima domain. Though the numbers of samurai appointed to posts in 1753 and 1862 were influenced by historical circumstances, the structure of the vassal band indicates an emphasis on roles for serving the ruler and his family, followed by posts relating to the military, especially in accordance with the situation near the end of the Edo period. In contrast, the proportion of those who were involved in civil administration was rather small.

The Proportion of Samurai in Civil Administration Relative to the Rural Population

Let us consider the civil administration from another angle. Table 3 contains information about four of the Hiroshima domain's seventeen counties in 1715, beginning with agricultural output, the numbers of villages and households, and their overall population. The middle columns of the table show the number of town magistrates or county magistrates engaged in administrative work in each county, as well as the number of local administrators,[28] who were burdened with substantial work. In total, the Hiroshima domain had twenty-seven county magistrates and town magistrates, and seventy-five local administrators who performed actual local administration duties. According to the "local rule" section of figure 3, there were twenty-eight county magistrates and town magistrates in 1753, so their numbers hardly changed from 1715. There were also seventy-five subordinates to the local rule division, though they are not indicated in figure 3. Area 1, "Villages around Hiroshima," refers to the villages in the direct vicinity of the castle town (*Jōka-machi*) of Hiroshima. There were seventeen such villages, containing a total of 893 households and a total population of approximately ten thousand.[29] Unlike the remaining counties in the table, this area had no county magistrate, because

TABLE 3. Hiroshima in 1715: Output, Population, and Government Officials

No.	County (*Gun*) name	Agricultural output (unit: *koku*)	Villages	Houses	Population	a. Town Magistrate (*Machibugyo*)	b. County Magistrate (*Koribugyo*)	c. Local Administrator (*Muramawari*)	a+b: Population per government one official (unit:person)	c: Population per government one official (unit:person)
1	Villages around Hiroshima	10,830	17	893	10,855	2	0	3	5,400	3,600
2	Numata county	20,562	31	7,677	24,896	0	2	5	12,500	5,000
3	Kamo county	56,868	90	20,109	60,669	0	2	7	30,000	8,700
4	Toyota county	56,224	85	18,744	55,701	0	2	7	28,000	8,000
	[omission : 13 counties]	329,759	624	112,312	346,561	0	19	53	18,240	6,500
	Total	474,243	847	159,735	498,682	2	25	75	18,500	6,650

SOURCE: Hiroshima-ken 1973.

it was under the jurisdiction of the town magistrate, who was in charge of the castle town. The three local administrators were thus under the town magistrate's command. The final two columns of table 3 show the population of each county per magistrate and per administrator, which was fifty-four hundred and thirty-six hundred, respectively, for area 1. Area 2 was the smallest in scale of all the counties; areas 3 and 4 were the largest.

Let us look at Toyota County (area 4) as an example. This county was about fifty-six thousand *koku* in size and contained eighty-five villages, eighteen thousand households, and fifty-five thousand people. Two county magistrates and seven local administrators were responsible for its governance. The tendency for this county and all of the others was to have a fixed number of two county magistrates and to adjust the number of local administrators according to the number of villages and the population. By comparing these numbers with the population, it can be concluded that each county magistrate had to administer a rural population of 28,000, and each local administrator administered 8,000. The averages across the entire domain were 18,500 people per town or county magistrate and 6,650 people per local administrator.

These numbers indicate that in the Hiroshima domain, a small number of government officials were engaged in civil administration. In fact, five hundred thousand people were administered by just one hundred samurai, a proportion that would have made it difficult for those samurai to grasp the overall conditions of village communities. Such numbers further suggest, as I have argued in this chapter, how few samurai there were engaged in civil administration.

The County Magistrate's Duties

Having established the small number of samurai appointed to the civil administration, it is now time to address the question: What work did they actually have to do? To answer this, let us take a look at the mid-nineteenth-century work journal of a county magistrate of the Kurume domain,[30] which was located in Kyushu. The Kurume domain was ruled by the House of Arima, which occupied an area of two hundred thousand *koku,* and contained a population of about 250,000 people in 550 villages (Nishimura 1980). This work journal, which belonged to the county magistrate of Mizuma County[31] in the Kurume domain, provides insight into his work. The journal begins with the names of eleven samurai who served as secretaries, treasurers, and village administrators[32] before moving on to work-related entries. According to the entries made by the county magistrate, he would hold meetings every winter with relevant subordinates to verify annual tribute collections and also meet with the village headmen's representatives. However, the journal does not contain detailed information about the collection of annual tributes, and while there is special mention of matters related to delayed payments of annual tribute to the ruler, this was limited to a minority of villages. This is probably because there was no need to write anything about prompt payments.

The entries corresponding to visits from the village headmen's representatives are also exceedingly short, which gives the impression that they were more of a formality than a forum for the discussion of actual business.

Other than tribute-related items, there are many entries about (a) public order, the police, and lawsuits; and (b) participation in the ruler's formalities. The police mentioned in the (a) entries were a part of the civil administration and, needless to say, persons whose duty was indispensable for the safety of society. However, an independent police force served a large part of the Kurume domain, and within the villages there were also neighborhood watch–style groups headed by village headmen's representatives, which meant that the county magistrate did not necessarily oversee everything. Rather than general police functions, it may be more accurate to say that it was special investigations for which the police force in the (a) entries was responsible. In particular, special mention in the journal was given to the discovery and control of gambling, which was a prohibited activity and punishable offense at the time. Suspects were arrested by the subordinates of the county magistrate, who intervened on behalf of the local community. With the possibility that nonsamurai investigators (who were subordinate to the village headmen's representatives) would be partial to the suspects, it made sense for prosecutors to pursue a fair investigation by the county magistrate. Religious rites for the ruler and his ancestors and visits to Buddhist temples (item [b]) were also among the country magistrate's important duties. The county magistrate was also in charge of matters like public declarations of filial piety, which were carried out in domains across Japan during this time.

THE DUTIES OF THE
SHOGUNATE'S CHIEF ADMINISTRATORS

As suggested by the aforementioned numbers and roles of samurai appointed to organizations on the ruler's side, vassals were relatively unconcerned with civil administration. This section will discuss the activities of officials in the *bakuryō*, or lands under direct control of the Tokugawa shogunate, with the intention of comparing them to those of the domains discussed earlier.

There were pockets of *bakuryō* all over the country, with about forty of the shogunate's officials *(hatamoto)* appointed as chief administrators *(bakufu dai-kan),*[33] who held de facto positions as leaders of their respective regions. These chief administrators were similar in stature to feudal lords, presiding over areas roughly equal in scale to those of minor *daimyo;* however, like the county directors and county magistrates of domains, they were also responsible for work related to civil administration.

Bakuryō in Kanto were presided over by chief administrators called *Kanto dai-kan,* whose office was established in Edo. Previous research on *Kanto daikan* has shown that they reported to work at this office more than three hundred days per year (Nishizawa 2004). This number varied in subsequent generations; there even appears to have been one instance where they reported to work in Edo 340 days out of the year. While such working conditions would seem to be rather cruel at first glance, normal working hours were from 10:00 AM to 2:00 PM, and sometimes they only had to work for two hours in the morning. It is supposed that their "desk work" consisted of duties such as communicating the shogunate's directives to the villages they governed, examining the reports received from villages, and offering judgments on individual court cases (Murakami 1970). However, judging by their working arrangement, it is difficult to imagine that their workload was very extensive; rather, it must have been quite light, at least most of the time.

The administrators of Nakano in Shinano province presided over one hundred villages in the *bakuryō* around their regional office (Nishizawa 2004). One might expect them to have worked and looked after their subjects from the regional office in Nakano, the local center of power.[34] However, in Nakano, subordinates were stationed at the regional office; the administrators themselves lived in Edo.[35] The extent of their visits to Nakano and the villages they governed was once a year in the fall—a mere twenty days' trip, of which ten were dedicated to village inspections. Though the goal of these trips was ostensibly the on-site verification of rice harvests, the mere fact of visiting as many as one hundred villages suggests that the administrators could not have conducted sufficient inspections. Ultimately their visits were nothing more than a formality.

The Career of Itaro Hayashi

Born in 1806 to the family of an official for the shogunate, Itaro Hayashi aspired to be a scholar (Murakami 1970, Yasuda 2009). Although Hayashi did become a scholar, he subsequently served as a chief administrator in many areas. At the beginning of the nineteenth century, the Tokugawa shogunate often appointed scholars to the post of chief administrator; other than Hayashi, however, nearly all of them resigned within the first year.[36] In that regard, Hayashi was a rare individual who left the scholarly world and would go on to hold various positions in civil administration.

From 1858 to 1862, Hayashi was appointed as a local administrator for Shibahashi in Dewa Province (the northeast region of Japan called Tohoku, ten days on foot from Edo), where he presided over a *bakuryō* encompassing one hundred villages. The regional office was in Shibahashi, but only a few of his subordinates were stationed there. Meanwhile, Hayashi worked from his residence in Edo, which he himself owned. He visited the area he governed for about two weeks each year, which means that he was in Edo for the remaining 350 days. Of course, it would have been impossible for Hayashi to complete one year's work in two weeks and oversee all of the villages that he managed. In view of this fact, the local administrators worked as direct managers under his supervision. The number of local administrators who held a post in Shibahashi is uncertain; however, in

Nakaizumi, where Hayashi began a new assignment,[37] there were initially twenty-six local administrators in 1853, and this number dropped to seventeen in 1858. In any event, what kind of work did the feudal lord's administrative organization do, with only twenty samurai for an area where tens of thousands of people lived? Hayashi recorded daily events, which included the activities being conducted in Shibahashi at the time.[38] His journal contains an enormous amount of information, but evidence of interaction with commoners and detailed entries about the civil administration are rare.

Many of his office hours were spent creating and signing documents and making plans, with almost no activities involving positive interventions in village communities. However, inspecting the Shibahashi regional office over a period of two weeks seemed to be a hard schedule. He was accompanied by a subordinate and finished the inspection of a village on the first day. This indicates that the chief administrator's visit was just a formality—an item to be checked off the list without involving the actual work of inspecting the village. Moreover, while Hayashi was staying in Shibahashi, he also observed how a copper mine in the area under the shogunate's jurisdiction was being developed and managed; he subsequently developed that mining project further. Although there are entries about matters other than the development of the copper mine, there are few indications that he had developed innovative policies. He tackled a lawsuit and satisfactorily addressed an incident that occurred in the copper mine project. On the other hand, Hayashi hardly mentioned management of the village, and neither did his subordinate. This suggests that local administrators tasked peasants with management of the village, which was probably because annual tribute collection and other duties did not entail much work.

Hayashi's record of his daily activities adds two additional points to what we have learned about local administration from early examples. First, the local officer did not always reside in his administrative area. Hayashi performed on-site inspections only once a year; it is uncertain whether he actually fulfilled his duties as a member of the civil administration in the area he governed. Second, local officers had very few subordinates. In one example, there were twenty subordinates, and in another case, only ten people worked for one local officer. This was thought to be a small number, and it is surprising that a single officer could administer one hundred villages containing tens of thousands of people.

The smooth functioning of the civil administration in early modern Japan required the active participation of the peasants, particularly the village officials. Indeed, the peasants' contribution to local administration is a distinctive characteristic of the society during this period. On the other hand, the suzerain authority's limited employment of samurai in the civil administration clearly indicates that they did not assign it much importance. One could also argue that they had created a very effective system for local administration, incorporating commoners that worked very efficiently, so they did not need to employ more samurai. Furthermore, the few samurai who did hold posts in the civil administration were not deeply involved with the villages they ruled and rarely even visited them. The level of rulers' involvement in the human side of local governance was therefore extremely low with respect to their provision of public goods.

This chapter looked at the specific relationship between rulers and villages with regard to the staffing of the civil administration. Earlier research has shown that rural governance functioned smoothly with the help of peasants *(muraukesei),*[39] but there has been little study of the staffing of administrative organizations.

As is evident from the appointment and roles of samurai in the Okayama and Hiroshima domains, not only did domains allocate only a small number of samurai to civil administration, but the samurai who were employed in that capacity did not live in the regions they ruled, severely limiting their opportunities to exercise their role as inspectors. It is not at all surprising, then, that such a state of affairs led to the active participation of a comparatively large number of village officials in civil administration. This is illustrated by the fact that the most salient tasks in the relationship between feudal lords and their subjects—conducting cadastral surveys and determining and collecting annual tributes—depended on the peasants. Moreover, in addition to the small proportion of samurai in civil administration compared to both vassal bands and the rural population, the civil administration's reliance on villages was also prompted by the rather light workloads of individual samurai.

Another major finding of this analysis, and one that may be regarded as another characteristic of early modern Japanese society, is the fact that peasants, who had to pay annual tributes, were not compensated by the load as employees.

PRIMARY SOURCES

Arimake Monjo (n.d.). *Kōribugyō Nikki* (The Country Magistrate's Journal), collection of Kurume City Main Library.

Takegaki Naomichi Nikki (The Journals of Takegaki Naomichi), in collection of Historiographical Institute of the University of Tokyo.

NOTES

1. For the details of annual tribute, see chapter 2 of this volume, by Masayuki Tanimoto.

2. The reforms of 1682 established the structure of village administration in the Okayama domain, which encompassed, for the most part, posts and hierarchy that were inherited by subsequent administrations (Taniguchi 1964).

3. These inspections were intended to inform subjects about ways to promote agricultural growth and to improve habits and customs.

4. The norm was for villages to nominate village officials and inform the county magistrate of the nominees, whom the magistrate would then appoint.

5. There are data to indicate that there were 721 villages in 1868 and that the rural population of the domain was 366,867 in 1721 and 346,866 in 1834 (Kanai 1953).

6. This religious inquisition, the *Shūmon aratame,* was the Edo shogunate's measure to ban Christianity and expose adherents. Families and individuals were asked about their religious affiliation (Buddhist sect) and had to prove that they were registered with a Buddhist temple. This information was recorded in the administrative documents.

7. Taniguchi (1964) states that local administrators treated the collection of tributes as their job, citing the "persuasion" of villages with declining production. However, it is unclear whether they actually collected the tributes.

8. The official titles of the Big Three varied from region to region and were sometimes changed over time, as in the case of the Okayama domain. In general, village headmen were called *shōya, nanushi,* or *kimoiri;* vice headmen were called *toshiyori* or *kumigashira,* and the peasants' representative was called *hyakushōdai.* Nevertheless, their respective job duties remained largely the same regardless of their title.

9. These two paths to assuming the post—by inheritance or by *irefuda* election—were the same in other domains as well. The vice headman could also be chosen by nomination of the village headman, in addition to either of those two methods.

10. For details of the *koku,* see the short introduction to part 1.

11. The village headmen's representative was called *ojōya* in the Okayama domain, but in other domains, other titles such as *ōkimori* and *warimoto* were used.

12. Organizations of multiple villages were called *kumi* or *kumiai.*

13. The village headmen's representative was chosen from among the village headmen.

14. Surveys of lands belonging to the shogunate were usually conducted by officials from the shogunate, but for the Kanbun-Enpō survey, neighboring domains were put in charge in order to prevent fraud by officials from the shogunate and by the peasants under its rule (Mori 1970).

15. Surveyors measured the land's productivity and ranked each zone. In the beginning, there were three levels: high, medium, and low.

16. Cadasters were land registers upon which the collection of tributes was based. Each cadaster was created in duplicate; the original was kept by the feudal lord, and the copy was issued to the village (Kanzaki 1983).

17. This Kan'ei survey was the only time that the Sendai domain carried out its own cadastral survey across the lands under its jurisdiction.

18. Each group consisted of four samurai.

19. In general, newly developed fields were exempt from consideration in the collection of tributes for the first five years.

20. This corresponds to the Okayama domain's county magistrate.

21. It is unclear how the actual yields were determined, but there is no evidence that the county magistrate or other samurai were actively involved.

22. This corresponds to the Okayama domain's local administrators.

23. Popular movements such as peasant uprisings and village riots raised the caliber of officials (Kurushima 1995).

24. This figure includes the ruler's close attendants (his direct servants), rear vassals (*their* servants), servants of samurai households, and their families.

25. The number of close attendants was 385 in 1619, but subsequently increased (Doi 2015).

26. Their actual numbers for each section are unclear, but it is assumed that samurai were employed in proportion to the number of official posts.

27. The Hiroshima domain built residences in Edo, Kyoto, and Osaka, in which some samurai were stationed permanently.

28. These are the same posts as county magistrate and local administrator.

29. All of the numbers for area 1 pertain only to the villages around the castle town. For reference, the population of the castle town itself was about thirty thousand.

30. Arimake Monjo n.d.

31. Mizuma County contained 130 villages and had a population of about fifty thousand.

32. These correspond to the local administrators. The county was divided into four regions, each governed by one administrator.

33. Chief administrators had greater authority than officials in the domain administration and often governed lands of between fifty thousand and one hundred thousand thousand *koku*. Some samurai inherited this post, whereas others were appointed by the domain and transferred to different regions, with the proportion of the latter increasing after the eighteenth century (Murakami 1970).

34. Regionally based chief administrators lived in buildings that housed both their private residences and the regional office.

35. Chief administrators had subordinates called *tetsuki* and *tedai,* of whom administrators generally had about twenty in total (Yasuda 2009).

36. There were many reasons, but ultimately, they were not cut out for politics, and it appears that the shogunate asked them to resign.

37. Prior to his appointment as an administrator for Shibahashi, Hayashi was an administrator for Nakaizumi in Tōtōmi province.

38. Yasuda 2003.

39. For details of the *muraukesei,* see the short introduction to part 1.

REFERENCES

Doi, Sakuji (2015). *Hiroshima Han* (The Hiroshima Domain). Yoshikawakōbunkan.

Hiroshima-ken (1973). *Hiroshima-kenshi Kinseishiryōhen,* vol. 1 (History of Hiroshima Prefecture, Early Modern Historical Materials, vol. 1). Hiroshima-ken.

——— (1984). *Hiroshima-kenshi Tūshi,* vol. 4 (History of Hiroshima Prefecture, vol. 4). Hiroshima-ken.

Kanai, Madoka (1953). "Hitotsu no han no sōjinkō" (Total Population of One Domain). *Nihon-rekishi* 67.

Kanzaki, Akitoshi (1983). *Kenchi: Nawa to Sao no Shihai* (The Land Survey: Rule to Be Established from a Rope and a Pole). Kyōikusha.

Kurushima, Hiroshi (1995). "Hyakushō to Mura no Henshitsu" (Change in Quality of a Farmer and the Village). In *Iwanami Kōza Nihontūshi,* vol. 15. Iwanami Shoten.

Morris, John Francis (2009). *Kinsei Bushi no Kō to Shi: Sendaihanshi Tamamushi Jūzo no Kyaria to Zasetsu* (The Public Job of the Samurai of Early Modern Japan, and a Private Life: Samurai of Sendai Career and Frustration which Tamamushi Jūzo Experiences). Seibundō Shuppan.

Mori, Sugio (1970). *Enpō Kenchi* (The Enpō Land Survey). Takaishi-shi Kyōdo-shi Kenkyūkai.

Murakami, Tadashi (1970). *Edobakufu no Daikan* (The Chief Administrator of the Edo Shogunate). Kokushokankōkai.

Nishimura, Mutsuo (1980). "Hanryōjinkō to Jōka-machijinkō" (The Domain Territory Population and Castle Town Population). *Rekishi-chirigaku* 111.

Nishizawa, Atsuo (2004). *Daikan no Nichijōseikatsu: Edo no Chūkankanrishoku* (A Local Governor's Everyday Life: The Middle Manager of the Edo Period). Kōdansha.

Ravina, Mark (1999). *Land and Lordship in Early Modern Japan.* Stanford University Press.

Sendai-shi (2001). *Sendaishi-shi Tsūshihen,* vol. 3 (History of Sendai City, vol. 3). Sendai-shi.

Shirakawabe, Tatsuo (2010). *Nihon Kinsei no Jiritsu to Rentai* (Self-Support and Solidarity of Early Modern Japan). Tokyo Daigaku Shuppankai.

Taniguchi, Sumio (1964). *Okayama Han* (History of the Okayama Domain). Yoshikawakōbunkan.

Watanabe, Nobuo (1983). "Sendaihan no Seiritsu" (Establishment of the Sendai Domain). In *Miyagi no Kenkyū*, vol. 3. Seibundō Shuppan.

Watanabe, Takashi (1989). "Bakumatsuisinki Niokeru Nōmin to Sonrakukyōdōtai" (Peasants and Village Communities during the End of Edo and the Early Meiji Restoration Period). In *Rekishi-hyōron 475*.

——— (2004). "Mura no Sekai" (The World in a Village Community). In *Nihon-shi Kōza*, vol. 5. Tokyo Daigaku Shuppankai.

——— (2008). *Hyakushō no Chikara: Edojidai kara Mieru Nippon* (Peasant's Capability: Japan Seen from the Edo Period). Kashiwa Shobō.

——— (2010). *Mura karamita Kinsei* (Early Modern Japan as Seen from the Village). Azekura Shobō.

Yasuda, Haruo, ed. (2003). *Hayashi Kakuryō Nikki*, vol. 5 (The Journals of Hayashi Kakuryō). Nihon Hyōronsha.

——— (2009). *Aru Bunjindaikan no Bakumatsu Nikki* (A Government Official Diary of Man of Culture). Yoshikawakōbunkan.

4

Outsourcing the Lord's Finance

An Origin of Local Public Finance in Early Modern Japan

Kazuho Sakai

Who did provide the public goods and how did they do so in the early modern Japan? This volume emphasizes on the role of "local notables"—comprising wealthy farmers, land owners, brewers, and local merchants who emerged from *hyakushō* (peasant) status, residing outside of the castle towns. Some recent research and other chapters in part 1 revealed that such local notables often played a greater role in the provision of local public goods in the late Tokugawa era than had previously been the case (Kikuchi 2003, Yoshimura 2013). However, it is not yet clear how they established a resource for financing the public goods. Although they had achieved authority in civil administration, it was not always accompanied by a corresponding transfer of revenues from feudal lords. The creation of a new financial basis for the provision of local public goods seemingly became an important problem for them. This chapter shows a pattern on how they created financial basis for the public goods provision based on a micro case study.

This chapter focuses on the outsourcing of the lord's finance and investigates how local notables changed the lord's finance, which was not able to satisfy demands for the public goods, and utilized it as the financial basis for the public goods provision. In the late Tokugawa era, rural economy based on market-oriented agriculture and proto-industry developed dramatically compared to urban economy, and new economic surpluses were formed and accumulated in the countryside (Shinbo and Saitō 1989). For example, it is known that the population of castle towns including Edo, Osaka, and Kyoto was stagnant or declining, whereas that of villages and country towns was increasing from the late eighteenth century to the nineteenth century (Smith 1989). However, feudal lords were unable to completely capture the benefits of those new surpluses under the annual tribute *(nengu)* system.[1] Consequently, most of feudal lords suffered fiscal deficits and fell into fiscal crisis (Tsuchiya 1927), and so more and more lords entrusted their fiscal management to local notables who lived in their domain and increased the management ability or fund-raising capability starting in the late eighteenth century.

On the other hand, similar tasks of fiscal management were also outsourced to wealthy financial merchants—such as rice brokers and money changers—in the castle towns, especially Osaka and Edo, where were the financial center of Japan (Mori 1970). We should focus on a difference between fiscal management by local notables in the countryside and that by wealthy financial merchants in the Osaka and Edo. The wealthy financial merchants, who weren't domain inhabitants, took on the fiscal management as a profit-seeking business, but the local notables could not pursue only self-profit. They, who were domain inhabitants, tribute-payers, and local administrators, had a direct responsibility to sustain the other domain inhabitants and regional society and worked as substitutes for their lords. Therefore, such outsourcing to the local notables changed the fiscal system into something more beneficial to local inhabitants than that to the wealthy financial merchants.

How did the local notables change the fiscal system by intervening in their lords' finance? To whom did the change become beneficial in the relationships between the lord, wealthy merchants in the castle towns, and local inhabitants in the countryside? Focusing on these questions, this chapter clarifies that local notables converted the lord's finance into the financial basis for public goods provision.

OVERVIEW OF THE CASE

Lord Tsuda

This chapter deals with a case of the outsourced lord's finance by focusing on the case of the *hatamoto* Tsuda clan. The reason for using this case is that we can overview the lord's finance overall based on the historical materials. Although it is not easy to overview the overall fiscal management in the lord's finance because of lack of historical materials, in this case it is fortunately possible due to abundant historical materials.

Hatamoto, like the *daimyō*, was also the domain lords who were direct vassals of the Tokugawa shogun. The dividing line between the *hatamoto* and the *daimyō* was the scale of the territory (income level), such as ten thousand *koku*.[2] *Hatamoto* was one type of feudal lord in the Tokugawa era, despite the domain's relatively small size of ten thousand *koku*. From a standpoint of domain inhabitants, there was no precise difference in governance between the *hatamoto* and the *daimyō*, but *hatamoto* didn't have alternate attendance *(sankin-kōtai)* duties like the *daimyō* and they lived in the shogunal capital, Edo all the time.

Even among the *hatamoto*, the Tsuda clan had a relatively large domain and notably high number of retainers. As of 1842, Tsuda clan ruled over fourteen villages, assessed at about 6,614 *koku,* in the Kantou region near Edo.[3] The Tsuda clan held as many as ninety-six retainers and two residences at Edo.[4] They always lived in the Edo clan residence and ruled the domain without putting in local officials or a provincial office. Then, they only dispatched their vassals to their domain if necessary, and much of local administration was entrusted to the village headmen of their domain in general.

Key Players

Merchants or village headmen in Sawara village of Tsuda domain, Shimousa province, played a key role in the outsourcing of fiscal management. Sawara was legally designated as a village throughout the Tokugawa era; however, Sawara was a famous country town in which many merchants and wealthy people resided.[5] Its economy grew significantly late in that period, when it capitalized on its sake and soy sauce brewing industries and its position as a port city on the lower Tone River, and thus became an urbanized commercial hub (Ishii and Uno 2000).

In this chapter, we will deal with the three types of key players in outsourcing fiscal management, (1) the chief manager, (2) the treasurer, (3) a syndicate group. (1) The chief manager *(makanai-yaku)* bore fiscal management responsibilities and held the authority to make decisions about anything concerning the outsourcing of fiscal management duties. The post was held by two men—namely, Hidekata Seimiya and Kageharu Inō. The Seimiya and Inō families were prominent merchants in Sawara and served as Sawara village headmen during the Tokugawa era. Under these two men, (2) the treasurer *(makanai-tōban),* a position held by two Sawara merchants, held all cash and was in charge of accounts. In addition, (3) a syndicate group *(goyōtashi)* comprising approximately ten Sawara merchants provided the working capital needed to run the finance apparatus. They were the wealthiest merchants in Sawara.[6]

Other Activities of the Chief Managers

Among key players, the chief managers, Hidekata and Kageharu, had the initiative and played the most important role. What kind of the social and economic activities other than those of fiscal management did they do? Both the Seimiya and Inō families were distinguished, longtime inhabitants of Sawara. Their children and grandchildren had been since the Meiji period among the area's renowned local notables, serving as mayors of Sawara and as members of the Chiba Prefectural Assembly. Both Hidekata and Kageharu lost their fathers when they were children; at tender ages they both became managing heads of their family businesses, and through their stewardship they reversed the waning fortunes of their respective houses. As managers, they succeeded in growing their family wealth. They also served as headmen of the Sawara village administration, where they worked hard on behalf of the local government.

As a scholar of history and geography, Hidekata left behind numerous works of his own authorship, and so subsequent generations do indeed recognize his name; however, few know about his work in the government as the headman of village administration during the Tokugawa era. After the Meiji Restoration, he was in charge of implementing land tax reforms in Sawara. It is also known that he went on to establish the financial administration of the new greater Sawara area, after it absorbed the surrounding villages. In addition, he oversaw the construction and improvement of roads connecting Sawara to the surrounding regions and funneled much of his own money into these projects.[7] Furthermore, he made generous donations to the construction of the new district office and police station. He adapted well to the demands of local government in post–Meiji Restoration society.

As for Kageharu, during the Tenpo Famine of 1836, he provided food relief each morning to some two hundred impoverished people and conducted other relief activities.[8] In 1861, a group of mutineers *(roushi)* from the Mito domain participated in an armed uprising in support of a campaign to revere the emperor and expel foreigners (the *sonnō-jōi* campaign). They murdered merchants in Sawara and demanded a large sum of money to finance their military efforts. Together with Hidekata, Kageharu negotiated with the mutineers while simultaneously petitioning the feudal lord to send retainers for their protection. He succeeded in resolving the problem and maintaining peace by taking defense measures on his own initiative, including the purchase of rifles. In his final years, his most significant achievement was the flood control work he undertook on the Tone River. Flooding was a serious and widespread problem for Sawara and its surrounding area. The river project expenses disbursed from the new external fund were used by Kageharu to conduct part of this flood control project.[9] The roles and functions that the internal reserved fund and the new external fund performed for the region were as an embodiment of the actions and initiative of Hidekata and Kageharu, who worked not only as chief managers, but also as merchants, domain inhabitants, and local notables.

CHANGES GENERATED IN THE OUTSOURCED LORD'S FINANCE

The outsourcing of fiscal management took place over a twenty-three-year period, from 1842 until the Tsuda family ceased to rule Sawara, in August 1864; the outsourcing of fiscal management was generally implemented as a reform measure to address financial crisis, and this was also true in the case of its implementation in Lord Tsuda's finance. In starting, the lord and the chief managers exchanged the contract. The contract stipulated that the chief managers were given complete discretion over where and how the annual tribute rice was sold, and how expenditures were disbursed in return for supplying a designated sum of money *(goyōdate-kin)* to the lord's residence in Edo.[10] In many cases, they sold the collected annual tribute rice for bidding in Sawara.[11]

In this outsourcing of fiscal management, the chief managers made Lord Tsuda's finance more beneficial to local inhabitants in the domain than their lord or merchants in the castle town, Edo. The chief managers' strategy for giving priority to local interests was based on four measures: (1) reduction in the lord's household expenses, (2) charging the "interest" only to lord's household expenses, (3) prior repayments to intradomain creditors, (4) the creation of an internal reserved fund.[12] Let us turn to an examination of each of these measures.

Reduction in the Lord's Household Expenses

The chief managers succeeded in reducing expenditure by more than 10% by cutting the lord's household expenses. Initially, they began to survey the fiscal health of the clan and domain and to plan in a detailed manner how to reduce its annual expenditures. The chief managers then investigated the amounts of annual income (annual tribute) from the previous twenty years and estimated standard annual revenues as about 1,931 *ryō* after considering changes in the rice price rate.[13] On the other hand, the chief managers lowered the salaries paid to retainers, maids, and servants working in Edo residences.[14] More importantly, following close inspection of the lord's daily life, he compelled the lord to accept changes that would lead to reductions in his living expenses. To achieve the objective of lowering annual expenditures, for example, the chief managers made the following demands of his lord.[15]

1. Anywhere the lord travels for the next three years must be by horse, and not by palanquin.
2. The lord, his family, retainer, and even his maids and servants must be dressed in low-priced clothes made of cotton.
3. The lord must take no more than fifteen baths per month.
4. Daily shopping is prohibited.
5. The sumptuous New Year's dinner must be served for no more than three days.
6. Firewood and charcoal must not be purchased in quantities exceeding those dictated by regulations.
7. One horse must be abandoned.
8. The lord and his family must live together on a single residence.
9. When a living residence can be sold at a high price, the lord must move to another residence, even if doing so is inconvenient.

By enacting these changes, the chief managers succeeded in reducing the lord's household expense by two hundred *ryō*, an amount equivalent to 10% of total annual expenditures (2,020 *ryō*). Consequently, they could estimate the standard annual expenditure as 1,820 *ryō* and generate fiscal surplus.

Charging the "Interest" Only to the Lord's Household Expenses

The chief managers separated lord's household expenses from domain administrative expenses, and seemed to treat the former as an unfavorable expense and the latter as a favorable one. This is because they consistently added a 10% extra charge, called "interest" *(rigin)*, only to lord's household expenses in spite of not doing so to the domain administrative expense. In other words, they deducted about 10% from the lord's household expense.

What is "interest"? Why was it added? "Interest" was consistently recorded in tandem with the lord's household expense in the budget, account statement, and account book. For example, on April 2, 1855, the chief managers paid and remitted thirty *ryō* to the lord in Edo. In the account book, thirty *ryō* and forty-five *monme* (equivalent to 0.75 *ryō*) were accounted as the lord's household expense for October and the three months' worth of "interest". It is thought that "three months" refers to the time period extending until the December 31 fiscal year end.

The reason why the "interest" was added is that the lord's household expense was advanced to the lord before the annual tribute income came in. The lord's household expense was paid every month, but annual tribute income was received only between October and the following March. This time lag was covered by short-term debts from the syndicate group and so on. Strictly speaking, the chief managers borrowed the money needed for the lord's household expense to remit it to the lord and repaid it with "interest" after annual tribute income came in. It is thought that the "interest" was charged because it was the cost of financing the lord's household expense.

However, it should be noted that no such "interest" was added to the domain administrative expenses when the expenses were made in the same way prior to the fiscal year end. For example, in the account book, 1.0625 *ryō* was recorded on April 24, 1855, as the expense for planting the seedling needed to maintain the forest in the domain, but no interest was charged on this expense.

Why did such a difference arise between household expenses and administrative expenses? Unfortunately, the chief managers did not tell us the reason directly, but we need to consider for whom these expenses were used. The lord's household expense on which the interest was charged was used primarily to maintain the lord's daily life at the Edo residence—something that would not have been considered a domain administrative expense. The details of the lord's household expense could be revealed by the estimate of the standard expenditure, which the chief managers made at the beginning of the outsourcing. According to the estimate, of the standard expenditure of 1,820 *ryō*, salary wage paid to retainers, maids, and servants accounted for 35.2%, gifts or party expenses for 9.2%, and clothing, food, and other living expenses for 55.4%.[16] These were a cost needed for the lord, his family, retainers, maids, and servants, not for the domain inhabitants. Now, we should turn our attention to the sense of interest. In general, interest is something that occurs when different economic agents share a lending relationship.[17] Therefore, the existence of an extra charge called "interest" indicates that the chief manager separated the lord's household from civil administration and considered the former as a domain outsider (external affair).

Prior Repayments to Intradomain Creditors

The chief managers strove to cut expenditures related to the lord's household, while at the same time actively repaying and greatly reducing the debt load. It is noteworthy that they paid off debts to intradomain creditors first, to others later. To understand the scale and trends of the long-term debt obligations that the Tsuda clan faced, see figure 4, which shows its total outstanding debt as of 1852: it amounted to 7,009 *ryō*. As its annual income in 1854 was approximately 2,000 *ryō*, this means that the long-term debt in 1852 was about 3.7 times greater than its annual income. However, in 1864, its total outstanding debt was reduced by half, to 3,794 *ryō*—an amount roughly 1.4 times greater than the annual income. We can see clearly that the chief managers' handling of finances resulted in a consistent decline in long-term debt.

However, in examining the pattern of debt reduction by region, one can see that these debts were not uniformly reduced. The historical source for figure 4 is a document written by the chief managers themselves, and it classifies the debt obligations as intradomain (Sawara and Izu)[18] or extradomain (Edo). Of these, debt owed to villages that are intradomain, aside from an increase of about 639 *ryō* in 1857, consistently declined as well. With average annual repayments of approximately 170 *ryō* over thirteen years, as shown in figure 4, by 1864, the size of the debt shrank to one-fourth of the initial outstanding long-term debt.

In contrast, debts owed that are extradomain were repaid at a rate of 50 *ryō* per year. Allowing for increased borrowing due to new loans in 1853, 1854, and 1856, this repayment rate is lower than that at which debt owed to areas within the domain were paid back. Furthermore, although old debts can be considered very long-term debt, they were frequently amalgamated with the debt owed to creditors in Edo. It is therefore estimated that the majority of debt was owed, in regional terms, to the extradomain. Accordingly, when such old debts are factored in, the subordinate status of the debt to the extradomain in relationship to that owed to others becomes even more prominent. In examining the trends in outstanding long-term debt, one can surmise that the chief managers prioritized the repayment of debt owed to intradomain creditors over that of debt owed to extradomain creditors.

The Creation of an Internal Reserved Fund

The chief managers allocated fiscal surplus not only to debt repayment, but also to creating a fund separate from a general account. This, referred to as Betsukado Tsumioki-kin, was the internal reserved fund (IRF) formed by depositing the

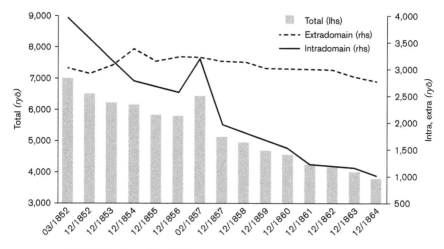

FIGURE 4. Outstanding Long-Term Debt
Source: The Archives of Seimiya Family, Bun 24–16.
Credit: Sakai 2014.

fiscal surplus, and kept and managed by the chief managers. This IRF had two roles: (a) lender who provided working capital needed to finance the lord's household expenses, (b) payer who spent on public goods for inhabitants living in the domain. Among these two roles, (a) is shown in figure 5 and figure 6, and (b) will be described in detail in the later section.

Figure 5 schematically illustrates the flow of funds in Lord Tsuda's finance. Referring to figure 5, let us further looking at figure 6. Figure 6 shows the quarterly balance of the cash flow statement on the general account of Lord Tsuda's finance in 1862. Importantly, the cash flow statement included the short-term debts, which were repaid within a fiscal year and were not accounted in the statement of account. An examination of figure 6 reveals that the remittances needed for the lord's household expense were paid every month in advance of the annual tribute income, which was received only between October and the following March. We can confirm that this time lag was covered by short-term debts from the syndicate group and the IRF. The syndicate group and the IRF were both repaid with interest of 10% per year when the annual tribute income came in. Strictly speaking, the short-term money from the syndicate group and the IRF was borrowed by the chief managers to send the lord's household expenses. In short, the syndicate group and the IRF financed the lord's household expenses through the chief manager. In examining the total amount of short-term debt paid each year from 1860 to 1864 from both the syndicate group and the IRF, we see that the syndicate group paid 72% of the total amount (9,628 *ryō*), and the IRF did 21%.[19] The syndicate group and the IRF played a critical role in providing the short-term money

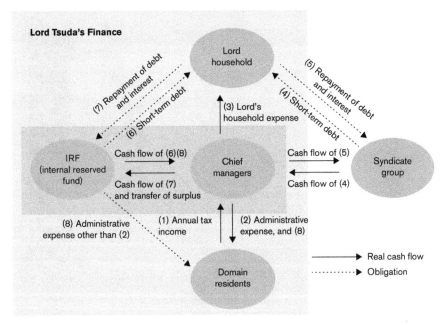

FIGURE 5. The Conceptual Diagram of Lord Tsuda's Finance
Credit: Sakai 2014.

needed to cover the lord's household expenses. In other words, the IRF formed in Lord Tsuda's finance functioned as a fictitious lender separately from the lord's household.

CREATION OF THE LOCAL "PUBLIC" FUND FOR PROVIDING PUBLIC GOODS

The Founding Source and Function of IRF

Then, what is the IRF used for? Where did the funds come from, and how were they used? In principle, it was the lord's deposit with the chief managers, but it was an involuntary deposit that the lord didn't have a free hand to control. Substantially, the IRF had the characteristic of the fund profitable for not only the lord but also local inhabitants. This will become apparent from the management and contents of the financial statements of the IRF. The asset and ledger of the IRF were kept by the chief managers. That ledger details the daily inflows and outflows of cash from 1842 until Sawara was no longer part of the Tsuda domain, in August 1864. Therefore, that ledger can make the balance sheet and profit and loss statement for the IRF. Table 4 shows balance sheet and profit and loss statement from 1842 to 1864.

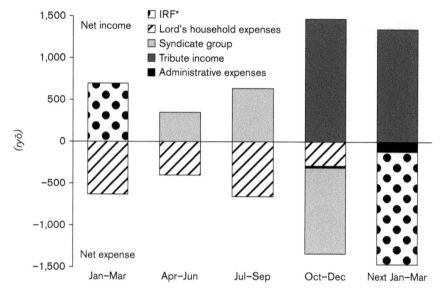

FIGURE 6. The Quarterly Balance of the Cash Flow on the General Account in 1862
Note: IRF includes the prior year fiscal surplus.
Source: The Archives of Seimiya Family, Bun 23–4.
Credit: Sakai 2014.

The net assets column of the balance sheet shows transfers from a general account surplus, as well as profit from the partial sale of rice deducted from the revenues in the general account statement. These were the primary funding sources of the IRF. Additionally, the assets and income columns show loans to the account for the lord's household and local merchants, suggesting that this was a money-making endeavor. The borrowers were primarily merchants like brewers and pawnbrokers in Sawara and wealthy farmers from the surrounding villages.

On the other hand, from the income statement you can see what the IRF was used for. The expenses column in the profit and loss statement of table 4 shows that 72.5% of the total revenue was spent from 1842 to 1864. Furthermore, in examining the breakdown of the expenses column 52.8% of the total expenses was used for long-term debt repayment, 23.3% was used for purchasing the military goods, and 20.4% was used for subsidies for the famine relief and civil engineering project in domain villages. This subsidy was obviously a public expense for the domain inhabitants, but what about other expenses? Based on the earlier-mentioned pattern of the long-term debt repayment, much of this repayment seems to be carried out against the intradomain creditors. In addition, the military goods were needed by the lord and retainers when they prepared for the defense against the arrival in 1853 of US Navy ships led by Matthew Perry,[20] and by the chief managers when preparing for the defense against the attack in 1861 of mutineers from the Mito domain. These expenses were omitted from the general account statement

TABLE 4. The Financial Statement of the IRF

Balance Sheet (August 1864)

(unit: *ryō*)

Assets		Liabilities	
Cash	66	Deposit payable	50
Short-term loans to the lord's household	1,152	Total liabilities	50
Long-term loans to the account for lord's household	100	Net assets	
Loans to local domain merchants	643	Fiscal surpluses from 1841 to 1863	789
Advance receivable	36	Profit from the sale of dedicated rice *(nengu)*	354
		(unknown)	500
		Net income	304
		Total net assets	1,947
Total assets	1,997	Total liabilities and net assets	1,997

NOTE: The unspecified loan had been recorded in the source at the beginning of a period. Thus, the author shows the loan as (unknown) in the net assets column.

Profit and Loss Statement (from June 1841 to August 1864)

(unit: *ryō*)

Expenses		Revenues	
Interest expense	22	Interest income gained from loans to the lord's household	175
Military goods	186	Interest income gained from loans to local domain merchants	903
Subsidies for the famine relief	143	Others	26
Subsidies for engineering project in domain villages	20		
Long-term debt repayment	422		
Others	7		
Total expenses	800		
Net income	304		
Total expenses and net income	1,104	Total revenues	1,104

SOURCE: The Archives of Seimiya Family, Bun 24–38, 24–40, 24–23, 24–41

and disbursed independent of the IRF. Considering the existence of the aforementioned expenses, it is likely that the IRF comprised fiscal surpluses generated by the chief managers during the fiscal management process, and that the fund was used to support the military activity and the civil administration.

From IRF to the Local Public Fund

What happened to the IRF after 1864? In August 1864, when Lord Tsuda ceased to rule Sawara the relationship between the chief managers and Lord Tsuda ceased to be one between a feudal lord and his subject. Thus, after that time, no new entries were made in the IRF ledger, which the chief managers kept. One concludes that the IRF left the hands of the chief managers and reverted to the lord. Is it true that the accumulated IRF money had disappeared in Sawara? The answer is no. Rather, a new local fund was restructured using the IRF as the funding source. In other words, the IRF effectively continued as a new local fund external to Lord Tsuda's finance, under a different name—namely, Sunshu-okatte Ingaikin.

In January 1865, the former lord Tsuda deposited seventeen hundred *ryō* (approximates to the net asset of the IRF, nineteen hundred *ryō*) with an annual 4% interest with the former chief managers, Kageharu and Hidekata.[21] They exchanged a contract for the deposit. This deposit became the founding source of the new local fund.

Why such a vast sum of money was deposited with former chief managers, instead of being invested elsewhere? The reason seems to be that Lord Tsuda could not take away this money from Kageharu and Hidekata due to their relationship built up over many years. As before, the former chief managers were still entrusted with the task of converting the annual tribute rice into money, which was primarily done in Sawara and in Choshi, the largest town in Shimosa province.[22] The direct funding source of the deposit was a portion of the money obtained from selling annual tribute rice extracted from the former Lord Tsuda's newly bestowed holding. Accordingly, they were the ones responsible for generating the seventeen hundred *ryō* in the first place. Had the outsourcing of the fiscal management system continued as before under the same framework, the seventeen hundred *ryō*—which was the annual tribute income—should have been returned to the IRF as a payment of short-term debt for remittance. It was better to keep the funds in the hands of the former chief managers. Wealthy farmers and merchants in the local domain were entrusted with these finance duties. In the process of performing these duties, they generated surpluses that they themselves oversaw and managed as a local fund. This historical experience shaped the former lord's subsequent financial management activities.

The deposit from the former lord had further increased to twenty-two hundred *ryō* by 1867.[23] However, it began to decrease after 1871 when the feudal domain system was abolished, and it shrank to one hundred *ryō* by 1875. From 1875 onward, the cumulative investment gains, which can be said to be equity capital, became major funding sources.[24] This fact indicates that the new local fund was external to the lord's finance.

The funds were used first to provide working capital to local merchants, and second to finance local public construction projects, including buildings and a civil engineering project on the rivers. Looking at the assets of the new local fund, somewhere from almost 70% to over 90% of them were allocated as loans to merchants in Sawara and the surrounding region;[25] this leads to the conclusion that this was the fund's primary purpose. Interestingly, the fact that most of the original capital for these loans came from deposits from the former lord was widely known among the merchants who were the recipients of this funding,[26] even well into the Meiji period in the 1880s. The existence of such financial basis seemed to be significant in providing liquidity and avoiding the shortage in the supply of working capital in the first half of Meiji period, when new financial institutions such as banks were established, while demand for funds was increasing due to the expansion of regional markets.

According to the detail of expenses, the new local fund was used to pay for the construction of Sawara's new police station in 1883. As one of Chiba prefecture's major towns, Sawara established a post office in 1872, the Katori district office in 1878, and the Kawasaki Bank in 1880 (Sawara town 1931). Sawara merchants made major contributions to these public building projects, in the forms of both land and money (Kawajiri 2003); however, the new local fund also played a role in subsidizing these projects. Furthermore, direct expenses related to a civil engineering project on the river were financed by the new local fund, between 1874 and 1881. This project rerouted the Tone River and constructed levies to prevent flooding. The river was dredged to allow ship access, and piping was laid and wells were dug to secure clean drinking water for the populace in the surrounding area. More than a total of 476 *ryō* had been spent for this project within seven years. Until a modern local administrative and financial system was established, the new local fund that was created by deposits from the former lord during the Edo period played no small role in the funding of the provision of local public goods, such as basic infrastructure. That is to say, this functioned as the local "public" fund.

We can confirm that the local notables to which the lord outsourced their fiscal management had structurally changed the fiscal system from something profitable for the feudal lord to something profitable for local inhabitants and regional society. This conclusion is supported by four notable findings—(1) reduction in the lord's household expenses, (2) charging the "interest" only to the lord's household expenses, (3) prior repayments to intradomain creditors, and (4) the creation of an internal reserved fund (IRF) generated by fiscal surplus.

With respect to (1) and (2), it was found that local notables had divided the lord's finance into two sectors—namely, the lord's household finance and the civil local (domain) finance—and tried to restrict the former. Furthermore, they reduced the lord's household expense, that is, salary wage, gifts or party expenses, and clothing or food, as well as other living expenses of the lord, his family, retainers, maids, and servants in the Edo residence.

Then, as the (3) finding indicates, all of this resulted in generating a fiscal surplus and local notables allocated most of the surplus to the active repayment of debts. However, they prioritized debt repayments to intradomain creditors, and repaid only a little money borrowed from extradomain creditors. In other words, these changes can be regarded as the local notable's attempt to prevent outflows of money to extradomain areas, including merchants in the castle town (Edo) and the lord's household, and instead retain them to accumulate money within the local domain.

This attempt also relates to (4). Some of fiscal surplus was reserved in local notables' hands to create the IRF: a deposit that was controlled and managed by them, and augmented by reinvesting in local merchants and their lord, rather than increase fiscal expenditures. In addition, this fund, which was managed separately from the general account and the lord's household, also provided the money needed to finance the military activities, civil engineering, or relief projects for domain inhabitants. That is, this fund worked to finance public goods provision.

As the IRF also had certain benefits for the feudal lord, its academic evaluations have not necessarily been uniform. However, the current study emphasizes that the lord did not have a free hand in managing these funds, which served as an involuntary deposit. The lord's ownership and use of this fund were restricted, and its management was strongly controlled through the will of local notables.[27] In this respect, the IRF had the characteristic of a local fund, rather than the lord's household fund. Therefore, even after the feudal lord–subject relationship was dissolved, a new local fund was re-created outside Lord Tsuda's finance, and the large amount of money accumulated within the old fund (IRF) was retained in the reginal society, well into the Meiji period. Furthermore, this money played more significant role in the provision of local public goods, such as public building projects or civil engineering projects.

On the other hand, feudal lords often entrusted some tasks of managing their finance to the wealthy financial merchants in Osaka or Edo, and some of these merchants also created reserved funds like the IRF (Takatsuki 2014). However, the fund created by them didn't finance local (domain) public goods and were never preserved in their hands after the Meiji Restoration. This difference in two reserved funds can be recognized as the difference of statue and purpose between wealthy financial merchants and local notables. Whereas wealthy financial merchants were only fiscal managers, local notables were not only fiscal managers but also local inhabitants and local administrators. Local notables had a direct responsibility to sustain the other local inhabitants and regional society and worked as substitutes for their lords in providing public goods.

In summary, local notables' intervention into the lord's finance draws a clearer distinct line between the lord's household finance and the civil local (domain) finance, and then generates a fiscal surplus by reducing the amount of money supplied to the lord, instead reserving it to create a local fund for providing public goods. Through this process—which may be understood as a silent conflict between the feudal lord and the local notables—they converted the lord's finance to a financial basis for the provision of public goods for the local inhabitants. This diversion can be recognized as one of the paths to the formation of the local public finance in the early modern Japan.

NOTES

1. In recent research, the effective national (Tokugawa shogunate) tax rate per gross agricultural product is estimated to decrease from 40% to less than 30% during the period from the mid-seventeenth century to the mid-nineteenth century, and per gross domestic product (GDP) from 30% to 16%–17% during the same period (Imamura and Nakabayashi 2017).

2. The size of a domain was measured in the income it was expected to produce, which was calculated in units of rice (i.e., *koku*, which is equal to one hundred liters of rice).

3. The archives of Seimiya family, Bun 4c–18. (This copy is preserved in Chiba Prefectural Archives.)

4. Seimiya, Bun 4c–12.

5. In 1810, the number of households is 1,301, the population is 5,335 people; in 1873 the number of households is 1,415, the population is 6,411. Generally, it is said that in Tokugawa Japan the average number of households in the village is one hundred and the average population is four hundred people (Watanabe 2008). The number of households and population of Sawara village is quite large compared to that of a standard village.

6. In 1864, as the lord levied a bond of about ten thousand *ryō* upon Sawara, they expended 75% (Sakurashi-shi Hensan Iinkai 1971).

7. Hidekata was awarded by Nīhari prefectural government in 1889 (Seimiya, Butsu7–54–14).

8. The archives of Inō family (Now preserved in National Museum of Japanese History), C–19.

9. Kageharu was awarded a type of medal with blue ribbon (for distinguished service in social and public works) by Meiji government in 1889 (Inō, E26–3).

10. Seimiya, Bun 4c-63-4.

11. The primary purchasers of the annual tribute rice—which constituted the bulk of this income—were Sawara's sake brewers and rice merchants (Seimiya, Bun 22–15, Bun 34–3–3, Bun 34–3–9, Bun 34–3–13, Bun 3–13–18, Bun 13–3–23). Aside from the chief managers, the existence of the Sawara merchants was extremely important to the outsourcing of fiscal management duties within the Tsuda domain.

12. If you want to confirm the detail and evidences, refer to Sakai 2014.

13. Seimiya, Butsu 2–57–4.

14. Seimiya, Butsu 4–57–1.

15. Seimiya, Bun 4c–63–4.

16. Seimiya, Butsu 2–57–1.

17. As compared with the contemporary corporate accounting, we can recognize this charge as the "internal interest" of the divisional performance. In addition, "internal interest" and the divisional system were observed in the accounting of wealthy merchants in early modern Japan (Nishikawa 1995).

18. Both Sawara and Izu were villages in Lord Tsuda's domain, but the chief managers didn't live in Izu. Therefore, they wrote in a distinction between Sawara and Izu.

19. Seimiya, Bun 23–5, Bun 23–6.

20. The Lord Tsuda and retainers armed themselves for the battle against the US Navy by the shogun's order (Inō, C–19).

21. Seimiya, Bun 3–10–32–4.

22. Seimiya, Butsu 2–44–1.

23. Inō, A42.

24. Inō, K369–1.

25. Inō, K369–1.

26. Inō, K539–2.

27. The recent studies in *daimyō* lord's finance has also revealed the existence of an IRF (Itō 2014). However, the IRF of *daimyō* lord's finance was controlled not by local notables (the governed) but by samurai (the governor).

REFERENCES

Imamura, Naoki, and Masaki Nakabayashi (2017). "Shotoku to Shisan no Bunpai" (Distribution of Income and Assets). In *Iwanami Kōza Nihon Keizai no Rekishi, Dai 2 kan, Kinsei:16seiki matsu kara 19seiki zenhan,* edited by Kyoji Fukao, Nofumi Nakamura, and Masaki Nakabayashi. Tokyo, Iwanami Shoten.

Ishii, Susumu, and Shunichi Uno, eds. (2000). *Chiba-ken no Rekishi* (History of Chiba Prefecture). Tokyo, Yamakawa Shuppansha.

Itō, Akihiro (2014). *Han Zaisei Saikō* (Re-Thinking of *Daimyō's* Public Finance). Osaka, Seibundō.

Kawajiri, Nobuo (2003). "Meiji-Jidai no Sawara no Gakkōkyōiku" (The Elementary School Education in Meiji Period, Sawara). *Sawara no Rekishi 5.*

Kikuchi, Isao (2003). *Kikin kara Yomu Kinsei-shakai* (Rethinking the Society of Early Modern Japan from Famine History). Tokyo, Azekura Shobō.

Mori, Yasuhiro (1970). *Daimyō Kinyūshiron* (Historical Study of *Daimyō's* Finance). Tokyo, Ōhara Shinseisha.

Nishikawa, Noboru (1995). "Kaikē Soshiki to Boki Gihō" (The Accounting Organization and Bookkeeping Method). In *Nihon Keieishi, Dai 1 kan: Kinseiteki Keiei no Tenkai,* edited by Shigeaki Yasuoka and Masatoshi Amano. Tokyo, Iwanami Shoten.

Sakai, Kazuho (2014). "Bakumatuki Hatamoto Zaisei no Henyō to Chiikikeiei" (Changes in a *Hatamoto* Lord's Finances and the Development of Local Management). *Shakai-keizai-shigaku* 80 (2).

Sakurashi-shi Hensan Iinkai (Compilation Committee of the History of Sakura City) (1971). *Sakurashi-shi* (The History of Sakura City). Dai 1 kan, Chiba, Sakura-shi.

Sawara-chō (Sawara Town) (1931). *Sawarachō-shi* (The History of Sawara Town). Chiba, Sawara-chō.

Shinbo, Hiroshi, and Osamu Saitō (1989). "19 seiki e" (Towards the Nineteenth Century). *Nihon Keizaishi Dai 2 kan: Kindaiseichō no Taidō.* Tokyo, Iwanami Shoten.

Smith, Thomas C. (1989). *Native Sources of Japanese Industrialization, 1750–1920.* Berkeley, University of California Press.

Sueoka, Teruhiro (1997). "Kinseikouki Sumitomo Ryōgaedana no Sougyou to Keiei" (The Establishment and Management of the Exchange Store by Sumitomo Family in the Late Tokugawa Era). *Izumiya Soukou* 21.

Takatsuki, Yasuo (2014). "Kinseichūkouki Osaka Kinyūshijyō Niokeru Tachiiri Shounin no Kinō" (Function of "the Privileged Merchants" in the Financial Market in Osaka during the Middle and Later Period of Early Modern Japan). In *Nihonshi kenkyū* 619.

Tsuchiya, Takao (1927). *Hōken Shakai Hōkai Katei no Kenkyu* (The Study of a Collapse of Feudal Society). Tokyo, Kōbundō.

Watanabe, Takashi (2008). *Hyakusyō no Chikara* (The Power of Peasants). Tokyo, Kashiwa Shobō.

Yoshimura, Toyoʻo (2013). *Nihonkinsei no Gyōsei to Chīkishakai* (Civil Administration and Regional Society in Early Modern Japan). Tokyo, Azekura Shobō.

PART II

Coping with Poverty and Famine

POOR RELIEF REFLECTS THE CHARACTERISTICS of a society in a given period in respect of who is regarded as being in charge of assisting the poor, what level of living standards is considered poor (that is, who is regarded as eligible for relief), and how much support is considered to be enough both in amount and in duration. Thus, a comparative approach toward poor relief history would be a suitable topic when discussing the historical role of public goods, or nonmarket activities, in the sustainability and reproduction of ordinary people's economic lives.

Although comparing historical evidence and the backgrounds of poor relief in different premodern European areas has already been attempted in previous studies, a more worldwide comparison including non-European societies remains to be carried out. In line with this aim, part 2 examines the characteristics of poor and famine relief in early modern Japan, England, Prussia, and China. Though the types of historical records used in each study differ widely, which means that approaches to the history of poor and famine relief will also differ, these four areas provide us with significant but complex viewpoints for discussing what factors affected the quality of relief, and how the public social space arose historically in each area in helping indigent people.

The first point is the type of polity. Japan and Prussia's states comprised lordships that inevitably brought about a decentralized state formation; this therefore necessitates research into the role of regional lords and the central government in poor relief and the relationship between them. On the other hand, states where lordships had little or no effect formed a rather centralized polity that enabled them to introduce a nationwide safety net system: with one Parliament and one system of law, England created the Old Poor Law system; Qing China, a state simply comprising the emperor, bureaucrats, and the subjects, enforced an empire-wide granary system.

The second viewpoint is the role of local communities. Although Japan and England differed widely on the type of state formation, both areas heavily depended on villages and parishes to operate poor relief activities, which put the public social space of relief at a micro communal level from the beginning. Prussia's villages also played a role in poor relief, but it was only after an increase in the number of those who were not protected by the traditional lordship *Gutsherrschaft* that the responsibility of villagers for providing poor relief arose at state-level politics.

Closely linked to the second point, the third is the viewpoint of micropolitics: face-to-face negotiations managed inside communities, or between lords and their subjects. Even in England, where poor relief was underpinned by national law, relief was not provided mechanically toward the indigents but was supplied through severe negotiations at the communal level that divided who was the "deserving" and who was not. Therefore, a close look at these face-to-face negotiations is required when we discuss the characteristics of poor relief in each area. In Japan and England, micropolitics in villages, parishes, and counties was the foundation of practicing poor relief, while face-to-face negotiations between a lord and his subject made sense in Prussia. Moreover, as the change in economic and social environments forced the Prussian state to become engaged in poor relief and made the role of villages a focus, micropolitics emerged even among the Prussian villagers in practicing relief in their own communities.

Under these perspectives, each case in our volume offers an abundant amount of new evidence that will pave the way for further comparative discussions.

In Tokugawa Japan, where no permanent poor relief system was incorporated at the state level, autonomous villages were delegated the primary responsibility for ensuring the subsistence of community members by their lords. This meant that the villages shouldered the formal and public role in relief activities, and each village decided independently when communal relief should be carried out, what the duration and amount should be, and who the "deserving" were at that time. Villagers maintained an attitude of willingness to provide relief when help from personal relationships became overburdened; on the other hand, they did not hesitate to shame and punish the recipients who were treated as dependents or a burden on their community. As shown in Mitsuo Kinoshita's chapter (chapter 5), all these characteristics of poor relief in early modern rural Japan were underpinned by the micropolitics that evolved in each individual village.

Thanks to its unique nationwide safety net system constructed after the late sixteenth century, studies on England outperform any other area in the world in investigating the details and realities of poverty and poor relief, which have been addressed at an individual level using quantitative data. Along with the accumulation of scholarship starting from the beginning of the twentieth century, detailed documents such as pauper censuses and petitions of the poor have enabled these high-level studies, that were themselves the result of micropolitics engaged in by the poor, ratepayers, overseers, and justices of the peace in each parish and county. In our volume, using 3,169 first-time petitions documented in Lancashire between 1626 and 1710, Jonathan Healey (in chapter 6) examines how the Old Poor Law's relief was incorporated into people's "economy of makeshifts," what kinds of causes of poverty were reported by the petitioners, which, in turn, shows what people expected the Old Poor Law to do, and how the Poor Law system contributed to the disappearance of famine in England after 1623.

While the micropolitics of poor relief in early modern Japan and England occurred spatially at the local community level, from the seventeenth century onward Prussia showed a different level of face-to-face politics in securing people's everyday lives: personal relationships between the demesne lords and their subjects. Takashi Iida (in chapter 7) shows what obligations of protection were owed by the lords to their tenants, and how extraordinary assistance was provided through lord-tenant negotiations. Furthermore, as lodgers who were not integrated into the lord's protection increased after the eighteenth century, poverty became a political and public problem that brought the role of state and village into focus. In Iida's chapter, what reaction was shown by the villagers is also discussed, which would indicate the Prussian type of micropolitics engaged in at the communal level.

Unlike these areas, Qing China holds a difficulty in examining poor and famine relief at the level of micropolitics. It stems from the scarcity of historical records, but this absence of documents itself may indicate the characteristics of relief in early modern China. On the other hand, Qing China's case teaches us how a huge granary system could be carried out throughout the empire. R. Bin Wong (in chapter 8) explains how the emperors, the officials both at the center and in the locales, and the local elites of eighteenth-century China together operated a large-scale granary system, and what ideological background motivated these players to maintain the granaries.

Closely drawn comparative discussions with dense historical evidence can lead us to a better understanding of the contemporary problem surrounding welfare systems, namely, stigma against relief recipients and the poor. Early modern Japan can be a suitable benchmark for this argument and is challenged by Kinoshita in chapter 5 by combining our case studies from the perspectives of micropolitics, targetism, and social sanctions. There are only four research areas in part 2, but the insights extracted from them are fruitful and may contribute to more advanced investigations in the future.

Mitsuo Kinoshita

5

Sanctions, Targetism, and Village Autonomy

Poor Relief in Early Modern Rural Japan

Mitsuo Kinoshita

Granting restricted relief and shaming the recipients before the community members are the symbols of poor relief in early modern rural Japan and the most notable facts in discussing worldwide poor relief history from a Japanese perspective. In this chapter, we use documents composed by village communities to examine who was in charge of assisting the poor in rural Tokugawa Japan, how it was managed, and why people were so eager to punish the relief recipients. While there were various types and providers of relief, both in urban and in rural parts of Japan,[1] we should focus foremost on the role of autonomous villages since they were the most important backbone of Tokugawa state and society.[2]

In premodern Japanese history, research on poor relief has not been as attractive a theme as in European scholarship,[3] but one may easily find many documents concerning poor relief in rural Japan, particularly after the seventeenth century. However, this abundance compares unfavorably with that of Europe, as in the eyes of Japanese historians, the depth and detail of historical records and studies on poverty and poor relief in early modern Europe appear astonishing. In European studies, as shown in Robert Jütte's introductory textbook (Jütte 1994), counting the total number of recipients or the expenditure of poor relief and tracing its historical transition after the sixteenth century would be an ordinary research method. On the other hand, it is almost impossible to do the same for early modern Japan; only after the Tokugawa state system collapsed and the Meiji government enforced the first poor law in 1874 (*jukkyū-kisoku*) could a statistical table of the poor be constructed.[4] In contrast to seventeenth-century England, there were no poor laws, poor rates, or regular doles in the era of Tokugawa Japan. Thus, the state system did not require regular censuses, accounts, or individual petitions of the poor. As we see in the following chapters, poor relief documents in the Tokugawa period were mostly made not at the state level but at the village level, and not for constant relief but for ad hoc assistance. Therefore, qualitative rather than quantitative approaches are required when assessing the characteristics of poor relief in early modern rural Japan.

As statistical research does not fit the case of Tokugawa Japan, qualitative inquiries overcome differences in historical sources and pave the way for comparative discussions in the same dimension, especially concerning the quality of rural micropolitics in poor relief, which has already been emphasized in studies of seventeenth- and eighteenth-century England (Hindle 2004, Healey 2014). In discussing these points, this study first shows why statistical approaches are difficult to use in understanding the case of Tokugawa Japan, where these difficulties stem from, and how this connects to the characteristics of Tokugawa Japan's poor relief practices: village autonomy, ad hoc attitude, targetism, and social sanctions.

DIFFICULTIES IN CALCULATING THE POOR

In spite of the absence of research that specializes in the history of poverty, previous studies of early modern Japan often used the term *hinnō* (poor peasants) by setting the poverty line at five *tan* (0.5 ha) of crop field or five *koku*, a number of the tax base calculated by the Tokugawa land tax system called the *kokudakasei* (*kokudaka* system).[5] However, neither the size of the cropland nor the amount of the tax base would prove suitable for quantifying the poor in rural Japan.

First, most peasants in the Tokugawa villages earned their livelihood by farming alongside several other types of work, such as wage labor, spinning, weaving, fishing, and selling firewood. Thus, their household income could not be easily estimated by the size of their crop fields alone. Second, the *kokudaka* system was not a tax based on the actual amount of each household's farm products. Previously, *kokudaka* (calculated by multiplying the size of cropland and its assessed value [*todai*] per one *tan* [0.1 ha] together)[6] was assumed to be equivalent or nearly equivalent to the real amount of agricultural produce. In recent studies, however, this assumption has been denied, and it is thought that through the medieval era to the early modern era, the estimated value of *todai* always meant *nengu* (land tax) itself, rather than products; thus, *kokudaka* could not be anywhere near equivalent to the amount of farm products; it was a tax base that was not supported by product surveillance (Ikegami 2004).

With these apparent weaknesses in proving household income, previous studies contain additional problems of defining the precise positioning of the poverty line and how it should be set; the calculation of household expenditure, which is as essential a procedure as income research is in the definition of poverty, was totally overlooked. *Hinnō* has been a popular term in historiographies of rural Tokugawa Japan, but in these respects, the ability to prove the calculations has remained so limited that the challenge persists as to how to investigate and quantify the poor in rural societies, or whether it is even possible given the scarcity of historical records that show the reality of peasants' household finances.

Currently, the only accessible document that indicates the real family budget is the account made by Tawara village in Yoshino county, Yamato province, in 1808.[7] To entreat their lord for tax reduction by emphasizing their household deficits, Tawara villagers researched the 1807 annual income and expenditure of all the community members, who constituted a total of forty-one households. Income content ranged from cash crops and labor wages to crops for home use. Expenditure research covered tax, interest on loans, diet grain (rice and barley), wages for laborers, fertilizer, and even private expenses for each household member. From these detailed data, new images of Tokugawa village life emerge at the level of household realities. Household income was not at all proportionate to each family's *kokudaka,* proving that *kokudaka* was not an appropriate indicator of poverty. The tax burden ranged widely from 7% to 87%, and almost every household was in the red, but even those high-tax-rated families who were deeply in debt did not always become bankrupt. Household deficits were mostly brought about by diet grain and private expenses, not by tax and interest; this indicated people's lack of intention to alter their living standards even if they were suffering from severe income deficits.

As indicated earlier, the account of Tawara village is an epoch-making document for early modern Japan studies, but despite the excellence of this record, the poverty line cannot be easily set for these forty-one households. Equivalized household disposable income, which is the most trustworthy indicator for counting the poor, could be calculated from the 1808 Tawara account by using the amount of annual income, tax, interest, agricultural expenses, and number of household members. However, the figures are dispersed, and this makes it additionally hard to even clarify which households are normal or middle-class, let alone poor. In Tokugawa studies, a huge barrier exists in investigating who the real *hinnō* are and how to quantify them through the calculation of peasants' household finances.

In contrast to the scarcity of family budget accounts, many villages documented the names and numbers of impoverished peasants, called *nanjūnin* or *konkyūnin,* in order to gain formal relief *(osukui)* from their lords. From these records, it seems that the total numbers and percentages of the poor in a given village could be easily calculated, but as shown in an example later, the matter is not so straightforward.

In 1866, rice prices skyrocketed in the Kinai district and villagers of the Odawara domain[8] in Settsu and Kawachi provinces (seventy-two villages, population greater than twenty-one thousand), who were used to purchasing rice because of their tendency to grow cash crops like cotton, entreated their lord to provide subsidies in order to save the *komae-nanjūnin,* the impoverished peasants. Fortunately, 150 *kan* in silver was granted as *osukuigin,* and the domain ordered the petitioner's leaders to have it allocated autonomously by each village. The Odawara domain did not give any instructions for provision standards, which left each village to decide for itself how and to whom benefits should be distributed. One village called Rokutan (Tanboku county, Kawachi province) divided the targets into three ranks: The first rank consisted of tenant households working hard in farming, but who were still in need of payments for diet grain and fertilizer; ten *monme* per person was given to seventy persons (12.5% of the total population of 556 persons in 131 households). The second rank consisted of tenants "in dire need" *(itatte-nanjū)*, and 14.5 *monme* was given to each of these 172 persons (30.9%). The third rank consisted of "the destitute" *(goku-nanjū)*, and 11 *monme* were given to each of 32.5 persons (5.8%). Among recipient households, household members who were working as servants for more than fifteen days a month were counted as half a person while those who were registered but apprenticed were not counted.[9]

While negotiating with their lord, the Settsu and Kawachi villages of the Odawara domain used the term *komae-nanjūnin,* a general word meaning "impoverished peasants." However, at the level of actual distribution by village autonomy, not every impoverished peasant was considered deserving of relief, and in the Rokutan village case, the main target was set for tenants. Therefore, even if a landowning household was in dire need or even destitute, it was not counted. Moreover, as shown by the difference between the unit cost of ranks two and three, "the destitute" were rated lower than tenants "in dire need," meaning that the real level of poverty was not the main standard for relief in Rokutan village at this time. Furthermore, the number of those who deserved relief in each rank was subject to change. The numbers shown earlier were the final result. In the documents submitted beforehand to the domain officers during negotiations, Rokutan village initially included twenty households (111 persons in real numbers, 19.9% of the total population) in the first rank, thirty-two households (116 persons, 20.8%) in the second rank, and thirty-four households (113 persons, 20.3%) in the third rank. In the actual relief provision, ten households, or fifty persons (42.5 persons at the allotment rate), were moved from rank one to rank two, and 16 households, or fifty-six persons (thirty-five persons), were moved from rank three to two. This indicates that the village tried to apply the highest unit cost, rank two, as much as possible to households in other ranks. How these decisions were made is not clear, but in any case, neither the documents drawn up before allocation nor those drawn up after allocation are reliable for measuring the total number of the poor or the degree of poverty in Rokutan village.

As the Rokutan village case shows, Tokugawa studies are blessed with documents counting the numbers of recipients for a certain relief case, but even those records would not be worthy of statistical analyses such as those being conducted in European studies. On the other hand, the difficulties associated with quantitative research reflect the characteristics of Tokugawa poor relief practices: who was thought to be the "deserving," what level of relief was considered to be enough, and who was in charge of assisting the poor. The discussion opens with where the primary responsibility of poor relief was laid in early modern Japan.

POOR RELIEF MANAGED BY VILLAGE AUTONOMY

Compared to the constancy, regularity, and legitimacy underlying the poor relief system of England after the seventeenth century, poor relief in early modern Japan could be characterized by its unsystematic and ad hoc nature. The position and attitude of lords were symbolic. As a compound state,[10] neither the "states" in Tokugawa Japan, the shogunate *(bakufu)*, nor the domains *(han)* attempted to enact a statute or form a permanent system to relieve the poor, and their basic policies toward poor relief were to leave it to the autonomy of villages and towns. In 1642, although the whole country had been suffering from famine since the previous year, the shogunate decreed that if a single peasant became sick and could not maintain his cropland, villagers in the same community should help that peasant with farming and making ends meet, especially with respect to tax payments.[11] The Tsu domain also ordered their subjects in 1643 to support hungry community members and, again in 1660, during a time of high crop prices in Yamashiro and Yamato provinces, ordered that each village had the responsibility to take care of those who were compelled to beg and keep them from seeking alms away from home.[12] Even when lords recognized their subjects' economic hardships, the primary responsibility for subsistence was delegated to the people's autonomy; as indicated by Keiko Yanagiya's study, it was only after communities were overburdened with poor residents and implored for formal relief *(osukui)* that governmental aid from the shogunate or domain was granted.[13] Some lords, such as the Nihonmatsu domain, introduced a subsidy system for newborns and the aged after the latter half of the eighteenth century,[14] but even within these relief systems, village autonomy still owed the poor the basic duty of support.[15]

In the absence of systematic formal relief and the obligation required of them, rural people mobilized every possible way to cope with poverty. This ranged from informal help by kin, neighbors, and economic relations (e.g., landowners and tenants), to assistance provided by various autonomous bodies, such as the *goningumi* (a neighborhood unit comprising every five households), village headmen *(shōya* or *nanushi)*, and the whole community. As in European poor relief history, these options were often combined, and support from autonomous communal bodies was recognized as actual formal and public relief by the villagers. This is why we can find so many documents concerning poor relief from archives kept by either the families of the headmen or the communities themselves.

Basically, the mobilization of these types of relief occurred in stages. First, households in hardship were expected to rely on their relatives, and if relatives became overburdened, communal formal support was enacted; *goningumi* bore the first stage, and when their limits had been reached, assistance from the whole community finally appeared.

While this step-by-step policy formed the basis of poor relief practice, people often avoided the exercise of communal formal help, and tried to shift the relief responsibility to the field of personal relationship, and especially to family and relatives as much as possible. In 1669, when one individual from Hari village (Yamabe county, Yamato province) became bankrupt through his unpaid tax and debt, the village attempted to transfer the responsibility of repayment to the bankrupt villager's brother, whereas the previous local custom rules had dictated that the prime duty of repayment was held by *goningumi,* not by relatives; Akatsuka village of Ito county, Kii province, enacted a village law in 1771 that announced the abolition of absorbing members' unpaid tax by the whole community and that now one's kin and descendants owed the payment duty; a law from 1775 in Kubota village (Heguri county, Yamato province) divided the relief responsibility between the community and the sector of personal relationship, providing that the *goningumi* would take care of the impoverished household so as not to become bankrupt, but once they went bankrupt, the responsibility of payment was to be shifted onto their relatives.[16] In the days of village autonomy, the rural societies of Tokugawa Japan vacillated between who should bear the final responsibility for poor relief: the public sector consisting of communal autonomous bodies, or the personal relationship sector including kin, descendants, and the indigents themselves.

AD HOC ATTITUDE DOMINATES

Poor relief, whether granted by lords or village autonomy, was provided on an ad hoc basis. In 1669, *Nara-bugyō,* the shogunal governor of Yamato province, intermittently bestowed rice porridge in alms *(kayu-segyō)* to beggars *(kojiki or hi'nin)* and starving people *(katsuebito)* in Nara city for about four months. While doing so, he did not forget to notify the people that this *osukui* would not be carried out often, and hence, they should take care of themselves so that they would not go hungry by their own actions.[17] The amount of governmental aid fluctuated dramatically as well: in 1729, the shogunate lent twenty thousand *koku* of grain for diet and seeds to his domain subjects, and more than 107,000 *koku* in 1732, but after an announcement in 1734 that severely restricted the lending aid policy, the amount of aid soon shrunk drastically; in 1844, only 294 *ryō* in gold was disbursed from the shogunate treasury for the same aims, yet by 1863, it suddenly ballooned to 33,125 *ryō.*[18] The childrearing subsidy system enacted by the Nihonmatsu domain in 1786 promised to grant a two- to three-year semiconstant allowance for third children, but first children were not eligible even if their parents were poor,[19] meaning that poverty itself was not the central target of this relief policy, let alone a permanent and regular support for the impoverished. The expression used in the financial accounts of the Matsue domain from 1767 to 1841 was more symbolic: expenditures for *osukui* were always classified as "extraordinary expenses" *(rinji-gonyūyō).*[20]

In accordance with this ad hoc attitude, there was no guarantee that lords would offer formal relief every time it was requested, even if the economic situation of the petitioners seemed similar. As shown in the previous chapter, villagers of the Odawara domain in Settsu and Kawachi provinces got 150 *kan* of *osukuigin* from their lord in 1866, a year when prices were particularly high. The next year, however, even though prices were still high and peasants again petitioned for relief, the Odawara domain did not easily consent to provide aid and probably rejected the petition.[21] Similar economic environments were not a sufficient condition to either grant or receive formal poor relief.

Thus, split decisions about *osukui* between domains were not unusual. Peasants of the Odawara domain in Settsu and Kawachi provinces succeeded in gaining formal relief in 1866, but that did not mean all residents in both provinces enjoyed the same benefits. While representatives of the petitioners were negotiating with Odawara domain officers in Osaka, one Kawachi village headman researched and reported on how other lords responded to people's requests for *osukui*: the Tatebayashi domain chose not to grant relief, but instead to lend rice from granaries one month earlier than usual (the domain had been lending rice annually during the sixth lunar month); the Koga domain did nothing.[22]

An ad hoc attitude also determined the shape and quality of the communal formal relief managed by village autonomy. The contents of financial statements for annual autonomous expenses *(muranyūyōchō)* reflect this trend. Poor relief expenditures rarely appear on these books, even if relief was provided through formally autonomous systems during a given year, which means that communal formal relief was not recognized as an essential running expense for daily self-governance.

The length and amount of relief was treated the same way. In 1801, when a peasant family headed by Kyūemon of Nonaka village (Tannan county, Kawachi province) fell into poverty due to sickness, his relatives and the *goningumi* paid for meals and assisted his family until they could earn their own living again. However, the burden soon surpassed the supporters' capacities, so they petitioned the village officers for help from the community, and were permitted to rent one *kan* in copper for buying diet barley. Fortunately, Kyūemon was allowed not only to pay no interest, but also to render the sum whenever he could in the future *(shusse-barai),* though this one *kan* was calculated by an estimate of just thirty day's consumption, four *gō* of barley a day for the whole family.[23] In addition, in 1866, when Rokutan village, one of the Odawara domain villages in Kawachi that received *osukuigin* that year, gave rice in alms to "the most destitute" residents *(gokugoku-nanjūnin)* in their community, the allowance was limited to sixty days and only one *gō* for each person per day.[24] The same amount of charity rice was allocated to "the destitute" *(goku-nanjūnin)* in 1867 at another Kawachi village called Wakabayashi, and was prepared for just twenty days.[25] Because of the fact that most rural people ate four to five *gō* of mixed grain a day at that time,[26] communal formal relief provided an absolutely insufficient amount and was strictly restricted within a given period as well. This suggests that people considered a limited safety net sufficient in both quantity and length of time; permanent, sufficient assistance was not thought to be required, even for the most desperate neighbors. Though granary systems, such as those in the Qing dynasty of China,[27] were created in rural Japan especially after the eighteenth century, they did not promise a constant and regular relief for the poor either.[28] The ability to be self-supporting was strongly demanded in the rural society of Tokugawa Japan, while the attitude of only occasional relief dominated the nation.

Because of the ad hoc character of relief, targets for communal formal relief differed from time to time in each village. As in other areas and eras, the aged, disabled, and sick tended to be the primary subjects, but there was no basic principle as to who would receive relief, and the criteria for identifying the "deserving" changed often. As shown in the previous chapter, in 1866 Rokutan village established the main relief target as the tenants, excluded needy landowning households as eligible for relief, and treated the tenants "in dire need" *(itatte-nanjū)* more favorably than "the destitute" *(goku-nanjū)*, who were supposed to be the most impoverished members in their community.

Given its ad hoc character, predictability, an important quality that Marjorie Keniston McIntosh perceived in institutionalized assistance to the poor in early modern England,[29] was not incorporated into poor relief in Tokugawa Japan. As the villagers of Odawara domain did in 1866, people often pleaded with their lords for *osukui* when they felt they could not make ends meet and expected their lords to be obligated to sustain their subject's subsistence. However, these measures did not result in a constant, regularized poor relief system, either nationwide or in regional domains, and perhaps, as Yanagiya suggests, the people themselves did not consider whether such access to predictable assistance would be formally constructed.[30] The ad hoc attitude to poor relief penetrated the state and society of early modern Japan; occasional relief was enough and no formal system prevailed.[31]

Therefore, quantitative approaches, such as calculating annual expenditures of poor relief in a lord's finances or those of an autonomous village, or counting the number and types of recipients continuously and systematically in a communal formal relief, are not only impossible but also meaningless in evaluating Tokugawa Japan's poor relief practices. Qualitative analyses are required, and the most attractive viewpoint to consider is the quality of village autonomy that shaped the substance of poor relief in each rural society: that is, where the "deserving" line was established, who was counted out, and what sense of value was used by each village's autonomous judgments concerning relief.

Although these standards were substantially set on a case-by-case basis, the way an individual worked seemed to be a key criterion in relief judgments. The

Rokutan village case in 1866 symbolizes this tendency: being a tenant was the primary concern, the laboring poor were treated lightly, and the actual condition of each household's living standard did not matter particularly. "Goodness" in everyday behavior seemed influential too. When Yamanobō village of Tōichi county, Yamato province, allocated seeds from its granary to the three ranks of the needy in 1800, households whose heads were regarded as "faithless" (*fujitsu*) or "selfish" (*wagamama*) were provided smaller amounts of relief than they should have been, even if their standards of living were ranked at the "destitute" (*goku-nan*) level.[32] These attitudes in communal formal assistance lead us to a serious problem surrounding poor relief in early modern rural Japan: social sanctions directed toward relief targets.

TARGETISM AND SANCTIONS

Before discussing the sanctions thriving in poor relief, we should briefly trace the history of targetism in Japan, the precondition of social practices that brings shame on relief recipients.[33] In the field of poverty research, selecting and naming one by one those who deserve relief and those who do not is called targetism or selectivism, which are antonyms of universalism. Targetism requires listing the names, numbers, ages, earnings, and health of each household of recipients or applicants for relief; thus in the periods that targetism prevailed, many kinds of historical documents concerning poor relief were completed, and fortunately have remained extant until today. The abundance of poor relief documents in early modern Japan and England is owed to this principle of targetism.

In Japanese history, targetism first appears in the eighth century, a period of forming a centralized state ruled by the imported Chinese law system called *ritsuryō*. The central government decreed in 718 that the primary responsibility to relieve those who were not able to earn their own living, such as the aged, orphans, the disabled, or the economically destitute lay with their kin. If nobody was suitable, then the micro administrative unit in the capital Heijōkyō and rural areas, the *bō* and *ri*, would offer some formal help.[34] Clear evidence of this kind of formal assistance, if any, is rarely found and it seems that the *ritsuryō* state paid no attention to providing constant relief to the needy. On the other hand, the formal relief called *shingō* was bestowed temporarily at special times, such as the enthronement of the emperor, or bad times, involving famine, plague, and disasters (Terauchi 1982). Targetism appears in these *shingō* cases. In 739, when *shingō* was undertaken in Izumo province, the names of recipients, the aged, orphans, and the destitute, were listed one by one in each community unit *gō* and *eki*.[35] The basic policy of registering "all" nations for centralized taxation and conscription enabled targetism in this kind of occasional formal relief.

As the *ritsuryō* state system collapsed in the tenth century, the targetism principle was abandoned. Throughout the medieval era, formal poor relief was rarely confirmed, apart from the almsgiving called *hi'nin-segyō*, which was temporarily provided by the shogunate or the imperial court in urban areas. However, even in this kind of charitable relief, alms were given to unspecified beggars (Mizuno 2013). Poor relief run by targetism vanished for centuries, both nationwide and at the community level.

Targetism reappeared in the seventeenth century as the Tokugawa shogunate began to govern the country and the family register system was introduced. Although we are rarely told about when targetism first started in Tokugawa Japan, the number of starving people during the years of famine from 1641 to 1642 was already minutely counted in formal documents,[36] which means that targetism was probably underway by that time. The histories afterward are shown in the previous chapters.

Poor relief managed by targetism seems to be more sophisticated than that directed toward unspecified individuals, but it inevitably brought harsh social sanctions against the recipients. The practice of shaming the recipients by coercing them to wear badges is well documented in studies of seventeenth- to eighteenth-century England,[37] but early modern rural Japan was no less eager than England to punish poor relief recipients. In 1837, a year when famine hit the whole country, eleven neighboring villages in Heguri county, Yamato province, made an agreement to take sanctions against the recipients of community almsgiving. For one generation, equivalent to about twenty to thirty years, recipients could not wear showy clothes, had to live a simple life, and were not permitted to wear *haori* (coat) and *setta* (high-grade sandals), a full dress for male adults, meaning that they had to attend community ceremonies, with shame, in ordinary clothes. Full members, including the children of each recipient household, were forced to sign their names to this agreement.[38]

Wakabayashi village of Kawachi province went further. As noted in the previous section, Wakabayashi village gave rice in alms to the destitute in 1867, and drew up a book listing the names of those who donated the charity and those who received it. In the same document, they blamed the recipients, stating that their economic hardship was brought about by their idleness, and instead of providing alms, the village coerced the recipients to live in disgrace for five years: the names of recipients were openly posted at the barbershop *(kamiyuidoko)*, where villagers gathered daily, as well as in front of each recipient's house; recipients could not wear or use *setta,* silks, or sunshades and were not allowed to drink a lot or go on trips, each of which symbolized a luxurious life; moreover, recipients had to assume an obsequious posture when they entered a donor's house.[39] Although the term of the sanctions was shorter than in the Yamato villages' case, having one's name conspicuously posted might have been a harsher stigma for the recipients, as harsh as the badges worn in early modern England. The price of depending on charity was not light in the age of targetism.

Furthermore, depending too much on your home community could cost you your right of residence: in 1699, Terada village of Kuze county, Yamashiro province, became so overburdened with taking over a bankrupt member's heavy unpaid tax that they finally decided to expel him from their community.[40]

In view of these facts, we may recognize why people in Tokugawa Japan endeavored to avoid depending on others' alms as much as possible and preferred to get relief through financial markets rather than almsgiving, even if they were in desperate need. When *osukuigin* was dispensed in 1866, Rokutan village also decided to lend or sell rice to the needy from the granary, either with no interest or at low prices. Low prices were set for each of the three ranks mentioned in the former chapter: rank one paid six hundred *monme* per one *koku*, rank two 550 *monme*, and rank three five hundred *monme*, while the market price was nine hundred to 950 *monme*. Moreover, the village suggested to "the most destitute" (*gokugoku-nanjūnin*) in rank three that the community was prepared to give in alms one *gō* of rice per person a day for sixty days. Three households accepted this suggestion, but most of the *gokugoku-nanjūnin* preferred to "buy" low-priced rice, so Rokutan village set their price at 450 *monme* for a maximum of two *gō* for each person per day.[41] Even though others regarded the destitutes' living standard as miserable, it did not mean that the destitute would easily choose the "cheapest" way to survive.

A few more affluent people behaved similarly. In 1850, at Minamiōji village of Izumi county, Izumi province, the economic situation was so difficult that 60 wealthy households decided to allocate charity rice, barley, and cash in copper to "the destitute" (*goku-nan*) for a while. Meanwhile, the middle-class residents (*chūbun-no-mono*), about 170 households, were facing the same hardships and were in great need as well. However, the middle-class not only refused to accept alms from others, but also refused to go begging outside their community, so, as a substitute, the village officers distributed several kinds of reserved funds to these residents.[42] In a sense of being "given" relief from others, accepting charity or reserved funds seems to be the same, but for the middle-class residents reserved funds were more acceptable since they themselves were investors of the funds; it relieved them of being haunted by the fear of being total "dependents" on their communities.

As in early modern Europe, seeking alms was not an unfamiliar choice to maintain subsistence in rural Japan, and begging was incorporated into the so-called economy of makeshifts, the household strategies for the survival of the indigent (Hufton 1974, King and Tomkins 2003). Nevertheless, there was a great difference between "buying," "renting," and being "given" when people decided to rely on others' help; the last was avoided as much as possible because it meant being labeled unequivocally as a dependent or burden on the community, and had a high chance of bringing social sanctions onto oneself as well.[43] A strong belief in evaluating highly the ability for self-support backed these judgments, and this attitude was so strong that it could force the poor to flee from home even if their community intended to continue supporting them. In Minamiōji village, in the middle of the nineteenth century, there was an impoverished household headed by a peasant called Hanbei. His family was in so much need that not only were relief from kin and *goningumi* provided, but creditors also suspended demands for payment until his finances improved. The community showed a positive attitude to maintaining his subsistence but, at last, Hanbei's family fled their home in 1846. The reason for their moonlight flight was a painful one; they felt so ashamed that they could not bear anymore to depend on others' help. (The Hanbeis came back to Minamiōji village five years later and described the circumstances of why they fled and how they lived during their time away.)[44] For peasants living in rural Tokugawa Japan, feeling sorry for neighbors' burdens and pride in economic independence could outweigh the objective conditions of being offered relief in one's home community.

THE HISTORICAL POSITION OF TOKUGAWA JAPAN IN DOMESTIC CONTEXT

Poor relief in early modern rural Japan was substantially managed by the micropolitics of each autonomous village, which means numerous types of relief could be provided depending on duration, amount, and target. Thus, the quantitative approaches familiar in European poor relief studies are not useful for describing Tokugawa Japan, at either the state or the community level. On the other hand, even in these case-by-case circumstances, we are able to confirm the common attitudes held toward poor relief, which penetrated rural society in Japan. A stress on each household's ability for self-reliance, or "self-help," formed the core of communal formal relief policies; an ad hoc attitude prevailed, and limited assistance in both quantity and duration was thought to be enough for even the most impoverished members. While the village community did not completely desert their indigent fellows and tried to support them as much as possible so as not to allow them to become bankrupt or totally hungry, once the recipients were regarded as a burden to the community, and especially when they were "given" communal help, then with the backup of targetism, harsh sanctions were implemented, even if the assistance was provided only occasionally.

From these characteristics of rural poor relief practices, several new historical images of the state and society of Japan can be discussed. First, the ad hoc attitude confirmed in *osukui,* the formal relief granted by the lords, can change our conventional view toward state power in early modern Japan. In previous studies, both the shogunate and the domains were regarded as holding "interventional" powers toward public welfare, especially in the seventeenth century, and as lords' finances got worse after the eighteenth century, the attitude toward *osukui* retreated. Reluctance to provide funds for granaries or lend grain to the needy was recognized as typical proof of the retreat of *osukui* policy.[45]

Certainly, as stressed in Masayuki Tanimoto's chapter in part 1, the interventional attitude toward building large-scale infrastructure, such as irrigation and urban development, tended to shrink after the eighteenth century, but that does not mean the political attitude toward public welfare, typified by poor relief, "retreated" as well. The facts were far different, and as this chapter indicates, the lords' principles for formal relief were established on an ad hoc basis from the beginning. Therefore, as also shown in part 1, expenditures for public welfare in the lords' finances remained low throughout the era of the Tokugawa shogunate. No evidence shows the historical transition from a "positive" attitude toward *osukui* to a "negative" one, and facts that had been recognized as showing this transition should be regarded as just a "ripple" in the vast ocean of occasional relief. Discussing whether the *osukui* policy "retreated" is out of the question in its historical context from the seventeenth century to the nineteenth.

Moreover, the lords and the shogunate in Tokugawa Japan are often said to have governed their subjects with the idea of a Confucian-style benevolent rule called *jinsei,* and the *osukui* policy has been described as the symbol of *jinsei* ideology.[46] Acceptance of *jinsei* thought may explain partly why early modern rulers granted more relief than their preceding medieval lords. However, considering the ad hoc attitude toward *osukui* policy, we should not emphasize the rulers' benevolent ideas in discussing the characteristics of poor relief in Tokugawa Japan. Repeatedly stressed in this chapter, the core of poor relief in early modern Japan lies in the micropolitics carried out in each autonomous village. Villagers of Wakabayashi in 1867 shamed the recipients on their own and not because of their lord's order.

The historical position of the attitude to self-reliance should also be afforded attention. Previously, the emergence of stressing the ability for self-support was thought to be a symptom of "modernization," and it was assumed that premodern Japan was transformed from a society essentially underpinned by people's mutual assistance to a "modern, competitive" society in which a strong belief in the ability for self-help existed.[47] However, as this study shows, self-supporting ability was strongly demanded from each peasant household from the beginning, and therefore, together with the combination of communal mutual assistance, Tokugawa villages vacillated throughout the era over which sector, personal or public, had the ultimate responsibility for saving the poor.

In the context of the Japanese history of poor relief, the Tokugawa era holds a unique and significant place. Even though an ad hoc attitude ruled poor relief in early modern Japan, both the lord and the communities did start to relieve impoverished households one by one, compared with the medieval era, when no active movement was made to assist the poor formally and individually for hundreds of years. On the other hand, the characteristics of poor relief in Tokugawa villages may have shaped the framework of the modern poor relief system, and even that of contemporary Japan. The modern poor relief system legitimated by the poor law *jukkyū-kisoku* of 1874 was known for its severe restrictiveness, shown in the extremely low ratio of recipients, compared with that of England under the Old Poor Law system.[48] Twenty-first-century Japan is not more accommodating of the poor than it was in the prewar era; although a new comprehensive relief system was started after 1950, the system has only covered 20% of the truly needy,[49] and in spite of this low ratio and insufficient allowances, a harsh stigma that involves treating recipients as "lazy" occurs repeatedly. According to *The Pew Global Attitudes Project 2007 Survey,* the Japanese seem to now be the "coldest" nation in the world in terms of supportive attitudes toward a governmental safety net.[50] Behind the restrictiveness incorporated into the modern relief system, Yoshimasa Ikeda perceived a deep gap that existed between the Tokugawa mutual assistance practices managed by people's autonomy and the modern relief system that imposed the poor law "from above" on the people as a blessing from the emperor and suppressed the former practices of development "from the bottom" into a nationwide public welfare system.[51] Certainly, we should not overlook the differences between the early modern and modern era, such as having a nationwide poor law system or not; however, more attention must be paid to the legacy or tradition that has survived from the seventeenth century onward. It must be remembered that targetism, restrictiveness, sanctions, and a strong belief in self-help were the most significant elements of poor relief in rural Tokugawa Japan.

A COMPARATIVE PERSPECTIVE OF JAPAN WITH ENGLAND, PRUSSIA, AND CHINA

As shown in the chapters in part 2, the characteristics of poor relief, as well as the types of historical documents concerning it, differed widely in early modern Japan, England, Prussia, and China. If the research areas are expanded, the differences will be diversified as well. Where numerous types of poor relief practices and systems might have prevailed, how can we compare them on the same dimension while not only mentioning the differences or varieties? An examination of how the vivid micropolitics at the communal level influenced the qualities of poor relief and whether sanctions were exercised against the recipients or not would be worth undertaking, because social sanctions and stigma surrounding poor relief, which made the welfare system work inefficiently, have been a big headache in several contemporary countries, and, therefore, research into the historical background to this problem is required acutely.

From this viewpoint, the historical experience of Tokugawa Japan would be a suitable benchmark for comparative discussions, as poor relief in early modern rural Japan was notably characterized by social sanctions and targetism implemented at the micropolitical level in autonomous villages. To conclude this chapter, we compare the characteristics of poor relief in Japan, England, Prussia, and China from the dimensions of micropolitics and social sanctions and then discuss the reason for the difference between areas where harsh sanctions were brought against the recipients and those that seemed to be not so eager about them.

From a Japanese perspective, the case of early modern England could be compared to that of Tokugawa Japan on the same dimension. As is well known, from the late sixteenth century onward, England constructed a unique, permanent, and nationwide poor relief system based on poor laws, poor rates collected from each parish, regular doles allocated weekly to the indigent, and a juridical system accepting complaints from applicants and recipients whose applications or allowances had been rejected or cut off by the overseers (Slack 1988, 1990, King 2000, Hindle 2004, McIntosh 2012, Healey 2014).[52]

It would seem that England was completely different from Japan, where no poor laws, poor rates, or regular doles existed in the same period.[53] However, if we adopt the viewpoint of targetism and sanctions, major commonalities surface: England's poor relief system was also well known for the severity of its distinction between the "deserving" and the "undeserving" and its harsh attitude in shaming the recipients by coercing them to wear badges.[54] While the two were differentiated by whether or not they had a systematic support structure for the poor, recipients of communal formal relief in both areas were treated in a similar way by the fellows of their own parish or village: as a burden on the community. As the sanctions in rural Tokugawa Japan were managed by the micropolitics in each autonomous village, so was England's badging policy determined by each parish and county's micropolitics, which consisted of negotiations and struggles between the poor, the ratepayers, the overseers, and the justices of the peace.

While, in Japan and England, the micropolitical method is suitable for looking inside each village or parish autonomy, in early modern Prussia under demesne lordship *(Gutsherrschaft),* the viewpoint of micropolitics is also useful in examining the personal relationships between the demesne lords and their subjects. The protection provided by the lords for the peasants (tenants), which was called *Konservation,*[55] is especially significant in discussing the history of poor relief from a comparative perspective.

In Prussia, in return for owning the peasant farm (the "upper ownership") and withholding the "lower ownership," lords accepted responsibility for their subjects' subsistence and had to protect their tenants' everyday lives. Demesne lords were required to provide farm equipment, livestock, seeds, and buildings when they first leased their farms to tenants, and, in some cases, even beds and kitchen utensils were prepared.[56] If tenants did not hold the lower ownership, lords were obligated to grant timber continuously in order to maintain tenants' buildings.[57] Moreover, as Takashi Iida's chapter in part 2 indicates, tenants could enjoy exemption from feudal rents in rebuilding their buildings, which were called "ordinary assistance." These protections by the lords were called *Konservation* and were not regarded as a "blessing" but as the lords' duty. Therefore, the cost of *Konservation* was not considered by the villagers to be a burden on their community, and would not provoke social sanctions against the recipients as well.

Of course, this does not mean that peasants in early modern Prussia lived peacefully under demesne lordship. Although providing timber allowance was the lords' duty, routine maintenance of farm equipment, livestock, and seeds was the

tenants' duty. If the tenants faced difficulties in performing this routine maintenance, they had an opportunity to receive "extraordinary assistance" from their
lords. However, as Iida's case study shows, whether the extraordinary assistance
would be granted or not depended on the negotiation between each lord and tenant, which was influenced by the availability of a worthy successor to maintain the
farm, and if the lord judged a tenant incompetent and ineligible for extraordinary
assistance, the tenant was evicted from his farm and downgraded to the status of
a lodger, even if he held the lower ownership. In the context of Prussian lordship,
targetism played a role in the bargaining for extraordinary assistance, which was
affected by the micropolitics between the demesne lords and the tenants.

On the other hand, as the population of lodgers grew during the eighteenth
century, poor relief for them became a political and public problem since they
were not integrated completely into the demesne lords' personal protection. Thus,
the Prussian state ordered each village to support their impoverished members,
but, as shown in Iida's chapter, the villagers' reaction was rather negative: as in
Japan and England, communal relief recipients were regarded as a burden on
the community, and the Prussian villagers were so reluctant to relieve the poor
that, in some cases, they even passed an impoverished lodger from one village to
another to cut the cost of communal relief as much as possible. Although villagers in Prussia did not shame the recipients by revealing their names or coercing
them to wear badges, probably indicating the differences in the level of communal
autonomy between Japan and England and Prussia, harsh sanctions in all areas
were underpinned by the micropolitics at the local community level.

In contrast to these cases, no social sanctions were imposed on the recipients
of poor relief in Qing China. As shown in R. Bin Wong's chapter, Qing China
developed a nationwide granary system which comprised "ever-normal granaries"
set in county seats, "community granaries" in the countryside, and "charity granaries" in major towns (Hoshi 1985, Will and Wong 1991). The ever-normal granary
was the core of the system and, in combination with the community and charity
granary, its main aim was stabilizing grain prices and relieving the poor by giving,
lending, and selling grain at reduced prices.

What is noteworthy about China's case is that, unlike Japan, where accepting
communal alms was avoided as much as possible because it meant being labeled
unequivocally as a dependent or burden on the community, no such stigma seemingly existed in China, and no social sanctions were imposed on the recipients of
free grain from these granaries. This difference probably depended on the degree
of "openness" to relief resources. While the substance of communal formal relief
in rural Tokugawa Japan was its restrictiveness underpinned by targetism, China's
granary system was actually open to anyone, including those who were not in
real need but wanted to make an easy profit from it: merchants often bought up
grain from the granaries for private resale, lowering the possibility of reduced-
price sales reaching the truly needy; corruption of officials who maintained the

granary system was always a headache for the authorities. Drawing up a list of the poor was attempted in some areas in the 1730s to the 1750s, but that targetism was not for selecting or excluding severely the "deserving" and "undeserving" but for protecting those who were eligible for granary sales or loans. Nevertheless, even this kind of listing did not work well in China because of the difficulties in locating and registering the poor.[58]

Previous studies have compiled detailed data on the holdings and balance of each type of granary in each area or the numbers of people fed by granary disbursals. On the other hand, investigating what kind of people required and utilized free grains, loans, or reduced-price sales is hard because of the scarcity of historical records, which means that applying the micropolitical method to Qing China is not so easy. However, though our inquiry faces these problems, we are still able to conclude that, thanks to the granary system's "open access" and profitable characteristics, grain recipients in China did not face shame and sanctions, and, ironically, that merit itself could also be an obstacle to efficient relief of the poor.

By comparing poor relief cases of Japan, England, Prussia, and China from the viewpoints of social sanctions, targetism, and micropolitics, we can gain an insight into what kinds of historical mechanisms provoked harsh sanctions against the recipients of communal formal relief in early modern societies.

As the cases of Japan and England show, targetism, alongside an efficient register system, was a necessary condition to shame the recipients before their community members. The contrast was with China, where malfunctioning targetism and open granaries made sanctions less likely, though they simultaneously made relieving the truly needy less efficient.

However, as the negotiations with the extraordinary assistance between the Prussian lords and the peasants indicate, targetism alone would not bring about sanctions toward the recipients of relief at the community level. A decisive factor seems to have been a feeling of resentment against being burdened by the recipients of communal relief, among the communal charity donors in Tokugawa and Prussian villages and the ratepayers in England parishes. In order to provoke social sanctions, communal relief should be a "public" affair rather than just a "formal" action. Thus, a viewpoint that favors micropolitics at the community level becomes significant since participating in communal politics is necessary to make the relief resources "public." Tokugawa Japan provides more interesting evidence that shows types of relief that were free from sanctions, which helps us to understand this mechanism. Whether the donors were all village members or only the wealthy villagers, once communal charity was provided through village autonomy, the almsgiving became a public affair and inevitably made the recipients a burden on the community. On the other hand, if the donor was a certain wealthy peasant and made the personal decision to grant charity, the almsgiving was regarded as a personal affair, which would not force the recipients to be a communal burden, let alone be punished by their village fellows. Formal relief from the lords, the *osukui,* did not also provoke sanctions at the community level, even if it was allocated through village autonomy. Though the actual resources of *osukui* came from the land tax collected from the villages ruled by each lord, alms from the lords were treated by the villagers not as a financial burden but as a "blessing" by the lords. *Osukui* was certainly "formal" relief but was assumed not to be "public" assistance, whereas communal relief underpinned by people's autonomy was regarded not only as actual formal help but also as a public service of one's community. Furthermore, as Japan shifted from a lordship state to a centralized nation at the latter half of the nineteenth century, the stigma surrounding poor relief went from a communal level to a national level. Although popular desire for sanctions managed at the micropolitical level in autonomous villages might have receded, the historical stigmatizing of relief recipients and the poor as dependent or lazy has become nationwide, as the expenditure on poor relief has become a matter of national interest.

Our volume may be the first attempt to compare poor relief in early modern societies, including not only European areas but also Asian areas, from the viewpoint of social sanctions, targetism, and micropolitics. Only four areas are chosen, but even with those limited cases, we are able to obtain a great insight into the historical background and mechanism of shaming the recipients of formal and public relief, which, regrettably, still survives in our twenty-first-century societies. If we broaden our research areas, another historical path may appear. In continuing this approach, not only will a newer image of each early modern society become clearer, but we will also come to a deeper understanding of the characteristics of our contemporary world.

NOTES

1. For relief cases such as almsgiving in urban areas, see Yoshida 1991, Kitahara 1995. Beggars, called *hi'nin,* often formed their own autonomous status groups (Tsukada 1987, Ehlers 2018).

2. For details of the autonomy operated in village communities, see Masayuki Tanimoto's and Kenichiro Aratake's chapters in part 1.

3. There are only two historiographies that specialize in the Japanese history of poverty and welfare from a long-term perspective: Yoshida 1984, Ikeda 1986.

4. For tables: Ikeda 1986, 192, 194, 304–307, 310, 312, 539–541, 696–700, Garon 1997, 43.

5. For a survey on previous studies, see Kinoshita 2017, chap. 1.

6. If one crop field is ranked as *jōden* (a fertile rice paddy) and its *todai* is set at 1.5 *koku* per 1 *tan,* the *kokudaka* of 5 *tan* of *jōden* will be 7.5 *koku.*

7. For details and analysis of each household's data, see Kinoshita 2017, chap. 2, 3.

8. Regional lords *(han)* in early modern Japan are usually translated as "domains," but considering Wenkai He's strict definitions of the "domain state" and "fiscal (tax) state," *han* should be considered as "tax state" as well, and a definite category for "domain (demesne)" should be applied in the same way to those such as *Gutsherrschaft* in Brandenburg-Prussia, as shown in Takashi Iida's chapter. In this chapter, we will use the term "domain" for convenience. See He 2013, 1–23.

9. Kinoshita 2017, chap. 6.

10. The notion of characterizing early modern Japan as a compound state and regarding domains as "'states' within a 'state'" is presented by Mark Ravina: Ravina 1999, 1–45.

11. *Tokugawa Kinreikō,* Zenshū 5, Sōbunsha, 1959, 154–155.

12. Fujita 1983, 51. *Tōdō-han Yamashiro-yamato-bugyō Kiroku,* Seibundō Shuppan, 1996, 62.

13. Yanagiya 2007, 254–255.

14. Drixler 2013, 158–169.

15. *Nihonmatsushishi,* 1, Nihonmatsu City, 1999, 706–720.

16. *Tōdō-han Yamashiro-yamato-bugyō Kiroku,* 380, *Hashimotoshishi,* Kinsei Shiryō 1, Hashimoto City, 2007, 94–95, *Andochōshi,* Shiryōhen Jōkan, Ando Town, 1990, 747–749.

17. *Nara-bugyōsho Kiroku,* Seibundō Shuppan, 1995, 163–174, 196.

18. Ōtomo 1982, 44, Ōguchi 1969, 37, Ōguchi 1981, 39, Ōno Mizuo, ed., *Edo-bakufu Zaisei Shiryō Shūsei,* Jōkan, Yoshikawakōbunkan, 2008, 368, *Edo-bakufu Zaisei Shiryō Shūsei,* Gekan, 39.

19. *Nihonmatsushishi,* 1, 718.

20. Yasuzawa Shūichi ed. *Matsue-han Deiri-shōran,* Hara Shobō, 1999, 33, 35, 57–67, 125, 165–171. Relief expenditures in the shogunate finance were also classified as "extraordinary expenses" *(rinji-gonyūyō* or *betsukuchi-haraikata)*: *Edo-bakufu Zaisei Shiryō Shūsei,* Jōkan, 363–370.

21. Kinoshita 2017, 263, 271.

22. Kinoshita 2017, 261.

23. *Fujiiderashishi,* 8, Fujiidera City, 1989, 133–134.

24. Kinoshita 2017, 241–242, 252.

25. Kinoshita 2017, 244.

26. Kinoshita 2017, chap. 2.

27. Hoshi 1985, Will and Wong 1991. See R. Bin Wong's chapter in part 2 as well.

28. Even in the case of Izumi province in 1803, where an allowance called "everlasting formal relief" *(ei-osukui)* was provided to an aged resident through the granary, "everlasting" in fact meant just one month's supply: Saito 2014, 299–301.

29. McIntosh 2012, 1–4.

30. Yanagiya 2007, 254–255.

31. The only exception would be the relief system introduced in Edo city in the late eighteenth century, which granted a constant allowance called *jōshiki-osukui* to those living in hunger with no supporters, such as orphans under ten, single people older than seventy who were also sick, and single youth who were chronically ill. Indigent families bearing sick members were also eligible: Yoshida 1991, 3–38, Garon 1997, 30–31.

32. *Jintarō Ichidaiki,* Seibundō Shuppan, 1994, 65–68.

33. Kinoshita 2017, chap. 8.

34. *Nihon Shisō Taikei,* 3 Ritsuryō, Iwanami Shoten, 1976, 235.

35. *Dainihon Komonjo,* 2, Tokyo Daigaku Shuppankai, 1901 (reproduced in 1968), 201–247.

36. Kikuchi 1997, 15–16.

37. Hindle 2004, 433–445.

38. *Ikarugachōshi,* Shiryōhen, Ikaruga Town, 1979, 493.

39. Kinoshita 2017, 244–245.

40. Okuda Shūzo, *Genroku Murakata Nikki: Minami-yamashiro "Ueda-shi Kyūki" wo yomu,* Bunrikaku, 1988, 75.

41. Kinoshita 2017, 223–224, 241–242.

42. *Okudake-monjo,* 6, Osaka Prefectural Library, 1971, 740.

43. Avoiding being "given" help from others demonstrates how loan agreements in everyday life were important for Tokugawa villagers. For details of microcredit in early modern rural Japan, see Ōtsuka 1996.

44. *Okudake-monjo,* 5, Osaka Prefectural Library, 1971, 781–783.

45. Fukaya 1986, 63–97, Fukaya 1993, 15–66, Kikuchi 2003, 185–220.

46. Fukaya 1993, 15–66, Ehlers 2018, 1–32.

47. Yasumaru 1974, 4–55; Makihara 2006, vii–viii, 78–80, 88–91, 139, 201–202, Garon 1997, 31–32.

48. Ikeda 1986, 192–198.

49. Iwata 2007, 71–73.

50. Only 59% of Japanese people agree that taking care of the poor is the state's or government's responsibility, while most countries' consensus on this issue reaches 80% to 90%: *World Publics Welcome Global Trade—But Not Immigration: 47-Nation Pew Global Attitudes Survey*, Pew Research Center, 2007, 22, www.pewglobal.org/files/2007/10/Pew-Global-Attitudes-Report-October-4-2007-RE-VISED-UPDATED-5-27-14 pdf.

51. Ikeda 1986, 194–198.

52. See Jonathan Healey's chapter in part 2 as well.

53. As Jonathan Healey insists, England outperformed other European countries as well in constructing a nationwide safety net, but even such countries (especially their urban areas) as France, Spain, Italy, Germany, and the Low Countries had a history of enacting poor laws, surveying the poor, and allocating regular weekly or monthly doles to the indigent, which did not exist at all in Tokugawa Japan: Healey 2014, 4, Jütte 1994, 45–58, 100–142, 201–203.

54. In Steve Hindle's study, cases of badging policy are found in more than eighty parishes in England from 1677 to 1790: Hindle 2004, 438–440.

55. Eddie 2013, 29–67.

56. Eddie 2013, 46.

57. For details, see Takashi Iida's chapter in part 4.

58. Will and Wong 1991, 398–399, 408.

REFERENCES

Drixler, Fabian (2013). *Mabiki: Infanticide and Population Growth in Eastern Japan, 1660–1950.* University of California Press.

Eddie, S. A. (2013). *Freedom's Price: Serfdom, Subjection, and Reform in Prussia, 1648–1848.* Oxford University Press.

Ehlers, Maren A. (2018). *Give and Take: Poverty and the Status Order in Early Modern Japan.* Harvard University Asia Center.

Fujita, Satoru (1983). "Kan'ei-kikin to Bakusei" (2) (The Shogunate Measures against the Kan'ei Famine). *Rekishi* 60.

Fukaya, Katsumi (1986). *Hyakushō-ikki no Rekishiteki-kōzō* (The Structure of Peasant Uprisings in Early Modern Japan). Azekura Shobō.

——— (1993). *Hyakushō-naritachi* (Peasants and Lords in Early Modern Japan). Hanawa Shobō.

Garon, Sheldon (1997). *Molding Japanese Minds: The State in Everyday Life.* Princeton University Press.

He, Wenkai (2013). *Paths toward the Modern Fiscal State: England, Japan, and China.* Harvard University Press.

Healey, Jonathan (2014). *The First Century of Welfare: Poverty and Poor Relief in Lancashire, 1620–1730.* Boydell Press.

Hindle, Steve (2004). *On the Parish? The Micro-Politics of Poor Relief in Rural England c. 1550–1750.* Oxford University Press.

Hoshi, Ayao (1985). *Chūgoku Shakaifukushi-seisakushi no Kenkyū* (The History of Social Welfare Policy in China). Kokushokankōkai.

Hufton, Olwen H. (1974). *The Poor of Eighteenth-Century France, 1750–1789.* Oxford University Press.

Ikeda, Yoshimasa (1986). *Nihon Shakaifukushi-shi* (The Social Welfare History in Japan). Hōritsubunkasha.

Ikegami, Hiroko (2004). "Kenchi to Kokudakasei" (Land Surveying and Taxation in Premodern Japan). *Nihonshi Kōza*, 5. Tokyo Daigaku Shuppankai.

Iwata, Masami (2007). *Gendai no Hinkon: Working-Poor, Homeless, Seikatsu-hogo* (Poverty in Contemporary Japan). Chikuma Shobō.

Jütte, Robert (1994). *Poverty and Deviance in Early Modern Europe.* Cambridge University Press.

Kikuchi, Isao (1997). *Kinsei no Kikin* (Famine in Early Modern Japan). Yoshikawakōbunkan.

——— (2003). *Kikin kara Yomu Kinsei-shakai* (Rethinking the Society of Early Modern Japan from Famine History). Azekura Shobō.

King, Steven (2000). *Poverty and Welfare in England, 1700–1850: A Regional Perspective.* Manchester University Press.

King, Steven, and Alannah Tomkins, eds. (2003). *The Poor in England, 1700–1850: An Economy of Makeshifts.* Manchester University Press.

Kinoshita, Mitsuo (2017). *Hinkon to Jiko-sekinin no Kinsei Nihonshi* (Poverty and Poor Relief in Early Modern Rural Japan). Jinbun Shoin.

Kitahara, Itoko (1995). *Toshi to Hinkon no Shakaishi: Edo kara Tokyo e* (The Social History of Poverty in Early Modern Urban Japan). Yoshikawakōbunkan.

Makihara, Norio (2006), *Minken to Kenpō* (People's Rights and the Constitution in Modern Japan). Iwanami Shoten.

McIntosh, Marjorie Keniston (2012). *Poor Relief in England, 1350–1600.* Cambridge University Press.

Mizuno, Tomoyuki (2013). "Chūsei no Shingō, Segyō, Fuse, Kanjin to Shōgun, Bakufu" (Relief, Charity, Fund-Raising, and the Shogunate in Medieval Japan). In *Fuyū to Hinkon*, edited by Kesao Ihara. Chikurinsha.

Ōguchi, Yūjirō (1969). "Tenpō-ki no Bakufu-zaisei" (The Shogunate Finance in the First Half of Nineteenth-Century Japan). *Ochanomizu Joshi Daigaku Jinbun-kagaku Kiyō* 22 (2).

——— (1981). "Bunkyū-ki no Bakufu-zaisei" (The Shogunate Finance in the 1860s Japan). *Nenpō Kindai Nihon Kenkyū 3 Bakumatsu Ishin no Nihon.* Yamakawa Shuppansha.

Ōtomo, Kazuo (1982). "Kyōhō-ki Gōson-chokoku-seisaku no Seiritsu-katei" (The Making of Rural Granary Policy in the First Half of the Eighteenth Century Japan). *Kokushigaku* 118.

Ōtsuka, Eiji (1996). *Nihon Kinsei Nōson Kinyūshi no Kenkyū: Mura-yūzūsei no Bunseki* (Loan Agreements in Early Modern Rural Japan). Azekura Shobō.

Ravina, Mark (1999). *Land and Lordship in Early Modern Japan.* Stanford University Press.

Saito, Hiroko (2014). "Kinsei Izumi no Sonraku-shakai ni okeru 'Konkyūnin' Kyūsai" (Rural Poor Relief in Early Modern Izumi Province, Japan). In *Kinsei Mibun-shakai no Hikakushi*, edited by Takashi Tsukada. Seibundō Shuppan.

Slack, Paul (1988). *Poverty and Policy in Tudor and Stuart England.* Longman.

——— (1990). *The English Poor Law, 1531–1782.* Cambridge University Press.

Terauchi, Hiroshi (1982). "Ritsuryō-shihai to Shingō" (The Ritsuryō State System and Shingō). *Nihonshi Kenkyū* 241.

Tsukada, Takashi (1987). *Kinsei Nihon Mibunsei no Kenkyū* (Status System in Early Modern Japan). Hyōgo Buraku-mondai Kenkyūjo.

Will, Pierre-Étienne, and R. Bin Wong (1991). *Nourish the People: The State Civilian Granary System in China, 1650–1850*. University of Michigan Center for Chinese Studies.

Yanagiya, Keiko (2007). *Kinsei no Josei-sōzoku to Kaigo* (Women's Inheritance and Caring in Early Modern Japan). Yoshikawakōbunkan.

Yasumaru, Yoshio (1974). *Nihon no Kindaika to Minshū-shisō* (Modernization and People's Thought of Japan). Aoki Shoten.

Yoshida, Kyūichi (1984). *Nihon Hinkonshi* (The History of Poverty in Japan). Kawashima Shoten.

Yoshida, Nobuyuki (1991). *Kinsei Kyodai-toshi no Shakai-kōzō* (Social Structure of the Metropolis in Early Modern Japan). Tokyo Daigaku Shuppankai.

Coping with Risk in the Seventeenth Century

The First Age of the English Old Poor Law: A Regional Study

Jonathan Healey

THE "OLD" POOR LAW

The English Old Poor Law was unique in early modern history, in that it was a *national* system of poor relief, funded by systematic taxation. It stipulated that each English and Welsh parish (there were around nine thousand at the time) was to collect money from those who could afford to pay, and to redistribute it to those of their poor neighbors who were unable to support themselves. From uncertain and somewhat faltering origins, it became established over the course of the seventeenth century to a point where it was probably transferring around £400,000 a year by the 1690s. This has been calculated as enough to feed about 5% of the population (Slack 1988, 170–173).

Why England developed this system before her neighbors is a difficult question. On the face of it, the challenges faced by the English in the sixteenth and early seventeenth centuries were no more acute than those anywhere else. As with much of Europe, rising population brought falling real wages: the numbers of those in poverty grew (Wrightson 2000). Certain economic and religious factors might have made the situation worse: England's monasteries were dissolved in the 1530s under Henry VIII, removing their traditional role in the support of the needy; the chantries, which supported many institutional forms of relief, were swept away in the 1540s during the more radical Edwardian Reformation (Fideler 2006). England may have been unusually capitalist, too, though this is arguable (Patriquin 2007). Certainly commentators at the time complained of enclosures, rising rents, and the engrossment of farms—though the old argument that these changes destroyed the peasantry can no longer be sustained (Whittle 2013). What seems to have happened is that population growth brought fissures among the peasantry: wealthy peasants—the "yeomen"—got wealthier, buying new consumer goods and rebuilding their houses into the handsome buildings that survive in the English countryside today (Wrightson 1977). Their poorer neighbors suffered, and it was these who provided the main "constituency" for the Poor Law. But many of these developments can be detected elsewhere in Western Europe. What—perhaps—was unique about England was the nature of the state. She was a unified political entity, with one Parliament and one system of law. Thus the Poor Law depended on statute law, and the political will among the governing class (from the Privy Council to local magistrates right down to parish officers themselves) to impose and manage it (Hindle 2004). Uniquely, it appears, in England this political will for a robust system of poor relief was there.

Central government played a major role in this, although there was also considerable local initiative. The early sixteenth century had seen attempts to encourage voluntary giving to the poor, but as the problem intensified in the latter half of the century Parliament increasingly turned to compulsory rating (local taxation). Important work by Marjorie McIntosh has shown many parishes in the south and east implementing rates and formal relief in the later sixteenth century, but the key acts were those of 1598 and 1601 (the latter slightly modifying the former) (McIntosh 2011). These codified existing laws that provided for a local taxation and support for the impotent poor, as well as for work to be created for those who were unemployed but able-bodied, but they also created an effective mechanism for the system's operation (Slack 1990). Thus the statute of 1601 ordered that overseers of the poor (the parish officers charged with the day-to-day management of the Poor Law) in each parish were to set to work "all such persons, married or unmarried, having no means to maintain them, use no ordinary and daily trade of life to get their living by," and relieve with cash "the lame, impotent, old, blind, and such other among them being poor and not able to work." Poor children, meanwhile, were to be apprenticed (43 Eliz. I, c. 2). This was to be supervised by magistrates, who effectively oversaw the overseers.

The English Poor Law thus created was, in a sense, a classical public good provider, although the exact nature of the "public good" has been a topic of debate. It has variously been credited with helping to foster social stability, end famine, and even underpin the economic risk-taking that allowed a large portion of the English labor force to specialize in industry (Solar 1995, Hindle 2000, Smith 2011). It was also a system in which the regional society played a major role. Setting aside the point that England was a relatively small country, and in population terms little larger than a province of China or of the Ottoman or Mughal Empires (to name but a few), one of the most fundamental tenets of the Poor Law was the devolution of its administration to a set of local institutions. Most fundamentally, its day-to-day operation took place at the parish level (or, in northern England, where parishes could be very large, at the level of the township). These were local, rather than regional, societies, but each parish was only semiautonomous of control from more obviously "regional" bodies. Most importantly, parishes and townships were subject to the jurisdiction of the magistracy: the body of amateur officials, usually gentry, that administered the English legal system at the regional level (Fletcher 1986). Particularly important were the counties, at which magistrates ("justices of the peace" or "JPs") sat as members of the "county bench," looking after local administration, and presiding over the county courts, known as "Quarter Sessions" (because they sat four times a year). In the early years of the Poor Law, Quarter Sessions played a major role in ensuring the implementation of Poor Law legislation, and throughout the Old Poor Law period (1598 to its drastic alteration by Parliament in 1834), magistrates at Quarter Sessions helped mold local practice by hearing appeals against local judgments on relief and "settlement" (the law that dictated which parish was obliged to relieve whom). By the latter part of the seventeenth century, if not earlier, many counties had devolved much of this business down to relatively new tier of government, the "Petty Sessions division," sometimes coterminous with the old "hundreds" at the subcounty level. Nonetheless, either by counties or by Petty Sessions divisions, the element of regional supervision over the more "local" parishes remained an important part of the Poor Law story. Indeed, it has been suggested—though not without question—that regional cultures of welfare existed by the eighteenth century at least. In the south and east, it is suggested, the regional welfare culture was relatively generous; in the north and west, meanwhile, the culture was one of parsimony (King 2000). Certainly spending per head was lower in northern and western counties, but whether this reflects a frugal regional welfare culture, or different economic needs and possibilities, remains open to debate.

The purpose of this chapter is to examine the role of the Old Poor Law as a provider of a public good. Obviously "public good" is a somewhat nebulous concept, but here I will define the key public good provided as the right of people not to starve to death, so long as they were willing (if not necessarily able) to work. This was not a new "right" in the seventeenth century, nor was it unique to England (Swanson 1997). But, with the Poor Law, England made a uniquely thorough attempt in the seventeenth century to turn a theoretical right into a real one. With this in mind, we can examine the reasons people called upon the Poor Law to support them, and use these to create a model of the social function of formal poor relief that will hopefully be useful for comparative purposes. In doing this, I would like to suggest that the prime function of the Poor Law was the provision of social security against personal, and household, economic risk. If the key public good underpinning the Poor Law was the right not to starve, this meant that it worked as a system of social insurance against the uncertainties of a harsh economic environment.

In keeping with the themes of the book, and in order to explore a critical issue, this chapter will focus its evidence on one "region," namely, the historic county of Lancashire in the northwest of England. This was clearly a "regional society" in a meaningful sense, although it was—of course—neither independent nor uniform. It was, indeed, economically quite diverse: mostly pasture farming, but with a distinction between the rough grazing of the uplands of the Pennines and southern Lake District and the plusher pastures of the lowlands (Walton 1987, Phillips and Smith 1994). It also had areas of good arable land, most notably the Fylde plain on the western seaboard. And it was an area of developing rural industries: woollens in the east, and cotton-using textiles in the southeast. In the southwest there was a growing metalwork industry reliant on local supplies of coal.

The chapter will begin by looking at the nature of Poor Law administration in our "regional society," arguing that county-level institutions were important in determining policy, and highlighting our key sources: petitions by paupers, archived by those county institutions. After this, it will discuss the "economy of makeshifts" in which formal poor relief operated: a term used by historians for the very diverse collection of "survival strategies" deployed by those facing hardship, on top of (but not excluding) application for support from the Poor Law. Next, we will consider what the evidence tells us about the nature of poverty as relieved (or expected to be relieved) by the Poor Law. Then, finally, I would like to say something about the role of the Poor Law in bringing about the end of famine in England, something that took place in the seventeenth century, at around the same time as the implementation of the Poor Law. I would like to suggest that this was not a coincidence. Indeed, Lancashire, as a regional society subject to famine until relatively late, constitutes a very valuable case study of this development.

LANCASHIRE AS A "REGIONAL SOCIETY"

Although England was unified by a monarchy, a parliament, and a system of law, it was also—in some senses—a patchwork of regions. Counties remained crucial focal points for peoples' political and social activities, particularly in the case of the landed gentry (for a sceptical discussion of this, see Holmes 1980). More generally, people were conscious that their lives were bounded by what was usually called their "country." This word has evolved to mean, in contemporary English, something akin to the "nation-state," but in the early modern period the word "country" usually referred to a smaller area, often unified by some economic or administrative characteristic. Famously, Wiltshire had its "chalk" country and its "cheese" country. Daniel Defoe, visiting the Sheffield area in the early eighteenth century, wrote about the "country called Hallamshire" (Hey 2016, 1–4). Such examples could be multiplied.

Where these regional units had administrative functions, most obviously in the case of counties but also with hundreds, Petty Sessions divisions, and other units, they played a major role in the formulation of Poor Law policy. In the early years of the system, counties and divisions can be seen directing parishes within their respective jurisdictions (Lister 1888, Royal Commission on Historical Manuscripts

1905). In the 1630s, with the royal government pushing for local enforcement, the Privy Council ordered justices in their divisions to push on with the implementation of the Poor Laws, and to report back (Quintrell 1980). Meanwhile, county government was crucial to the reimplementation of formal poor relief in the aftermath of the first Civil War (1642–1646), albeit this time under pressure from below (Hindle 2008). Nonetheless, the growth of poor relief was always driven by a dynamic interaction between national regional and local institutions. Each component was important.

In Lancashire, the administrative landscape was perhaps especially complex (Healey 2010a). Because parishes were very large, the fundamental unit of administration gradually became the township—an old subdivision of the parish. Confusingly, parishes did still maintain a role in some areas, especially where the level of poverty was uneven across a large parish, and thus the parish served as a useful mechanism for redistribution of expenditure across space. These were then subject to higher jurisdictions: most immediate were Petty Sessions divisions, which covered a group of parishes, and theoretically met as a body of magistrates every six weeks. Above these were the institutions of the county, although because Lancashire was quite large and suffered relatively poor communications these county institutions actually met in four separate locations: at Lancashire for the north of the county, at Preston for the middle areas, at Manchester for the southeast, and alternating between Wigan and Ormskirk for the southwest. In addition, Lancashire's justices met to discuss administration at "Sheriff's Table," during the biannual visitation by the Assize judges on circuit out of London.

Central to the operation of this administrative web was the system of appeal, often by petition, whereby those with a grievance against some local decision took their case to higher institutions. Crucially, decisions made in townships could be appealed upward. Increasingly, it would seem that Petty Sessions divisions were taking these cases on, but happily for historians, Quarter Sessions heard many thousands of these cases across the seventeenth century. Thus, from the end of the Civil War to the first decade of the eighteenth century magistrates heard an average of nearly fifty new cases relating to the relief of individual paupers coming up to Quarter Sessions every year. On top of this, they also dealt with appeals for habitation orders and settlement cases. Of course, compared to the number of people relieved in the county without such appeals, these are small numbers, but these were likely to have been the most contested, borderline cases. They could thus set important precedents. Appeals also generated documentation, and in some cases, actual petitions survive.

ASKING FOR POOR RELIEF

These surviving petitions are the crucial sources for this chapter. Some 3,169 initial petitions survive for the county (i.e., excluding those whose case had already been heard and were thus contesting some aspect of a former order). In order to understand the importance of these as sources, it is worth noting how they differ from other material relating to the English Poor Law (Healey 2014). The system of parochial poor relief was, quite apart from anything else, an impressive bureaucracy. In theory, each parish or township was to write up lists of both taxpayers and recipients of poor relief. At least from the middle decades of the seventeenth century, it seems that the majority of parishes did this. Only a minority of these survive, but where they do they are extremely useful sources, and historians have used them to recover local poor relief policies, and some data about the number and nature of the poor in receipt of relief. The big problem, of course, is that such accounts are records of relief rather than poverty. They can tell us *what* people got, but they do not necessarily tell us *why* they needed it. For this, historians have had to be more creative. Sometimes, they have used the (sadly rare) pauper censuses that survive for some English towns. Because these often collected more data about recipients (such as information about earnings, family sizes, or infirmities) they can be mined for insights into the question of who got poor relief (Pound 1971, Slack 1975, Healey 2010b). Alternatively, historians have deployed "nominal record linkage" (the linking of names found in Poor Law records with those in other sources) to gain similar insights. In particular, they have linked records of Poor Law payments to "family reconstitutions," which give basic demographic data about parishioners. This is a time-consuming methodology, and it is subject to some important source biases—most notably its difficulty in "seeing" the migrant poor—but it has nonetheless underpinned some important and influential studies of poverty and its relief (Wales 1984, Newman-Brown 1984, Williams 2011).

An issue with all of these sources is that they are "top down": that is, they do not give the poor a voice of their own. In recent years, historians of the Old Poor Law have developed a much greater interest in sources that record some element of the "voices" of the poor (Hitchcock, King, and Sharpe 1997). For the eighteenth and nineteenth centuries, there now exists a vibrant literature on pauper letters—sources generated when a pauper who lived in a parish different from their place of formal "settlement" applied back to that parish of settlement for relief (Sokoll 2001). These are incredible sources, which in many cases appear to have actually been written by the paupers themselves. None, or very few, survive for the seventeenth century, but for this period there are sometimes archives of pauper petitions, such as the many thousands that survive for Lancashire. In most cases, these petitions were created when a poor individual had been refused relief by their parish or township, and were thus appealing over the heads of local officers to the magistracy in the hope of a more favorable hearing. In the process, the pauper described what conditions had left them in poverty, as well as (sometimes) giving information about their strategies of *avoiding* destitution.

They need to be read carefully, however. So far as can be seen, petitions of the period were rarely actually written by the poor. They were at best "hybrid voices" in which the stories of the poor were transmitted to paper and thus to the court and to history by the scribe. Indeed, they follow a well-established epistolary form, starting with a salutation, following with a narrative of the reasons for poverty, and ending with an appeal to the conscience and benevolence of the magistrates, and usually an offer to pray for their soul (Jones and King 2015). They are instrumental documents: they had a specific political purpose—getting a dole—which means they are not objective records of the past. Nor are they necessarily a representative sample of the poor themselves: they normally refer to cases in which the pauper had been refused relief in the first instance. As has been noted, they were probably representative of the most controversial cases.

This all said, petitions—particularly their narrative section, in which the would-be pauper set out the reasons for her or his poverty—present an exciting opportunity for historians to explore why some people needed poor relief, and what they expected of the Old Poor Law. Before we do this, though, we need to say something about issues of reliability. Clearly, as these were instrumental documents, they cannot necessarily be taken as unproblematic records of "historical truth." Rather, they are a representation of poverty aimed at provoking sympathy and (ultimately) a dole. Nonetheless, petitioners were subject to a series of checks, which likely prevented them from lying outright. As petitioners tended to be illiterate, the scribe would have acted as a potential moral check on any obvious falsehoods. Meanwhile, petitioners appear to have been expected to present petitions in person, and to have been subjected to some kind of cross-examination in court. Moreover, townships aggrieved by particularly serious falsehoods could themselves appeal successful petitions, allowing them to present contrary evidence. In most cases, petitions seem to have been successful, and not to have generated an appeal: this probably speaks to their general accuracy as a record of individual hardships. Finally, even if we refuse to trust a single statement in any of the petitions as representative of historical "truth," then they still exist as representations of deserving poverty: they can be taken, at the very least, as powerful statements of what people *expected* the Poor Law to do. The remainder of this chapter will tackle this question in more detail, focusing on the evidence contained in the Lancashire petitions. It first points out that formal poor relief existed as one part of a wider "economy of makeshifts," before discussing the kinds of economic misfortune that brought people to need poor relief, and then finally exploring the suggestion that the Old Poor Law was an important factor in the disappearance of famine from England in the seventeenth century.

THE "ECONOMY OF MAKESHIFTS"

It has become clear in the last couple of generations of Poor Law scholarship that formal poor relief was just one way in which those in poverty supported themselves (Ben-Amos 2000, Boulton 2000, King and Tomkins 2003, Muldrew and

King 2003, Hindle 2004, 15–95, Ben-Amos 2008). The petitions, for example, show paupers getting help from their kin, or neighbors. Grace Rydings of Heywood, for example, told in 1656 that she

> hath been sick about two months and having but 3d a week allowance was enforced to go abroad for relief and coming to one James Hardman's house being in the parish of Middleton for an alms [sic] was so sick and weak that she could not go again into the parish of Bury neither hath any place of abode but for the space of 12 days hath been at the said James Hardman's house and put him to cost and trouble. (LA, QSP/124/18)

Sometimes petitioners worked for small wages. Anthony Higginson of Priest Hutton recalled in 1656 that, when able of body, he had undertaken "so hard a labour or another lawful calling as killing of foxes, badgers and other devouring creatures which he much used when he was not otherwise employed" (LA, QSP/129/5). Some, meanwhile, admitted to begging for alms, though they might profess a reluctance to keep doing so. In 1663, for example, Jane Seed of Ribchester stated that she went begging for relief, but was "ashamed" to have to do so (LA, QSP/234/16). Others still stated that they had sold their possessions: land, cows, even the clothes from their back, to pay for their relief (Healey 2014).

The existence of such strategies of "making shift" is, of course, well attested by existing scholarship. Ilana Krausman Ben-Amos, for example, has shown how "gifts and favours" were crucial to social relations at all levels of wealth (Ben-Amos 2000, Ben-Amos 2008). The importance of formal charity as part of a "mixed economy of welfare" was emphasized most effectively by Joanna Innes, while a recent project has done much to recover the importance of almshouses to the support for the vulnerable (Innes 1996, Broad 1999, Goose, Caffrey, and Langley 2016). Meanwhile, although there is surprisingly little evidence for it in the Lancashire petitions, it has long been supposed that the poor were often able to make use of common land to help make ends meet (Neeson 1993).

Slightly ambiguously, formal poor relief existed as part of this "economy of makeshifts," and there is no necessary reason to think that paupers saw the taking of relief from the parish as especially different from taking it from their neighbors as charity. But formal relief also clearly existed in part to plug the gaps in this "economy of makeshifts." It is, for example, implicit in petitions that one of the reasons people might need parish support was that their attempts to "make shift" had failed. They needed relief because they had no kin, because their neighbors were exhausted, because they had sold all their goods and had none left, or because they were too sick to beg relief from door to door. It is thus possible to argue that one of the functions of poor relief was to provide support where structural changes were making the wider "economy of makeshifts" less capable of supporting the marginal population. So, as enclosure removed common land, as people moved more and perhaps fractured their relationships with kin and neighbors, or as certain industries ebbed and flowed (perhaps most obviously the destruction of hand spinning at the end of the eighteenth century), in each of these cases formal poor relief picked up some of the slack. More generally, this emphasizes the point that poor relief existed within a wider social environment: need was dictated not just by the availability of resources, but also by cultural norms. It was accepted, as we shall see, that women should earn less than men, and this patriarchal assumption had consequences for the nature of poverty: it meant you were more likely to be poor if you were female (Bennett 1992). Ethical considerations, particularly notions of distributional justice, were also a part of this: petitioners might ask for relief "as may stand with justice and equity and as is usual in such cases," or they might claim their circumstances were "fitter for a swine then a Christian who is of the age of 65 years and lame" (LA, QSP/52/14; QSP/129/5; cf. QSP/197/15; QSP/570/2). Such statements betoken ethical ideas about acceptable and unacceptable levels of deprivation, and these clearly conditioned peoples' expectations of the Poor Law.

THE CAUSES OF POVERTY

The key pieces of information in petitions, though, are the causes of poverty reported by the petitioner. The main ones mentioned were old age, sickness, and family breakdown.

Forty-three percent of the petitioners complained of old age. This, they said, brought crippling decrepitude—failing eyesight, reduced mobility. William Oldham of Heaton Norris summed the problem up when he claimed poverty in 1691 through the "weakness in body and other infirmities always attending upon old age." He was eighty-two (LA, QSP/699/3). The key problem was simply that it was very hard for the aged to earn their living. John Burrow of Skerton was explicit about this in 1649 when he complained that "of late infirm and decrepit old age hath taken his work from him that he cannot neither will people have him to work as formerly" (LA, QSP/9/2). Alice Simpson, also of Skerton, petitioned in 1658 that she was "now far stricken into years, and of late grown blind, so that she is not any longer able to labour for her liveing or to help herself in any sort" (LA, QSP/153/7). Such examples could be multiplied many times over.

Neither were falling incomes the only problem. Senility and weakness of body also meant that individuals needed help to complete previously simple domestic tasks. Sometimes this help could be offered as charity by well-meaning neighbors, but if this was not available domestic assistance had to be paid for. Jane Bridge of Fazakerley, for example, pleaded in 1662 that she was "now somewhat aged & grown so infirm & weak of body, that your petitioner is not able to work for her living, & many times your petitioner's said weakness is so extreme that had she meat your petitioner were not able to feed herself" (LA, QSP/223/20). And in 1694, William Makater of Upholland provided a graphic image of old age, with him "now scarce able to perform a day's work, and his wife so extreme impotent that she is scarce able to crawl or go about" (LA, QSP/742/2).

Around 50%, on the other hand, claimed poverty on account of being ill. In fact, "old age" and "sickness" were clearly sometimes related, and it may well be that in some senses they were seen as two sides of a broader concept of bodily "impotence." Although this is an idea that awaits its historian, the notion of the poor, impotent body was probably a crucial cultural idea underpinning poor relief in the period. Among those who were not also old, this figure was 55%. Given the vagueness of the petitions, and the unsophisticated medical knowledge of the time, we cannot read too much into the different diseases reported. Lameness and blindness were very common complaints, but others told of palsies, agues, the King's Evil (scrofula), falling sickness, and mental incapacity. Elizabeth Dandy of Tarleton told JPs in 1701 that she was troubled with "a mazyness in her head that she is ready to fall if she doth not support herself by taking hold of some table or stool to help her" (LA, QSP/860/51). Isabel Hardman of Manchester had—in 1699—"a melancholy man to her husband," and as a result "none of your petitioners family hath had or eaten any bread for the space of 3 days last past" (LA, QSP/833/18). One couple suffered a "surfeit of cold," while another man told of being "very sore broken in his private parts" (LA, QSP/828/37; QSP/630/17). Anne Orrell of Pemberton was given poor relief in 1700 after being poisoned by her lover, the toxin being administered in a cup of sugary water he had given her to toast their marriage (LA, QSP/848/17). Pregnancy, while not—of course—a sickness, was often written about in similar terms: in its final stages it acted as a form of bodily infirmity, reducing one's ability to work. In 1688, Elizabeth Renshaw of Stretford petitioned that she had been widowed, and was great with child, and "is not able to work any longer by reason of her bigness with child" (LA, QSP/646/4). Just under 2% of petitioners referred to current or recent pregnancy.

Petitions also recounted cases of people suffering mental disabilities, including those from birth, and those of more recent onset. One of the most vivid examples is Mary Hill of Manchester, who in 1706 told of how her husband "has been melancholy for thirty years last past and now is wholly distracted and raving mad," leaving her fully "employed in attending and looking after him" (LA, QSP/945/5). Others told of accidents. In 1658, John Singleton—a servant from Broughton-in-Amounderness—needed poor relief after he was lamed by falling off a ladder (LA, QSP/162/1). John Renshall of Stretford claimed in 1655 that he was doubly unlucky. He had been blind in one eye for ten years, having been "at work making hedge for Sir Cecil Trafford, Knight, hastily stooping down chanced to hit his [other] eye upon an hazel stick & thereby lost the sight thereof" (LA, QSP/120/8). There were also cases of injuries in coal mines and one petitioner who was hurt building a bridge (e.g., LA, QSP/224/6).

The third major stated cause of poverty was household breakdown. Some 40% of petitions referred to being single, either through widowhood or, in many cases, through simple abandonment. This was a more serious problem for women than men, indeed only two male petitioners told of being abandoned by their wives (though several did mention being widow*ers*). The problems of family breakdown were essentially twofold. First, in a society that tended to ascribe fairly inflexible economic roles to men and women, families needed to pool what were then thought of as "male" and "female" activities. Hence the difficulty felt by widowed husbands. John Howard of Chadderton is a good example. He petitioned in 1670 that

> his vocation is what he can get with following and driving of two little horses loaded with coals or other loading what he can procure from one place to another, so as your petitioner by his calling is much forced to bee from his children and cannot be without someone amongst his children to dress and order them. (LA, QSP/360/13)

Second, marriage served as a form of risk-pooling in a difficult economic environment. Two incomes were always better than one. William Nicholson of Ulverston recounted in 1659 that, as he aged and his eyesight failed, his wife had been "his helper and the best comfort he had under God" (LA, QSP/173/7). And expressing the same sentiment from a rather different angle was Thomas Singleton of Wharles, who in 1660 lamented that he and his wife had become so destitute that "neither of them [were] able to look to one another when in any sickness or misery" (LA, QSP/198/36). Ultimately, though, family breakdown *was* gendered: it was a more serious occurrence for women than it was for men. This was an issue of culture and social structure: England was a patriarchal society where the earning power of women was lower than that of men.

Children were another element that could unbalance the family economy. It is not easy to get much meaningful quantitative information from the petitions, because paupers appear to have mentioned children who had evidently already left home. But it is worth noting that 43% of the petitioners mentioned having one or more children—and some had quite impressively large families: nine or ten children in a handful of cases.

Rather less frequent, but still important, were those who told of being unemployed—or faced with what we might call a "cost of living crisis"—and those who had suffered some environmental misfortune such as fire, flood, or theft. John Leigh of Walton-le-Dale is an example of the latter. He petitioned in 1678 that he and his wife were

> now reduced into poverty by reason of the two late great floods which happened in Walton aforesaid about the 11th of September a year ago at which time your petitioner lost ten acres & a half of wheat, barley, & oats besides the washing down of your petitioner's hedges and your petitioner further sheweth that your petitioner the year after for bread, corn, seed & other necessaries became indebted in the sum of fifty pounds by reason whereof your poor petitioner is clearly ruined & undone. (LA, QSP/483/7)

As for economic crises, the best thing is to count the number of petitions received on over time, and to look for peaks. There were peaks in 1638, 1647–1650, 1657–1662, 1674–1675, and 1699–1700. During these, it was not uncommon for petitioners to complain of high prices, or of the lack of available work, or simply of the "hardness of the times." In 1648, for example, William Ward of Alkrington reported that he and his wife were "especially now of late by reason of the scarcity of bread & hardness of the times both of them . . . brought into extreme want & misery" (LA, QSP/8/7). "I have but very little work," Rebecca Hopwood told Manchester JPs in 1699, "and everything is very dear" (LA, QSP/828/31).

Essentially, then, the fact petitioners were asking for support in times of family breakdown, sickness, old age, and other crises suggests that they construed the Poor Law as a system of support in the face of certain forms of economic risk. What unified these risks was that they caused people either to need more money or to have more difficulty in earning money, and that they occurred through no fault of the petitioner. The Poor Law was, then, a form of public good that provided support for people in the face of misfortune (if we can, indeed, describe old age—or having "too many" children—as misfortune). This fits with, and indeed expands upon, the work of scholars—such as, recently, Samantha Williams—who have emphasized the importance of "life-cycle poverty," in other words, poverty that hits households at certain semipredictable moments in the family life-cycle (youth, old age, widowhood, and a period in middle age when families were "overcharged with children" [Williams 2011]). It is also worth noting the concept of "nuclear hardship" (Laslett 1988). This emphasizes the importance of the nuclear household in early modern England, stressing its autonomy and weak interactions with kin, and posits this as a reason for the reliance in England on the "collectivity" to provide insurance against starvation. This argument has been questioned, on the grounds that kin interactions were not necessarily as weak as once thought, and because the English household was perhaps more flexible than the model allowed (Reay 1996). But, at its fundamentals, it is hard to argue against the idea that those in receipt of poor relief needed it, in part, because their kin networks were unable to protect them from misfortune. The Poor Law can thus be seen as providing a public good that—arguably—in other societies may have been provided by more flexible forms of household formation and by kin.

THE DISAPPEARANCE OF FAMINE

England suffered its last famine in 1623, and even this was a regional affair. We know relatively little about famine in earlier periods, although there was clearly major crisis in the years around 1315–1321, a famine in 1438, and recurrent crises in the reign of Henry VIII (Kershaw 1973, Pollard 1989, Sharp 2016). There is evidence for starvation, even in Westminster, in the late 1550s, although this is hard to disentangle from a much wider set of epidemics at the end of that decade. We get onto safer ground in the later sixteenth century, once we have access to vital registration data in the form of parish registers, and studies have suggested severe hunger coupled with an epidemic (perhaps typhus) in 1587–1588, a famine in 1597, and a regional famine in 1623 (Appleby 1978, Walter and Schofield 1989). After this, there were no more English famines, despite periods of bad harvests in the later 1640s, the 1690s, and at other times. In the 1720s, high prices coincided with high mortality, but this was explicitly considered an epidemic by contemporaries, and the geography of mortality does not fit what we would expect from a famine (Healey 2008). Other countries, within the British Isles and beyond, continued to suffer famines long after England had stopped doing so (Ó Gráda 2009). Scotland suffered widespread starvation throughout the seventeenth century, and especially during the "Ill Years" of the 1690s. Ireland, of course, remained famine prone in the eighteenth and nineteenth centuries. The worst famine was probably that of 1740–41, known as the "Year of Slaughter." In Europe, famines continued to occur into the eighteenth century, although they were in decline by the early nineteenth. The history of famine in Asia and Africa is long and heartbreaking.

England, then, was unusual in its early "escape" from famine, something that demands explanation. Partly, no doubt, it was a reflection of growing wealth, and growing purchasing power on the international grain market. Improved local distribution networks, greater crop diversity, and of course access to colonial sources of food (including Ireland) undoubtedly also helped. The role of government is less clear. Ironically, indeed, formal government intervention in the grain market largely ceased at around the time that famine did, so it is hard to argue that this was a successful weapon in the war on hunger (Outhwaite 1981).

The Poor Law, on the other hand, seems likely to have had a role. There is, indeed, considerable circumstantial evidence for this. The geography of the spread of poor relief, for example, seems to fit quite well with the retreat of famine. In the 1590s, at a time when formal poor relief was only weakly implanted, even in the South, famine was general. By 1623, formal poor relief appears to have been much better established in the South, but hardly so in the North. That year, famine hit the North, but not the South. After 1623, formal poor relief became more solidly embedded in northern parts; the dearths of 1630–1631, 1637, and 1647–1650 were ridden out without mass starvation. There is evidence from poor accounts that relief costs could and did rise to meet peaks in the price of food. At Amersham (Buckinghamshire), for example, overseers in 1631 gave additional money to their poor "which have not of the weekly collection to buy corn in the time of dearth" (CBS, PR4/12/2, 41). In 1730, William Stout of Lancaster reported, "[t]he last year, being a dearth of corn, increased the poor, so that our poor tax was advanced from one hundred to two hundred pounds a year" (Stout 1967, 207). Moreover, as we have seen, the record of the Lancashire petitions shows very noticeable peaks in 1637, 1647–1650, 1658–1662, 1674–1675, and 1699: all of these were years of high prices.

If we are to postulate a relationship between the English Poor Law and the decline of famine, then we might also speculate as to how this relationship might have worked. Most obviously the Poor Law had the power to prop up people's "exchange entitlements" (Sen 1981). Thus, where food was available but was simply unaffordable (because of either high prices or low incomes), transfer payments through the Poor Law might ensure that everyone could eat. A more subtle reason, though, might relate to the impact of the Poor Law on migration patterns during crises. Disease was, it seems, usually the major proximate killer in famines. In Continental Europe, it has been pointed out, institutions of charity and formal poor relief tended to be strongly centered on the cities and towns (Smith 2011). This meant that, when poor harvests struck, the poor were forced to flee to urban centers to get poor relief, and as they did so they crowded in poorly sanitized suburbs. This dislocation, and particularly the movement of underfed people to crowded areas, greatly exacerbated the spread of disease, and thus of famine mortality. In England, by contrast, poor relief was available at home, even in rural parishes. This meant there was less imperative to migrate in search of succor, and thus disease spread less readily. Such a relationship makes logical sense, and indeed was sometimes visible to contemporaries. The town of Lamport in Somerset, for example, clearly saw the failure of poor relief as potentially leading to the spread of disease. During a plague outbreak in 1641 they complained to Bath Assizes that a tax for the relief of the poor was not being paid, "whereby the poore inhabitants of the said towne are like to famish or to breake into partes adjacent for releefe which may scatter a further infection" (Cockburn 1971, 4).

There is, of course, no reason that the two explanations are mutually exclusive. Both, however, do depend on there being enough food going around for everyone to eat. The Poor Law can only, therefore, be part of an explanation for the disappearance of famine; improved food security must have been important too. But it seems a strong likelihood that a robust, national system of transfers to the poor played a considerable role.

COPING WITH RISK

The Poor Law provided security against economic misfortune for everyone who was prepared to work. Given the character of the economy of early modern England this misfortune usually entailed bodily infirmity through either old age or sickness—"impotence" in the language of the time—but it could also encompass the exposure to economic hardship through the death of a spouse. This was serious for women and men, but it was always more serious for the former. The Poor Law helped protect against misfortune, but that misfortune itself was a product of the social and cultural landscape of the age. It was conditioned by the nature of the economy, by the demographic environment, by cultural notions of social justice and of the role of kin, and of course by the dead hand of patriarchy. Within this, though, the public good ultimately provided by the Poor Law was social security against misfortune.

The role of the "regional society" in the provision of this public good was, however, somewhat ambiguous. There were, of course, many different entities that could claim to be "regional societies" in England, including counties, hundred, Petty Sessions divisions, older territorial units such as Baronies, and even some of the larger parishes. The sheer "localness" of Poor Law administration should never be underestimated: each parish—in large measure—set its own policies based on local conditions. The character of the local economy and the local availability of non–Poor Law charitable resources both colored the response to poverty in each individual parish (Broad 1999). Nonetheless, the focus here on county records, heard by magistrates, emphasizes the importance of regional institutions. These, because they had clear policy influence, helped implant a regional dimension to the operation of poor relief. The early modern "regional society" *was* undoubtedly an influence on the provision of this particular public good.

What the developmental impact of the provision of social security as a public good was is hard to say, but it is nonetheless worth asking. England was not, of course, the only country that provided such a safety net, though at this point it seems to have been the only country that operated a national, tax-funded system of poor relief based on the redistribution of cash to the needy poor. It seems likely that it played a role in the contemporaneous disappearance of famine. Whether it also helped underpin the industrial development that was just starting and was to transform England, Britain, and the world in two centuries will have to remain a matter for speculation.

MANUSCRIPT SOURCES

Lancashire Archives, Quarter Sessions Petitions, QSP: 1648–1710.
Centre for Buckinghamshire Studies: Parish Records, PR/4/12/2.

PRINTED SOURCES

Appleby, Andrew B. (1978). *Famine in Tudor and Stuart England*. Liverpool, Liverpool University Press.
Ben-Amos, Ilana K. (2000). "Gifts and Favors: Informal Support in Early Modern England." *Journal of Modern History* 72:295–338.
———. (2008). *The Culture of Giving: Informal Support and Gift-Exchange in Early Modern England*. Cambridge, Cambridge University Press.
Bennett, Judith M. (1992). "Medieval Women, Modern Women: Across the Great Divide." In *Culture and History, 1350–1600: Essays on English Communities, Identities and Writings*, edited by D. Aers, 147–176. Hemel Hempstead, Prentice-Hall.

Boulton, Jeremy (2000). "'It Is Extreme Necessity That Makes Me Do This': Some 'Survival Strategies' of Pauper Households in London's West End during the Early Eighteenth Century." *International Review of Social History,* Supplement 8, 47–70.

Broad, John (1999). "Parish Economies of Welfare, 1650–1834." *Historical Journal* 42:985–1006.

Cockburn, James S., ed. (1971). *Somerset Assize Orders, 1640–1659.* Somerset Record Society 71, Frome.

Fideler, Paul A. (2006). *Social Welfare in Pre-Industrial England.* Basingstoke, UK, Penguin.

Fletcher, Anthony (1986). *Reform in the Provinces: The Government of Stuart England.* London, Yale University Press.

Goose, Nigel, Helen C. Caffrey, and Anne Langley, eds. (2016). *The British Almshouse: New Perspectives on Philanthropy, ca. 1400–1914.* Milton Keynes, Family and Community History Society.

Healey, Jonathan (2008). "Socially Selective Mortality during the Population Crisis of 1727–1730: Evidence from Lancashire." *Local Population Studies* 81:58–74.

——— (2010a). "The Development of Poor Relief in Lancashire, c. 1598–1680." *Historical Journal* 53:551–572.

——— (2010b). "Poverty in an Industrializing Town: Deserving Hardship in Bolton, 1674–99." *Social History* 35:125–147.

——— (2014). *The First Century of Welfare: Poverty and Poor Relief in Lancashire, c. 1620–1730.* Woodbridge, Boydell.

Hey, David (2016). *The Grass Roots of English History: Local Societies in England before the Industrial Revolution.* London, Bloomsbury.

Hindle, Steve (2000). "The Growth of Social Stability in Restoration England." *European Legacy* 5:663–676.

——— (2004). *On the Parish? The Micro-Politics of Poor Relief in Rural England, c. 1550–1750.* Oxford, Oxford University Press.

——— (2008). "Dearth and the English Revolution: The Harvest Crisis of 1647–50." *Economic History Review* 2nd Ser. 61, Supplement 1, 64–98.

Hitchcock, Tim, Peter King, and Pamela Sharpe, eds. (1997). *Chronicling Poverty: The Voices and Strategies of the English Poor, 1640–1840.* London, Palgrave Macmillan.

Holmes, Clive (1980). "The County Community in Stuart Historiography." *Journal of British Studies* 19:54–73.

Innes, Joanna (1996). "The 'Mixed Economy of Welfare' in Early Modern England: Assessments of the Options from Hale to Malthus (c. 1683–1803)." In *Charity, Self-interest and Welfare in the English Past,* edited by M. Daunton, 139–180. London, University College London Press.

Jones, Peter, and Steven King (2015). "From Petition to Pauper Letter: The Development of an Epistolary Form." In *Obligation, Entitlement and Dispute under the English Poor Laws,* edited by P. Jones and S. King, 53–77. Newcastle, Cambridge Scholars Press.

Kershaw, Ian (1973). "The Great Famine and Agrarian Crisis in England, 1315–22." *Past and Present* 59:3–50.

King, Steven (2000). *Poverty and Welfare in England, 1700–1850: A Regional Perspective.* Manchester, Manchester University Press.

King, Steven, and Alannah Tomkins, eds. (2003). *The Poor in England, 1700–1850: An Economy of Makeshifts.* Manchester, Manchester University Press.

Laslett, Peter (1988). "Family, Kinship and the Collectivity as Systems of Support in Pre-Industrial Europe: A Consideration of the 'Nuclear Hardship' Hypothesis." *Continuity and Change* 3:153–175.

Lister, John, ed. (1888). *West Riding Sessions Rolls, 1597/8–1602.* Yorkshire Archaeological Society Record Series, 3, Leeds.

McIntosh, Marjorie K. (2011). *Poor Relief in England, 1350–1600.* Cambridge, Cambridge University Press.

Muldrew, Craig, and Steven King (2003). "Cash, Wages and the Economy of Makeshifts in England, 1650–1800." In *Experiencing Wages: Social and Cultural Aspects of Wage Forms in Europe since 1500,* edited by P. Scholliers and L.D. Schwarz, 155–182. Oxford, Oxford University Press.

Neeson, Jeanette M. (1993). *Commoners: Common Right, Enclosure and Social Change in England, 1700–1820.* Cambridge, Cambridge University Press.

Newman-Brown, William (1984). "The Receipt of Poor Relief and Family Structure: Aldenham, Hertfordshire, 1630–90." In *Land, Kinship and Life-Cycle,* edited by R. Smith, 405–22. Cambridge, Cambridge University Press.

Ó Gráda, Cormac (2009). *Famine: A Short History.* Oxford, Oxford University Press.

Outhwaite, R. B. (1981). "Dearth and Government Intervention in English Grain Markets, 1590–1700." *Economic History Review,* 2nd Ser., 34:389–406.

Patriquin, Larry (2007). *Agrarian Capitalism and Poor Relief in England, 1500–1860: Rethinking the Origins of the Welfare State.* Basingstoke, UK, Penguin.

Phillips, C. B., and J. H. Smith (1994). *Lancashire and Cheshire from AD 1540.* London, Routledge.

Pollard, Anthony J. (1989). "The North-Eastern Economy and the Agrarian Crisis of 1438–40." *Northern History* 25:88–105.

Pound, J. F., ed (1971). *The Norwich Census of the Poor, 1570.* Norfolk Record Society, 40, Norwich.

Quintrell, Brian (1980). "The Making of Charles I's Book of Orders." *English Historical Review* 95:376, 553–572.

Reay, Barry (1996). "Kinship and Neighbourhood in Nineteenth-Century Rural England: The Myth of the Autonomous Nuclear Family." *Journal of Family History* 21:87–104.

Royal Commission on Historical Manuscripts (1905). *Report on the Manuscripts of the Marquess of Lothian.* Preserved at Blickling Hall, Norfolk. "Orders concerning the Statute for the Releif of the poore agreed at Ilmynster, the 11th of April [1601?]." London, His Majesty's Stationery Office.

Sen, Amartya (1981). *Poverty and Famines: An Essay on Entitlement and Deprivation.* Oxford, Oxford University Press.

Sharp, Buchanan (2016). *Famine and Scarcity in Late Medieval and Early Modern England: The Regulation of Grain Marketing, 1256–1631.* Cambridge, Cambridge University Press.

Slack, Paul, ed. (1975). *Poverty in Early Stuart Salisbury.* Wiltshire Record Society 31, Devizes.

——— (1988). *Poverty and Policy in Tudor and Stuart England.* London, Longman.

——— (1990). *The English Poor Law, 1531–1782.* Basingstoke, UK, Penguin.

Smith, Richard (2011). "Social Security as a Developmental Institution? The Relative Efficiency of Poor Relief Provisions under the English Old Poor Law." In *History, Historians and Development Policy: A Necessary Dialogue,* edited by C.A. Bayly, V. Rao, S. Szreter, and M. Woolcock, 75–102. Manchester, Manchester University Press.

Sokoll, Thomas, ed. (2001). *Essex Pauper Letters, 1731–1837.* Records of Social and Economic History, New Series, 30. Oxford, Oxford University Press.

Solar, Peter M. (1995). "Poor Relief and English Economic Development before the Industrial Revolution." *Economic History Review,* 2nd Ser., 48:1–22.

Stout, William (1967). *The Autobiography of William Stout of Lancaster, 1665–1752.* Edited by J.D. Marshall, Chetham Society, 3rd Ser. 14, Manchester.

Swanson, Scott G. (1997). "The Medieval Foundations of John Locke's Theory of Natural Rights: Rights of Subsistence and the Principle of Extreme Necessity." *History of Political Thought* 18:399–459.

Wales, Tim (1984). "Poverty, Poor Relief and the Life-Cycle: Some Evidence from Seventeenth-Century Norfolk." In *Land, Kinship and Life-Cycle,* edited by R. Smith, 351–404. Cambridge, Cambridge University Press.

Walter, John, and Roger Schofield (1989). "Famine, Disease and Crisis Mortality in Early Modern Society." In *Famine, Disease and the Social Order,* edited by J. Walter and R. Schofield, 1–73. Cambridge, Cambridge University Press.

Walton, John (1987). *Lancashire: A Social History, 1558–1939.* Manchester, Manchester University Press.

Whittle, Jane, ed. (2013). *Landlords and Tenants in Britain, 1440–1660: Tawney's Agrarian Problem Revisited.* Woodbridge, Boydell Press.

Williams, Samantha A. (2011). *Poverty, Gender and Life-cycle under the English Poor Law.* Woodbridge, Boydell Press.

Wrightson, Keith (1977). "Aspects of Social Differentiation in Rural England, c. 1580–1660." *Journal of Peasant Studies* 5:33–47.

——— (2000). *Earthly Necessities: Economic Lives in Early Modern Britain.* London, Yale University Press.

7

Coping with Poverty in
Rural Brandenburg

The Role of Lords and State in the
Late Eighteenth Century

Takashi Iida

While the Prussian Kingdom rose to become one of the European great powers through expanding its army, territories, and economic power during the eighteenth century, it still had a highly feudal structure characterized by demesne lordship *(Gutsherrschaft)*, specifically in its provinces east of the Elbe River. The Hohenzollern monarchs were not only sovereigns of the Prussian state but also the lords of their domain estates that they owned just as noble lords owned their own estates. The income from domain estates increased remarkably and took a significant part of Prussian public finances throughout the eighteenth century (table 5).

In East Elbian Prussia, demesne lordship developed in the fifteenth and sixteenth centuries and existed until dissolution through the "peasant emancipation" that began in 1807 as a part of the Prussian reforms. Demesne lords had one or more estates as their landed properties, which comprised not only farms that their subject peasants held in hereditary or leasehold tenure, but also their own demesne farms and forests. The tenant peasants were obligated to pay feudal rents in kind, money, or labor. As the lords' demesne farms enlarged, they compelled peasants to render even more labor services, often with draught animals. To ensure such labor, the lords restricted their peasants' freedom to leave the farm and even required the peasants' children to work as servants, also known as *Gesinde*. Thus, entire peasant families became hereditary subjects *(Erbuntertanen)* to their particular lords. The subjects were also subordinated to their lords' judicial right.[1] While the lords thus strengthened their rule over their subject peasants, they were also obligated to support these subjects. The lords were obligated to grant timber to (re)build and repair buildings on peasant farms, especially in case of leasehold tenure, as well as

TABLE 5. Development of Public Finances of Prussia, 1713–1806

	Income from domain estates (Million rt)	Tax (Million rt)	Total pure state revenue (Million rt)	Military Expenditure (Million rt)	Number of military personnel	Population
1713	1.6	2.4	3.4	2.5	38,000	1,600,000
1740	3.3	3.6	7	5–6	72,000	2,200,000
1786	6–7	10–11	23	12–13	195,000	5,400,000
1806	7–8	16	27	16–17	250,000	10,700,000

SOURCE: Schmoller 1898, 180.
NOTE: rt = *Reichstaler.*

to provide peasants with firewood, litter, and fodder from their forests, as will be detailed in chapter 13 of this volume. Otherwise, they were generally obligated to support their subjects in case of need.

In his study from 1887 of the "peasant emancipation" from the demesne lordship in Prussia, Georg Friedrich Knapp wrote a pioneering description of the East Elbian demesne lordship and gave a picture of the subject peasants as generally impoverished, unmotivated, and incapable of development under oppressive feudal lordship, despite being on the verge of emancipation. He illustrated their deep dependence on their lords for a wide range of life's necessities, suggesting that there was a region where "many subjects openly say that they do not regard it as an injustice to steal their lords' goods, and do not call it theft, but nourishing by the lords."[2] Thereafter, for a century, the image of the patriarchal care of East Elbian lords for their subjects became a tradition in the scholarship,[3] although counterevidence was cited as well.[4] However, the traditional image was fundamentally challenged by new research beginning in the mid-1980s, which offered a more dynamic and diverse view of the peasants' economy and society under the demesne lordship.[5] Since then, the image of generally impoverished and dependent East Elbian peasants can no longer be upheld. Nevertheless, it is still worth focusing on the lords' obligations and practices to support their subjects' lives, which varied according to the conditions.[6]

However, the lords were not solely responsible for supporting impoverished people. During the eighteenth century, the Prussian state sought to provide relief to the impoverished people through village or town communities.[7] This was all the more necessary because of the emergence of a new type of rural populace. After the resettlement of peasant farms that had been deserted because of the Thirty Years' War, the Prussian state's population growth policy meant to ensure a large army (table 5) led to an increase in the number of cottage residents. Among them, the lodgers *(Einlieger)* especially were free persons who, in contrast to subject peasants of feudal estates, could leave an estate freely but were more likely to fall into poverty. These landless people were beyond the control of each feudal estate and were to be supported publicly by the state authorities or each village and town community.

This chapter illustrates how this dual system of poor relief functioned in rural Brandenburg in the late eighteenth century, focusing on the case of the royal domain of Alt-Ruppin, one of the fifty-four royal domains in the Kurmark (the greater part of Brandenburg comprising the Altmark west of the Elbe River and East Elbian areas down to the Oder River surrounding Berlin). Around 1800, the Alt-Ruppin domain comprised two towns and twenty-seven villages.

RURAL POPULATION, SOCIETY, AND ECONOMY IN LATE-EIGHTEENTH-CENTURY KURMARK

During the eighteenth century, rural Brandenburg experienced rapid population growth and social differentiation. Between 1725 and 1800, the number of rural establishments in the Kurmark increased from 35,784 to 65,804. While the number of peasant farm holders *(Bauern* and *Kossäten)* remained almost constant at around twenty-eight thousand, because of the impartibility of the farms, the number of cottage residents *(Büdner* and *Einlieger)* increased from 7,930 to 36,345.[8]

In the royal domain of Alt-Ruppin, the number of large peasants *(Bauern)* and small peasants *(Kossäten)* was almost unchanged at around 420 and 110 between 1764 and 1800. While farms passed undivided to a single child, noninheriting heirs were compensated with a portion with which they married into a peasant farm, set up a cottage, or rented it. Consequently, the cottage-resident class repeated their self-reproduction and became denser, because there was almost no chance of upward social mobility to the farm-holding class.[9] Between 1764 and 1800, the number of cottagers *(Büdner),* who owned a cottage, remained also constant at 124 after the rapid increase in the 1750s. However, lodgers *(Einlieger)* who rented a cottage that was built mostly on a peasant farm increased rapidly from 135 in 1764 to 322 in 1800 (see table 8 in chapter 13). Cottagers and lodgers usually earned their living as laborers, handicraftsmen, or soldiers. In this social differentiation, poverty became concentrated among the cottage-resident class, especially among lodgers.

In the last decades of the eighteenth century, the social disparity between peasant farmers and cottage residents widened. In this period, rural Brandenburg experienced an agrarian boom, in which grain prices almost doubled, because of increasing demands from industrializing England, the growing population of Berlin, and increasing number of local cottage residents.[10] While increasing grain prices benefited peasant farmers, they disadvantaged cottage residents as grain consumers. This contrast increased poverty and issues pertaining to the cottage-resident class. However, the peasant-farmer class was also never free from poverty, as the next section examines.

COPING WITH IMPOVERISHED FARM HOLDERS

When a tenant peasant family was impoverished, the feudal lord's authorities immediately handled this matter. It was no wonder because the impoverishment inevitably affected the economy of the tenant farm that made up the lord's landed property. According to the Prussian General Legal Code *(Allgemeines Landrecht für die preußischen Staaten)* of 1794,[11] every lord was obligated to look after his subjects unstintingly in case of need (II 7 §122). However, he was entitled to evict his peasant subjects not only in case of rebelliousness or crime (§289, §290, §291) but for economic reasons as well. An eviction could take place if the peasant ruined his farm and its appurtenances through slovenly economy (§288), if he wasted the loan (§292), or because of old age or an incurable disease rendering him incompetent to manage his farm economy (§293). The reason for evicting a peasant was based on his "incompetence" *(Untüchtigkeit)* in maintaining his farm economy. The lords required that a farm holder retain the number of livestock and maintain farm buildings such as houses, stables, and barns. Indeed, every usu-fructuary holder and owner of peasant farms in the royal domains could obtain the necessary building timber from the royal forest free of charge or by paying one-third of the cost respectively.[12] In the case of rebuilding, they could enjoy the "ordinary" assistance of *Baufreiheiten,* an exemption from feudal rent for specific years. Otherwise, the farm holder himself was responsible for retaining the number of livestock and maintaining buildings. How did the feudal authorities actually cope with an impoverished farm holder between their obligation to support him and their right to evict him? The following case of a farm-owning small peasant *(Erbkossät)* named Joachim Siering in the village of Schönberg in the royal domain of Alt-Ruppin[13] serves as an illustration.

On April 21, 1784, Joachim Siering petitioned his lord, King Friedrich II, for extraordinary assistance to reconstruct his living house, stable, and barn, which were beyond repair. Since he had taken over the farm from his father, he kept it as a "most faithful subject," put great effort into cultivating it, and repaid part of the loan on it. However, "as an impoverished man," he could not afford to reconstruct the farm buildings. He attributed his poverty to family misfortunes. His mother had a lame hand, and of his seven children, one had a lame hand and stiff arm, and another a bandy leg. Siering had also been sick for a long time. In addition, two horses had died the previous winter.

Questioned by domain officials, the village headman of Schönberg named Döring confirmed that the difficulties of Siering's farm economy mainly originated in his unfortunate family circumstances: when he inherited his father's farm twenty years earlier, it was already not mortgage-free, and he could marry only a poor woman with a dowry of ten *Reichstaler*. His family then grew, and of his seven children, four were still infants, and two were handicapped, as Siering complained. Furthermore, while supporting his growing family, he had to give a portion of retirement to his father for ten years and to his still-living mother, who was too infirm to work, for twenty years. Döring blamed him only for the frequent death of his horses, as Siering was engaged in transporting wares to different markets for handicraftsmen and tradesmen, which exhausted the animals, resulting in improper cultivation of the crop fields. Otherwise, Döring did not blame Siering for anything, and attested that he was never lazy in his farm economy.

Based on this attestation, the domain official of Alt-Ruppin gave his opinion to the Board of War and Domains in the Kurmark *(Kurmärkische Kriegs- und Domänenkammer)*. His opinion was that Siering was a worthy recipient of extraordinary assistance, with which he could restore the farm economy "with the largest possibility." However, the Board did not accept this proposal, because the assistance cost 327 *Reichstaler*, which, while enough to rebuild the farm and complete the livestock, was too much for a small peasant farm. Thus, on March 26, 1785, the Board decided that Siering should sell his farm to someone capable of renovating it.

This decision suggests that unfortunate family circumstances such as Siering's were not reason enough for a peasant to be allowed to keep his farm by obtaining extraordinary assistance from the lords. In the late eighteenth century, the lords in the Kurmark saw good prospects of finding a satisfying successor. Population growth and the drastic rise of grain prices meant that there were usually several well-off applicants waiting to obtain a vacant farm or marry a widowed farmer, among which the lords could choose the highest bidder.[14] In this situation, lords could hardly decide to let an impoverished peasant remain as a farm holder by generously granting him extraordinary assistance.

Indeed, lords could make a different decision when a competent successor was not available. From the end of the Thirty Years' War to the early eighteenth century, the lords prioritized the restoration of devastated farms. A "people shortage" and agrarian depression made this restoration difficult. As such, they were forced to keep a farmer regardless of how poverty-stricken he was. Even after restoration was completed, it was sometimes impossible to find a person willing to take on a ruined farm, especially when it was on poor soil and saddled with heavier labor obligations. In this case, the lords had to leave in place the impoverished farmer who had ruined the farm and provide him with extraordinary assistance.[15] However, these cases became more infrequent toward the late eighteenth century, because of the population growth and the agrarian boom. Thus, an impoverished peasant like Siering had less opportunity to keep the farm.

Before the eviction was decided, Siering started to find a purchaser who could both afford to renovate the farm buildings and livestock and provide him and his family with at least free lodging on the farm. After much meandering, on May 2, 1786, the Board finally approved purchase of Siering's farm by Christoph Hartmann, a large peasant in Schönberg. Hartmann offered to renovate the farm only if he received extraordinary assistance of sixty *Reichstaler* from the royal budget. In addition, he permitted Siering and his wife to live in a cottage, which was to be built on the farm, free of charge and for life, and offered the land culti- vated annually with two *Metzen* (6.87 liter) of flax seed free of charge, as long as one of them was alive. As owner of another farm, Hartmann had to agree to hand over Siering's farm to one of his sons or a competent person in five years, because no person was allowed to have two farms. However, until then, Hartmann could permit Siering's family members to live in their original house and, while doing so, build a cottage into which they could move when handing over the house to a new farm owner.

Thus, forced transfer of the farm to a well-off successor helped the lords to minimize their costs of renovating the farm and the farm-leaving peasant family to obtain support for their future lives from the farm. However, it was uncertain whether the successor was ready and able to take on such support.[16] Even when support was offered from a new farm holder such as in Siering's case, it was usually temporary, because the new holder was interested in using his cottage to support his own family or for rent. Furthermore, on an impartible peasant farm in early modern Germany, it was usually the case that new people successively came to hold the farm through remarriage with a widowed farm holder, which meant that the interests of earlier farm-holder families were not really considered.[17]

After Joachim Siering and his wife died, the free lodging and free use of land cultivated with flax were no longer guaranteed for their handicapped children. Thereafter, they could not enjoy the support from the farm owners, which was authorized by the domain authorities, and had to rely on relief from their close relatives or, if not, on public relief, as was the norm for impoverished persons liv- ing in a cottage.

COPING WITH THE POVERTY OF
COTTAGE RESIDENTS

While tenants of peasant farms were usually subjects *(Untertanen)* of feudal lords and thus were not entitled to leave the farms without the lords' consent, lodgers *(Einlieger)* were free persons, who could move to another estate without seeking the lords' consent.[18] However, the lords' authorities reserved the right to consent to admission of lodgers in the estate,[19] and levy *Schutzgeld* (protection money) on them: in case of the royal domains, one *Reichstaler* on a lodger couple and twelve *Groschen* on a single lodger. Therefore, at least every six years, when the lease of a domain to the domain official was renewed, the domain authorities com- piled a list of all the lodgers, who rented a cottage in the domain with his or her

TABLE 6. Number and Life Circumstances of Lodgers in the Rural Settlements in the Royal Domain of Alt-Ruppin, 1771–1783

	1771	1777	1783
Lodgers (total)	149	170	168
Impoverished, without means, supported, begging	7	12	27
Elderly, sick, handicapped, single mothers, invalid soldiers	-	19	13

SOURCES: BLHA, Rep. 2, Kurmärkische Kriegs- und Domänenkammer, D. 16367, fol. 124–8, 402–3; D. 16368, fol. 88–92, 198–9; D. 16369, fol. 39–44, 92–4.

family or alone, to estimate the income generated by the *Schutzgeld*. The lists also included information on each lodger's life circumstances that could affect ability to pay *Schutzgeld*. Table 6 is an extract of three available lists of lodgers in the Alt-Ruppin domain, which were drafted for the domain lease every six years, from 1771, 1777, and 1783. Over time, the number of impoverished lodgers—indicated as "impoverished," "without means," "supported," or "begging"—increased from seven to twenty-seven, and their proportion among lodgers also increased from 4.7% to 16.1%. In addition, several lodgers were not indicated as impoverished but had difficulty—indicated as being "elderly," "sick," "handicapped," "single mothers," and "invalid soldiers"—and were likely to fall into poverty. Thus, the domain authorities cleared from paying *Schutzgeld* all impoverished lodgers and those having difficulty, as well as all soldiers.

However, it was not up to the domain authorities but the state authorities to provide for the impoverished lodgers. That is, feeding and clothing the poor was practiced not in the feudal patrimonial space but in the public space, where the state authorities charged each village community with the task regardless of whether it belonged to a royal domain or a noble estate. Starting in 1725, the Prussian state repeatedly ordered the judicial authority of each village or town community to establish its treasury to support the impoverished people living in the village or town. The main motive of these orders was that, from day to day, still more paupers and beggars were rushing to the city of Berlin from other towns and the countryside. Generally, however, the village communities remained passive and reluctant in this task. According to a study and report from 1745 on village communities in the district *(Kreis)* of Ruppin, many villages had not established a treasury and some that had had ceased its operation. In fact, in the nine villages in the royal domain of Lindow, which were in 1764 incorporated in the Alt-Ruppin domain, the treasury ceased in 1735, when the yearly cash contribution by villagers stopped. Instead, community members took turns to feed or clothe the impoverished, which, according to the report, was easier for them than making a yearly cash contribution to the treasury. In eight villages originally belonging to the Alt-Ruppin domain, where a treasury had established in and around 1725 and still existed in 1745, the yearly contribution was not fixed, except in one village.[20] By 1769 and 1773, the number of the villages with treasuries or collecting boxes for the impoverished had increased. However, in several villages, contributions remained irregular.[21]

The village communities were cautious not only in their fixed contributions to the treasury, but also in supporting the local impoverished people, especially in the 1790s. To clear the country and towns in the Kurmark of beggars, three houses for impoverished and invalid people were established from 1791 on. A house for four hundred beggars and two hundred invalids was established near the town of Strausberg, and another for two hundred beggars and one hundred invalids was established near each of the towns of Wittstock and Brandenburg.[22] However, since the establishment of these public houses for the impoverished on the provincial level, many problems occurred pertaining to the local impoverished people, who were meant to be supported in each village. As reported in the inspection protocol of 1797 on villages in the royal domain of Alt-Ruppin, local impoverished people were oppressed in the most outrageous ways.[23] These problems generally occurred in the Kurmark.[24]

The problems were related to the then custom that only a person who had lived for three years in a village was recognized as a local impoverished person eligible for support from the village community.[25] The inspection protocol of 1797 on villages in the Alt-Ruppin domain reported three common patterns to the problems experienced. First, it was conjectured that a person or his children would become a burden on the village community, because of disease, old age, or having no close relatives. In this case, if the person had not yet lived for a full three years in the village, he was driven out toward the end of this period, at the risk of not being readmitted elsewhere. Second, if a person had already lived in a village for three or more years, the opposite scenario often occurred, especially in the case of an invalid soldier. Because the village community was obligated to support him, he behaved as he pleased and often neglected his obligation to serve as a herdsman. Third, an elderly person qualified as a local impoverished person who was eligible for relief by a village and, while still willing to work, could not find employment in the area. However, he could not leave for another village, because he would not be accepted elsewhere due to the risk of having to support him and his children in the future.[26]

Reluctant to take on tasks pertaining to relieving impoverished people, villages shifted the responsibility onto the parties close to the impoverished. The village of Herzberg refused to support orphaned children, whose father had moved to the village less than three full years before his death. Ultimately, the children's relatives offered to support the orphans provided that the village of Herzberg fed them with a few *Scheffel* of rye.[27] Furthermore, the village of Wildberg adopted a measure whereby each cottage owner had to support impoverished lodgers living in his cottage to reduce the collective burden of the villagers. Unfortunately, this led to the cruel practice of driving lodgers between cottages after the lease period.[28]

Remember that according to the 1797 inspection protocol, each village adopted its cruel policy toward those lodgers likely to fall into poverty after the houses for impoverished and invalid people were established in the Kurmark. Another report of the same year also observed the emerging phenomenon of accommodation shortages for lodgers.[29] However, while this was not common, there had been similar incidents previously in the Kurmark. Jan Peters found a case from 1728, in which an impoverished, elderly, sick woman was passed from one village to more than ten other villages across the border between Saxony and the Kurmark without being accommodated until she ultimately died. Peters argued that this organized form of collective refusal to accommodate a person in need of help was already familiar to the villages.[30] This likely long-established merciless practice of village communities became common after the provincial houses for impoverished and invalid people were established. Thus, the village communities forced their responsibility onto the provincial institutions.

In the Kurmark Brandenburg, feudal lords were obligated to support their impoverished subject peasants unstintingly. However, only in cases in which a competent successor was lacking was an impoverished peasant allowed to keep the farm while enjoying extraordinary assistance from his lord. In the late eighteenth century, which was characterized by population growth and the agrarian boom, lords generally had good prospects for replacing an impoverished peasant with a competent successor selected from several applicants. Even in this case, the lords did not leave the evicted family to fend for themselves, but arranged as far as possible for the new peasant farmer to support the evicted family by accommodating them in a cottage on the farm or offering life's necessities, albeit for a limited time.

An increasing number of cottage residents, especially lodgers, suffered more frequently from poverty in the late eighteenth century. Indeed, the feudal lords helped impoverished lodgers in their estates by not holding them liable for the *Schutzgeld* payment. However, it was the task of the state authorities to provide for the impoverished lodgers, who could freely move over the boundary of feudal estates. To remedy the problem of the paupers or beggars rushing to the city of Berlin, the state ordered each village community to relieve the poor in the village by establishing a treasury for that purpose. However, the villages were never willing to take on this task. They did not always carry out the order to give a yearly or monthly fixed contribution to the treasury to assist the impoverished. The villages were inclined to shift the responsibility of support to the close relatives of local impoverished people or the owner of the cottage in which an impoverished lodger lived. Often, the villages refused to accept a lodger in prospective poverty and passed him from one village to another to avoid the future responsibility of having to support him and his family. This cruel practice of village communities, which had likely been long established, became common in response to the establishment of the houses for impoverished and invalid people on the provincial level in 1791.

NOTES

1. Rösener 1994, 104–124.

2. Knapp 1887/1927, 1:78.

3. Wald 1934, Lütge 1960, 381–382.

4. Spies 1972, 390, Berdahl 1988, 53–54.

5. Harnisch 1989a, part 3, 87–108. For a survey of the new research, see Kaak 1999, Finlay 2001, 282–284, Cerman 2012.

6. As the latest research, see Eddie 2013.

7. Harnisch 1989b, 216–217.

8. Harnisch 1994, 21. See also Wunder 1996, 82–84.

9. Iida 2010, 130.

10. Harnisch 1984, 27–58, Harnisch 1986.

11. *Allgemeines Landrecht für die preussischen Staaten von 1794.* Textausgabe mit einer Einführung von Hans Hattenhauer, 3. ed. (Neuwied: Luchterhand Verlag, 1996).

12. See chapter 13 in this volume.

13. Brandenburgisches Landeshauptarchiv, Potsdam, Germany (hereafter: BLHA), Rep. 7, Amt Alt-Ruppin, No. 530, See also Iida (2010), 111–21.

14. Harnisch 1989a, 96, 101, Enders 1989, 272.

15. Iida 2010, 126–128.

16. Iida 2010, 124–126.

17. Iida 2010, 170–180. See also Schlumbohm 1994, Rouette 2003, and Rouette 2006.

18. *Allgemeines Landrecht für die preussischen Staaten von 1794,* II 7 §113, 121.

19. *Allgemeines Landrecht für die preussischen Staaten von 1794,* II 7 §114.

20. Geheimes Staatsarchiv Preußischer Kulturbesitz, Berlin-Dahlem (hereafter: GStAPK), Tit: CCII, Armen-Sachen, no. 4, fol. 95–101.

21. BLHA, Rep. 7, Amt Alt-Ruppin, no. 118.

22. Friedrich Wilhelm August Bratring and Otto Büsch, *Statistisch-Topographische Beschreibung der gesamten Mark Brandenburg: mit einer biographisch-bibliographischen Einführung* (1804–1809, repr., Berlin: Walter de Gruyter, 1968), 237–38.

23. BLHA, Rep. 7, Amt Alt-Ruppin, no. 115, fol. 115.

24. GStAPK, Tit: CCII, Armen-Sachen, no. 4, fol. 235.

25. This qualification was based on the paragraph 15 of the edict of April 28, 1748, that, within two weeks, foreign beggars should leave Prussian Kingdom and native beggars should return to their home villages and towns, in which they were born or lived for the last three years (GStAPK, Tit: CCII, Armen-Sachen, no. 4, fol. 186, 237).

26. BLHA, Rep. 7, Amt Alt-Ruppin, no. 115, fol. 115.

27. BLHA, Rep. 7, Amt Alt-Ruppin, no. 115, fol. 141.

28. BLHA, Rep. 7, Amt Alt-Ruppin, no. 115, fol. 115.

29. GStAPK, Tit: CCII, Armen-Sachen, no. 4, fol. 235.

30. Peters 1991.

REFERENCES

Berdahl, Robert M. (1988). *The Politics of Prussian Nobility: The Development of a Conservative Ideology, 1770–1848*. Princeton, Princeton University Press.

Cerman, Markus (2012). *Villagers and Lords in Eastern Europe, 1300–1800*. Basingstoke, UK, Palgrave Macmillan.

Eddie, Sean A. (2013). *Freedom's Price: Serfdom, Subjection, and Reform in Prussia, 1648–1848*. Oxford, Oxford University Press.

Enders, Lieselott (1989). "Bauern und Feudalherrschaft der Uckermark im absolutistischen Staat." *Jahrbuch für Geschichte des Feudalismus* 13.

Finlay, Mark (2001). "New Sources, New Theses, and New Organizations in the New Germany: Recent Research on the History of German Agriculture." *Agricultural History* 75.

Harnisch, Hartmut (1984). *Kapitalistische Agrarreform und industrielle Revolution: Agrarhistorische Untersuchungen über das ostelbische Preußen zwischen Spätfeudalismus und bürgerlich-demokratischer Revolution von 1848/49 unter besonderer Berücksichtigung der Provinz Brandenburg*. Weimar, Hermann Böhlaus Nachfolger.

——— (1986). "Peasants and Markets: The Background to the Agrarian Reforms in Feudal Prussia East of the Elbe, 1760–1807." In *The German Peasantry: Conflict and Community in Rural Society from the Eighteenth to the Twentieth Centuries*, edited by Richard J. Evans and W. R. Lee. New York, St. Martin's.

——— (1989a). "Bäuerliche Ökonomie und Mentalität unter den Bedingungen der ostelbischen Gutsherrschaft in den letzten Jahrzehnten vor Beginn der Agrarreformen." *Jahrbuch für Wirtschaftsgeschichte* 1989, part 3.

——— (1989b). "Die Landgemeinde in der Herrschaftsstruktur des feudalabsolutistischen Staates: Dargestellt am Beispiel von Brandenburg-Preußen." *Jahrbuch für Geschichte des Feudalismus* 13.

——— (1994). "Der preußische Absolutismus und die Bauern: Sozialkonservative Gesellschaftspolitik und Vorleistung zur Modernisierung." *Jahrbuch für Wirtschaftsgeschichte* 1994, part 2.

Iida, Takashi (2010). *Ruppiner Bauernleben, 1648–1806: Sozial- und wirtschaftsgeschichtliche Untersuchungen einer ländlichen Gegend Ostelbiens*. Berlin, Lukas.

Kaak, Heinrich (1999). "Brandenburgische Bauern im 18. Jahrhundert: Sozialgeschichtliche Forschungen in mikrohistorischer Perspektive." In *Leben und Arbeiten auf märkischem Sand: Wege in die Gesellschaftsgeschichte Brandenburgs, 1700–1914*, edited by Ralf Pröve and Bernd Kölling. Bielefeld, Verlag für Regionalgeschichte.

Knapp, Georg Friedrich (1887/1927). *Die Bauernbefreiung und der Ursprung der Landarbeiter in den älteren Theilen Preußens*. 2 vols. 2nd ed. Munich and Leipzig, Duncker & Humbolt.

Lütge, Friedrich (1960). *Deutsche Sozial- und Wirtschaftsgeschichte. Ein Überblick*. 2nd ed. Berlin, Springer.

Peters, Jan (1991). "Das unbarmherziges Dorf: Eine verhaltensgeschichtliche Studie aus dem südlichen Främing (1728)." *Jahrbuch für brandenburgische Landesgeschichte* 42.

Rösener, Werner (1994). *The Peasantry of Europe*. Oxford, Blackwell.

Rouette, Susanne (2003). "Erbrecht und Besitzweitergabe: Praktiken in der ländlichen Gesellschaft Deutschlands, Diskurse in Politik und Wissenschaft." In *Ländliche Gesellschaften in Deutschland und Frankreich im 18. und 19. Jahrhundert*, edited by Reiner

Prass, Jürgen Schlumbohm, Gérard Béaur, and Christophe Duhamelle. Göttingen, Vandenhoeck & Ruprecht.

——— (2006). "'Hofesbande'—Bauernfamilien, Verwandtschaft und Besitz im münsterländischen Diestedde im 19. Jahrhundert." In *Generationengerechtigkeit? Normen und Praxis im Erb- und Ehegüterrecht 1500–1850*, edited by Stefan Brakensiek, Michael Stolleis, and Heide Wunder. Berlin, Duncker & Humblot.

Schlumbohm, Jürgen (1994). "The Land-Family Bond in Peasant Practice and in Middle-Class Ideology: Evidence from the North-West German Parish of Belm, 1650–1850." *Central European History 27.*

Schmoller, Gustav von (1898). *Umrisse und Untersuchungen zur Verfassungs-, Verwaltungs- und Wirtschaftsgeschichte*. Leipzig, Duncker & Humblot.

Spies, Klaus (1972). *Gutsherr und Untertan in der Mittelmark Brandenburg zu Beginn der Bauernbefreiung*. Berlin, J. Schweitzer.

Wald, Annmarie (1934). "Die Bauernbefreiung und die Ablösung des Obereigentums—eine Befreiung der Herren?" *Historische Vierteljahrschrift 28.*

Wunder, Heide (1996). "Agriculture and Agrarian Society." In *Germany: A New Social and Economic History*, vol. 2, *1630–1800*, edited by Ogilvie Sheilagh. London and New York, Arnold.

8

Coping with Poverty and Famine

Material Welfare, Public Goods, and Chinese Approaches to Governance

R. Bin Wong

This chapter on Chinese efforts to cope with the problem of poverty and the threats of famine differs from other chapters in this part of the book regarding the spatial scale on which it addresses the topic. It places local activities within a much larger spatial frame than even the English case study since England is spatially and demographically so much smaller than China. England's population of less than six million and China's some two hundred million around 1750 mean China's efforts at addressing poverty and famine affected a population many times the size of England's. The two other case studies of early-modern-era approaches to poverty and famine stress actions taken within small spaces—Japanese efforts within the village and Prussian efforts by lords spanning a number of villages. In China, most county-level officials in the eighteenth century organized their efforts far from the political center and relied in part on the organizational efforts and financial resources of people without any formal positions in the government; in this respect their activities resembled those we have seen in our other case studies. But because their efforts together were part of a virtually empire-wide system, certainly in terms of population if not including some of the newly subjugated Inner Asian components of the empire, the centrally coordinated activities created public goods on spatial and demographic scales dwarfing those found elsewhere. To understand how and why policies to address poverty and relieve famine occurred on such a large scale in eighteenth-century China, a brief introduction to the ideological foundations of Chinese approaches to poverty as part of a broader focus on issues of material welfare provides some background to eighteenth-century policies that are designed to sustain people through times of harvest hardship, and that are especially mindful that poorer people needed help on a more regular basis.

THE IDEOLOGICAL AND INSTITUTIONAL BACKGROUND TO FOOD SUPPLY POLICIES

Between the sixth and third centuries BCE, a number of Chinese political thinkers conceived social order and the viability of political rule to be linked in a direct manner that provided part of the basis for the subsequent imperial era's approach to governance. The ruler's political success depended on his ability and commitment to benefiting the people (利民 *limin*). By formulating policies intended to promote common people's material welfare, rulers could achieve both social stability and political acceptance. Governments could appeal to their subjects to support them in their competition with rival governments for territory and subjects during the Warring States era (475–221 BCE). Such demands for service in times of war made more sense when understood by people to be coupled with the means to secure a livelihood. This approach to governance recognized the limited organizational capacity that rulers could call upon to enforce their will through coercion and encouraged rulers to recognize that meeting their desires for wealth and power over the long run were more likely to be achieved by promoting the ability of people to produce more output than by impoverishing them in the short run through high taxation. Reputation as a benevolent ruler in a time of intense political competition made more likely that subjects would not flee and even encouraged those suffering hardship from other rulers to settle in his territory (El Amine 2015).

Chinese concerns for the material welfare of the people in subsequent centuries covered at least three areas—the circulation of resources and goods in society, the possession of the means to produce for one's needs, and intervention by the state when the production and circulation of grains failed to provide for people due to either poverty or dearth. Framing direct state interventions to address poverty and dearth became elements of an approach to governance known as *jingshi* (經世 statecraft) intended to foster "learning of practical use to society" (經世之用 *jingshi zhi yong*) in the late twelfth and early thirteenth centuries; the statecraft tradition informed policy discussions and choices in subsequent centuries, taking particular salience in moments of crisis but present as a backdrop to conceptions of state approaches to popular material welfare more generally (Hymes and Schirokauer 1993). To understand how the issue of poverty and dearth figured in the more general context of statecraft governance, this chapter considers the circulation of food supplies among resources more generally and efforts to promote common people's capacities to achieve material security through their own labors, before considering directly the eighteenth-century recognition of the desirability to intervene against vulnerability to harvest fluctuations and, in extreme situations, famine.

THE IMPORTANCE OF MARKETS AND THE
CONSTRUCTION OF AN EIGHTEENTH-CENTURY
COMMERCIAL AGRARIAN EMPIRE

The notion of the emperor anchoring his authority and demonstrating his virtue (and hence legitimacy) according to his concern for popular material welfare began to be persuasive in the Han dynasty (206 BCE–220 AD), China's second imperial dynasty and the first to last beyond its founding emperor. A Confucian political logic of conceiving the state's support to rest upon a society of small-scale agriculturalists whose taxes would support the government depended upon insulating them from the predations of large land-owning lords to whom they could be reduced to some form of tenancy or servitude. Promoting popular welfare was thus one political strategy for creating a political base of support and avoiding the emergence of powerful families who could challenge imperial authority and power; at times more an aspiration than a reality, the logic nevertheless indicates a general frame of reference within which the use and hence flows of resources could be imagined and thus pursued. The fifteenth-century scholar Qiu Jun included in his discussion of the principles for the management of wealth a logic traced to what had initially been a divination text but became between the sixth and third centuries BCE a cosmological and philosophical text, the *Yijing (Book of Changes),* addressing the unity of opposites and processes of change moving both cyclically and through historical time. Using the *Book of Changes* as a reference point, Qiu Jun discusses the movement of resources from the government to the people and from the rich to the poor; both movements promise future increases in wealth from which either the government or the wealthy would benefit. Government financial management, in Qiu Jun's formulation, matters not only to a successful state but also to a prosperous society. Conceived properly and pursued effectively, state fiscal policies not only avoid harming the people greatly, but indeed also provide the basic conditions for increasing social wealth based on how resources flow within society and between the government and its subjects. Such resource flows became part of a far larger circulation of goods through markets in subsequent centuries.[1]

During the Song dynasty (960–1279) China experienced what Mark Elvin famously called a "medieval economic revolution" based on improvements in agricultural productivity, largely owing to the expansion of paddy rice agriculture, the expansion of water transport for goods, and the emergence of merchants independent of the kinds of state regulation present in earlier centuries and the expansion of market networks (Elvin 1973). After 1500, regional merchant groups and two especially prominent merchant groups associated with the northern province of

Shanxi and Huizhou prefecture in the eastern province of Anhui with empire-wide networks moved increasing amounts of diverse goods between counties, across provincial borders, and even greater distances where riverine transportation was well developed and maintained. Craft production, which had been more town-centered than rural-based in Song times, had become increasingly common among rural households who pursued a combination of crops (including cash crops) and crafts for which market exchange was essential. This meant the economy was both largely agrarian and commercial at the same time. Moreover, this economic expansion took place within an empire that provided, over great distances for considerable segments of time, the relatively peaceful and secure conditions that enabled trade to proceed relatively free of disruption and dislocation caused by violence, be this widespread banditry or more problematic war making of the sort that became increasingly present across the European landscape of the early modern era (Rosenthal and Wong 2011, 89–91).

The contrast between European interstate competition and a largely peaceful Chinese empire became more vivid in the eighteenth century when two especially activist emperors dominated the country from the 1720s into the 1790s. The priority placed on the circulation of goods, in particular grain, was made plain by the Yongzheng emperor (r. 1723–1735), who often opposed the efforts by officials in the provinces to impede the commercial flow of grain for fear that exports from their jurisdictions could create shortages amid possibilities of poor harvest (Abe 1957). Since grain on markets flowed from areas with prices lower than those to which it was being shipped, it made sense from a supply and demand perspective to uphold the free circulation of grain. Chinese notions of circulation related the logic of circulation to that of balance, in this case balancing supply and demand indicated by price differences. Officials also had concerns regarding balancing grain prices through the year. Market prices were lower when the fall harvests were reaped and far higher in the lean spring season when the past year's harvests had been depleted. To meet this annual cycle of price fluctuations, ever-normal granaries (常平倉 changping cang) were established in each of more than thirteen hundred county seats and charged with selling grain in the spring to lower market prices and restocking in the fall after harvests brought prices down below those at which officials had sold grain the previous spring. These granaries in turn formed the core of a broader set of civilian granaries that were a major line of defense against conditions of serious dearth that threatened famine, a subject to be explored further in this chapter (Will and Wong 1991).

Another indication of the relatively favorable conditions for trade in eighteenth-century China compared to conditions in Europe was the low transit taxes levied in China. European rulers relied heavily on commercial taxation to satisfy their growing appetites for fiscal resources needed to pursue war making with one another. China lacked such demands as there were no threats of war making within China corresponding to the European space within which war making was a chronic threat. With low commercial taxes, all domestic trade with the exception of salt avoided the heavy hand of the state. Salt production and distribution were administered by the state; production was legally limited to households registered for this purpose and distribution was limited in principle to merchants who had purchased licenses authorizing them to participate in the trade within the areas for which their licenses applied (Chiang 1983). Restricting legal participation in the salt trade to a small set of merchants fostered the emergence of a few very wealthy merchants, a common outcome of restricting access to a market—the state garnered revenues from these individuals, who in turn enjoyed the privilege of limited competition from other sellers of salt, much as Dutch and English merchants who were members of their respective chartered companies engaged in Asian trade benefited from the limits to competition from other Dutch and English merchants not part of the chartered companies. In China more generally, however, the state favored market competition and the presence of multiple buyers and sellers, which made less likely the presence of a few merchants able to manipulate prices by holding supplies off the market to drive up their subsequent profits. This was especially the case for the case of grain, the staple so basic to people's material security. Officials criticizing merchant hoarding of grain to drive up prices on local markets were simply one small part of a far larger set of policies intended to manage food supplies in a manner that assured poorer people access to grain at prices they could usually afford.

The eighteenth-century Chinese state's antipathy toward merchants manipulating prices to garner profits beyond those possible on markets with large numbers of buyers and sellers applied to domestic markets but not to those merchants licensed to engage in trade with foreigners. The Canton system (1757–1842) limited foreigners to the single port of Guangzhou, where they were allowed to do business with a specific group of merchants licensed for this purpose (Wakeman 1978). While the fortunes of these Chinese merchants certainly fluctuated, the possibilities of making large sums of money meant a few of them became famously wealthy. In the preindustrial era when trade was the likely arena in which money could be made, restricting access to markets usually in exchange for the state gaining fiscal benefits turned some commerce into a kind of capitalism, especially when we recognize as a key feature of capitalism the ability of a small number of firms or individuals to dominate leading sectors of the economy, which is seen among the early modern Dutch and English companies engaged in Asian trade and subsequently in the industrial era among the late-nineteenth- and early-twentieth-century American and German firms in chemicals, steel, and railroads. Eighteenth-century China's general antipathy to market concentration in the hands of a few entrepreneurs not only made the emergence of such key capitalist traits less likely, but also enhanced the likelihood ordinary people would benefit from markets as consumers. To assure that most farmers could enjoy opportunities to benefit from markets as producers who sold their crops and crafts commercially, officials also had to be concerned about the impact of rents on tenants. Thus, eighteenth-century officials continued to recognize the ideal of limiting landlord exactions on tenants even as they proved unable to prevent the basic negative impacts that tenants could suffer at landlord hands. While landlords and market supply concentration in the hands of capitalists were both present possibilities, state policies to promote circulation of grain freely to benefit peasants who could be either producers or consumers for commercial grain were a key component of efforts to maintain a stable food supply. These were efforts designed to promote a well-functioning structure for circulation of grain. But as population rose, grain production also had to rise in order to meet increased demand. For this reason a second cluster of official efforts was directed to increasing grain production.

STRATEGIES TO PROMOTE MATERIAL WELFARE: SUPPORTING THE INFRASTRUCTURE FOR PRODUCTION

Officials supported both extensive and intensive increases in grain production. Extensive growth occurred when land-poor peasants migrated to areas with more abundant opportunities to open barren land and turn it into productive fields. The state at times offered a grace period before taxes would be levied on newly opened fields to facilitate owner investment in making the land productive. Migration was a form of circulation of people that complemented the circulation of goods, in the broad spirit of balancing people and resources through movements found in fifteenth-century Qiu Jun's remarks noted earlier. Where markets moved commodities from areas of low prices to those with higher ones, migration moved labor from areas with limited farm land to those places where land clearance for fresh cultivation was more easily pursued. Officials further supported such migrations by also encouraging the transfer of what were deemed the best technologies of crop cultivation and craft production from more developed areas to poorer ones. All these efforts entailed some form of circulation—of people and knowledge to complement market-based movements of commodities (Wong 2014). While our contemporary categories of analysis regard markets as the site for private transactions because ownership is vested in individuals or families and not the government, the eighteenth-century Chinese government played a significant role in assuring the success of markets as part of a larger vision of resources and people staying in balance through the movements of each.

Complementing extensive expansion of grain production was the intensified use of land through irrigation. This technology, virtually absent in Europe, but found in Northeast, South, and Southeast Asia, as well as China, depended on multiple levels of water control management and coordination among several parties. Given its far larger size and population, Chinese officials had more water control issues in general to consider on a larger spatial scale than did other Asian countries. Not surprisingly, the historical importance of water management to China and to Asia more generally has long been recognized. We can divide the bulk of the literature into one of three categories—those stressing an authoritarian top-down perspective, those focused on local communities that have a bottom-up perspective, and those studies addressing interactions of local actors and state agents. Karl Wittfogel made famous the top-down perspective, while Japanese historians, notably Morita Akira, have contributed a community-centered bottom-up perspective for China (Wittfogel 1957, Morita 2002). Other scholars have either examined complementary and coordinated efforts of the Ming and Qing governments and elites to finance and organize the maintenance of water control works or noted the competition between elite efforts to create new polder lands and official priorities on assuring free-flowing transportation routes (Li Cho-ying 2012, Will 1985, Perdue 1982).

None of the scholarship on water control issues to date has been intended to highlight the public goods dimension of official interventions. Takehiko To's study in part 3 does this for China's capital region during the eighteenth century. The challenge for us more generally in a volume on public goods regarding water control is to discover relationships among different spatial levels of organization from those headed by state officials at the top to others managed by local villagers at the bottom. In the Nobel laureate Elinor Ostrom's analysis of "common pool resources," the eighth and last principle for effective organization of activities such as water control, she speaks of "nested enterprises."[2] The "nested" nature involves the coordination above the level of different groups each organizing common pool resources drawing upon the same water sources. Some mix of state and local community efforts was present most everywhere irrigation was an important economic practice, but Chinese approaches to mobilizing and managing resources and labor needed to maintain water control works for irrigation and transportation also evolved across diverse kinds of terrain and on an especially large spatial scale. Chinese efforts also fluctuated over time, affected by a changing cast of competing priorities, especially clear after the mid-nineteenth century, when higher-level officials were more likely to be constrained in their resources and abilities to intervene in water control issues.

State efforts made at the center, provincial, and county levels to promote independent peasant household production of grain and its commercial circulation suggest political appreciation for a well-functioning economy based on private property. Clearly, some of these efforts, like the infrastructure for agricultural production that forms the subject for part 3 of this volume, entailed recognition of nonmarket and nonprivate property features of the economy. To address dearth and poverty directly, official and elite efforts beyond the production and commercial circulation of grain were mounted to form a separate kind of public goods provision.

EIGHTEENTH-CENTURY EFFORTS TO RELIEVE
FAMINE AND MANAGE FOOD SUPPLIES

In preindustrial societies where the vast majority of sedentary populations are engaged in agriculture or, as in the Chinese case, in other craft-related pursuits, economic instabilities came in two temporal forms both tied to agricultural harvests. First were the annual variations in food supply availability tied to the harvest cycle—grain is plentiful and cheap after the fall harvests and scarce and dear in the months directly preceding the annual harvests. Second were the variations in the size of harvests, with a sequence of mediocre or bad harvests increasing the likelihood of severe dearth. Addressing seasonal fluctuations in grain availability targeted poor people specifically, seeking to assure them grain at lower prices or loans of grain. Severe annual shortages posed threats to people more generally and carried with them a potential to undermine social stability. Because the political legitimacy of Chinese governance depended in principle on officials averting or at least mitigating the impact of severe dearth, famine relief was a key component of effective food supply policies during the eighteenth century.

During this period, famine relief involved selection of multiple policies from a repertoire of techniques developed over the previous several centuries. These policies that were mobilized into an intensive campaign to relieve a famine were one kind of government provision of a social or public good. They were in turn embedded in a broader system of granaries utilized in a more routine fashion over more than a century, infused with new supplies of grain through major initiatives to augment granary reserves and with supplies reduced by both deliberate policy decisions and bureaucratic neglect. This apparatus was flanked by the grain price reporting system that provided officials from county to the capital with data on the conditions of grain supplies on markets across the empire (Will and Wong 1991).

Inspired by political principles defining a Chinese approach to governance first articulated roughly two millennia before and drawing on institutions formed over several preceding centuries, eighteenth-century policies formulated by the Chinese state reveal three important attributes of the Chinese state's approach to public or social goods. First, the state considered providing famine relief or building granaries to store grain to be a responsibility of officials across the empire, from those at the center to those in locales at opposite ends of the empire. Second, providing famine relief and grain storage was the shared responsibility of local elites, attesting to the elements of a governance agenda that they shared for maintenance of domestic social order. Third, in the extreme conditions of sequential bad harvests due to flood, drought, or pestilence, famine relief efforts required extraordinary mobilization of resources and human effort, creating a campaign-level intensity well beyond what routine bureaucratic or social action entailed. Food supply interventions were both a kind of social good and a social service performed directly by various levels of the state and elites outside the bureaucracy. Their effectiveness made the economy work more smoothly.

Eighteenth-century institution building for grain storage and the implementation of famine relief drew more immediately and concretely upon policies formulated beginning in the Southern Song (1127–1279). The institutional basis for managing food supplies formulated during this period created an alternative to Northern Song (960–1127) "big government" associated with Wang Anshi, even as it affirmed the importance of popular material welfare. Almost all these efforts depended on the combined complementary efforts of local officials and local elites to forge and maintain institutions of local order. These included granaries to store grain, charitable estates the incomes from which went to aid indigent kinsmen or other local residents, and organizing emergency famine relief measures in times of acute harvest failure (Hymes and Schirokauer 1993). A similar reliance on local efforts to store grain and relieve famine that were part of late Ming dynasty (1368–1643) governance can be placed in a larger context to include social commitments to charity inspired by Buddhism (Smith 2009). This kind of situation is consistent with emperors and the central government bureaucracy being neither interested nor able to create much in the way of grain storage across the empire, a situation easily accommodated by an influential strand of late-twentieth-century scholarship that has claimed the late Ming government to be largely ineffectual (Huang 1981). But even as the Wanli emperor (r. 1472–1620), typically viewed as a weak and ineffectual ruler, was embroiled in major disputes with high-level officials over the selection of his heir apparent, leading to his refusal to meet with current officials or appoint new ones, the state ruling in his name was able to mount a famine relief campaign in 1592 that prepared local reports, released grain from the local granaries, and remitted land taxes in areas hardest hit by poor harvests (Des Forges 2003, 34–35).

However modest and infrequent local efforts to relieve potential famine in the late sixteenth century were, they appealed to principles and policies developed over earlier centuries. Their existence, in contrast to a total absence of grain storage and famine relief, made plausible the efforts to create more robust policies in the eighteenth century. These were pursued through the three kinds of practices introduced earlier—bureaucratic action, elite efforts, extraordinary campaigns—practices that were also responsible for eighteenth-century Chinese efforts to provide public goods and services more generally. For subsistence issues specifically, officials spearheaded, in response to imperial instructions, the formation of an empire-wide system of centrally monitored granaries storing hundreds of thousands of tons of grain both for annual use to mitigate seasonal fluctuation in grain prices and for relieving subsistence crises in more difficult years. Each of the empire's more than thirteen hundred counties reported their granary reserves at the beginning and close of the year as part of an annual accounting of reserves, distributions, and replacements. Provincial governors summarized their county reports and forwarded their summaries to the center. Behind this system of accounting was an even more remarkable bureaucratic procedure that entailed each county magistrate reporting to the provincial governor every ten days the high and low prices for each of the grains commercially available on markets within his jurisdiction. These reports were summarized on a monthly basis for dispatch to the center for central government officials to review and when necessary report to the emperor regarding extremely high prices over a widespread area that required a famine relief campaign (Will and Wong 1991). Pierre-Etienne Will has analyzed the famine relief campaign mounted in response to the famine of 1743–1744 in the capital province of Zhili. Officials conducted surveys of the severely affected locales to assess the number of victims and severity of the famine in particular areas. They implemented a range of policies including remitting land taxes, setting up rice gruel stations, releasing local granary reserves, and seeking to move grain themselves into the most badly affected areas (Will 1990).

The manner in which the eighteenth-century state provided grain as a public good qualifies in at least three ways sometimes skeptical and even negative views of the state. First, the state's chronic anxieties over big government and bureaucratic mismanagement, which historians have echoed, depended first on Chinese political leaders developing a rule-governed, vertically integrated bureaucracy that could identify violations of expected official behavior. The bureaucracy comprised highly educated individuals, increasing numbers of whom were selected based on their exam performance and were forbidden to serve in their home provinces and typically moved from post to post every few years so that they became less likely to promote local interests or develop long-standing relations to be exploited for illicit private gain. Chinese principles of governance in general and concern for material welfare more specifically could not have been pursued across such a large territory and impact such a large number of people without one of the world's largest and more effective bureaucracies operating virtually continuously for roughly a millennium before the fall of the Qing dynasty in 1911. Even though an activist central state had been soundly rejected in principle during the twelfth century, the eighteenth-century central state was able to build an empire-wide system of civilian granary reserves that enlisted the active commitments of local elites to contribute and manage some of those reserves.

A second way grain provision to address poverty and dearth qualifies images of a weak and ineffective state comes through understanding that the agenda constructed by the central government was largely shared ideologically and institutionally, not only with officials at lower levels of the bureaucracy, but also by local elites. This fact helps explain why it was still possible in the nineteenth century, when the initiative to sustain local institutions from the center waned and threats to domestic social order and new kinds of international political challenges both grew, for some local officials and local elites to keep up local granaries, and in moments of acute crisis for larger-scale efforts at famine relief to be planned and implemented by higher-level officials. The elasticity and flexibility of Chinese governance in practice made the durability of its principles more lasting. The third possible revision to some of the conventional views of the early modern Chinese state considers how governance was not a matter simply for government officials but in practice a set of efforts shared with elites. Perhaps not surprisingly this meant there was no simple and sharp distinction between what was considered "official" and what was considered not "official," suggesting the inability of our conventional notions of public goods based on our more general conceptual divide between public and private to help us understand how public goods were in truth conceived and created in eighteenth-century China.

The problems of poverty and challenges of famine relief were addressed by government and elites in ways that spanned any conventional distinction between public and private.[3] The significance of famine relief and the maintenance of granaries officially managed and others officially monitored go beyond their being an example of public finance or more specifically the addressing of a basic human need as a social or public good. Because officials understood and undertook these activities in the context of both private market activities and local village-level informal exchanges, early modern Chinese conceptions of social or public goods continued to conform in important ways to ancient Chinese understandings of how state management of resources matters to social order and political legitimacy.

BEYOND THE BINARY OF PRIVATE AND PUBLIC GOODS

The binary between public and private to describe the economic character of goods and services in modern societies is inadequate to address policies designed to prevent or at least reduce the problems of poverty and dearth in early modern China. Without a better taxonomy of methods for the allocation of goods and services beyond the conventional public-private dichotomy, it remains difficult to locate the related roles of officials from the center to the county level and of elites resident in their local communities in affecting the problems of poverty and dearth. For managing grain supplies, official actions complemented those of local elites and of merchants. From a vantage point of Chinese approaches to governance, the state's water control efforts and grain storage policies were both conceived with the intent of creating benefits for the people. This principle certainly was not uniformly sustained through the centuries, across China's vast territories, and for all of its large population. But it did shape early-modern-era policy intent and motivate multiple concrete attempts to provide famine relief, to create institutional structures to store grain in advance of extraordinary need, and to use such reserves on smaller-scale routine levels to aid poorer people on an annual basis. The central state's specific efforts were located within a broader mix of official, local elite, and local community efforts.

Chinese sources on famine relief, granary storage, and water control suggest the limited legibility about their origins, intent, and impact that we can gain by limiting our analysis to the conventional categories of modern economics, in particular the division of all goods and service into either private or public. This chapter suggests that there was a broader spectrum of mechanisms to allocate goods and services in early modern China than the private-public binary can accommodate. At the same time it links the basic principle from ancient times of benefiting the people to (a) early-modern-era Chinese campaigns to relieve famines, (b) efforts to build and maintain granary reserves to help meet extraordinary events and intervene more routinely to help people through seasonal supply fluctuations, and (c) managing the economy's water control infrastructure. These activities exemplify key components of the Chinese understanding of governance. Before we formulate assessments of the successes and failures of this system of governance, this review of famine relief and food supply stresses a need to take its measure by combining an understanding of what governance principles led the Chinese to attempt their food supply interventions through categories of analysis not typically deemed relevant to our evaluations of early modern Europe.

In the Chinese case of addressing poverty and dearth, we can see behind these efforts a broader approach to promoting material welfare and benefits for common people that was inspired by an ideology of governance that linked the state's material resources (fiscal base) and symbolic viability (political legitimacy) to its performance of effective governance. These appear most clearly developed in the eighteenth century and rely on efforts of both officials and local elites, with officials themselves serving at different administrative levels. The diminished role of the nineteenth-century central state to monitor and control grain reserves across the empire did not prevent local actors from mounting their own efforts without higher-level supervision; indeed, the relative contraction of central efforts made regional and local efforts even more important and more salient. The effectiveness of local grain storage efforts was far less affected by what other locales did or did not do than were the efforts of local officials and elites facing water control issues because their concerns were connected to those of their neighbors in ways that depended to some degree on the nested enterprises of organized effort to manage water use, as Elinor Ostrom and her collaborators identified as a general issue around the globe, especially in more recent times. Because larger-scale coordination of dredging and dike repairs spanned many small communities and even crossed administrative boundaries, nineteenth-century officials remained more involved with larger water control projects than they did with coordinating the uses of granary reserves. Only after the collapse of the Qing dynasty in 1911 did there begin roughly four decades in which the absence of much effective government at provincial or regional levels, not to mention at a national scale, meant that the provision of public goods by Chinese regimes was far more meager than typical in the early modern era. This situation would be reversed after 1949 when the state took upon itself ever more responsibility for allocating resources, goods, and services, even as it curtailed the use of markets in the name of socialism, extracted surpluses from agriculture to fund industrialization, and, as part of the follies of the Great Leap Forward (1958–1962), seriously exacerbated the impact of natural disasters and bad harvests beginning in 1959.

From the vantage point of this volume, which highlights early modern Japanese practices as a baseline against which to evaluate and compare public goods provision in other countries, the Chinese case of addressing poverty and dearth doesn't fit the increased visibility of very local organizational efforts in Japan as a new early modern phenomenon that led to new kinds and scales of social or public services. Chinese practices, in particular those affecting poverty and dearth, involved official and nonofficial actors at central, provincial, county, and subcounty levels. The increased relative importance of lower-level official and local elite efforts in nineteenth-century China occurred in conditions quite different from those marking the earlier emergence of Japanese public goods provisioning considered in part 1 of this volume. What the Japanese and Chinese cases do, however, share in the provision of early modern goods and services is a poor fit with the conventional modern economics distinction between public and private goods. The same is, in fact, also true of early modern European efforts to address the increased insecurities of poorer strata of society because these activities tend to be overshadowed by the seemingly relentless expansion of fiscal extraction to finance growing military forces. It is too easy to imagine that in Europe military defense was the only public good being produced in the era rather than simply the most visible. When we step outside of Europe we have a better chance of appreciating more common economic challenges that people and their governments faced and the distinctive ways such challenges were met through the provision of public goods. The early modern ideologies and institutions responsible for addressing famine and poverty varied in scale and substance across Eurasia. Chinese practices creating what we consider public goods to address these challenges in the eighteenth century were notable for the unparalleled spatial and demographic scales they aimed to achieve and the results they did in fact produce. Even when falling short of stated ideals, they created material realities dwarfing those inspired and organized within any other polity of the era.

In conclusion, it may seem implausible that eighteenth-century Chinese policies toward dearth and poverty could matter to the modern era. Certainly from the vantage points of modern state construction in much of Europe and in Japan, nineteenth-century Chinese changes reduced the scale of intervention to relieve poverty and dearth. If, however, we move forward to consider policies toward food supply pursued at various points after 1949 we can identify a persistent concern regarding promoting production and availability of grain, especially for the poorer members of society, most vulnerable to subsistence challenges. These policies were, to be sure, quite different both among themselves and compared to policies of earlier eras. But they stemmed from similar political anxieties and drew upon a menu of policy choices containing ingredients also found in early modern Chinese menus of policy choices. We can recall the slogan "take grain as the key link," which accompanied policies to promote and even coerce the planting of grain crops begun in the early 1960s to achieve grain self-sufficiency across China's many diverse locales in response to the recent disastrous famine years. We might also remember that China's current era of economic transformation started simply enough in late 1978 as a kind of tweaking of the socialist planned economy designed to offer peasants greater incentives to increase grain production in order to stave off possibilities of dangerous levels of dearth. Such historically recent and yet very different kinds of reactions to anxieties about grain production and the possibilities of dearth are in fact responses to far older issues for which Chinese approaches to governance had already long grappled and in the eighteenth century specifically achieved considerable evidence of success.

NOTES

1. Qiu Jun, *Daxue yanyibu* (Supplements to Expositions on the Great Learning), juan 21 "Licai," part 2 (General discussion of financial matters, part 2). Siku quanshu edition. (Complete Library of the Four Treasuries.)

2. Ostrom (1993) formulated eight principles for the effective organization of common pool resources.

    1. Clearly defined boundaries
    2. Proportional equivalence between benefits and costs
    3. Collective-choice arrangements
    4. Monitoring
    5. Graduated sanctions
    6. Conflict resolution mechanisms
    7. Minimal recognition of rights to organize
    8. Nested enterprises

3. These and other traits of Chinese state activities and relations between officials and elites and common people, especially those related to political economy, are examined in Wong 1997.

REFERENCES

Abe, Takeo (1957). "Beikoku Jukyū no Kenkyū: 'Yōsei-shi' no isshō toshitemita" (Grain Supply and Demand during the Yongzheng Reign). *Tōyōshi- kenkyū* 15 (4): 120–213.

Chiang, Tao-Chang (1983). "The Salt Trade in Ch'ing China." *Modern Asian Studies* 17 (2): 197–219.

Des Forges, Roger (2003). *Cultural Centrality and Political Change in Chinese History: Northeast Henan in the Fall of the Ming.* Stanford University Press.

El Amine, Loubna (2015). *Classical Confucian Political Thought: A New Interpretation.* Princeton University Press.

Elvin, Mark (1973). *The Pattern of the Chinese Past.* Stanford University Press.

Huang, Ray (1981). *A Year of No Significance: The Ming Dynasty in Decline.* Yale University Press.

Hymes, Robert, and Conrad Schirokauer, eds. (1993). *Ordering the World: Approaches to State and Society in Sung Dynasty.* University of California Press.

Li, Cho-ying (2012). "Beneficiary Pays: Forging Reciprocal Connections between Private Profit and Public Good in Hydraulic Reform in the Lower Yangzi Delta, 1520s–1640s." *T'oung Pao* 98:385–438.

Li, Lillian (2007). *Fighting Famine in North China: State, Market, and Environmental Decline, 1690s–1990s.* Stanford University Press.

Mori, Masao (1969). "Jūroku-Jūhachi Seiki Niokeru Kōsei to Jinushi-Denko Kankei" (Famine Relief and Landowner-Tenant Relations from the Sixteenth to Eighteenth Centuries). *Tōyōshi-kenkyū* 27 (4): 69–111.

Morita, Akira (2002). *Shindai no Suiri to Chiikishakai* (Qing Dynasty Water Control and Local Society). Chūgoku Shoten.

Ostrom, Elinor (1993). "Design Principles in Long-Enduring Irrigation Institutions." *Water Resources Research* 29 (7): 1907–1912.

Perdue, Peter (1982). "Water Control in the Dongting Lake Region during the Ming and Qing Periods." *Journal of Asian Studies* 41 (4): 747–765.

Pomeranz, Kenneth (1993). *The Making of a Hinterland: State, Society, and Economy in Inland North China, 1853–1937.* University of California Press.

Rosenthal, Jean-Laurent, and R. Bin Wong (2011). *Before and Beyond Divergence: The Politics of Economic Change in China and Europe.* Harvard University Press.

Smith, Joanna Handlin (2009). *The Art of Doing Good: Charity in Late Ming China.* University of California Press.

Wakeman, Frederic, Jr. (1978). "The Canton Trade and the Opium War." In *The Cambridge History of China,* edited by J. Fairbank, 163–212. Cambridge University Press.

Will, Pierre-Etienne (1985). "State Intervention in the Administration of a Hydraulic Infrastructure: The Example of Hubei Province in Late Imperial Times." in *The Scope of State Power in China,* edited by Stuart Schram, 295–348. SOAS and Chinese University Press.

——— (1990) *Bureaucracy and Famine in Eighteenth-Century China.* Translated by Elborg Forster. Stanford University Press.

Will, Pierre-Etienne, and R. Bin Wong (1991). *Nourish the People: The State Civilian Granary System in China, 1650–1850.* University of Michigan Center for Chinese Studies.

Wittfogel, Karl (1957). *Oriental Despotism: A Comparative Study of Total Power.* Yale University Press.

Wong, R. Bin (1997). *China Transformed: Historical Change and the Limits of European Experience.* Cornell University Press.

——— (2014). "China before Capitalism." In *Cambridge History of Capitalism,* vol. 1, *The Rise of Capitalism from Ancient Origins to 1848,* edited by Larry Neal and Jeffrey Williamson, 125–164. Cambridge University Press.

PART III

Building Infrastructure

IN PART 3, WE PRESENT CHAPTERS discussing the construction and maintenance of physical infrastructure for water control including dikes and irrigation and for transportation including roads and waterways. As mentioned in chapter 1, these facilities are weak in nonexcludability, as they have attributes of "club goods," which places them between "pure" public goods and "private goods" suitable for market transaction. Potential investment, therefore, could be sourced from profit-driven private entities to the "public" entities such as the state. Historically, it is well known that the profit-based construction and maintenance of toll roads, known as "turnpike," played a significant transportation infrastructure role in early modern England.

Although the emergence of profit-based and market-oriented investment in physical infrastructure deserves further discussion, our intention in part 3 is to focus on nonprofit projects provided by rulers, including monarchs, feudal lords, and nonrulers such as community-related entities, discussing the diverse patterns in building physical infrastructure within nonprofit-based activities. The motivations and social structures that urged rulers or community leaders to undertake such projects are our main concerns, as these points are expected to relativize the influential framework of the state-market dichotomy frequently applied for explaining the difference between the providers of "private goods" and public goods.

From this point of view, the infrastructure building in early modern Japan provides us with intriguing examples to be discussed. The chapter by Junichi Kanzaka (chapter 9) discusses how paddy acreage was expanded and maintained from the seventeenth century to the nineteenth century in Japan, mainly focusing on the building of water control facilities. Although rulers such as the Tokugawa sho-gunate and other domain lords (*daimyōs*) carried out large-scale civil engineer-ing works for expanding paddy lands in the seventeenth century, the initiative for investing in land improvement and maintenance of water control facilities moved to nonrulers such as entrepreneurial individuals and village communities from the eighteenth century onward. The chapter emphasizes the strength of village communities that were based on irrigation and drainage systems, and the role of regional society, which consisted of leagues of villages that had means of set-tling conflicts among villages over water control. These findings reveal that the nonprofit-based providers, including rulers and nonrulers, were not uniform in terms of motivation and ability, and their composition may change according to the time periods.

The combination of rulers and nonrulers in committing themselves to the big project of infrastructure building will be discussed further in the next chapter by Heinrich Kaak (chapter 10). The chapter deals with the state-run water control projects in early modern Prussia, which constructed and maintained huge dikes to enable the expansion of land for cultivation and protection of existing land from floods. Under direction of the king, dike associations comprising lords and villages took responsibility for the construction and maintenance of dike parts related to their areas of interest. Their contributions were occasionally enforced through the military force executed by the state, namely, the king. In evaluating the success of these projects, the author explains that the king's initiative was not based on any benevolent interest for the well-being of his subjects, but rather provided for an immediate fiscal advantage for the state treasury.

The chapter by Takehiko To (chapter 11) focuses on the rulers' initiative in pursuing water control policy during a period of the thriving Qing dynasty in eighteenth-century China. In fact, the embankment managing system discussed in this chapter was funded through focused public investment in expanding inhabitable and cultivatable land. In addressing flood control and irrigation policy in the Jifu region near Beijing, the capital of Qing China, the author highlights the strong leadership of the emperor and the intelligent agenda-setting by the governor general and governor. The author believes this to be a contemporary example of good governance and the concept of a "shapeless treasury," in which the development of arable land has the same effect as a state treasury or grana-ries in coping with famine and poverty. Assuming the common feature of agricul-ture, the difference in the strength of rulers' initiative in infrastructure building between Tokugawa Japan and Qing China is distinctive.

In addition to these three chapters mainly discussing water-controlling proj-ects, the last chapter focuses on the transport facilities of roads and waterways. As mentioned earlier, profit-based "turnpike" was prevalent in early modern England, whereas it was the rulers' task to construct and maintain major trunk roads in early modern Japan. Sascha Bütow points out in chapter 12 that the king of the Holy Roman Empire advocated the concept of *bonum commune topos* (good governance for the people), taking responsibilities in constructing and maintaining the traffic ways to legitimize his rule. This idea was built on the success of medieval communities that were responsible for traffic and road construction in Brandenburg-Prussia. The author insists that this sense of governance legitimacy has been carried forward into contemporary law in the Federal Republic of Germany.

These four cases illustrate the significant role that rulers played in building physical infrastructure in early modern periods. However, it also highlights a motivation away from enhancing societal well-being and more toward increasing state's or lords' treasury revenues besides the existing idea of "good governance" by the ruler. The combination of a king, lords, and other nonruling people was also an important factor in the case of dike associations in Prussia, whereas the role of village and regional societies was clear in eighteenth- and nineteenth-century Japan. These diverse patterns within nonprofit-based activities reflected the socio-economic background of each society at the time, and may have had an influence on the formation of the social welfare system in present states.

Masayuki Tanimoto

The Development of Civil Engineering Projects and Village Communities in Seventeenth- to Nineteenth-Century Japan

Junichi Kanzaka

In Japan, civil engineering projects have played an important role in the development of agriculture. Building dikes, canals, and ponds substantially expanded the amount of irrigated land. Furthermore, draining lakes and the sea reclaimed a great deal of land. These investments in field expansion, as well as the rise in productivity per acre, contributed greatly to the advancement of agriculture in Japan (Ishikawa 1967, Booth and Sundrum 1985). It is true that, sometimes, village communities opposed civil engineering projects. However, in many cases, village communities promoted field expansion and land improvement projects in Japan. Indeed, at the beginning of the Tokugawa period, large-scale projects by governments often promoted the establishment of close-knit rural communities. Government projects encouraged the growth of villages consisting of autonomous small households. Thereafter, villagers accumulated wealth and began carrying out civil engineering projects by themselves. In the nineteenth century, village communities played a very important role in building facilities for irrigation, drainage, and reclamation. Villagers supported or initiated water management projects by making plans, providing labor, and, sometimes, funding capital. Furthermore, the close social network encompassing villages based on the water control system helped settle disputes among several villages. Prominent figures in regional society arbitrated many conflicts outside of government courts.

To examine the relationship between the development of civil engineering projects and the growth of village communities, section 2 of this chapter provides an overview of the increase in paddy acreage between the seventeenth century and the nineteenth in Japan, based on the database of civil engineering projects. Section 3 analyzes the relationship between the growth of villages and government civil engineering projects. Section 4 analyzes the communal functions of village communities and regional societies. Section 5 concludes the chapter.

EXPANSION OF PADDY ACREAGE

Civil Engineering Projects

This analysis examines the effect of several civil engineering projects by calculating the acreage of paddies created by each individual project. In Japan, cultivated land mainly consists of paddies where rice grows and dry fields where wheat and other crops grow. Since irrigated paddies are usually more productive than dry fields are, the Japanese community tirelessly built water management facilities to convert wastelands and dry fields to paddies. Three such facilities are especially important, namely, dikes, canals, and ponds. First, dikes were constructed to control the flow of rivers. Many Japanese rivers flowing from mountains frequently change their courses on alluvial fans and flood plains. Therefore, peasants began to cultivate the soil and build new villages on former flood plains only after the construction of dikes. Thereafter, they built canals along former river courses to irrigate new paddies. Second, canals were sometimes dug without building dikes. Long canals of more than ten thousand meters were often constructed using advanced techniques, such as topography analysis to let water go down shallow slopes and the construction of tunnels and siphons to lead water beyond all obstacles. Finally, ponds were constructed where sufficient water was not available from river flows. In some places, a sophisticated system for the connection of several ponds was developed to stabilize water supply (JSCE 1936).

In this way, the Japanese built several facilities to provide paddies with sufficient water. In 1907, the Ministry of Agriculture and Commerce of Japan investigated the hydrological condition of paddies (MAC 1909). In the 1910s, the Japanese began to use power pumps for irrigation and drainage. Furthermore, as explained later in more detail, in the 1920s, the government began to subsidize the cost of large civil engineering projects. Therefore, the investigation of developments in 1907 reveals the achievements of privately financed projects utilizing the natural flow of water, indicating the sources of irrigation and the manner in which sufficient water was provided. The survey shows 65.5% of 2,738,508 hectares of paddies were irrigated by water coming from rivers. Almost all of this water is assumed to have been distributed through canals. Next, 20.7%, 5.3%, 1.3%, and 1.0% of paddies were irrigated by ponds, fountains, wells, and lakes, respectively. In addition, the investigation indicates that 22.3% of paddies were irrigated plentifully, and 58.5% of paddies were irrigated properly. Therefore, more than 80% of paddies had sufficient water. Since the survey shows the data by district *(gun)*, I calculate the river irrigation rate (hectares irrigated by rivers divided by total hectares) and the sufficient irrigation rate (the ratios of hectares irrigated plentifully, properly, and insufficiently were

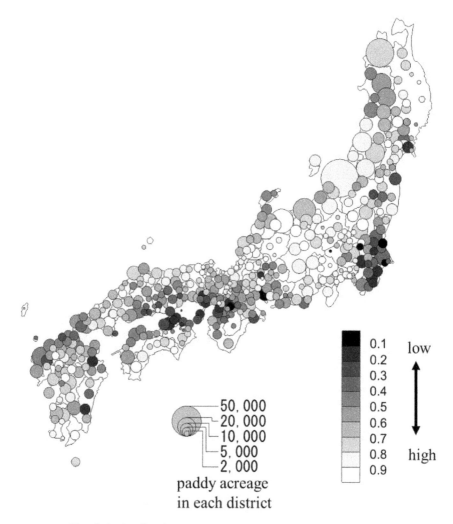

FIGURE 7. River Irrigation Rate in 1907
Source: Data from MAC 1909.

tentatively weighted by 1.0, 0.5, and 0.0, respectively, and summed), and I show the distributions of the two rates in figures 7 and 8. On the one hand, figure 7 reveals that the river irrigation rate varied widely across districts. Each district adopted its own suitable method for irrigation. In the regions around the Seto Inland Sea and the Bōsō Peninsula, where there are no large rivers, ponds provided water to many paddies. On the other hand, figure 8 also shows that the sufficient irrigation rate was not so different between each district. It was less than 0.35 in only 9.1% of districts, and there was no area where districts with a lack of water supply

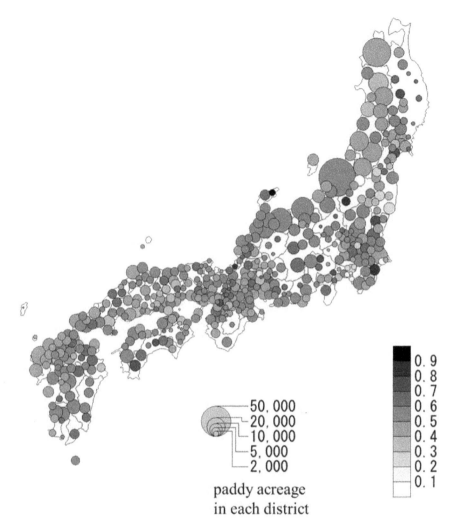

50, 000
20, 000
10, 000
5, 000
2, 000

paddy acreage
in each district

0. 9
0. 8
0. 7
0. 6
0. 5
0. 4
0. 3
0. 2
0. 1

FIGURE 8. Sufficient Irrigation Rate in 1907
Source: Data from MAC 1909.

were concentrated. Until the beginning of the twentieth century, each individual district throughout Japan had developed its own appropriate irrigation system.

Increase in Irrigated Paddies

How did the Japanese expand the acreage of irrigated paddies? Since there are no comprehensive statistical data on arable land before 1874, I estimate the increase in paddy acreage before 1873 in two ways. First, the paddy acreage at the beginning and the end of the Tokugawa period was estimated based on existing historical documents. Following Miyamoto's calculation based on a land survey executed by Hideyoshi Toyotomi, who politically unified Japan's archipelago in the late sixteenth century, the total acreage of the arable land is estimated as 2,064,657 *chō*[1] at the end of the sixteenth century. Furthermore, assuming half of the arable land comprised paddies, the paddy acreage was 1,032,328 *chō* (Miyamoto 1999).[2] Next, using data from the survey for Land Tax Reform by the Meiji Government, the acreages of total arable land and paddies in 1872 are calculated as 3,476,844 *chō* and 1,842,066 *chō*, respectively (APDLTR 1953–1957). Therefore, paddy acreage increased by 809,738 *chō* during the Tokugawa period. However, these numbers are calculated according to *kyū-tanbetsu*, or acreage measured by traditional methods. Meanwhile, the Meiji government eagerly reexamined the acreage of arable land by utilizing common national measures and adopting a strict approach to calculating acreage (Sasaki 2016, 311), and, as a result, the revised acreage *(shin-tanbetsu)* was 42.9% larger than former acreage *(kyū-tanbetsu)*.[3] Hence, the acreage in the Tokugawa period may have been underestimated in comparison with that in the later period.

Second, the growth in paddy acreage is estimated based on the data of each individual civil engineering project. In 1926, the Ministry of Agriculture and Commerce of Japan conducted its survey of civil engineering projects in the Tokugawa era in order to examine the origins of customary irrigation rights (MAC 1926). A decade later, the ministry's research was revised by the Japanese Society of Civil Engineering, and the number of listed projects increased from about 1,171 to 1,585. Based on the revised survey, Miyamoto (1999, 38) estimates the acreage of cultivated land, and Nakamura (1968) calculates the "real amount of production" in Tokugawa Japan. Nevertheless, the estimates are insufficient because they simply count the number of construction projects, ignoring the scale of each. Therefore, as to 2,857 projects registered by the two surveys (MAC 1926, JSCE 1936), and some other documents (Akita-ken ECLIH 1985, Ishikawa-ken ECLIH 1986, Niigata-ken ECLIH 1986, Toyama-ken ECLIH 2004), I built a database recording information on who carried out each project, when it was accomplished, and how many acres were affected in the process. The total acreage of the affected area of the listed projects is 492,203 *chō*; this total accounts for 58.0% of the aforementioned paddy expansion during the Tokugawa period. Since villagers often increased their production simply by expanding their paddies to the adjoining land *(kirizoe-shinden)* without records, the database of civil engineering projects does not fully capture the activities of peasants. Nevertheless, the accumulated acreage data of affected individual projects can be assumed to indicate the principal trend of paddy expansion.

The database reveals that there were three periods of paddy expansion from the end of the sixteenth century to the nineteenth century.[4] Figure 9 shows the increase of paddy acreage in the Tokugawa period. First, until around 1680, paddy

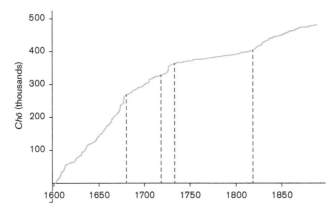

FIGURE 9. Increase of Paddy Acreage of Tokugawa Japan
Source: The database mentioned in the text.

acreage expanded greatly. This expansion is sometimes called the "great reclama-tion" and is considered to have begun in the sixteenth century in advanced regions (Saito 1988, 173). Public investment in controlling rivers and the construction and maintenance of canals and ponds converted barren wasteland into fertile paddies and fields. In the early seventeenth century, local governments carried out many large projects to improve public infrastructure, which stabilized the production of peasant households and encouraged them to create a close-knit community.

However, the growth hit an environmental limit. Since severe deforestation due to paddy expansion as well as logging for a construction boom had caused landslides and floods by the late seventeenth century, the shogunate and the domain government restrained paddy expansion. For example, in 1666, the sho-gunate government issued the Regulation for Conserving Mountain and Rivers *(Shokoku-sansen-okite)* to prevent erosion and floods in the Kinai region, and it prohibited deforestation in the mountains and encouraged tree planting (Totman 1998). Then, from the 1680s onward, the growth in paddy acreage slowed down. The second period of paddy expansion began with an announcement by the sho-gunate government to encourage the creation of new paddies in 1722 (Kimura 1964, 58). In this period, governments carried out large-scale public works, such as reclaiming land from lakes. For example, Yasubee Izawa, a shogunate official, directed the reclamation of Minuma and Iinuma in 1727, and that of Shiunji in 1733. Nevertheless, the development did not last very long. Paddy expansion stagnated for about eighty years from 1736 to the 1810s. Then, in the 1820s, the third period of paddy acreage expansion began. Paddy acreage increased mainly as a result of the construction of canals and reclamation of land from the sea. Village communities that had accumulated wealth played an important role at this stage. This expansion continued beyond the Meiji Restoration in 1868, and ended in 1880. Thereafter, a slow-down period lasted until 1905.

Growth of Productivity

The civil engineering projects not only increased the acreage of paddy fields but also laid the foundation for the growth of land productivity per acre. Tokunaga (1997) states that agricultural development in Tokugawa Japan consisted of three phases: namely, the construction of irrigation facilities, greater input of fertilizer, and the amelioration of cultivation tools. "Since agricultural production is based on natural factors such as land, water, and plants, we should build water management infrastructure first" (Tokunaga 1997, 15). Then, on the well-irrigated paddy fields, peasants started to apply fertilizer efficiently, and practiced deep tillage. In fact, after many great civil engineering projects were accomplished in the seventeenth century, peasants raised the intensity of agricultural production. During the eighteenth and early nineteenth centuries, to increase fertilizer inputs, many peasants began to use purchased fertilizers, such as sardine meal and the residue from pressing oil. Furthermore, they developed a variety of hoes and sickles with specific uses for different stages of production (Miyamoto 1999, 46).

Since, as mentioned before, irrigation systems were developed throughout Japan, peasants were able to carry out intensive agriculture in almost all districts. As a result, land productivity grew in all of Japan and the gap in land productivity between advanced and backward regions reduced. In the early Tokugawa period, peasants in several provinces in western Japan yielded more than twice the amount of products than in the backward northeastern provinces. Nakamura (1968) estimates land productivity in each province *(kuni)* in 1700, by dividing *kokudaka* in 1697–1702 by the acreage of arable land in 1716–1747. *Kokudaka* are land values measured by the amount of estimated rice yield based on land surveys. Although, from the eighteenth century onward, the *kokudaka* usually underestimated the real quantity of output,[5] *kokudaka* in 1697–1702 is assumed to reflect actual products. In the early Tokugawa period, the average product per *tan* of seventy provinces (Echizen is excluded)[6] was 0.94 *koku,* the standard deviation was 0.28, and the coefficient of variation was 0.29. Next, I estimate the land productivity in the beginning of the Meiji era based on governmental surveys on the yield of "paddy and non-glutinous rice" in 1877–1881 (Umemura et al. 1966, 38). The data reveal two facts. First, land productivity had increased during the eighteenth and nineteenth centuries. The average product per *tan* of seventy-one provinces was 1.31 *koku,* or 39% higher than what it was around 1700. This must have been the result of the development of intensive cultivation. Second, the difference in the productivity among the provinces had reduced. The standard deviation of *koku* per *tan* of seventy-one provinces was 0.26, and the coefficient of variation was 0.20, or 31% lower than what it was around 1700. While the productivity in the advanced Kinai area rose, the productivity in the backward area such as the northeastern and Kantō areas increased by a greater amount. The establishment of water management systems in every corner of the country enabled this growth in productivity throughout Japan.

In sum, civil engineering projects expanded paddy acreage and promoted the rise of land productivity in Tokugawa Japan. How did local government projects promote the creation of a village community? How, in turn, did wealthy villagers begin to help carry out projects?

DEVELOPMENT OF VILLAGE COMMUNITIES AND CIVIL ENGINEERING PROJECTS

The Growth and Decline of the Projects of Indigenous Magnates

Before the Tokugawa period, village communities did not play an important role in managing water resources. In the sixteenth century, powerful individuals carried out civil engineering projects. Indeed, in Kinai, the most advanced region, indigenous magnates usually controlled irrigation and drainage. Although historians refer to the magnate in several ways, such as *dogō* (powerful local clan), *ji-zamurai* (vernacular warriors), or *shō-ryōshu* (minor seigniors), its central feature was performing large-scale cultivation by employing several *genin,* or servants, who were personally subordinate to the magnate. The indigenous magnates engaged servants to build ponds or canals for irrigation and drainage. Furthermore, the magnates controlled resources in the woodlands. Private facilities for water management and the control of woodlands were important sources of a magnate's regional power. In local settlements, several small peasant households also cultivated their fields, only with their family's labor. Although the peasants were not personal subjects, they had to follow the magnate's orders to obtain permission to use the irrigation facilities and woodlands. Therefore, the peasants provided labor for the maintenance of the facilities (Asao 1967).

Nevertheless, large-scale civil engineering projects by local governments in the "great reclamation" from the sixteenth century undermined the power of local magnates. Note that there were two types of local governments in charge of water control in the Tokugawa period. First, in the regions where a lord, or *daimyō,* exclusively ruled a large territory, his officials carried out water management and flood control. I call this type of government a "domain government." However, not all the domains had a territory large enough to have sole control over a river. Second, in Kinai, around Kyōto and Ōsaka, and Kantō, around Edo, many domains intermingled with one another. Therefore, a shogunate magistrate, or *bugyō,* presided over the construction and maintenance of dikes, canals, and ponds for irrigation and drainage in the region (Ōtani 1996, Mizumoto 1993, 267–301). I call this type of government a "magistrate government." In the early seventeenth century, the magistrate government promoted several large-scale projects in Kinai. For example, in 1608, the great repair work of the Sayama Pond in Kawachi within Kinai improved the irrigation of the surrounding regions. The peasants benefited most from the project since they became less dependent on the private facilities of indigenous magnates. Now, the peasants requested equal treatment of water management.

Furthermore, Toyotomi's nationwide land survey from 1582 to 1598 registered many former servants who had served indigenous magnates as independent holders of land titles. They also benefited from improvements in infrastructure. Then, in each village, a cooperative community consisting of autonomous peasant households emerged (Asao 1967, Mizumoto 2008, 129–139).

In the advanced regions, the power of indigenous magnates declined as a result of the increase in governmental projects. Nevertheless, in the backward northeastern and Hokuriku regions, the domain government utilized indigenous magnates to develop many paddies and fields. For example, in Mutsu province under the Hirosaki domain government, from 1619 to 1687, if an indigenous magnate developed a new village at his own cost, he was given a fief, or *jikatachigyō*, of thirty or fifty *koku*[7] and was then employed as a lesser vassal, or *shochigyō* samurai. However, since the increase in fiefs did not improve the finances of the domain government, the fief system was abolished in 1687. Afterward, the *shochigyō* moved to the castle town as samurai and obtained a stipend, or became peasants by returning the samurai title. Then, the domain government directly managed large-scale projects called *mikura-ha*; until 1730, they established 201 new villages by building canals and reclaiming land from marshes. These projects by the domain government were sharply in contrast with the previous small-scale projects by indigenous magnates (Kikuchi 1977, 70–77, Kikuchi 1986, 635–729). Moreover, in other backward regions, indigenous magnates and samurai vassals carried out civil engineering projects and expanded paddies. For example, in the Aizu domain government, samurai vassals and indigenous magnates established *hōkōnin-shinden* and *mitate-shinden*, respectively, and in the Akita domain government, samurai vassals developed *sashigami-kai* (Miura 1983). Nevertheless, as in the Hirosaki domain government, in the late seventeenth century, the shogun and *daimyō*, or the heads of local governments, removed the vassals and some of the magnates from their fiefs to control the peasants directly. The *daimyō* provided samurai vassals staying in castle towns with "an amount equivalent to the expected income from that man's original fief" (Gordon 2003, 15). Thereafter, village communities, in cooperation with local governments, played an important role in public investment.

In the seventeenth century, local governments dominated the techniques in these large-scale projects. Until the sixteenth century, the advanced regions of Kinai had had several groups of craftsmen who specialized in building dikes and dams. Local government officials employed them or learned techniques from them (Miura 1984). Furthermore, in the seventeenth century, the shogun and *daimyō* built castles and dug new mines. The construction techniques developed in these projects were employed in the construction of dikes, canals, and ponds. Government officials were required to have advanced techniques for water management. Therefore, "in guidebooks, or *jikata-sho*, which instructed officials on how to control people, there were many explanations of techniques for controlling rivers and irrigating paddy" (Tsukamoto 1984, 197). Nevertheless, it should also be known that government officials were not able to complete projects without the support of local people who were aware of the detailed conditions of rivers and lands. Hence, the officials usually employed a few villagers as their assistants (Nishida 1984, 228–229).

Civil Engineering Projects by
Local Governments and Village Communities

In Tokugawa Japan, there were two types of construction projects for dikes, canals, and ponds. *Go-fushin* was carried out at the expense of shogunates or local governments, whereas *ji-fushin* was carried out at the expense of village communities (Ōishi 1960, 75). Furthermore, there were four varieties of *go-fushin*: first, *kōgi-fushin*, whose cost was borne only by the shogunate; second, *otetsudai-fushin*, where the shogunate ordered domain governments to contribute money and labor to shogunate construction projects; third, *kuniyaku-fushin*, where the magistrate managed the projects in an area consisting of several small domains by allocating the cost to surrounding villages; and fourth, *ryōshu-fushin*, where each domain government carried out projects in its own territories. Out of the four varieties of *go-fushin*, the first three were usually carried out on a temporary basis for disaster recovery or large-scale projects (Ōtani 1996, 133). In *kuniyaku-fushin*, villagers were sometimes asked to work without receiving wages. The dikes and canals constructed in the project were public goods that benefited villages by preventing floods and improving water management, but the villagers sometimes complained about the "excessive" burden. For example, in 1678, the villages in the shogun domain requested an exemption from providing laborers, since they had already undertaken other government work (Murata 2009).

The activities of village communities were often connected with public investments by local governments. In particular, during the seventeenth century, the domain government carried out river-controlling projects that provided a basis for other projects. For example, in Muko-gun of Settsu province, the Amagasaki domain government built the dikes of the Muko River and dug new ponds and canals. Thereafter, wealthy villagers invested in building branch canals and expanding paddies on the western side of the river. In the process, village communities played an important role. Villagers in the irrigated areas cooperated in order to maintain irrigation facilities and allocate water "equitably." As Mizumoto (2002, 45) states, "The civil engineering projects involved several villages in the new irrigation system and strengthened the mutual relationship among the villages." Furthermore, in Etchū province, which has seven major alluvial fans, public investment by the Kanazawa domain government on the construction of the dike to control rivers promoted the expansion of paddies. For example, starting in 1670, the government built a large dike to control the Shō River to prevent floods. This construction encouraged village communities to expand paddies and fields

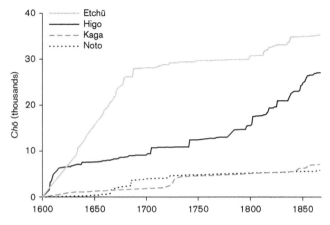

FIGURE 10. Increase in Paddy Acreage in Kaga, Noto, Etchū, and Higo Provinces
Source: The database mentioned in the text.

significantly. Imamura (2014) shows that the new arable lands were created not only by establishing new villages on the alluvial plains, but also by increasing paddy acreages in existing villages. Village communities supported the projects. After 1660, they had to provide thirty workers per one hundred *koku.* Furthermore, "in principle, villagers living downstream were in charge of cleaning the river bottom to maintain the banks *(kawayoke)* and maintaining canals, although the local governments provided subsidies if the cost was too high" (Saeki 2007, 153).[8] In Etchū province, paddy acreage increased by 34,400 *chō* from around 1600 to 1872, which is in contrast with a moderate increase of only sixty-eight hundred *chō* in Kaga province under the same local government, namely, the Kanazawa domain government (Figure 10). Since Kaga province was a more advanced region, there was only a bit of room for the expansion of paddies.

Merchant-Initiated Reclamation

In Tokugawa Japan, there were some individual merchants who promoted civil engineering projects. Furthermore, they sometimes became landlords of the newly reclaimed land and collected rents from the tenants. These merchants may correspond to entrepreneurial individuals in England and the Netherlands that undertook land improvement projects. In England, landlords promoted enclosures to improve productivity and raise rents, and farmers also brought about land improvements through drainage, fencing, or the erection of new buildings. Then, farmers had the "tenant right" to be compensated for their investments (Overton 1996, 162–184). In the Netherlands, wealthy town dwellers made large-scale investments to reclaim new polders, since "large landownership was dominant there from the outset" (van Bavel 2001, 17). These civil engineering projects increased agricultural production by expanding cultivated land and improving land or labor productivity. In Japan, however, the activities of merchants were not always praised. They sometimes contradicted the interests of the shogunate and domain government. Matsuyoshi (1936/1955) states that "merchant-initiated reclamation (chōnin ukeoi shinden)" undermined the "feudal agrarian system." Nevertheless, the policies of shogunate governments on merchants' projects were not consistent. In 1687, the government prohibited merchant-initiated reclamation. In 1722, merchants were permitted to develop new paddies and obtain rents from tenants since the shogunate hoped that the new villages built by merchants would stabilize rural society, by absorbing the surplus population in the surrounding villages (Kimura 1964, 52–54, Ōishi 1973, Kikuchi 1977, 516). For example, on the eastern side of the Muko River, merchants from Ōsaka and Amagasaki invested in building new paddies in the seventeenth century (Mizumoto 2002, 48–50).

Nevertheless, the merchants' projects in Japan are not regarded as similar to entrepreneurial individuals' projects in England and the Netherlands for three reasons. First, their contributions were limited. The database of civil engineering projects shows that the acreage constructed by merchants was only less than 5% and the projects were concentrated around big cities, such as Edo and Ōsaka. Second, many government officials and scholars continued to criticize merchants' projects. Even after the shogunate's authorization, Kyūgu Tanaka blamed merchants for "deceiving and slandering others for money and engaging themselves just in obtaining their own profit" and recommended utilizing "the knowledge in villages and hamlets" (Tanaka 1721/1996, Kurachi 2008, 75–78). Finally, whereas villagers often resisted the entrepreneurial projects in Europe (Blum 1978), village communities usually helped merchants create new paddies in Japan. In practice, villagers used their knowledge to gain profits even from merchants' projects. Nakai states that, in new villages, merchant landlords maintained social order and promoted agricultural production with the strong connection with surrounding village communities, and therefore, "merchants carried out the projects by parasitizing existing village communities even in the most commercialized region around Ōsaka, although it is supposed that the tenancy relationship in merchant-initiated reclamation was contractual and free from communal constraint" (Nakai 1956, 219). Thus, villagers supported civil engineering projects by merchants, as well as by local governments.

The Rise of Contributions by Village Communities in the Nineteenth Century

In a later period, the contributions of village communities increased further, and the distinction between go-fushin by the local government and ji-fushin by village communities became obscure. When the scale of go-fushin projects was not so large, wealthy villagers sometimes took the initiative in the project. Indeed, go-fushin projects executed by local governments were not always effective. In 1721,

Tanaka criticized *go-fushin* for its inefficiency and recommended a procedure to carry out *go-fushin* by which local villagers first requested a project and then local governments assessed it. If the project was found to be good, the government would subsidize it. In these cases, the villagers provided labor and shared the financial burden with the government. Nagatsuma calls this "the subsidization of government construction and maintenance" (Nagatsuma 2001, 35).

In the paddy expansion from the 1820s onward, the role of wealthy villagers was prominent. Many domain governments had suffered from financial debts that were so severe that they were not able to afford to pursue civil engineering projects. Meanwhile, some villagers had accumulated wealth and carried out large-scale projects without support from their local governments. To avoid the risk of a shortfall in capital, villagers sometimes formed a new type of organization for investment. Yanagita, a famous folklorist, contrasts "cooperative" construction of new paddies with projects "led by one leader" (Yanagita 1931/1991, 247); thus, cooperatively reclaimed districts often have place names such as Sōbiraki (literally meaning "collectively reclaimed"). Kikuchi calls this cooperative organization *hyakushō yoriai shinden* (peasant cooperation to develop new paddies), which collected from many peasants like a joint-stock company and allocated new paddies according to the amount contributed (Kikuchi 1977, 304–305). For example, in Bizen province in 1852, a peasant cooperation reclaimed land from the sea to build 730 *chō* of paddies. It collected 1,015 *kan* worth of silver from 336 peasants. However, the cooperative organization did not eliminate the risk entirely. The manager spent his own entire fortune on the project and became bankrupt.

By the development of techniques as well as the improvement of finance, village communities contributed to civil engineering projects in the nineteenth century. At that time, some villagers had acquired advanced techniques for constructing dikes, canals, and ponds. As mentioned earlier, in the seventeenth century, government officials nearly monopolized water management techniques. However, afterward, villagers improved their techniques and the high-level skills began to spread directly to other villagers. "As villagers in several regions communicated with each other and broadened their perspectives, their knowledge and skills were able to be interconnected without the mediation of government officials" (Tsukamoto 1984, 225). Then, to carry out *go-fushin,* some local governments employed capable villagers. For example, in Etchū province, Dōsan Shiina, born in a family of wealthy peasants in 1790, constructed several canals until he was in his thirties. Since he displayed great talent in these projects, the Kanazawa domain government asked him to give them advice on the construction and maintenance of dikes and canals in 1829, and appointed him as a manager of development of new paddies. Thereafter, he directed several projects in Etchū, Noto, and Kaga provinces, including Jūni-kanno canal irrigating 652 chō. Shiina had sophisticated techniques for planning a waterway route, measuring slopes, and building facilities. Although it is not known as to who taught him these skills, there must have been several opportunities for wealthy villagers to learn advanced techniques in rural society. For instance, in the same province, Nobuyoshi Ishikuro, born in another family of wealthy peasants in 1760, studied Japanese mathematics and astronomy, and acquired enormous skills in measurement and calculation (Jūnikanno-yōsui-tochikairyōku 1985).

Furthermore, wealthy villagers sometimes took the initiative in carrying out many *go-fushin* activities, which were supposed to be done by the local government. For instance, in Higo province, under the Kumamoto domain government, a regional and originally nongovernmental association of villages *(tenaga)* managed almost all civil engineering projects. Then, wealthy peasants *(sou-shōya)*, who managed the association, were treated as local government officials. Since the *tenaga* was incorporated into the administrative system of the local government, civil engineering projects were usually regarded as "public." The MAC (1926) labels them as "governmental," and, furthermore, Kimura states that all projects in Higo province were managed by the Kumamoto domain governments (Kimura 1964, 179–181). However, the *tenaga*, rather than the local government, carried out projects. Yoshimura states that "in the early Tokugawa period, authorities of the shogun and *daimyō* executed civil engineering projects for river control and water management by organizing teams of vassals and the labor services of peasants. These were the most important public activities and duties by such authorities in order to justify their control over peasants. Nevertheless, in later periods, the civil engineering projects were conducted not by the authorities of the shogun and *daimyō,* but by the *tenaga*" (Yoshimura 2013, 113). The development of regional associations promoted civil engineering projects. Yoshimura indicates that in Higo province, the nineteenth century was "the age of civil engineering for water management." Some *tenaga* built several canals for expanding new fields and others reclaimed land from Yashiro Bay on a large scale. For example, Yabe *tenaga* planned to build Tsūjunkyō canal consisting of a ditch of forty-two kilometers, a siphon, and an aqueduct. Since the *tenaga* was creditworthy enough to borrow from the domain government, wealthy villagers, and merchants, it was able to pay the huge construction costs. The *tenaga* refunded the debt from the profit of newly reclaimed paddies (Yoshimura 2013, 405, 408–453). Then, the paddy acreage in Higo province increased significantly, as figure 10 shows.

Major contributions by wealthy villagers to civil engineering projects continued beyond the political transformation by the Meiji Restoration in 1868. Many projects were carried out with private capital. For example, in 1879, the Aichi prefecture government permitted two wealthy villagers, Hyomatsu Okamoto and Ihachiro Iyoda, to build canals for irrigating infertile fields in Hekikai-gun. To carry out this project, Okamoto and Iyoda invested their own fortune. Furthermore, they persuaded five others to join the project by explaining the profitability of the investment. In 1881, they accomplished the construction, and the canal was named "Meiji canal." It created eighty-eight hundred *chō* of new paddies and improved the hydrological condition of forty-five hundred *chō* of old paddies. The large cost of the project was compensated by the income from distributing water. Okamoto and Iyoda had spent too much money in this project and were bankrupt, while the five investors gained profit by obtaining new paddies (Kondo 1929, 193–197, Hatate 1977, 105–110). Until 1881, the Japanese economy had grown based on brisk economic activity, mainly in the countryside. As Saito and Tanimoto state, "The period between the early nineteenth century and Matukata Deflation (1881–1886) was the period of rural centred development" (Saitō and Tanimoto 1989, 226). The increase in civil engineering projects sponsored by wealthy villagers was an aspect of the "rural centred development." However, a rural depression caused by the Matsukata Deflation hindered the accumulation of wealth by villagers. Thereafter, the pace of paddy acreage growth slowed down. The growth of paddy acreage stagnated until the 1910s, when paddy acreage started to increase greatly, again. While from 1874 to 1880, paddy fields expanded by 914 *chō* per year, from 1880 to 1905, it extended by 536 *chō* per year. Then, from 1905 to 1930, paddy acreage increased 1,352 *chō* per year (Umemura et al. 1966, 216). However, this time, government funds rather than the private capital of wealthy villagers played a very important role. With the Reclamation Assistance Act of 1919, the government began to subsidize the rent of the capital for the project. Furthermore, after the Ministry of Agriculture and Commerce of Japan issued a Notification to Subsidize Projects for Improving Irrigation and Drainage (1923), a government fund was injected into large projects affecting five hundred hectares or more (Imamura 1977).

COMMUNAL FUNCTIONS OF JAPANESE VILLAGES

Functions of Village Communities

In Tokugawa Japan, village communities or leagues of villages played crucial roles in many civil engineering projects. The principal reason for the positive role of village communities is that paddy cultivation in Japan necessitated close cooperation within and among villages. Since every paddy in a village shared an irrigation system, the mismanagement of one plot affected the entire village adversely. One household's negligent water management could interfere with its neighbors' water supply (Watanabe 2008, 81–85, Kanzaka 2018). Reflecting the communal character of cultivation, Japanese peasants did not believe that they had exclusive rights to a plot even if they cultivated it. At the end of the nineteenth century, a Japanese peasant stated, "the surface layer of the land belongs to me, the middle layer belongs to my village, and the deepest layer belongs to Heaven" (Sakane 2011, 137). They still had the idea that possession in the village should be common. Yanagita states, "the idea that 'land in a village should be used by the [members of] the village' has its origin in history and still has a surprisingly strong influence in today's society" (Yanagita 1931/1991, see also Sakane 2011, 140–141). This notion of property rights did not match the European view. Therefore, even after the Japanese made the Meiji Civil Code by studying European laws in 1898, customary rules continued to control life in each village. Peasants were expected to work together and help one another. In the beginning of the twentieth century, village communities still had effective control over land transfers and field utilization. Even if some outsiders, such as town merchants, became absentee landlords, the villagers required the landlords and their tenants to follow the rules of cultivation of the village (Saito 1989, 223–254). Therefore, landlords were not able to buy and sell land freely.

In the Tokugawa period, strong village communities sometimes prevented land-improving projects but, other times, promoted agricultural development. In some cases, villagers opposed the development of new paddies, since this development would reduce the amount of grassland needed to fertilize paddies. In this respect, Japanese peasants seem to have behaved in the same way as many European peasants did, in resisting the enclosure of commons (Blum 1978, 292). Tokugawa peasants made a fertilizer called *karishiki* from grass and young leaves. The area of grassland and mountain necessary for providing the fertilizer was ten times larger than the size of the cultivated land area. Therefore, for example, when there was a plan to turn grassland into paddies in Yamashiro province in 1702, villagers opposed the plan because it would cause a shortage of fertilizer as well as the runoff of soil. Furthermore, at the beginning of the eighteenth century, a shogunate official lamented that "it has become difficult to find land on which new paddies could be developed," and stated that "recently grassland [*magusa-ba*] has been turned into paddies. Since the grassland is the place that supplies fertilizer and feeds horses . . . this type of new paddy development is unfavorable" (Mizumoto 2003, 70–71).

Meanwhile, in other cases, cooperation in villages based on communal property supported the construction and maintenance of public goods. Indeed, village communities were suitable for improving and maintaining irrigation facilities. Hayami and Godo (2002) state that communities were usually superior to markets and the state in the supply of "local public goods" because "the community relationship is effective in preventing free-riders." Members who did not join collective works, such as the construction and maintenance of irrigation canals, would be severely sanctioned by the village. In addition, Yanagita states that "the negligence of just one or two people will cause failure in community-based works, such as destroying insects and weed seeds and repairing canals and roads . . . Japanese villages avoid this risk by old customs, while many other law-governed countries do this by enactment" (Yanagita 1931/1991, 261–262, see also Sakane 2011, 138–139). Since maintenance systems based on village communities worked well, local governments and wealthy villagers invested in water management facilities.

The Function of Regional Society

Close connections in Tokugawa Japan were not just found within each village. Several villages in a region were closely interconnected. The villages had to cooperate to maintain the facilities and allocate water. Tokugawa Japan had many leagues of villages that cooperated to control irrigation and drainage. The league also preserved commons and worshiped a common local Shinto deity. For example, in Kizu-gō of Yamashiro province, there was a league of nine villages consisting of about eleven hundred households. Since the territory of the nine villages was divided into more than ten lordships, the league played a key role in preserving order. The league kept control of a total of eleven irrigation ponds and five canals and rivers. About twenty-five village officials in this league frequently communicated with one another to reconcile the interests of each village. The officials usually joined the meetings of the league more frequently than every other day (Mizumoto 1993, 154–159).

Within the league, however, villages not only cooperated, but also fought over the allocation of water. Villages that were situated upstream or whose ancestral members had greatly contributed to building the facilities had an advantage in accessing irrigated water (Kitamura 1950, 208–214). To maintain or to eliminate discrimination, each village pursued its own interests. Furthermore, the construction of new canals and ditches also caused trouble. The establishment of a new sluice gate on a river could prevent downstream villages from being sufficiently irrigated. In addition, new drainage ditches could emit water and create a nuisance for other villages. Therefore, there were many disputes over irrigation and drainage (yōsui-sōron) in Tokugawa Japan. The irrigation-drainage disputes were fought and settled in three characteristic ways. First, players in the disputes were usually not individuals, but village communities. When they litigated disputes, both the plaintiff and the defendant were usually village communities. Especially in the first half of the eighteenth century, most documents describing the rights and practices of irrigation and drainage were signed in the name of the village (Watanabe 2007, 181–185, Mizumoto 1993, 4–7).

Second, many disputes were settled out of court. Prominent figures and officials staying in neighboring villages arbitrated several conflicts between villages. As mentioned before, officials in the same league of villages frequently communicated with one another in daily life. This close relationship helped bring about reconciliations. Certainly, some disputes went to government court, but it was not unusual for government officials not to decide but instead to ask the village officials to reconcile (Watanabe 2007, 182). For example, the disputes over canals and commons between several villages in late-eighteenth-century Odawara domain government were settled using the following process. Since voluntary reconciliation by neighboring villages had failed, the two parties brought the matter before the court of the domain government. However, government officials did not make a decision, but instead ordered the prominent figures of neighboring villages to arbitrate the dispute. Then, the arbitrators managed to settle it. Thus, local governments and village communities cooperated to maintain the social order. On the one hand, "the government officials utilized practical knowledge and functions for the reconciliation of the arbitrators based on village society"; on the other hand, "the arbitrators negotiated with parties backed by the authority of the local government" (Mizumoto 2008, 327–328).

In early modern Japan, many civil engineering projects were carried out, and paddy acreage was expanded, especially from the sixteenth century to 1680, from 1722 to 1736, and from the 1820s to 1880. Then, until the beginning of the twentieth century, each individual district throughout the country of Japan had developed its own appropriate irrigation system. From the seventeenth century to the nineteenth, village communities or leagues of villages played an important role in many civil engineering projects. The activities of village communities were connected with public investments by local governments through irrigation and drainage networks. Government projects made it possible for villagers to create new paddies and fields. Furthermore, in practice, village communities sometimes initiated the promotion of public projects subsidized by the local government. The strength of a village community lay in the irrigation and drainage system, which were closely connected with the production activities of each household within a village.

Even after Western-style Civil Code was established in 1898, customary law governed many land transactions and water management in rural society. However, in the beginning of the twentieth century, well-developed irrigation systems based on cooperation among and within village communities became regarded as an obstacle to the growth of agriculture in Japan. The Ministry of Agriculture and Commerce of Japan believed that customary irrigation rights of village communities prevented the expansion of paddies and caused instability in the water supply, and tried to eradicate these customary rights. Furthermore, in 1923, "to modernize irrigation facilities and to deny customary irrigation rights effectively," the Ministry decided to carry out large-scale projects supported by the national budget (Imamura 1977, 138). Whereas, in the Tokugawa period, investments by local governments were promoted and supported by the community-based irrigation mechanism, in the twentieth century, the government made investments to abolish the traditional irrigation system and established a "modernized" water management mechanism.

NOTES

This work is supported by JSPS KAKENHI grant number 15K03589.

    1. One *chō* is 9,917.4 m² and is almost equal to one hectare. Hence, one *chō* is 2.45 acres. However, the actual area of *chō* varied according to place and time in the Tokugawa period.

2. Okura-shō (1927) provides paddy acreage data from 1716 to 1748 (the Kyoho to Enkyo eras), although its original source is unknown. Using this data, the paddy acreage in the early eighteenth century is calculated as 1,643,450 *chō*, whereas the total acreage of arable land is 2,969,714 *chō*.

3. So far, the revised acreage has been regarded as almost 50% larger than the former acreage (Sasaki 2016), since APDLTR (1953–1957) records the revised paddy acreage as 2,622,593 *chō* and the former acreage as 1,701,149 *chō*. However, this calculation is not correct. The former acreage does not include the paddy acreage in the Nagasaki and Ishikawa prefectures. Therefore, to calculate the increase from the former acreage to the revised acreage, the acreage of these two prefectures should also be excluded in the estimation of revised acreage. Then, the revised acreage is rectified to 2,423,474 *chō*. Hence, the increase rate is 42.9%. Furthermore, the former paddy acreage, including that in the omitted districts, was estimated as 1,842,104 *chō*.

4. The estimation is different from that of Miyamoto since he shows that arable land increased more in the late seventeenth century than it did in the early period, and there was not a rapid increase of arable land between the 1720s and 1730s (Miyamoto 1999, 38). Since he calculates the field expansion without considering the scale of each project, Miyamoto underestimates the effects of great projects in the early seventeenth century and from the 1720s to the 1730s.

5. It is because in land survey investigations, peasants hid some paddies and fields to evade tax and, furthermore, the domain government that conducted the land surveys did not report the real situation to the shogunate. Kawamura 1984, 159, 246, 263.

6. *Kokudaka* of 1697–1702 in the Echizen province is considered much higher than the real productivity; a contemporary stated that "the *kokudaka* had been determined improperly to pretend about the high productivity of the domain." Fukui-ken 1994.

7. One *koku* is equal to 180 liters. However, the actual volume of *koku* varied according to place and time.

8. In 1732, the shogunate also stated that each village had to provide fifty workers per 100 *koku* at its own cost, and the shogunate would give wages to additional laborers.

REFERENCES

Akita-ken ECLIH (Editing Committee of Land Improvement History) (1985). *Akitaken Tochi-kairyō-shi* (A History of Land Improvement in Akita). Akita, Akitaken Tochi-kairyō Jigyō-rengo-kai.

APDLTR (Association for Publishing Documents about Land Tax Reform) (1953–1957). *Meiji-shonen Chiso-kaisei Kiso-shiryō* (Basic Document about Land Tax Reform during the Early Meiji Period). 3 vols. Tokyo, Yūhikaku.

Asao, Naohiro (1967). *Kinsei Hōken-shakai no Kiso-kōzō* (The Basic Structure of Early Modern Feudal Society). Tokyo, Ochanomizu Shobō.

Blum, Jerome (1978). *The End of the Old Order in Rural Europe*. Princeton, Princeton University Press.

Booth, Anne, and R. M. Sundrum (1985). *Labour Absorption in Agriculture*. Oxford, Oxford University Press.

Fukui-ken (1994). *Fukui-kenshi: Tsūshihen3, Keisei 1* (A History of Fukui Prefecture: Early Modern, Part 1). Fukui, Fukui-ken.

Gordon, Andrew (2003). *A Modern History of Japan: From Tokugawa Times to the Present*. Oxford, Oxford University Press.

Hatate, Isao (1977). "Tochi-Kairyō wo Ninatta Hitobito" (People Who Carried Out Land Improvement Projects). In Imamura et al. 1977.

Hayami, Yūjiro, and Yoshihisa Godo (2002). *Nōgyō-keizai-ron* (Agricultural Economics). 2nd ed. Tokyo, Iwanami Shoten.

Imamura, Ikuko (2014). *Kinsei-shoki Kaga-han no Shinden-kaihatsu to Kokudaka no Kenkyū* (A Study of the Development of New Paddies and the *Kokudaka* of Kanazawa Domain Government in the Early Tokugawa Period). Toyama, Katsura Shobō.

Imamura, Naraomi (1977). "Tochi-Kairyō Eno Kokka no Tōjō" (The Entry of the National Government into Land Improvement Projects). In Imamura et al. 1977.

Imamura, Naraomi, Toshiro Sato, Hiroyasu Shimura, Satoshi Tamaki, Eijuro Nagata, and Isao Hatate, eds.(1977). *Tochi-kairyō Hyakunen-shi* (One Hundred Years of History of Land Improvement). Tokyo, Heibonsha.

Ishikawa, Shigeru (1967). *Economic Development in Asian Perspective*. Tokyo, Kinokuniya.

Ishikawa-ken ECLIH (1986). *Ishikawa-ken Tochi-kairyō-shi* (A History of Land Improvement in Inshikawa). Ishikawa, Ishikawa-ken Tochi-kairyō-jigyō Rengō-kai.

JSCE (Japanese Society of Civil Engineering) (1936). *Meiji-izen Nihon Doboku-shi* (A Pre-Meiji History of Civil Engineering in Japan). Tokyo, Iwanami Shoten.

Jūnikanno-yōsui-tochikairyōku (1985). *Jūnikanno Yōsui-shi* (A History of Jūnikanno Canal). Toyama, Chūetsu.

Kanzaka, Junichi (2018). "The Scattered and Intermingled Field System of Japan Compared to the Open-Field Systems of Europe." In *Peasants and Their Fields: The Rationale of Open-Field Agriculture, c. 700–1800,* edited by C. Dyer, E. Thoen, and T. Williamson. Turhout, Belgium, Bropls.

Kawamura, Hirotada (1984). *Edo Bakufu-sen Kuniezu no Kenkyū* (A Study of Pictorial Maps Collected by the Edo Shogunate). Tokyo, Kokon Shoin.

Kikuchi, Toshio (1977). *Shinden Kaihatsu* (Development of New Paddies). Tokyo, Kokon Shoin.

——— (1986). *Zoku Shinden Kaihatsu* (Development of New Paddies, Part 2). Tokyo, Kokon Shoin.

Kimura, Motoi (1964). *Kinsei no Shinden-mura* (Newly Developed Villages in the Tokugawa Period). Tokyo, Yoshikawakōbunkan.

Kitamura, Toshio (1950). *Nihon Kangai-suiri-kankō no Sshiteki-kenkyū* (A Historical Study of Customs of Irrigation and Water Management). Tokyo, Iwanami Shoten.

Kurachi, Katsunao (2008). *Tokugawa-Shakai no Yuragi* (The Destabilization of Tokugawa Society). Tokyo, Shōgakkan.

Kondo, Sentaro (1929). *Meiji-Nenkan Kangai Haisui Jigyō Shiryō* (Record of the Project for Irrigation and Drainage in the Meiji Period). Tokyo, MAC.

MAC (Ministry of Agriculture and Commerce) (1909). *Ta no Kangai-haisui ni Kansuru Jōkyō Chōsa* (Survey on the Irrigation and Drainage of Paddies). Tokyo, MAC.

——— (1926). *Kyūhan-jidai no Kouchi-kakuchō-kairyō-jigyō ni Kansuru Chōsa* (Research on the Expansion and Improvement of Fields in the Tokugawa Period). Tokyo, MAC.

Matsuyoshi, Sadao (1936/1955). *Shinden no Kenkyū* (A Study of New Paddies). Tokyo, Yūhikaku.

Miura, Kaiichi (1984). "Chūsei no Doboku to Shokunin-Shūdan" (Civil Engineering and Craftsmen Group). In *Doboku* (Civil Dngineering), edited by Akeshi Amakasu et al. Tokyo, Nihon-hyōron-sha.

Miura, Tetsuro (1983). *Akita-han Niokeru Shinden Kaihatsu* (The Development of New Paddies in Akita Domain). Tokyo, Kokon Shoin.

Miyamoto, Matao (1999). "Quantitative Aspects of the Tokugawa Economy." In *The Economic History of Japan,* edited by Akira Hayami, Osamu Saitō, and Ronald P. Toby. Oxford, Oxford University Press.

Mizumoto, Kunihiko (1993). *Kinsei no Gōson-jichi to Gyōsei* (Autonomy and Administration of Village Leagues in the Tokugawa Period). Tokyo, Tokyo University Press.

——— (2002). *Ezu to Keikan no Kinsei* (Pictorial Maps and Landscapes in the Tokugawa Period). Tokyo, Azekura Shobō.

——— (2003). *Kusa-yama no Kataru Kinsei* (Grassland Mountains in Tokugawa Japan). Tokyo, Yamakawa Shuppansha.

——— (2008). *Tokugawa no Kokka Dezain* (Tokugawa's Design for State Building). Tokyo, Shōgakukan.

Murata, Michihito (2009). *Kinsei no Yodogawa Chisui* (Water-Control of the Yodo River in the Tokugawa Period). Tokyo, Yamakawa Shuppansha.

Nagatsuma, Hiroshi (2001). *Hojokin no Shakai-shi* (A Social History of Subsidy). Kyoto, Jinbun Shoin.

Nakai, Nobuhiko (1956). "Shōnin-Jinushi no Shomondai" (Several Problems on Merchant Landlords). In *Meiji-ishin to Jinushi-sei* (Meiji-Restoration and Landlord System), edited by Rekishigaku-kenkyūkai. Tokyo, Iwanami Shoten.

Nakamura, Satoru (1968). *Meiji-ishin no Kisokōzō* (Basic Structures of the Meiji Restoration). Tokyo, Mirai-sha.

Niigata-ken ECLIH (1986). *Niigata-ken Tochi-kairyō-shi* (A History of Land Improvement in Niigata). Niigata, Niigata-ken Tochi-kairyō Jigyō-rengō-kai.

Nishida, Masaki (1984). "Kawayoke to Kuniyaku Fushin" (Controlling River and Government-Sponsored Constructions). In *Doboku* (Civil Engineering), edited by Takeshi Amakasu et al. Nihon-hyōron-sha.

Ōishi, Shinzaburo (1960). "Bakuhan-Taisei-Shakai no Kōzō" (The Structure of Shogunate System Society). *Rekishigaku-kenkyū* 242:72–80.

——— (1973). "Kinsei-Chūki no Shinden Seisaku" (The Policy of Creating New Paddies in the Middle of the Tokugawa Period). *Gakushūin Daigaku Keizaironshū* 10 (3): 59–76.

Ōkura-shō (1927). *Dai-nippon Sozei-shi* (Financial History of Great Japan). Tokyo, Ōkura-shō.

Ōtani, Sadao (1996). *Edo-bakufu Chisui-shi Seisaku-shi no Kenkyū* (A Study of the History of the Tokugawa Shogunate's Policy of Controlling Rivers). Tokyo, Yūzankaku.

Overton, Mark (1996). *Agricultural Revolution in England: The Transformation of the Agrarian Economy, 1500–1850.* Cambridge, Cambridge University Press.

Saeki, Yasukazu (2007). *Kinsei Tonami-heiya no Kaihatsu to Sanson no Tenkai* (The Exploitation of the Tonami Plain and the Development of Dispersed Villages in the Early Modern Period). Toyama, Katsura Shobō.

Saito, Hitoshi (1989). *Nōgyō-mondai no Tenkai to Jichi-sonraku* (The Development of Agrarian Programs and Autonomous Villages). Tokyo, Nihonkeizai Hyōronsha.

Saitō, Osamu (1988). "Daikaikon, Jinkō, Shōnō Keizai" (Great Reclamation, Population, and Peasant Economy). In *Keizai Shakai no Seiritsu* (Emergence of Economic Society), edited by Akira Hayami and Mataro Miyamoto. Tokyo, Iwanami Shoten.

Saitō, Osamu, and Masayuki Tanimoto (1989). "Zairai-Sangyō no Sai-Hensei" (Restructure of Indigenous Industries). In *Kaikō to Ishin* (The Opening Ports and the Meiji Restoration), edited by Mataji Umemura and Yuzo Yamamoto. Tokyo, Iwanami Shoten.

Sakane, Yoshihiro (2011). *Ie to Mura: Nihon Dentō-shakai to Keizai Hatten* (Family System and Village: Economic Development and Japanese Traditional Society). Tokyo, Nōsangyoson Bunkakyōkai.

Sasaki, Hiroshi (2016). *Chiso-Kaisei to Meiji-Ishin* (Land Tax Reform and Meiji Restoration). Tokyo, Yūshisha.

Tanaka, Kyūgu (1721/1996). *Minkan-seiyō*. Revised by Sunao Murakami. Tokyo, Yūrindo.

Tokunaga, Mitsutoshi (1997). *Nihon Nōhō-shi Kenkyū* (A Study of Cultivation Methods in Japan). Tokyo: Nōsangyoson Bunkakyōkai.

Totman, Conrad (1998), *The Green Archipelago: Forestry in Pre-Industrial Japan*. Athens, Ohio University Press.

Toyama-ken ECLIH (2004). *Toyama-ken Tochi-kairyō-shi* (A History of Land Improvement in Toyama). Toyama, Toyama-ken Tochi-kairyō-jigyō Rengo-kai.

Tsukamoto, Manabu (1984). "Yōsui-Busin" (The Construction of Canals). In *Doboku* (Civil Engineering), edited by Takeshi Amakasu et al. Nihonhyōron-sha.

Umemura, Mataji, Saburo Yamada, Yujiro Hayami, Nobukiyo Takamatsu, and Minoru Kumazaki (1966). *Agriculture and Forestry, Estimates of Long-Term Economic Statistics of Japan*. Vol. 9. Tokyo, Tōyokeizai Shinpōsha.

Van Bavel, Bas J. P. (2001). "Land, Lease and Agriculture: The Transition of the Rural Economy in the Dutch River Area from the Fourteenth to the Sixteenth Century." *Past and Present* 172:3–43.

Watanabe, Takashi (2007). *Gōnō, Sonraku-kyōdotai to Chiikishakai* (Wealthy Peasants, Village Communities, and Regional Society). Tokyo, Kashiwa Shobō.

——— (2008). *Hyakushō no Chikara* (Power of Peasants). Tokyo, Kashiwa Shobō.

Yanagita, Kunio (1910/1976). *Jidai to Nōsei* (Agricultural Policy throughout the Ages). In *Yanagita Kunio Zenshū* (Collected Works of Yakagita Kunio), vol. 29. Tokyo, Chikuma Shobō.

——— (1931/1991). *Nihon Noumin-shi* (A History of Japanese Peasants). In *Yanagita Kunio Zenshū*, vol. 29. Tokyo, Chikuma Shobō.

Yoshimura, Toyoo (2013). *Nihonkinsei no Gyōsei to Chiikishakai* (Civil Administration and Regional Society in Early Modern Japan). Tokyo, Azekura Shobō.

10

Rulers and Ruled in Flood Protection during the Eighteenth Century

The Prussian Example

Heinrich Kaak

PROJECTS ON THE ODER, NETZE, AND
WARTHE FROM THE EUROPEAN PERSPECTIVE

The Prussian diking and cultivation of the river bottomlands during the eighteenth century attracted significant attention, not least because it involved the risky plan of rerouting a section of the Oder River at the northern end of the Oderbruch.[1] Moreover, the Prussian King, Frederick William I (1713-1740), and his son, Frederick II (1740-1786), declared the project a special goal of the state, made a strong financial commitment, and ran the risk of failure (Gudermann 1999, 352-354).

Certainly, the diking resulted in the expansion of high-quality royal agricultural lands from which the state itself benefited directly. Here, however, the question will be investigated to what extent there were broader objectives, above all, the protection of inhabitants, with their homes and farmland, their animals and their production, from the frequent flooding. The regions' climate improved and it became viable to invest in infrastructure. The exploitation and securing of Prussia's best farmlands resulted in an increase in the yields of everyone involved in agriculture. As a result, it was possible to expand the food supply in the country. The river bottomlands, considered in the context of the widespread serfdom, became a model system of agriculture with secure ownership and freedom of movement for small producers. The Prussian state—until this time an agricultural state—offers interesting insights into these interrelations. Nonetheless, such measures were in no way unique in Europe.

THE PREHISTORY OF FLOOD CONTROL AND
COASTAL PROTECTION IN EUROPE

The first documented flood control structures on European rivers were in Mycenaean Greece in Orchomenos around 1500 BCE (Knauss 1990, 23, Knauss 1987, 106-107), and later in Koroneia in Kopais (Greece) in the first century CE, which was under the reign of the Roman Emperor Hadrian (Fossey 1991, 5-26). There are further indications of river dikes constructed during the Roman Era, including Italy, the Netherlands, Central Europe, Romania, and Great Britain— where several shipping canals were dug and provided with dikes (Winkander 2000, 321-330). Dike building then subsided until the end of the early Middle Ages, from which point there are indications that levees and dikes existed on estuaries and rivers with flat shores. This was the case on the Loire (France), which had levees in the ninth century and partly dikes in the twelfth century (Garcia and Pusch 2002, MGH, 301). Facilities for flood control also existed in the Po Valley (Italy) in the twelfth century. This older trend was also strong in Central Europe, where "all of the larger rivers and most streams . . . [had] been changed considerably since the early Middle Ages" (Jäger 1988, 18). Indeed, dikes were built on the Lower Rhine (Germany/the Netherlands) in the ninth century. The Dutch worked on the Elbe (Germany) during the twelfth century (Schmidt 2000, 106-107, Hofmeister 1981, 7, Boeselager 2003, 234), and the Vistula (Poland) was diked in the thirteenth century (Ehlers and Winkel 1947, 8), while the Oder (Germany) received its first dike in the fourteenth century.[2] Dike work, drainage, and cultivation were done on numerous other rivers in Central Europe, including the Scheldt and the Meuse (Belgium/the Netherlands), the Ems and the Weser (Germany) (Berendsen and Stouthammer 2001, 13, Allemeyer 2006, 35-37, Peters 2005, 26-27), the Danube (Germany to Hungary), and the Vltava (Czech Republic).[3]

Outside Central Europe, in 1703, Dutch engineers helped establish the Russian city of St. Petersburg where the Neva River flows into the Baltic Sea.[4] Dike work was first done on the Rhône (France) in the mid-eighteenth century and on the Tisza (Hungary, Serbia) at the end of that century (Szűcs 2010, 243-245). Dikes were built on the Sava (Slovenia, Croatia) and on the Drava (Croatia, Hungary) in the eighteenth and nineteenth centuries.[5] In England, dikes were built on the River Tweed around 1800, and on the Thames and the River Severn at the end of the nineteenth century.[6]

Although river dikes were presumably developed before sea dikes, river dikes were significantly influenced by the diking of the sea. The first Roman reports about life on the North Sea, by Pliny the Elder in the first century CE and Tacitus around 100 CE, describe the extremities of life in living among the tides and cold, the storms and rain. At Isca Augusta, near Caerleon in Wales, structures dated to

(74-75 CE) protected the community from the ocean (Rippon and Cameron 2006, 76, Campbell 2012, 176). Archeologists have also shown that an early sea dike near a farm at Feddersen Wierde, situated on the North Sea coast of Lower Saxony (Germany), was built in the first or second century CE (Krämer 1984). Additional sea walls on the North Sea coast were built in Flanders (Belgium) before the end of the tenth century, while additional ring dikes were built around farms and villages on the German North Sea coastline in c. 1000 CE (Ey 2005, 147-149).

Dike construction on rivers and on the coast is thus a technology dating back millennia, which indicates that people in Europe, especially in the south, west, and center of the continent, developed and secured areas to deal with a lack of space and good conditions for settlement made so urgent by the circumstances of the time. This trend continues—although it is increasingly controversial—to this day.

DIKE CONSTRUCTION AND MAINTENANCE

In addition to protecting existing settlements and agricultural areas, both river dikes and sea walls were used to reclaim land that was particularly fertile for agriculture and suitable for new settlement.

Sea Dikes: At first, construction and maintenance went hand in hand. This was the case in certain areas on the North Sea coast until the eighteenth century. Originally, coastal inhabitants made the decision to erect and construct dikes on their own. Rulers of the areas in which dikes were built granted coastal dwellers who took the initiative more autonomy than the inhabitants of the interior because the extreme conditions on the coast did not permit effective feudal control. Given the weakness of princely rule, North Sea inhabitants became "peasant republicans" (Urban 1991, 50, 59, 119). The more secure the land became, so the infrastructure became more developed, and income increased—resulting in greater danger of a hostile takeover. In 1500, the Danish king's first attempt to subjugate the area failed and the peasant republic subsequently flourished. The second attempt was successful, however, and the region was more firmly incorporated into the Danish kingdom in 1559 (Bohn 2006, 41, 57).

The coastal strategy of territories and states began to change in the sixteenth century. Like many other areas, they became actively involved in dike matters—particularly once traditional oral coastal law was codified.[7] At the same time, technological improvements were often triggered by periods of heavy storms. Indeed, after the Burchardi Flood of 1634—also known as the second "Grote Mandränke"[8]—Johann Claussen Rollwagen, the new *General-Deichgraf* of Duke Frederick III of Gottorp (1616-1659), launched a new section of dikes on the west coast of Schleswig-Holstein, while reorganizing construction so that it was no longer the communal task of marsh inhabitants but performed by professionals. Thereafter, the responsibility of the inhabitants was focused more on dike maintenance—and they were no longer able to keep the new land for themselves as a result. This intervention of the territorial state was further strengthened after the Christmas Flood of 1717, which was known as the largest flood at the time and claimed more than eleven thousand victims.[9]

River Dikes: The existence of river dikes in the Middle Ages and early modern period has been frequently documented.[10] Northwestern continental Europe and western Central Europe seem to have preceded eastern Central Europe: that is, the technological transfer moved from west to east. The Dutch were the leaders in coastal protection and other forms of hydraulic engineering (Tols and Langen 2000, 358–366). Indeed, a large portion of the land in the Netherlands was created artificially—from dikes, diked marshland, canals, locks, and drainage equipment—and later became farms, villages, and towns. Broad sections of land below sea level were secured and developed as highly productive agricultural areas, and the first pumping facilities powered by wind (wind pumps)[11] were implemented in the region. In the twelfth century, the inhabitants of Friesland and Dithmarschen were the first eastern Europeans to learn from the Dutch. In roughly 1530, Frisian Mennonites (a Protestant religious denomination) were invited to cultivate the lower Vistula (Ludwig 1961, 34). As noted earlier, the first hydraulic engineers from the Lower Rhine came to Brandenburg-Prussia during the seventeenth century.

Immediately after the Thirty Years' War (1618–1648), Elector Frederick William of Brandenburg granted the Havelbruch—a small area north of Berlin—to the nobleman Jobst Gerhard von und zu Hertefeld of the Lower Rhine for diking and cultivation. In the model village of Neu Holland, settlers from the Lower Rhine followed the Dutch tradition in receiving rights of quasi-ownership, exemption from the requirement to perform servile labor, and freedom of movement in exchange for independently working and securing the land (Peters 1989, 18–30). In this small experimental area, dike maintenance appears to have been left to the new settlers as no dike decree is known to exist. In the rural world east of the Elbe, which was characterized by personal and manor serfdom, this concept was intended to spur emulation by the feudal lords of Brandenburg. It had limited success at first. The reconstruction of dikes was undertaken on the Elbe during the late seventeenth century; while the Havelland Luch (*CCM,* Part VI, Nachlese, "No. XVIII") and the Rhinluch—areas near the Havelbruch—were cultivated in the eighteenth century. These were all state initiatives. In 1717, at the same time that the Christmas Flood hit the northwest, Frederick William I ordered the construction of a dike to protect the upper Oderbruch. This dike and the security it provided became a model for further land cultivation projects in absolutist Prussia in the eighteenth century (cf. part 2 on dike construction and maintenance on the Oder, Netze, and Warthe in the eighteenth century).

There are three early modern variants based on similar needs. The North Sea dike variant displays a democratic-communal structure, which continued to exist despite increasing encroachment by states or territories. River dike construction increasingly fell under the influence of territories. After the seventeenth century, the differences between the variant of the northwest German territories—which were based more on class structure—and that of the more strongly authoritarian regions of eastern Brandenburg-Prussia and Prussia were, in essence, slight. In eastern Prussia, the local feudal lords with their extended estates were much more directly and energetically involved in the organization of dike maintenance, and they assumed a dominant role as a result. In western territories, the nobility—who were more dependent on rent income—tended to exercise their influence on events surrounding the dikes indirectly through the territorial estate assemblies (Melchers 2002, 43–45 et passim).

The necessity of building and maintaining dikes was perceived in various ways by those concerned. In places like the Netherlands, potential danger was extremely high and the necessity was repeatedly reinforced by flooding. When dikes were breached, floods affected not only areas reclaimed for extensive agriculture but also villages and towns, particularly as settlement increased. Such conditions made the obligation of dike construction and maintenance fully acceptable. This continues to be the case today, especially following the trauma of the floods of 1953. Resistance was more likely where new sea walls were to be built by state decree. The fishermen of the Oderbruch in Brandenburg had lived with floods for centuries, and rightly viewed their existence as threatened by dike construction in the eighteenth century (Kaak 2004a, 224, Kaup 1994, 126–127).

For centuries the area of northwest Germany, Belgium, and the Netherlands has been densely packed with people, industry, agriculture, energy production, and transportation infrastructure. Consequently, there is a problem in that old mine tunnels still exist under the mighty dikes of the Lower Rhine and several of its tributaries (Ruhr)—which complicate present-day dike maintenance (Tittizer and Krebs 1996, 34).

In order to build the dikes and ensure their safety, organizational forms had to be found and developed.

ORGANIZATIONAL FORMS: DIKE BANDS OR DIKE ASSOCIATIONS

There can be no negligence in the maintenance of flood control facilities, which demands considerable energy. From practical experience on a small scale, in instances where all interested parties were more or less equally affected, neighborly pressure at first helped dike and levee construction. The next level at which construction took place was the parish (the lowest church district), which included several villages. The dike associations grew and existed nearly everywhere that dikes and levees were built, whether on the sea or rivers. These still exist today as organizations in which membership is mandatory and which require work and monetary payments (Allemeyer 2006, 84–85, 91–93).

On the sea, Dike associations have existed in the Netherlands since the twelfth century. In Schleswig-Holstein (Germany) they were at first called "dike bands." As the scope of projects grew, the number of dike associations decreased to a few with complex hierarchies governing numerous sub-dike associations. These associations were affected by a trend toward legal standardization, which was being introduced by the northwestern territories of the Holy Roman Empire of the German Nation, to which the Netherlands belonged until 1648. During the early modern period these territories—counties of East Friesland and Oldenburg; the Free City of Bremen; as well as the duchies of Bremen, Lüneburg, and Holstein—took control of dike supervision in a stepwise manner. Thus, the dike associations in East Friesland lost their autonomy in the sixteenth and seventeenth centuries: placed under the supervision of the state police, they lost the authority to establish their own statutes but maintained the right to elect their officers (Jakubowski-Tiessen 1992, 228). The dike associations on Schleswig-Holstein's west coast corresponded to the parishes. The parish reeve was also the dike count, and therefore a member of the territorial administration. The dike judge—who was in charge of the inspection of certain sections of the dike, made neglect and damage public, and summoned those remiss in their official duties—was democratically elected by the dike band cooperative. Two to three dike inspections were performed annually by local commissions (Allemeyer 2006, 88–89). With the decree of January 29, 1800, King Christian VII of Denmark (1766-1808) created "a uniform legal basis" for Schleswig-Holstein in the "Entire State" of Denmark (which included Norway, Iceland, Greenland, and Schleswig-Holstein). As a result, the state controlled dike construction, without the dike associations losing their cooperative structure (*CSVV*, cf. Nawotki 2004, 179).

On the rivers: The northwest German political entities noted earlier also controlled river dike matters. Many other territories of the Holy Roman Empire, and later the German Confederation and Empire, acted in a similar manner, as construction measures on rivers also covered higher regions. Representative of the numerous policies of the early modern period is the Braunschweig-Lüneburg Dike Decree of 1664, which governed the dikes on the Elbe north of Hamburg. As in the aforementioned regions, local interested parties *(Deichinteressenten)* were formed into groups in which membership was mandatory. Dike sections and the property behind the dike were joined indivisibly, and dike sections were indicated by marked posts. The so-called *Ober= Haupt= und Amt=Leute*—the hierarchy of supervisors—was named by the territories and designated dike panels for three-year periods.[12] The democratic-communal structure of the North Sea was thus not duplicated here.

In 1695, further up the Elbe in Brandenburg, a dike decree for the Altmark area was issued based on that of 1476. It was intended to spur reconstruction after the Thirty Years' War.[13] The dike captain was nominated by the aristocracy of the

Altmark and confirmed by the elector. The decree also specified how many deputies from the nobility, towns, villages, and individual farms had to participate in the upper and lower inspection of the dike (Tit. I). More broadly, this decree comprised regulations for the dike inspection (Tit. II), detailed how the dike was to be maintained (Tit. III), and concluded with a comprehensive dike roll of the upper and lower districts. With this Elector Frederick III of Brandenburg (1688/1701-1713) issued in concession to the nobility a decree that did not leave any room for bylaws of the dike unions.

The dike decree of 1717 issued for the upper Oderbruch was based on that of the Altmark. The decree for this area described the division of responsibilities following dike construction. A small staff comprising representatives of the king performed inspections of the dike in cooperation with the *Deichinteressenten,* and distributed repair jobs and penalties. However, the dike union did not have the freedom to adopt a charter, and its members did not have the right to elect dike representatives. Farm owners played an important role among the deputies due to the size of their land and their ruling position in the villages of their areas.[14] The General State Laws for the Prussian States of 1794 declared that dike affairs were "determined by special river, dike and riverbank decrees."[15] This was not amended until 1818, when the influence of aristocratic deputies in the dike associations decreased to the advantage of the urban and rural inspectors, and when local dike administrators were selected by dike association members—as specified by the Prussian "Law Regarding Dike Affairs" in 1848 (*GSPS*, 57, §15., f., cf. Rönne 1863, 610—613). These concessions to democracy resulted from the Revolution of 1848, when Prussia briefly opened the doors to change. In 1853, however, the Amendment of the Dike and Riverbank Decree for the Bottomlands in Lebus did not result in any fundamental changes, it essentially confirmed the altered division of property. Between 1861 and 1895, four melioration associations and dike subassociations were established within the dike organization of the lower Oderbruch.[16]

Dike affairs in the Oderbruch were part of a larger movement. Indeed, the *Yearbook of Official Statistics of the Prussian State* lists ninety-four dike associations with a total of 465,250 hectares of protected land in the nine "old provinces" of Prussia in 1866.[17] These were almost exclusively river and Baltic Sea dike associations. In 1867, almost the entire German North Sea coast—including the annexed regions in northwestern Germany—were part of Prussia (Dörr 1995, 259-263). The upper and lower Oderbruch merged into a single association in roughly 1900. Dike associations shared the costs of construction with the Prussian state, each paying half (Spiegelberg 2001, 106-109).

The "Prussian Water Law" of 1913 treated the dike associations as water cooperatives and upheld members' right to select governing boards themselves (Bochalli 1913). The Water Association Law of 1937 unified water and dike affairs throughout Germany; based on the principles of the National Socialist regime, this law once again eliminated the right of members to select officers—a right that had existed since 1848.[18] When the united dike association of the Oderbruch protested the establishment of two armament firms in 1938, it was punished by having both its responsibilities for serious flood control and its authority to collect membership dues reduced. In 1940, all dike associations and subassociations of the region were merged into the Oderbruch Dike Association. The Second World War (1939–1945) had catastrophic effects on the dikes on the Oder. Indeed, the local dike commissions were only able to resume their work provisionally in 1947, and cooperation with sites on the east bank—now part of Poland—did not come to pass. The passage of the Law on the Dissolution of Common Separations, Interested Parties, Associations (Gesetz über die Auflösung der gemeinschaftlichen Separations-Interessenten-Vereinigungen) of 1951 by the parliament of the German Democratic Republic resulted in the dissolution of the dike association of the Oderbruch in 1953. Moreover, local commissions and melioration societies, which had been reestablished, were once again placed under the strict political oversight of state enterprises and institutions. A dike association with its own charter was not created again for a long period of time (Spiegelberg 2001, 106-109). In 1991, the Oderbruch Water and Soil Association was established from these groups and responsibilities. Consequently, the idea of a dike association on the basis of German federal law, and with its own charter (§6) and responsibilities (§2, §54), was also revived in 1991.

Today, the German government has largely taken over the financing of coastal protection and river dikes, while the federal lands take part in planning financing and construction. The main dike associations contribute significantly to making buildings secure and providing for dike defense in disasters. They also function as contractors of construction work. Contemporary dike associations are statutory corporations *(Körperschaften des öffentlichen Rechts)* that elect their representatives democratically.[19]

ENFORCEMENT

The collective construction of flood control structures demands a strict conception of facility maintenance, especially for those living behind the dike. Mutual supervision sufficed when neighbors organized the dike among themselves. When the scale of the work grew, however, keeping them in good working order without officials, inspections, and government enforcement was not feasible in the long run. The more centralized the organization, the greater the tendency of individuals to shirk their responsibilities. This is shown clearly by the struggles of officials in charge of the construction and maintenance of new dikes and levees on rivers and the sea. Whether cooperatively developed or imposed from above, the means of enforcement must be available.

In northern and eastern Germany in the Middle Ages, the *Sachsenspiegel* was the universal code of law.[20] Its most important passage regarding dike construction was "Villages located on the water that have a dike must maintain their portion of the dike in good order. However, if flooding occurs which breaks the dike, everyone on the dike is required to help rebuild it. Those who do not do their part forfeit their right to property behind the dike."[21] A shortened form of this was passed into laws and oral tradition as "Anyone who won't dike must step aside."[22] This principle was first codified as the *Spadelandsrecht* in 1557 (Allemeyer 2006, 84-86), and remained in force until the twentieth century. This essentially meant that anyone who was unable to participate in dike construction lost their property and had to leave the area. This drastic law reflected the tense situation near the sea. The dike court—or shovel court—provided that anyone who could no longer work on the dike had to stick their shovel in their section of the dike, or an inspector would issue the last warning when a *Deichinteressent* had neglected his responsibilities (Kühn 1992, 83).

Prussia was not the only land that used so-called military execution (against those who failed to pay their dues or work their share). It was also widely used for various purposes in other territories, as well as on the North Sea coast. Indeed, the practice was documented in East Friesland, Oldenburg, the duchy of Bremen, as well as in Holstein and Schleswig in even more severe forms than on the Oderbruch. Even after the Christmas Flood of 1717, *Restanten*—outstanding payments—were rigorously collected. This indicates that the readiness to work the dikes decreased following this disaster. Certainly, settlements were destroyed and many people drowned in areas immediately bordering the North Sea, while survivors were traumatized. Those in more distant areas considered themselves less threatened, and refused to contribute to the massive reconstruction project. The more forcefully rulers pushed the work, the more serious were local conflicts (Jakubowski-Tiessen 1992, 173-176, 243-244). Ultimately, territories and states— with the higher-level perspective, comprehensive planning, and effective means of enforcement—prevailed. Indeed, the Braunschweig-Lüneburg dike decree (1717) provided that a hand be chopped off for the crime of moving a marker post, while those guilty of the "malicious" breaching of the dike were burned alive. The Prussian state guaranteed the implementation of the requirements of this decree with "military execution" and, after 1754, prosecuted acts of sabotage with *Karrenstrafe* (hard labor while chained to a cart)—a relatively mild punishment compared to those of Bremen and Verden.[23]

SECONDARY EFFECTS

The draining of an area resulted in the sinking of the water table, a change in climate, as well as a decrease in the variety of plants and animals. During the dike work on the Warthe, for instance, parts of the farmland on hillsides in the Warthebruch dried out, further disadvantaging inhabitants for whom the old settlements on the edge of the marsh had already become a legal detriment (Kaak 2012, 75). In 1800, Friedrich Wilhelm August Bratring quoted the opinion of King

Frederick William III's personal physician that the air had become "cleaner and more healthy since the reclamation of various marshes and the felling of forests because nothing blocks the winds blowing through" (Bratring 1968, 32-33). This characterization represents the opposite of what is called for today. A diminishing variety of species in the Oderbruch was evident in the eighteenth century. The town of Wriezen was no longer able to function as the Oderbruch's central fish market, which had supplied Berlin primarily.[24] This was considered collateral damage by contemporaries.

The stronger the continuous line of dikes was built, and the more the river's course was shortened, the higher and stronger dikes had to be. This is true of the North Sea, where flood barriers and the shortening of dikes reclaimed land from the sea. It is also true of rivers, where straightening and narrowing had the same result.[25] In 2013, heavy flooding due to heavy rainfall ("centenary extreme event") affected eight of sixteen German federal lands: Passau experienced its heaviest flooding in five hundred years, while the Rhine, Elbe, Mulde, Saale, Oder, Lusitanian Neisse, Danube, and Inn were particularly affected. Flooding along many European rivers—including the Danube, Drava, Vltava, and Vistula—prompted the rethinking of matters. Making facilities higher and stronger had done little to diminish the danger. In view of climate change, measures to return land to rivers have been called for with increasing frequency. Experts have also argued for the creation of flood polders—diked-in areas intended to take in large masses of water—and rain retention basins on tributaries of larger rivers. The renaturation of the riparian zones is supposed to return flora and fauna to their old variety once again (Jakubowski-Tiessen 2009, 181).

DIKE CONSTRUCTION AND MAINTENANCE ON THE ODER, NETZE, AND WARTHE IN THE EIGHTEENTH CENTURY

In 1709, another bout of serious flooding occurred in the Oderbruch, upsetting its already limited agricultural production. As a result, Frederick William, who would become King in Prussia in 1713, decided to protect the upper Oderbruch with a uniform dike. This was not to ensure the continued existence of agriculture, but to significantly expand production on the monarchy's most fertile lands with settlers recruited from abroad (Wentz 1930, 101). This took place approximately eighty kilometers east of Berlin in Brandenburg, the central province of the state of Prussia.

While the king was pressing for economic progress and settlement in the sparsely populated backwaters of Prussia; the head bailiffs on the estates of the Order of St. John *(Amtmänner)* and royals, as well as the noble manor lords *(Gutsherren)* with their feudal operations, were striving to secure and expand their areas of cultivation. Meanwhile, the peasants required continuity, at minimum, to raise their livestock. It is less clear how local feudal lords were involved in securing

MAP 2. Colonization of the Oderbruch during the Reign of Frederick II
Source: Stier 1957, 69.

the dikes—that is, in an important administrative duty—and what advantages and disadvantages that such involvement brought them. The sequence of events is illustrated by occurrences in the upper Oderbruch between 1716 and 1717. This also provides insight into dike construction in the lower Oderbruch, the Netzebruch, and the Warthebruch. (See map 2.)[26]

PUBLIC GOODS IN THE EARLY MODERN PERIOD

In contemporary theory, the term "public goods" encompasses a nearly unlimited set of tangible and intangible measures taken by governments (or their official representatives) on the national, provincial, regional, and local level to guarantee or improve the peace, security, and social justice at all or any level using specific

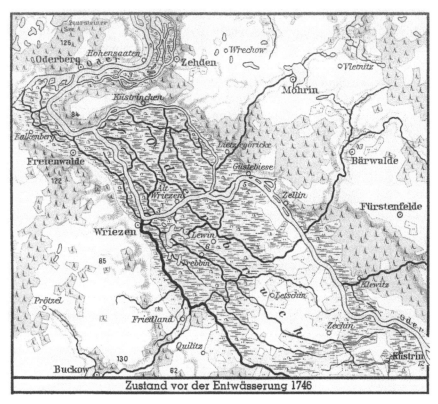

MAP 2. Continued

educational, cultural, and technical standards (Becker 2002, Ledyard 1995, 111–194). While the scope of government involvement was more modest in the early modern period, there are fundamental patterns of thought and action that are comparable. These involve national defense, the rule of law, ensuring production and foodstuffs, the safety of roads, as well as guaranteeing the basic principles of religion. Rulers also act on behalf of those who do not share costs, and can establish methods of enforcement to maintain specific needs (Hattenhauer 1996, 600-602, 734).

The problem of securing and cultivating river bottomlands in Brandenburg in the eighteenth century is particularly revealing in this regard. The late Middle Ages saw several attempts at flood control on the Oder, in the form of dikes that protected several villages. In the sixteenth century there was a continuous line of dikes for a small portion of the Oderbruch,[27] but this was partially destroyed in the Thirty Years' War (1618-1648) and fell into disrepair thereafter. In the eighteenth century, construction plans reemerged on a brand new scale when the Oderbruch, the Netzebruch, and the Warthebruch were extensively drained and settled using state resources. The population increased significantly in the area near the dikes, and rivalries arose between the old peasants and the new colonists. There was particular resistance from the original inhabitants—especially fishermen—who could not or would not support the changes. To give the project some security, the state issued decrees regarding dike maintenance and integrated both local feudal lords and communities into the system.

The scope of responsibilities expected of local feudal lords—particularly the manor lords and head bailiffs of royal property and those of the Order of St. John—as part of the state measures to ensure flood control in the eighteenth century must be taken into consideration. This includes examining which duties regarding the supervision of the protection system were specifically assigned to them, what methods of enforcement were at their disposal, how inspection worked in tandem with other duties, how effective their contribution to the linking of feudal and state activities actually was, and how finances were organized. Evidently, the organization of these matters was almost automatically given to local feudal lords, who were already firmly entrenched in land ownership, the control of the courts, and the administrative apparatus. A question arises regarding the extent to which these additional responsibilities altered the relationship between rulers and local communities.

When King Frederick William I of Prussia made the decision to dike the upper Oderbruch, he proceeded with all due caution—it was, after all, his first large project of this type. On December 30, 1716, he issued a preliminary dike and riverbank decree so that, as the final version read, "all interested parties better understand such a useful work and are able to inform themselves about it" (*CCM*, Part IV, 2nd Section, IV Cap., "No. XVIII," cc. 303). Such need was established on the assertion that

> Our [royal] in Amt Lebus, as well as many noble villages on the Oder and the lowlands, or located in the so-called marshes, are flooded almost yearly by the rising and overflowing of the waters of the Oder, and their farmlands, pastures, and droveways are laid waste to the great detriment and inconvenience of Ourselves and Our subjects.[28]

Compounding matters,

> it could not be countered with adequate effort or precaution, not only because many localities lacked the necessary supervision, but also because a few localities which own farmland and pastureland in marshes have contributed or performed very little toward the conservation of existing dams or ponds; others, in contrast, had to build and maintain more dams than they were able to afford, as well as the ponds laid in such a way on the edge or banks of the river, as to be almost completely unprotected from its attack and its violence. (*CCM*, Part IV, 2nd Section, IV Cap., "No. XVII," cc. 294-295)

As expressed in the preamble of the decree of June 1717, suggestions for improvement were received and the decree was significantly expanded—by means of the dike roll, for example (*CCM*, Part IV, 2nd Section, IV Cap., "No. XVII," cc. 294-295).

As such, the king recognized a serious problem, identified the causes, and understood that inhabitants were not in a position to take common action on their own. Realizing that there was no other institution that—given the conditions of the time—possessed the power, means, and authority to rectify the problem and provide a lasting solution, King Federick William I ordered the large construction project. As the recognized ruling power, he subsequently issued a decree on his own authority that integrated all concerned parties into a system of controls and services. He committed all parties to serve the power of the state, but above all to each one another as neighbors—thereby endeavoring for the fair distribution of burdens. In the medium term, obedience was rewarded with improved quality of life, while negligence or resistance was threatened with penalties up to and including military intervention to compel service. However, the king's initiative was not purely intended for the well-being of his subjects. The expansion of farmland, as well as of both agricultural production and population, was also in the narrow interests of the state. To a large extent, the area to be diked comprised royal domains and thus provided the state with an immediate fiscal advantage.

DISTRIBUTION OF LAND AND RESPONSIBILITIES IN
THE UPPER ODERBRUCH IN 1716

Except the *Immediatstadt* Küstrin,[29] the area planned for dikes comprised three *Mediatstädte*[30] of Lebus, Göritz, and Seelow, as well as forty-one villages. Of these forty-four settlements, nineteen had agricultural operations that were manorial and twenty-two did not,[31] while three villages had become purely manorial operations. The *Mediatstädte* and twenty-one villages were located on royal demesnes (twenty-two on the Lebus demesne, and two on the Quartschen demesne).[32] Fourteen villages were on land owned by the nobility (twelve noble, two *Adelslehne*).[33] Two were on land of the Order of St John, two on that of the Margrave of Brandenburg-Sonnenburg, and one on university property. As nearly all land in Prussia east of the Elbe was divided into local feudal districts, the *Mediatstädte* as well as all the villages and manorial operations were under feudal seigneurial.[34] Altogether the agricultural area of the lords in twenty-five villages of the upper Oderbruch comprised about a quarter of the total area: that is, barely 23%—a relatively low percentage. Elsewhere in East Elbian Prussia, such land comprised about 40% of village acreage at the time. This is because land in the Oderbruch was difficult to convert to agricultural uses prior to 1717, and was less interesting for manorial use as a result. The peasants of the villages where there were no manorial operations were also bound by the feudal system and required to perform servile labor.[35]

Given the scale of the construction plans and the ever-present doubt regarding its feasibility, only the state was able to take the initiative, as well as provide financing and organization. In any case, rather than weak local dikes, it was a matter of building a continuous fifty-kilometer-long dike (50.721 kilometers) on a middle-sized European river. This dike was intended to channel the waters of the Oder into a narrowed course, and thus had to be higher and significantly stronger than anything similar that had been previously built in Prussia. Under the supervision of royal director of Agriculture, Martin Friedrich von Creutz, a continuous wall was built on the east side of the river's main course from Lebus to Zellin in 1716-1717. This was followed by the Royal Dike Decree of 1717 (*CCM,* Part IV, 2nd Section, IV Cap., "No. XVIII"), which created a dike association in the upper Oderbruch to assign maintenance duties, as well as govern the villages, demesne farms, and estates located in outlying areas that did not directly border the dike. This association was not organized as a purely cooperative and autonomous body—behind everything stood the Prussian state with its laws and enforcement measures. In the implementation of the project, that royal lands dominated the upper Oderbruch was a distinct advantage for Frederick William I. After all, the king himself was the largest feudal lord in the area. The dike decree also included the dike roll, in which were entered all interested parties—so-called *Deichinteressenten*—from the royal demesne and manor farms of the nobility down to the owners of small sub-farms, as well as the dike portion of each (Dike roll, *CCM,* Part IV, 2nd Section, IV Cap., "No. XVIII," cc. 305-326). According to this directory, which was given in rods (3.777 meters), royal estates accounted for more than twenty-six kilometers—that is, over 50% of the total length of the dike (6,573 rods for the Lebus estate and 340 rods for the Quartschen estate). As such, the king was able to influence dike construction and maintenance decisively through the royal head bailiffs who administered his lands. Similarly, the villages and estates of the Order of St. John and those of the Margrave of Sonnenburg—all of which were owned by Margrave Karl Albrechts of Brandenburg-Sonnenburg, a member of the Prussian royal family—totaled 1,490 rods. In addition to these, villages that were held by nobility or that were part of noble fiefs (held by seventeen noble families and their lines) accounted for 4,217 rods. Finally, 1,075 village peasants were listed in the dike roll. The allocation of the rods reveals the social structure of village mayors, farmers, cottagers, small farmers, and other peasants. Their section of the dike amounted to 9,722 rods of a total 13,429. They were thus the portion most heavily burdened with maintenance work (72%) and, as shown later, even more duties. (See table 7.)

THE ROLE OF THE LOCAL FEUDAL LORDS

Given the limited technological, communication, and transportation capacities in the early modern period, the practical securing of dike facilities in Prussia was a local duty. According to the *Realprinzip,* everyone who had land in the protected area was required to participate in flood control measures (Führ 1967, 5, Kluth 1997, 164-165). They were bound to this by a system that combined governmental legislation with forms of self-administration. Under a small staff of government officials, the *Deichinteressenten*—as members of the dike association—were required to act in accordance with the principles established by the king in the dike decree, particularly in securing the dike at their own expense and keeping drainage ditches in the diked area in good order. At the same time, the *Deichinteressenten* were integrated into the system as so-called *Mit-Urteiler,* or coinspectors. This applied to representatives of feudal property holders, as well as to the Church and feudal

TABLE 7. Dike Assignments in the Upper Oderbruch, in Rods/Feet

Feudal Lordship	Item	Rods/Feet	Peasants	Rods/Feet	Fd. Op.	Rods/Feet
Roy. Demesnes (incl. L., G. &. S.)	25 ½	6.913/2	649	5.855/10	9	1.057/4
Noble Manors & Adelslehne	12 ²/₂	4.217/2	235	2.712/6	16	1.504/8
Order of St. John, Commanderie	3	963/5	77	577/5	2	386/0
Mgr. of Sonnenburg, Demesne	1 ½	617/4	106	552/4	1	65/0
University of Frankfurt/Oder	1	24/0	8	24/0	—	—
Total Villages (incl. L., G. & S.)	44	12.735/1	1.075	9.722/1	28	3.013/0
City of Küstrin (incl. New. Ch.)	1	694/0	n. i.	n. i.	1	88/0
Total	45	13.429/1	1.075			3.101/0

NOTE: Item = villages and towns; Fd. Op. = feudal operations; roy. = royal; incl. L. G. & S. = villages on the royal demesnes including the small towns of Lebus, Göritz, and Seelow; Mgr. of Sonnenburg = Margrave of Brandenburg-Sonnenburg; incl. New. Ch. = incl. land of the Chamber of royal demesnes of the New March of Brandenburg; n.i. = no information.

holders of farmer, cottager, small landholder, and tenant parcels who were represented by their village mayors (village leader and village judge) and jury men (assessors of the village court) (*CCM,* Part IV, 2nd Section, IV Cap., "No. XVIII," ch. X, cc. 332–333).

Local feudal lords (two head bailiffs of royal estates as representatives of the king, noble manor lords, the master of the knights, and a commander of the Order of St. John, as well as the city as a bearer of feudal rights) were included. They were affected in three ways:

1. As owners of manorial agricultural operations in the bottomlands, each of whom had to maintain their own sections of the dike for their own interest and those of the dike association;
2. As *Mit-Urtheiler* of the dike area who shared responsibility for dike inspection and for determining what work and penalties were necessary;
3. As manor and judicial lords—that is, as local rulers—of peasants living in the villages (*CCM,* Part IV, 2nd Section, IV Cap., "No. XVIII," ch. X, cc. 332–333).

THE LEADING ROLE OF THE NOBILITY AND OTHER BEARERS OF FEUDAL RIGHTS IN THE EAST ELBIAN COUNTRYSIDE

The free settlement relationships were established in Brandenburg in the course of the eastward expansion during the Middle Ages (after 1150); thereafter, settler society was refeudalized. In the late thirteenth century, the first monasteries were enfeoffed with villages, which until then had been part of the margravate. This was followed by the granting of fiefs in and around the villages to the knights who had conquered Brandenburg for the margraves. As such, the system of feudal lord-ship with tribute—at first minor services—and of the manor lords as the full own-ers of the farms was revived. In 1319, the death of Margrave Waldemar destroyed Brandenburg's internal stability for the next century. Monasteries, the nobility, religious orders, and cities obtained additional rights from the territorial sovereign—particularly judicial lordships, which the documents termed the "higher and lower courts" (Assing 1995, 140, 156-157, Winkelmann 2011, 146-147). It was at first a question of dispensing justice, which strengthened manorial authority vis-à-vis their peasants, and of the court income obtained therefrom. The responsibility for local administration thus resulted in the increasing prominence of magistrate character. This seigneurial authority was replaced by manorial authority in the sixteenth century. Village inhabitants were made manorial subjects (personal serfs in areas near Brandenburg's eastern border) who were obliged—besides paying cash rents—to perform servile labor, were bound to the soil (the personal serfs bound to the feudal lord), and were subject to weak ownership rights *(lassitisches Recht)*, and their children were forced to work in the manor house and farms *(Gesindezwangdienst)*.[36] Owning large manors, lords exercised seigneurial and jurisdictional control, as well as patronage of the church. They were, in modern parlance, the local tax authorities, registration office, trade licensing office, officers of the local church, and the largest commercial enterprise; they also controlled the mills and breweries that peasants had to use. Moreover, because they filled peasant positions and had the right to approve marriages, they had considerable influence on individual peasant families.

In 1653, Elector Frederick William of Brandenburg further strengthened the position of the local feudal lords—especially the nobility—based on claims of runaway peasants, entitlement to "unreasonable" servile labor, and the continu-ance of personal serfdom in areas where it already existed. Noblemen were to fill higher positions in public administration and the military. These concessions and offers were made by the elector in exchange for the power to raise taxes at his own discretion, and to free key policy issues from the influence of the territo-rial estates. Before the start of dike construction, bearers of feudal rights consti-tuted an unavoidable force in the rural power structure. Since local nobles were extremely wary of interference in their home domains, they carried out the lowest duties of the military administration (Harnisch 1996, 141, 144), and took over the duties of school patronage after the introduction of compulsory school attendance (Neugebauer 1985, 255-260). The princely estates into which the elector or, after 1701, king divided his land were very similar to the farms of the nobility. These large operations were called *Vorwerke*. Beginning in the time of Frederick William I, these royal estates, or *Ämter*, were leased to citizens. While *Amtmänner* acted economically like noble landowners and were responsible for numerous magistrate issues, they did not exercise any higher judicial authority and were bound by instructions in many areas—such as dike construction. All in all, the legal and ownership conditions of peasants on the estates of the king and the Order of St. John, as well as of the towns, were organized in a more tolerable manner than on the estates of the nobility (Müller 1981, 318).

THE FUNCTIONS OF THE DIKE ASSOCIATIONS
AFTER 1717

The highest supervisory responsibility was held by the captain of the dike of the upper Oderbruch, under whom were two dike counts each responsible for half of the dike's length. Under these dike counts were three dike masters who performed inspection functions, as well as enforcement functions with *Deichinteressenten* who had shirked their duties. *Deichinteressenten* were required to appear in their respective dike sections twice a year as *Mit-Urtheiler* before the dike inspection commission. The captain of the dike recorded damage and the penalties incurred. Fines and levies were to be settled on this occasion between the authorities and village mayors (*CCM*, Part IV, 2nd Section, IV Cap., "No. XVIII," ch. XV. and XVI., cc. 336–340). A dike financial official kept records of the dike association's income and outlays. Six pfennig per dike rod were to be paid annually; this money and any fines collected were used to pay state employees and to finance any construction that individual villages and so on were unable to perform themselves. (See figure 11.)[37]

At first glance, it would appear that a group of *Deichinteressenten*—who were equals in principle—were considered *Mit-Urtheiler* and that *Deichinteressenten* were distinguished solely by the length of their dike section and not by their social status. However, the head bailiffs and the noble manor lords actually had more power than other commission members. Whether nobles exercised the authority themselves or were represented by subordinates (administrators)—due to their other duties as officers or government officials—they nonetheless organized the affairs of their villages and farming property themselves and were involved in all important affairs of their peasants at the lowest judicial level ("self-acting manor lords") (Kaak 1995, 78). While ruling over farm and village, they were closely linked to the possessions of the peasants. In the first half of the eighteenth century, the manorial parcels of land were complexly intertwined with those of the peasants (Kaak 1991, 69). The head bailiffs and manor lords had the right, derived from their judicial authority, to receive servile labor from their peasants (farm work, haulage service, and extraordinary services). This constituted a large percentage of the labor performed on the demesnes and manors in the eighteenth century. The maintenance of the lord's dike rods became a new area in which peasant farmers, cottagers, and the like could be utilized as servile laborers—and a shifting line formed between dike labor and extraordinary labor as a result (Kaak 1999, 138–144).

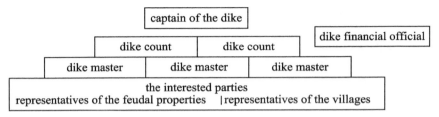

FIGURE 11. Organigram: The Hierarchy of the Dike Control (Upper Oderbruch)

MEANS OF ENFORCEMENT AND
ADDITIONAL PROJECTS

The use of means of enforcement refers to subsequent projects. The most serious punishment that the master of the dike could threaten or impose was so-called military execution. In August 1716, King Frederick William I ordered all regiments in the area to be at the ready to compel the necessary support efforts. This principle was confirmed in the dike decree of 1716 (*CCM,* Part IV, 2nd Section, IV Cap., "No. XVII," cc. 304). The general threat of this particular measure was clearly sufficient for construction work up to 1717. However, disputes over additional dikes increased in the face of the earlier project's consequences. The waters of the Oder had been pushed toward the east bank and larger quantities flowed through the Oderbruch into the lower marshlands, which acted as collecting tank. The construction of 1716-1717 forced a continuation of the enforcement measures, which in turn led to the heightened potential for conflict.

The use of military execution did not entail individuals being put to death. Rather, it involved situating soldiers in the houses of rebellious peasants, and putting pressure on them to provide shelter and food; it was intended to create a willingness to perform work and make payments. Manor lords also made use of this execution when peasants refused to perform other servile labor, as the conditions in which the law could be used were not stipulated precisely. As such, a gray zone developed. This included the use of military service, which manor lords often used to shield their land and peasants, while noble officers—often manor lords themselves—supported them (Kaak 2010, 182-184, 268-270).

As larger and more complicated work was undertaken to build dikes in the lower Oderbruch, attempts to sabotage construction emerged in 1747. Consequently, Frederick II increased the degree of punishment and ordered the use of the *Karrenstrafe* against saboteurs. In the *Karrenstrafe,* infringers were made to work on the construction of fortifications while chained to carts for weeks or months on a diet of bread and water (Kaak 2010, 183, 370). This affected the fishermen, whose basis of existence worsened radically after the area was drained; while the lives of farmers, cottagers, and the like improved.

Despite the complications, dike construction and the cultivation of the lower Oderbruch, between 1747 and 1752, proved a great success in terms of both economics and propaganda. Although the first generation of new settlers was not free of servile and menial labor duties, they did have a right to their land that resembled real ownership—unlike the older *lassitisch*[38] peasant inhabitants. Once again, the king was dominant and controlled nearly half of all the developed parcels. The previously mentioned margrave and master of the knights, Karl Albrecht, who owned more than a quarter of the cultivated area, also played an important role in the central Oderbruch. It was he who established colonist villages and demesnes on the Quilitz and Friedland margravate estates and on the neighboring Grüneberg estate of the Order of St. Johns. Noble families and cities shared a further area (Kaak 2012, 179-180). Indeed, while this dike was "only" about forty kilometers long, the effort and risk were greater. This risk was due to shortening of the Oder by some twenty kilometers using a canal, and because drainage facilities played a much larger role. According to the dike decree of 1769, the *Deichinteressenten* of the upper Oderbruch also shared the responsibility for sections of the lower Oderbruch (*NCC*, Vol. IV, 1769, "No. 7," cc. 5123-5125).

As a result of the success of dike construction in the Oderbruch, Frederick II was overly hasty in ordering the cultivation of the Netzebruch and Warthebruch in 1770. After the Netzebruch had been successfully drained, the Dike, Riverbank, and Trench Decree for the bottomlands was issued in 1779 (*NCC*, Vol. VI, 1779, "No. XLII"). In the beginning, favorable weather resulted in settlement of the areas in the lower Warthe before the dike there was completely finished. In 1775, however, a flood destroyed much of the finished work in the Warthebruch. Furthermore, the topography of the area was more difficult to convert to a closed polder landscape than the Oderbruch had been. There were parallels between the lower Warthe and the upper Oderbruch: in the latter, dike work and cultivation were performed around the royal Lebus estate, while in the former it was the Order of St. John with its extensive holdings at the Hospitaller Sonnenburg estate (10,000 ha) that determined the course of events (Kaak 2012, 183–184). The nobility played a smaller role than the Order, colonizing cities, and middle-class property owners. The original idea of Frederick II and his youngest brother August Ferdinand—who became the master of Knights of the Order of St. John in 1763—was to provide large parcels of land for the settlement of more significant colonists (economically stable, full acquisition areas, or *Vollerwerbsstellen*) and thus provide a model for melioration on the manor estates of the other feudal landowners. Consequently, a dike decree was issued in 1802 (*NCC*, Vol. XI, 1802, "No. XX.").

WHO ACHIEVED WHAT IN PARTICULAR?

The cultivation of the lowlands of the Oder, Netze, and Warthe showed itself to be an extremely successful project in several respects. The protected farmland with its dikes and drainage facilities became a symbol of Prussia's talent for innovation in the public opinion of the rest of Europe.

This reclaimed land was seen as the act of a far-sighted king. At first, however, this was only true to a certain degree in the upper Oderbruch. Gottfried Wentz writes in his publication on the history of the Oderbruch:

> In the reorganization of the conditions in the upper Oderbruch, the king [Frederick William I] was thinking and acting like a large landowner. The intrinsic value of viable farms as economic factors was not recognized, rather rural inhabitants were considered only in their capacity as villeins, a source of service and payment. (Wentz 1930, 169)

Indeed, after 1722, an expansion of the already-dominant royal properties in the Oderbruch took place in the upper Oderbruch, first because the king claimed large portions of the cultivated land for his own estates, and second because he purchased the noble villages of the families von Burgsdorf, von Kameke, von der Marwitz, von Pfuhl, and von Sydow. While property of the nobility totaled about 30% of the dike rods in the upper Oderbruch in 1717, it began to decline. Indeed, the very large Lebus royal estate acquired so much new farmland and so many new settlers that it was subdivided several times after 1736. In addition, two new estates were established. Although Friedrich Wilhelm I's governmental activities in this area did resemble those of a large landowner, Wentz's criticism is grossly exaggerated. He overlooks that first of all the king protected the inhabitants—including those who did not own land and who were thus not obliged to make payments or provide service—and he ordered the construction of infrastructure in the populated areas. Not until the second step did he help the state project *Bruchkultivierung* (marsh cultivation) achieve a new scale. Without subscribing to the Oderbruch mythos, one can say that an important development was then completed, one that had been conceived as part of an entire spectrum of innovative political measures.

When his son Friedrich II continued the colonization of the lower Oderbruch shortly after 1750, he was able to take advantage of organizational models that helped him protect inhabitants and to expand agriculture in the river bottomlands, which in turn supported other state goals. The fact that in the Seven Years' War he risked everything he had achieved is another story.

In 1752, Margrave Karl Albrecht, the master of the Knights of the Order of St. John, started establishing colonies and demesnes on the order's properties in the central Oderbruch before expanding this work to his neighboring margravate leased estates. The work complied with the ideas of Frederick II; however, as Frederick's older relative, he took the liberty of proceeding according to his own plan. His successor, Prince August Ferdinand, Frederick's younger brother, was faced with a much larger task on the Warthe and took a largely subordinate role to the king as a sort of junior partner. Under his tenure, numerous colonies and demesne farms—some with foreign names (Ceylon, Havannah, Pensylvanien, Philadelphia, Saratoga, Savannah, Sumatra)—were established. And indeed, the revenues of the Order of St. John doubled between 1763 and 1811.

In the lower Oderbruch, nobility with 18% of the land were involved in reclamation, while in the Warthebruch, where even less noble colonies were established, Lords von Waldow and von Wreech were particularly conspicuous in this regard. Town property played a bigger role than it did in the Oderbruch. Indeed, the town Landsberg an der Warthe on its own outperformed by far the limited reclamation activities of the towns Oderberg, Wriezen, and Freienwalde.

In principle, Frederick William I and Frederick II pursued economic goals when they reclaimed land while the nobility focused on business goals. Despite serious setbacks the kings, the margrave, and the prince were successful in creating fundamentally secure farmland of the highest profitability out of the river bottomlands, securing the existing royal villages—as well as those of feudal lords and towns. They also succeeded in significantly concentrating the population through settlement under improved law and in stabilizing the general provision of foodstuffs. The amount of time and the cost of reclaiming land increased significantly from one area to another. The large requirement spent by the state treasuries on construction was money the kings considered well spent. This was easy to accept because the royal property in Oderbruch grew along with its resident population. This well-secured and highly productive agricultural area provided additional income for state coffers, which could be used to improve infrastructure inside and outside the dike area (waterways, canals, bridges, postal systems), to create a school system as well as to improve the quality of the science, and, last but not least, to strengthen the standing army.

However, in the Warthebruch the stated goal of settling large areas with large numbers of colonists was only partially achieved. Because of dwindling demand from prospective settlers, part of the land was formed into demesne farms that also proved to be extremely productive.

The situation of the long-established manor subjects or serfs only improved slowly during the diking and cultivation. Their rights of possession improved in small steps but they were only rarely able to win their freedom. A number of them were even placed on *Kleinststellen* under conditions similar to the corvee system to work the new demenses of the Order of St. John.

When most of the new settlers enjoyed personal freedom and were free from servile labor duties, able to develop their own production, largely independent of one another, and unencumbered by the three-field system, an important goal had been reached (Kaak 2004b, 99–101). However, the influence on noble landholders was tentative.

In the marsh areas all of this contributed to the self-esteem of the inhabitants because it strengthened their awareness gradually of their own share in progress and in the increasing income. For this they continued to deal with manorial lords and the managers of the princely estates on many issues. Like the royal and the Order's demesnes, as well as the noble manors, the villages also were members of the dike associations. The delegation of responsibility had been experimented with in the upper Oderbruch, and later used in the rest of the Oderbruch, as well as the Netzebruch and

Warthebruch. Even if compulsory membership involved onerous work and financial burdens, it demonstrated that the population of the cultivated bottomlands accepted the region—with its steadily improved dike and drainage facilities—as its own.

NOTES

1. This contribution uses the older German names for these rivers: Netze (now Noteć) and Warthe (now Warta).

2. Until 1316, the Neuzelle monastery built a dike along the Oder and the Lausatian Neisse. Cf. Krüger and Oelze 2014, 330.

3. Danube: Mohila and Michlmayr 1996, Géra n.d. Moldava: Neuhäusl, Moravec, and Neuhäusl-Novotná 1965, 401.

4. Müller 1813, 503-504. To date, there have been 295 floods in Saint Petersburg. To control the flooding of the Great Neva, its shores and the three main canals were lined with Karelian granite.

5. Sava: Maissen 2002, 478-479. Drava: Michor 2014, 351-352.

6. Tweed: Boucher 1963, 130. Thames: Porter 1998, 192-193, 227, 264. Severn: Knapp 1979, 70.

7. The dike decree of Eiderstadt of 1595, the dike decree of Tondern of 1619, Royal Danish dike decree of 1634.

8. Menschentränke = Großes Ertrinken; a flood in which many people drowned.

9. In particular, Jakubowski-Tiessen 1992, 57-59, Egidius 2003, 104-105. General-Deichgraf = supreme dike reeve.

10. This is indicated by the Dutch dike decree of 1253, the dike decree of Düsselt and Cleverham of 1323, the first dike decree of Cleves of 1343, and the dike decree of Bremen of 1473. Cf. *ALZ*, col. 732.

11. Beginning in the sixteenth century, although some hold that they originated in the fourteenth century. Cf. Gasch and Twele 2013, 342.

12. *CBLLG*, Cap. VIII, Sectio 4: Von Teich = Sachen, "Nr. LXXII," §§15, 19, 192, 193. Ober = , Haupt =, und Amtleute = supreme supervisors, district, and local magistrates.

13. Dike roll: *CCM*, Part IV, 2nd Section, IV Cap., "No. VIII," cc. 273-286. Cf. Berghaus 1845, 218.

14. Schulze 1890, 378: Deichverbände and 416: Gesetz über das Deichverbändewesen von 1848.

15. *PrALR*, 1089. Intentional breaching of the dike in which flooding results in fatalities was punishable by death.

16. Spiegelberg 2001, 106-109. On the development of the dike associations in Prussia, cf. Armenat 2010, 116-118.

17. *JbSPS*, 80. Until 1866, in northwest Germany only North Friesland was part of Prussia (1744-1807); the kingdom was the dominant state in eastern Germany with a considerable exclave on the Rhine. The north German sea dike associations are not included here because Prussia did not annex a large part of north Germany until 1867.

18. Merck 1962, 732–733: "Instead of by an election, the chairman and his deputy were named to their office by supervisory authorities." The law remained in force in the FRG until 1991, when a series of sections were declared void and the law was supplemented by another state law. Its by-laws were enacted by its supervisory authorities.

19. There are, for example, twenty-two dike associations in Lower Saxony, ten in Schleswig-Holstein, two in Bremen, and one in Hamburg. Length of dike sections, for example: eleven dike associations on the Aller (Lower Saxony) with 69.1 kilometers, an average of 6.28 kilometers of dikes per dike association.

20. 1220-1235 recorded by Eike von Repgow, with partial effect until the introduction of the Civil Code in Germany 1900.

21. "Swelke dorp bi watere lieget unde enen dam hebbet, die sie vor der vlut bewaret, jewelk dorp sal sinen deil des dames vestenen vor der vlut. Kumt aver die vlut unde brict sie den dam, unde ladet

man mit deme gerüchte dar to, die binnen deme damme geseten sien, svelk ir nicht ne helpt büten den dam, die hevet verworcht so gedan erve als he binnen deme damme hevst." Cf. *SSp, L, V.*

22. "Keen nich will dieken, de mut wieken" or "Wer nicht will deichen, der muss weichen." Cf. Kühn 1992, 83.

23. *DOHB,* 83, § 1: "shall be burned according to the common rights." Cf. Allemeyer 2006, 103, Mellmann 1795, 126.

24. Richness in fish: cf. Christiani 1855, 13–16. Loss of the richness: cf. Kaup 1994, 126–128. Resistance of the fishermen: cf. Wentz 1930, 111–114, 118.

25. Rita Gudermann counts the Oderbruch after the dike construction and bursting of dikes in the years 1770, 1771, 1780, 1785, 1829, and 1830 and so on. Cf. Gudermann 1999, 376.

26. On the activities of Frederick II, also see Kouschil 2012.

27. Wentz 1930, 97: "Beginning around the end of the sixteenth century, lively attention was paid to dike facilities on the Oder."

28. CCM, Part IV, 2nd Section, IV Cap., "No. XVII," cc. 294-295. Amt Lebus = royal demesne of Lebus.

29. Immediatstädte *(civitates)* were directly under the head of state (here the electors of Brandenburg, after 1701 kings of Prussia) and were thus independent of local feudal lords.

30. Mediatstädte *(oppida)* were under local feudal lords. Regarding the *Mediatstädte* in Lebus, cf. Vetter 1996.

31. Here feudal operations are understood to cover the large manor farms of the nobility and the demesnes of the king, as well as the Order of St. John, and other village lords—including universities.

32. Royal estates were feudal districts comprising several villages and demesnes; they were also called domains. The town of Seelow was part of the royal Lebus estate.

33. A noble family's fief possession that was part of a tenure of another noble family, feudal corporation, and so on.

34. The German Reich of 1871 was divided into two parts of similar size by the Elbe River, of which the northeastern (i.e., the East Elbian part) was more heavily dominated by the nobility.

35. For example, the villages of Gusow and Platkow were without manorial operations under the same noble lord, although the peasants from Platkow had to work in Gusow; similarly, the margravate peasants from Quappendorf had to serve at the manor of Quilitz, cf. Kniehase 1995, Kaak 2010, 76–77.

36. Kaak 1991, 224, Neugebauer 2009, 175. Lassitischer Besitz = Lassbesitz = ceded *(überlassen)* to the peasants for their use. Gesindezwangdienst = compulsory farm service of the subject children.

37. 80.574 d = 3.357 1/4 gr = 279 3/4 Taler.

38. See note 36.

REFERENCES

Literature

Allemeyer, Marie Luisa (2006). *"Kein Land ohne Deich—!": Lebenswelten einer Küstengesellschaft in der Frühen Neuzeit.* Max-Planck-Institut für Geschichte 222. Göttingen, Vandenhoeck & Ruprecht.

Armenat, Manuela (2010). *Die "vollkommene Ausbildung" der Schwartzen Elster: Eine multidimensionale Studie zur Wasserwirtschaft und zum Kulturlandschaftswandel, 1800–1945,* Münster, Waxmann.

Assing, Helmut (1995). "Die Landesherrschaft der Askanier, Wittelsbacher und Luxemburger (Mitte des 12. bis Anfang des 15. Jahrhunderts)." In *Brandenburgische Geschichte,* edited by Ingo Materna and Wolfgang Ribbe, 85–168. Berlin, Akademie.

Becker, Hartmuth (2002). *Die Kategorie öffentlicher Güter als Grundlage von Staatstheorie und Staatswissenschaft.* Berlin, Duncker & Humblot.

Berendsen, Hendrik J. A., and Esther Stouthammer (2001). *Palaeographic Developement of the Rhine-Meuse Delta*. Assen, Koninklijke Van Gorcum.

Berghaus, Heinrich (1854). *Landbuch der Mark Brandenburg und des Markgrafthums Nieder-Lausitz in der Mitte des 19. Jahrhunderts*. Vol. 1. Brandenburg/Havel, Verlag Adolph Müller.

Bochalli, Alfred, ed. (1913). *Die Wassergenossenschaften nach dem neuen preußischen Wassergesetze: Kommentar zum dritten Abschnitt des Wassergesetzes unter besonderer Berücksichtigung der wasserwirtschaftlichen Meliorationen mit den einschlägigen Ministerialerlassen*. Berlin, Parey.

Boeselager, Elke Freifrau von (2003). "Sturmfluten an der norddeutschen Küste im Mittelalter—Erlebnis und Konsequenz." In *Natur im Mittelalter: Konzeptionen—Erfahrungen—Wirkungen. Akten des 9. Symposions des Mediävistenverbandes*, edited by Peter Dilg, 227-242. Berlin, De Gruyter.

Bohn, Robert (2006). *Geschichte Schleswig-Holsteins*. Munich, C. H. Beck.

Boucher, Cyril T. G. (1963). *John Rennie, 1761-1821: The Life and Work of a Great Engineer*. Manchester, Manchester University Press.

Bratring, Friedrich Wilhelm August (1968). *Statistisch-topographische Beschreibung der gesamten Marck Brandenburg*. Critically reviewed and improved new edition. Veröffentlichungen der Historischen Kommission zu Berlin 22. Berlin, De Gruyter.

Campbell, Brian (2012). *Rivers and the Power of Ancient Rome*. Chapel Hill, University of North Carolina Press.

Christiani, Walter (1855). *Das Oderbruch: Historische Skizze*. 2nd ed. Wriezen/Oder, E. Roeder.

Dörr, Oliver (1995). *Die Inkorporation als Tatbestand der Staatensukzession*. Berlin, Dunker & Humblot.

Egidius, Hans (2003). *Tod und Verderben an der Nordseeküste von Flandern bis Jütland*. Varel, CCV Concept Center.

Ehlers, Paul, and Richard Winkel (1947). *Bau, Unterhaltung und Verteidigung der Flussdeiche*. 2nd ed. Berlin, Wilhelm Ernst & Sohn.

Ey, Johannes (2005). "Früher Deichbau und Entwässerung im nordwestdeutschen Küstengebiet." In *Ruralia V: Water Management in Meval Rural Economy*, edited by Jan Klápště, Jean-Michel Poisson, and André Bazzana, Památky Archeologické, Supplementum 17, 146-151. Prag, Instituye of Archaeology.

Fossey, John M. (1991). "The City Archive at Koroneia." In *Studies in Boiotian Inscriptions*, edited by John M. Fossey, Epigraphica Boeotica 1:5-26. Amsterdam, Brill.

Führ, Heinz-Bodo (1967). *Das Selbstverwaltungsrecht der Wasser- und Bodenverbände unter dem Einfluß staatlicher Finanzhilfen*. Berlin, Ernst-Reuter-Gesellschaft.

Garcia, Xavier-François, and Martin Pusch (2002). "Ökologische Auswirkungen unterschiedlicher Verbauungsweise an Elbe, Loire und Garonne im Vergleich." In *Die Elbe—Neue Horizonte des Flussgebietsmanagements. 10. Magdeburger Gewässersemeinar*, edited by Walter Geller et al., 305-306. Stuttgart, Leipzig and Wiesbaden, Teubner.

Gasch, Robert, and Jochen Twele, eds. (2013). *Windkraftanlagen: Grundlagen, Entwurf, Planung und Betrieb*. Wiesbaden, Teubner.

Géra, Eleonóra (n.d.). "Entwässerung von Sümpfen und Landnutzung in Ofen-Pest und seiner Umgebung im 18. Jahrhundert." In *Migration und Melioration in der*

Habsburgermonarchie im Vergleich zu Preußen und anderen deutschen Saaten zwischen 1700 und 1850, edited by Márta Fata.

Gudermann, Rita (1999). "Zur Bedeutung der friederizianischen Landeskulturmaßnahen—Mythos und Realität." In *Leben und Arbeiten auf märkischem Sand: Wege in die Gesellschaftsgeschichte Brandenburgs 1700-1914,* edited by Ralf Pröve and Bernd Kölling, 351-377. Bielefeld, Verlag für Regionalgeschichte.

Harnisch, Hartmut (1996). "Preußisches Kantonsystem und ländliche Gesellschaft: Das Beispiel der mittleren Kammerdepartements." In *Krieg und Frieden: Militär und Gesellschaft in der frühen Neuzeit,* edited by Bernhard R. Kroener and Ralf Pröve, 137-165. Paderborn a. e., Schöningh.

Hattenhauer, Hans, ed. (1996). *Allgemeines Landrecht für die preußischen Staaten von 1794.* 3rd expanded edition. Neuwied a. e., Luchterhand.

Hofmeister, Adolf E. (1980). *Besiedlung und Verfassung der Stader Elbmarschen im Mittelalter,* Vol. 2, *Die Hollerkolonisation und die Landesgemeinden Land Kehdingen und Altes Land.* Veröffentlichungen des Instituts für Historische Landesforschung der Universität Göttingen 14. Hildesheim, Lax.

Jäger, Helmut (1988). "Frühe Umwelten in Mitteleuropa." *Siedlungsforschung. Archäologie-Geschichte-Geographie* 6:9-24.

Jakubowski-Tiessen, Manfred (1992). *Sturmflut 1717: Die Bewältigung einer Naturkatastrophe in der Frühen Neuzeit.* Munich, De Gruyter.

Jakubowski-Tiessen, Martin (2009). "Naturkatastrophen: Was wurde aus ihnen gelernt?" In *Umweltgeschichte und Umweltzukunft: Zur gesellschaftlichen Relevanz einer jungen Disziplin,* edited by Patrick Masius, 173-186. Göttingen, Universitätsverlag Göttingen.

Kaak, Heinrich (1991). *Die Gutsherrschaft: Theoriegeschichtliche Untersuchungen zum ostelbischen Agrarwesen.* Veröffentlichungen der Historischen Kommission zu Berlin 79. Berlin and New York, De Gruyter.

――― (1995). "Vermittelte, selbsttätige und maternale Gutsherrschaft, Formen gutsherrlicher Durchsetzung, Behauptung und Gestaltung in Quilitz-Friedland im 18. Jahrhundert." In *Konflikt und Kontrolle in Gutsherrschaftsgesellschaften,* edited by Jan Peters, 54-117. Göttingen, Vandenhoeck & Ruprecht.

――― (1999). "Brandenburgische Bauern im 18. Jahrhundert: Sozialgeschichtliche Untersuchungen in mikrohistorischer Perspektive." In *Leben und Arbeiten auf märkischen Sand: Wege in die Gesellschaftsgeschichte Brandenburgs, 1700-1914,* edited by Ralf Pröve and Bernd Kölling, 120-148. Bielefeld, Verlag für Regionalgeschichte.

――― (2004a). "From Fishing Village to Farming Village: Quappendorf an der Oder in the Eighteenth Century." In *Modernisation and Tradition: European Local and Manorial Societies, 1500-1900,* edited by Kerstin Sundberg, Tomas Germundsson, and Kjell Hanssen, 222-242. Lund, Nordic Academic Press.

――― (2004b). "Ländliche Bevölkerung zwischen Anpassung und Offensive: Wege der sozialen und wirtschaftlichen Behauptung von Dörfern im zentralen Oderbruch zwischen 1720 und 1850." *Zeitschrift für Agrargeschichte und Agrarsoziologie 52: Themenband: Agrarentwicklung im 18. und 19. Jahrhundert:* 84-101.

――― (2010). *Eigenwillige Bauern, ehrgeizige Amtmänner, distanzierte fürstliche Dorfherren: Vermittelte Herrschaft im brandenburgischen Alt-Quilitz im 17. und 18. Jahrhundert.* Berlin, Berliner Wissenschaftsverlag.

——— (2012). *Korporative Gutsherrschaft und Agrarinnovationen in Preußen—der Johanniterorden auf seinen neumärkischen Ämtern 1750 bis 1811.* Berlin, Berliner Wissenschaftsverlag.

Kaup, Martina (1994). "Die Urbarmachung des Oderbruchs: Umwelt-historische Annäherung an ein bekanntes Thema." In *Umweltgeschichte—Methoden, Themen, Potentiale: Tagung des Hamburger Arbeitskreises für Umweltgeschichte,* edited by Günther Bayerl, Norman Fuchsloch, and Torsten Meyer, 111-133. Hamburg, Waxmann.

Kluth, Winfried (1997). *Funktionale Selbstverwaltung: Verfassungsrechtlicher Status—verfassungsrechtlicher Schutz.* Tübingen, Mohr Siebeck.

Knapp, Brian J. (1979). *Elements of Geographical Hydrology.* London, George Allen & Unwin.

Knauss, Jost (1987). *Die Melioration des Kopaisbeckens durch die Minyer im 2. Jt. v. Chr. Generelle Forschungsergebnisse, 1985-1987.* Wasserbau und Siedlungsbedingungen im Altertum 2. Munich a. e., Technische Universität München.

——— (1990). "Zur Datierung der Deukalionischen Flut in der Kopais." *Teiresias* 20:19-25.

Kniehase, Friedrich (1995). *Das Oderbruch: Slawische und deutsche Siedlungsgenese seit dem hohen Mittelalter.* Leverkusen, Verlag für geographische und historische Wissenschaften.

Kouschil, Christa (2012). *Landesausbau in der Neumark unter Friedrich II. Bäuerliche Besitz- und Abhängigkeitsverhältnisse im unteren Warthebruch (18. Jahrhundert bis Mitte des 19. Jahrhunderts).* Berlin, Edition Bodoni.

Krämer, Rosemarie (1984). "Damm und Deich." In *Reallexikon der germanischen Altertumskunde,* edited by Johannes Hoops and Heinrich Beck, Vol. 5, *Chronos-Dona,* 222-223. 2nd, rev. and expanded ed. Berlin and New York, De Gruyter.

Krüger, Frank, and Marko Oelze (2014). "Das Deichbauprogramm an der Oder—der Praxistest 2010." In *Vorsorgender und nachsorgender Hochwasserschutz: Ausgewählte Beiträge aus der Fachzeitschrift Wasser Wirtschaft,* edited by Stephan Heimerl and Heribert Meyer, 330-337. Wiesbaden, Springer Vieweg.

Kühn, Hans Joachim (1992). *Anfänge des Deichbaus in Schleswig-Holstein.* Heide, Boyens Buchverlag.

Ledyard, John O. (1995). "Public Goods: A Survey of Experimental Research." In *The Handbook of Experimental Economics,* edited by John H. Kagel and Alvin E. Roth, 111-194. Princeton, Princeton University Press.

Ludwig, Karl Heinz (1961). *Zur Besiedlung des Weichseldeltas durch die Mennoniten: Die Siedlungen der Mennoniten im Territorium der Stadt Elbing und in der Ökonomie Marienburg bis zur Übernahme der Gebiete durch Preußen 1772.* Marburg, J. G. Herder-Institut.

Maissen, Anna Pia (2002). "Pferde, Schiffe und eiserne Träume: Die Verkehrsinfrastruktur Kroatiens in der zweiten Hälfte des 19. Jahrhunderts und die Rolle Baron Lazar Hellenbachs in der Eisenbahnfrage." In *Wege der Kommunikation in der Geschichte Osteuropas,* edited by Nada Boškovska, Peter Collmer, Seraina Gilly, Rudolf Mumenthaler, and Christoph von Werth, 275-502. Cologne, Weimar, and Vienna, Böhlau.

Melchers, Thorsten (2002). *Ostfriesland: Preußens atypische Provinz? Preußische Integrationspolitik im 18. Jahrhundert.* Thesis, University of Oldenburg.

Mellmann, Johann Dietrich (1795). *Einleitung in das gemeine Damm = Deich = Siel = und Schleusen = Recht.* Altona and Leipzig, Kavensche Buchhandlung.

Merck, Wilhelm (1962). *Deutsches Verwaltungsrecht.* Vol. 1. Berlin, Duncker & Humblot.

Michor, Klaus (2014). "Die Obere Drau in Kärnten—ein Beispiel für Hochwasserschutz mit Mehrwert." In *Vorsorgender und nachsorgender Hochwasserschutz: Ausgewählte*

Zusammenstellung rund um das Thema Hochwasser, edited by Stephan Heimerl and Heribert Meyer, 351–358. Wiesbaden, Springer Vieweg.

Mohila, Peter, and Franz Michlmayr (1996). *Donauatlas Wien: Geschichte der Donauregulierung mit Karten und Plänen aus vier Jahrhunderten/Atlas of the Danube River Vienna: A History of River Training on Maps and Plants of four Centuries.* Vienna, Österreichischer Kunst- u. Kulturverlag.

Müller, Christian (1813). *Sankt Petersburg: Ein Beitrag zur Geschichte unserer Zeit in Briefen von 1810, 1811 und 1812.* Mainz, Florian Kupferberg.

Müller, Hans Heinrich (1981). "Domänen und Domänenpächter in Preußen im 18. Jahrhundert." In *Moderne Preußische Geschichte 1648–1947: Eine Anthologie,* edited by Otto Büsch and Wolfgang Neugebauer, Veröffentlichungen der Historischen Kommission zu Berlin 52, vol. 1, 316–359. Berlin and New York, De Gruyter.

Nawotki, Kathrin (2004). *Die schleswigsche Deichstavengerechtigkeit: Vom 17. Jahrhundert bis in die Gegenwart: Eine gewohnheitsrechtliche Superfizies in nordfriesischen Deichgrundstücken und ihre Entwicklung.* Frankfurt/Main, Internationaler Verlag der Wissenschaften.

Neugebauer, Wolfgang (1985). *Absolutistischer Staat und Schulwirklichkeit in Brandenburg-Preußen.* Introduction by Otto Büsch. Berlin, De Gruyter.

——— (2009). "Die Krise des 17. Jahrhunderts in Brandenburg-Preußen." In *Handbuch der preußischen Geschichte,* edited by Wolfgang Neugebauer and Frank Kleinehagenbrook, Vol. 1, *Das 17. und 18. Jahrhundert und Große Themen der Geschichte Preußens,* 145–178. Berlin and New York, De Gruyter.

Neuhäusl, Robert, Jaroslav Moravec, and Zdenka Neuhäusl-Novotná (1965). *Vegetace CSSR: Synökologische Studien über Röhrichte, Wiesen und Auenwälder,* Vol. A1. Prague, Československá Akademie Věd.

Peters, Jan (1989). "Historische Einführung: Neuholland von den Anfängen bis zur Mitte des 18. Jahrhunderts." In *Märkische Bauerntagebücher des 18. und 19. Jahrhunderts: Selbstzeugnisse von Milchviehbauern aus Neuholland,* edited by Jan Peters, Hartmut Harnisch, and Lieselott Enders, 18–80. Weimar, Böhlau.

Peters, Klaas-Heinrich (2005). "Organisation des Küstenschutzes und Wandel des Deichrechts von den Anfängen bis zur Gegenwart." In *Ostfriesland und das Land Oldenburg im Schutz der Deiche,* edited by Christoph Ohlig, Schriften der Deutschen Wasserhistorischen Gesellschaft 6, 25–30. Siegburg, Books on Demand.

Porter, Dale H. (1998). *The Thames Embankment: Environment, Technology, and Society in Victorian London.* Akron, OH, University of Akron Press.

Rippon, Stephen, and Nigel Cameron (2006). *Landscape, Community and Colonisation: The North Somerset Levels during the 1st to 2nd millenia AD.* York, Council for British Archaeology.

Rönne, Ludwig von (1863). *Das Staats = Recht der Preußischen Monarchie.* Vol. 2, pt. 2. Leipzig, Brockhaus.

Schmidt, Martin (2000). *Hochwasser und Hochwasserschutz in Deutschland vor 1850: Eine Auswertung alter Quellen und Karten.* Munich, Oldenbourg.

Schulze, Hermann (1890). *Das Preussische Staatsrecht auf Grundlage des deutschen Staatsrechts.* Vol. 2. Leipzig, Breitkopf & Härtel.

Spiegelberg, Karl (2001). *Das Oderstromsystem: Eine Dokumentation.* Frankfurt an der Oder, N. O. Agentur Neue Odersche Verlags- und Medien-GmbH.

Stier, Hans-Erich, ed. (1957). *Völker, Staaten und Kulturen: Ein Kartenwerk zur Geschichte.* Berlin, Georg Westermann.

Szűcs, Linda (2010). "Auenbewirtschaftungsformen an der Theiß." In *Schauplätze und Themen der Umweltgeschichte: Umwelthistorische Miszellen aus dem Graduiertenkolleg. Werkstattbericht,* edited by Bernd Herrmann and Ulrike Kruse, 237–249. Göttingen, Universitätsverlag Göttingen.

Tittizer, Thomas, and Falk Krebs, eds. (1996). *Ökosystemforschung: Der Rhein und seine Auen: Eine Bilanz.* Berlin and Heidelberg, Springer.

Tols, Richard S. J., and Andreas Langen (2000), "A Concise History of Dutch River Floods." *Climatic Change* 46:357–369.

Urban, William L. (1991). *Dithmarschen: A Medieval Peasant Republic.* Lewiston, ME, Edwin Mellen Press.

Vetter, Klaus (1996). *Zwischen Dorf und Stadt—die Mediatstädte des kurmärkischen Kreises Lebus: Verfassung, Wirtschaft und Sozialstruktur im 17. und 18. Jahrhundert.* Weimar, Böhlau.

Wentz, Gottfried (1930). "Geschichte des Oderbruchs." In *Das Oderbruch,* vol. 1, edited by Peter Fritz Mengel, 85–238. Eberswalde, Verlagsgesellschaft R. Müller m. b. H.

Winkander, Charlotte (2000). "Canals." In *Handbook of Ancient Water Technology,* Technology and Change in History 2, edited by Örjan Wikander, 321–330. Leiden a. e., Brill.

Winkelmann, Jan (2011). *Die Mark Brandenburg des 14. Jahrhunderts: Markgräfliche Herrschaft zwischen räumlicher "Ferne" und politischer "Krise."* Studien zur brandenburgischen und vergleichenden Landesgeschichte 5. Berlin, Lukas.

SOURCES

ALZ (Allgemeine Literatur-Zeitung vom Jahre 1808), vol. 2, Halle-Leipzig, 1808, "Num. 219. Allgemeine Literatur-Zeitung, Mittwochs, den 27. Julius 1808," col. 729–736.

CBLLG (Chur = Braunschweig = Lüneburgischer Landes = Ordnungen und Gesetze), Lüneburg, 1744, Cap. VIII, Sectio 4: Von Teich = Sachen, "Nr. LXXII. Fürstliche Braunschweig-Lüneburgische Teich = Ordnung, wornach sich die Unterthanen an der Elbe zu achten de 1664," 189–195.

CCM (Corpus Constitutionum Marchicarum), edited by Christian Otto Mylius, Berlin-Halle, 1737–1755.

—Part IV, 2nd Section, IV Cap., "No. VIII. Neu = revidirte und confirmirte Teich = Ordenung in der Alten = Marck, zu sambt denen Teich = Rollen in beyden Schauen. Vom 20. Decembr. 1695," cc. 255–286.

—Part IV, 2nd Section, IV Cap., "No. XVII. Teich = und Ufer = Ordnung. Vom 30. Decembr. Anno 1716," cc. 293–304.

—Part IV, 2nd Section, IV Cap., "No. XVIII. Sr. Königl. Majest. in Preussen, und Churfürstl. Durchl. zu Brandenburg, etc. Teich = und Ufer = Ordnung, in der Lebusischen Niederung an der Oder. De dato den 23. Junii 1717," cc. 303–340.

—Part VI, Nachlese, "No. XVIII. Graben = und Schau = Ordnung über das im Havelländischen Creyse belegene Nauensche Luch, de dato Berlin, den 31ten Augusti 1724," cc. 69–74.

CSVV (Chronologische Sammlung der im Jahre 1800 ergangenen Verordnungen und Verfügungen für die Herzogthümer Schleswig und Holstein, die Herrschaft Pinneberg, Graffschaft Ranzau und Stadt Altona), Kiel, 1801, "Nr. 5. Patent, betreffend die einzuführende Aufsicht über die Deiche der sämtlichen Marsch-Commünen, adlichen Marschgüter und octroyierte Koege in den Herzogthümern," 4-9.

DOHB (Deich = Ordnung für das Herzogthum Bremen, wie dieselbe in verschiedenen Stücken geändert und verbessert worden, publiciret Stade, den 29. Julii 1743), Stade, 1852, "Cap. 16. Von Strafe derer, so mit bösem Vorsatz die Deiche durchstechen oder sonst beschädigen," 83-84.

GSPS (Gesetz = Sammlung für die Königlichen Preußischen Staaten), Berlin, 1848, "Nr. 2933. Gesetz über das Deichwesen. Vom 28. Januar 1848," 54-60.

JbSPS (Jahrbuch für die amtliche Statistik des preussischen Staats), vol. 3, edited by Koenigliches Statistisches Bureau, Berlin, 1869, Belastung und Entlastung des Grundeigenthums, "B. Die Landesmeliorationen und ihr Schuldenwesen," 79-82.

MGH (Monumenta Germaniae Historica: Capitularia regum Francorum), 2 vols., edited by Alfred Boretius and Viktor Krause, Hanover, Hahn, 1883-1897, vol. 1, "Nr. 148. Capitula Missorum. 821," 300-301.

NCC (Novum Corpus Constitutionum Prussico-Marchicarum), edited by Samuel von Cocceji, Berlin, 1753-1822.

—Vol. IV, 1769, "No. 7. Königlich Preußische Teich = und Ufer = auch Graben = und Weg = Ordnung in dem auf beyden Seiten der Oder, zwischen Zellin und Oderberg belegenen neu bewalleten und urbar gemachten Nieder = Bruch. De Dato Berlin, den 23. Jan. 1769," cc. 5121-5334.

—Vol. VI, 1779, "No. XLII. Deich = Ufer und Graben = Ordnung für das Ober = und Nieder = Netz = Bruch. De Dato Berlin, den 14. December 1779," cc. 1631-1692.

—Vol. XI, 1802, "No. XX. Deich = Ufer = Graben = und Schau = Ordnung für das Warthe = Bruch. De Dato Berlin, den 27sten März 1802," cc. 785-838.

PrALR (Das Allgemeine Landrecht für die Preussischen Staaten), vol. 1, Sachen-Recht, edited by Carl Wilhelm Zimmermann, Berlin, 1850, Part II., tit. XX, 17th Section, "§. 1585. Von vorsätzlich verursachten Ueberschwemmungen," 1089-1090.

SSp (Repgow, Eike von, Der Sachsenspiegel, niederdeutsches Rechtsbuch, 1220-1235), liber secundus.

Infrastructure Maintenance in the Jifu Region, Beijing Metropolitan Region during the Eighteenth Century

Takehiko To

During the eighteenth century, China proper was under the rule of the Qing Dynasty founded by the Manchus at the beginning of the seventeenth century. By the middle of the eighteenth century, the Qing Dynasty had become a vast empire; it directly controlled the Manchu heartland and the eighteen inner provinces of China, and had annexed the Mongolian territories and Tibet and extended its power into Central Asia, and entered into a tribute system with Korea, Ryukyu, and Vietnam. It was also engaged in trade with Russia and Japan. Qing relationships with neighboring countries were based on a system that that reflected relative power, distance, and importance. The Qing Dynasty brought stability to East Asia through its skillful foreign policy, which was known as *Pax Manchurica.*[1]

Domestically, the Qing rulers took over the Ming bureaucratic institutions, adding on the new Board for the Administration of Outlying Regions to supervise newly incorporated territories, and establishing the Grand Council to strengthen the efficiency of the administrative structure.[2]

Global deflation during the "Crisis of the Seventeenth Century" affected China in the form of the Kangxi Depression *(Kangxi Gujian).*[3] As overseas trade declined and less silver came in from abroad, the economy contracted. Once this cycle had concluded, the economy entered a new stage of prosperity, which lasted from the end of the seventeenth century to the first half of the nineteenth century. As commodity prices rose the consumption of cereal products and the production of handicraft goods and luxury products flourished. China also benefited from the long reigns of three generations of comparatively wise emperors who reigned for over 130 years—the Kangxi Emperor (1662–1722), the Yongzheng Emperor (1723–1735), and the Qianlong Emperor (1736–1795)—a time that came to be known as the golden age of the Qing.[4] This period could be extended by a further forty or so years, leading up to the Opium War in 1840, and could be called the "Long Eighteenth Century of Qing Rule."[5] This chapter focuses on water management practices in the Jifu (Beijing Metropolitan) Region, during the eighteenth century.

GEOGRAPHIC CONDITIONS

Beijing served as the capital of the Qing dynasty, and the region known as "Jifu," that is, the region around the capital, was known during this era as Zhili province. Jifu signifies land that is directly controlled by the emperor, while "Zhili" means "direct control." This region, which is now administratively under partly under the Beijing Metropolitan government and partly under and Hebei province, covered over three hundred thousand km², and was roughly the size of present-day Germany. Registered land that was subject to tax levies totaled 65,719,000 *mu* (or approximately forty thousand km²) in 1753.[6]

The region has a warm, continental monsoon climate: winters are cold with little snow, while summers are hot with heavy rains. The average temperature is around 10°C, and the average annual rainfall on the plains is around five hundred to six hundred meters (about a third of that received in Japan). Rain is particularly scarce during the spring, autumn, and winter, and the land is often arid.

The Jifu Region is part of the North China Macroregion described by G. William Skinner.[7] A macroregion is a physiographical regional division created for natural and economic reasons by a river catchment, and differs slightly from administrative regional divisions. The Jifu Region is in the northern part of the North China Macroregion, while in the west, hilly terrain runs along a large mountain range, and alluvial plains created by the Hai River system lie in the east. The North China plains were located downstream of the Yellow River prior to the Common Era, and though they have developed since ancient times, it is likely that cotton production was only just possible in coastal areas after the tenth century, given the alkaline soil (the result of salt accumulation), which was a consequence of overdevelopment in ancient times. Grain production was insufficient to support the consumption needs of the region, and the capital population relied on grain imports from the south (through the grain tribute, or *caoyun,* system).[8]

POPULATION

Political stability and favorable economic conditions allowed for rapid population growth. China had a population of approximately 150 million people at the beginning of the seventeenth century; by the eighteenth century this number had grown to two hundred million. It continued to grow to three hundred million by the end of the eighteenth century.[9]

Various strategies were implemented across China to cope with the increasing population. Sichuan province in the Upper Yangtze Macroregion developed its mountainous regions to cultivate New World crops like maize, sweet potatoes, and potatoes.[10] The Jiangnan Region in the Lower Yangtze Macroregion, which was already an economically advanced region, developed its handicraft industries (such as cotton and silks), and continued further along the path of urbanization as a means of absorbing the growing population. Meanwhile, Fujian province in the Southeast Coast Macroregion, which in comparison was struggling economically, avoided experiencing severe population pressures when millions migrated abroad to Southeast Asia and elsewhere as overseas Chinese, or *Huaqiao*.

The population was also growing remarkably fast in the North China Macroregion, though this region did not have access to resources such as under-developed land as in the Sichuan Region or commodity production levels such as those in the Jiangnan region. Between 1580 and 1660 the region's development cycle was affected by the crises that occurred as the Ming dynasty declined, namely, famines, epidemics, rebellions, and invasions, and the confusion that resulted as power was being transferred to the Qing. The population initially peaked in 1580 at twenty-eight million, then grew sharply under the Qing to five times that size by 1850, when it reached 120 million.[11] Economic activity also peaked around this time, and Beijing's population reached approximately one million. Jifu province had to expand into previously uninhabitable areas to cultivate land for the province's growing population, which was also the main pressure behind the region's efforts to maintain infrastructure through public works.

ASPECTS OF LOCAL SOCIETY

At the beginning of the Ming dynasty (early fifteenth century) the administrative management of local societies was entrusted to self-governing organizations in rural areas known as *li*. However, reforms to the tax system (i.e., the introduction of the Single Whip Reform, or *yitiao bianfa*) at the end of the Ming dynasty (six-teenth century) changed the situation; land and corvée were combined into a single payment in silver, rather than in kind; people began paying their taxes directly to the government in silver. Authority over local society was transferred from the *li* to the magistrate, and the infrastructure maintenance that had previously been carried out autonomously by local social organizations became the responsibility of the magistrate.[12]

At the same time, the central government's control of magistrates tightened significantly, and performance evaluations were based primarily on a magistrate's ability to collect taxes and maintain order. Under Qing rule, magistrates were not permitted—under the Avoidance System—to serve in their place of birth, and in principle they were expected to change posts every two to three years.

Under these circumstances, local elites found it necessary to negotiate with the magistrate to protect their region's interests. Composition of the elite varied in different regions: in economically developed regions like Jiangnan, retired officials. (Those who had advanced in civil service examinations to the highest status of *jinshi* [a graduate of the imperial examination] and *juren* [provincial graduates], collectively known as gentry *[xiangshen]*, had a great deal of power.) Meanwhile in Jifu, the local elite included many lower degree holders such as *sheng yuan* (a student of a prefectural or county school) and *jian sheng* (a student of the Imperial Academy), in which case the magistrate had the most power.[13] Since the region was very close to the center of national power in Beijing, government policies had a comparatively direct impact, and, in fact, the Kangxi Emperor and the Qianlong Emperor often visited the Jifu Region, thereby ensuring the concrete manifestation of their policies.

CHALLENGES FACED BY THE QING DYNASTY IN THE SEVENTEENTH CENTURY

When the Kangxi Emperor assumed direct rule in 1667 he intended to address three issues: the Three Feudatories *(sanfan)*, the grain tribute system *(caoyun)*, and flood control of the Yellow River *(hewu)*. The Three Feudatories were a military and political issue related to the suppression of rebellions led by Wu Sangui, who had previously helped the Qing shore up control over China proper, while both the grain tribute system and the flood control system for the Yellow River related to infrastructure. The Jiangnan Region was the economic center of Ming and Qing China, and important industries were concentrated there, including the production of commodities such as raw cotton, the silk and cotton textile handicraft industries, and the production of salt. In addition to this concentration of wealth it was also a cultural center, producing a relatively large number of successful candidates in the imperial civil service examinations.

Beijing, however, was the capital and political center, and, as a result, various resources were transferred from the south to the north. The Grand Canal system, which extended approximately twenty-five hundred kilometers from Hangzhou to Beijing, served as a major transportation artery, and was used in the grain tribute system to transfer wealth from the south to the north: every year, four hundred thousand to five hundred thousand tons of grain were transported to Beijing from the rice bowl in the middle of the Yangtze River Basin (Huguang Region), through the Jiangnan Region. This transfer of wealth served to ensure the unity of an empire in which the politics and the economy were divided between the north and the south. When this north-south structure broke down at the end of the nineteenth century, the empire began to split apart. In other words, maintaining the Grand Canal's infrastructure played an important role in the empire's survival.

The second major infrastructure concern is North China was related to the Yellow River; successive dynasties concentrated enormous quantities of energy in controlling the river. The Yellow River, flowing through the loess highlands of Northwest China, gathered a high sediment content, which resulted in frequent flooding. From ancient times, skill in controlling the Yellow River had served as a marker of the legitimacy of China's rulers. As a result, the scholarly officials, who in general paid little heed to technology, devoted great effort to flood control, which they frequently discussed, and about which they amassed a wealth of literature.

The Qing dynasty was no exception. The Kangxi Emperor appointed Fu Jin (1633–1692) as the director-general of River Conservation in 1677. Fu Jin developed a successful flood control program for the Yellow River, but even Jin's comprehensive plan could not prevent the continuing erosion of the river's embankments, and the Qing was forced to conduct constant maintenance. Just prior to the eighteenth century the central government paused in its nationwide focus on infrastructure maintenance and public works related to the grain tribute system and flood controls on the Yellow River, and embarked instead on redeveloping and improving the regions surrounding the capital.

FLOOD CONTROL AND IRRIGATION POLICIES IN THE JIFU REGION DURING THE EIGHTEENTH CENTURY

Some of the improvements in regions surrounding the capital included developing flood control measures for the Yong-Ding River and other rivers. Work also commenced on rice paddy development projects, albeit temporarily.

Flood Control on the Yong-Ding River

The Yongding River originates in Shanxi province, crosses over the Taihang Mountains, and passes through the Marco Polo Bridge (*Lu Gou* Bridge) to the southwest of Beijing, where it joins the sea east of Tianjin. Fortified embankments had been constructed around Beijing to protect the capital during the Ming dynasty, but the river's lower reaches had been neglected, and the river, which was much like the Yellow River in that it had high sediment levels, frequently changed course, and the roads that intersected with the river were frequently damaged by floods. Local gazette records from the Late Ming era clearly described the loss of life and fortunes whenever the river flooded, but local officials only addressed the issue in a palliative manner, while suggesting that prayers be offered during religious services.

Under the Kangxi Emperor high waterworks policies were implemented by the central government on stretches of the Yongding River downstream of Beijing, and the first embankments were constructed as far as the middle basin in 1698. It was at this time that the Kangxi Emperor gave the Yongding River its name,

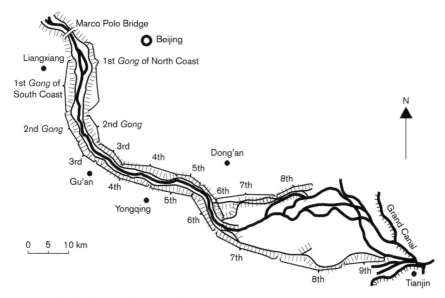

MAP 3. The Flood Control System of Yongding River

meaning "the river of eternal stability." The embankments were extended a further sixty kilometers downstream in 1700, and then to the outskirts of Tianjin in 1726. This expanded the area that could be inhabited and cultivated within the sphere of the embankments, and also made possible the cultivation of fertile soil known as *yudi* on the riverside land, which the government leased to farmers. Consequently both the population and productive capacity increased, though the establishment of a fixed waterway concentrated sediment deposits outside the embankments, and made it necessary to dredge the river constantly to protect the raised riverbed. Moreover, when the embankments were breached, the damage to human settlements was greater than it had been prior to this construction.

The Qing government responded to this problem by establishing jurisdictional regions of about five to fifteen kilometers known as *gong* on the northern and southern banks of the Yongding River to maintain its embankments, and appointed an assistant magistrate to oversee them; it also established jurisdictions known as *hao* every five hundred meters, and stationed soldiers to guard the embankments. (See map 3.) Ultimate overall responsibility for flood control of the Yongding River was initially given to the central government's Board of Works but was later transferred to the governor general of Zhili province. The yearly cost of the *gong* was between one hundred thousand to two hundred thousand taels,[14] at a time when major works were being conducted for around twenty thousand taels in normal circumstances; these costs were borne entirely by the central government. (At the time, central government reserves were around twenty millon taels.)

Approximately thirty thousand workers could be mobilized for a single project. In 1738, 190,000 taels were spent building a large stone facility like the Jinmen Sluice to act as a lock to control water volume. Three hundred dredgers (five to six meters long) and nine hundred dredge workers were usually employed in areas where downstream deposits of sediment had gathered. They dredged two to three *fang* (one *fang* is approximately 3.3 cubic meters, or approximately four to six tons) of mud per day, in five-day periods when water levels were high, from March to May and August to October. However, the operation of these dredgers ceased in 1764.

Since maintenance costs were very high, a proposal was made by the scholar official Jiagan Sun (1683–1753) in 1740 to abandon the embankments, and instead follow a low waterworks policy of "governing without governing" that returned the river to a pre-1698 state. Jiagan Sun argued that only one or two villages would be harmed in the case of a flood, and mitigating this damage would cost only one-tenth of the costs that would be incurred if the embankments burst.[15] The Qianlong Emperor supported this policy and even adopted it for a time, but in the following year (1741) there was such widespread and severe flooding that it was subsequently impossible to rehabilitate the people and redevelop the area. In the flood's immediate aftermath, embankment-based flood control policies (i.e., high waterworks) were once again adopted, and they were retained until the end of the Qing.

Flood controls of the Yongding River were most effective during the early years of the Qianlong Emperor's reign. Under Guancheng Fang (1698–1768)[16] a Han official—who had held the position of governor general of Zhili from 1749 to 1768 and who had previously been successful in the disaster relief efforts of 1743[17]—conducted thorough surveys of downstream sediment deposits in 1752 and 1755, and the course of the river was subsequently changed multiple times by moving embankments. These were major projects that involved moving residences, farmland, and graveyards, but they were successfully implemented according to plan.

The Qianlong Emperor had great faith in Guancheng Fang, and often met with him for face-to-face discussions unrelated to formal work-related instructions or reports. Furthermore, they occasionally communicated by exchanging poetry, which implied their real intentions, which they were unable to express in the formal official documents. This method was used when they committed to make flood control policies for the Yongding River as well. The Qianlong Emperor once asked Guancheng Fang for how many years it would be possible to maintain the river's course, to which the official replied that it could last for twenty years. However, when asked what would happen afterward, he was unable to provide an answer.[18] Essentially, the river's embankments would require constant maintenance. In 1773, twenty years after Guancheng Fang first changed the course of the river, his successor Yuanli Zhou initiated the Great Works (*da gong*), a large-scale maintenance project that ended up being the last comprehensive work undertaken during the Qing. At its conclusion, only embankments that burst as a result of water damage were dealt with.

The 1748 local gazetteer of Dongan County, located in the Yongding River valley basin, recorded a series of questions and answers between local elites and the local magistrate (the editor) concerning flood control of the Yongding River.[19] One of the first questions expresses local dissatisfaction with flood control measures on the Yongding River, and asks if there is any basic policy for flood control of the river. The local magistrate responds that unfortunately there is no basic policy, and no way to avoid the build-up of sediment downstream, thereby making it necessary to deal with the matter on a continuing basis. This could be taken to suggest that the local magistrate is expressing responsibility for the river's maintenance.

Other Rivers

Apart from the Yongding River, four other rivers once flowed in the Jifu Region: the north canal, the south canal, Daqing River, and Ziya River. These were different from the Yongding River, in that they were used as transportation routes. For example, the Ziya River was used to transport salt produced in the Tianjin Region upstream, and was an important river for the nation's finances, because of the state's monopoly on salt at the time, which meant that the central government controlled its production and distribution. It was also an important route for commerce, as it was used to transport grains and raw cotton from upstream regions to Tianjn. This led to the serious challenge of drafting a flood control policy that would maintain the route while protecting the farmland and residences in the area around the river.

Work on embankments for the Ziya River began at about the same time as for the Yongding River in 1700, under the Kangxi Emperor's high waterworks policies. While this limited unforeseen flood damage and expanded the cultivatable and inhabitable land around the river, it also resulted in more serious damage whenever a flood occurred, and the embankments required constant maintenance, thereby necessitating the stationing of officials at strategic points along the river, albeit on a smaller scale than on the Yongding River. The ultimate authority lay with the governor general of Zhili province, as was the case as for the Yongding River.

Different flood control policies were implemented on the river during the Yongzheng and Qianlong years according to the prevailing conditions. For example, the governor general of Zhili province, Guancheng Fang, seriously altered the course of the river in 1753. However, whereas the central government bore most of the costs for the Yongding River, financial responsibility for the Ziya River lay with the regional government, and ways had to be found to cover these costs, such as by charging interest on loans from the government to pawnshops (*yingyun shengxi yin*). During the Qianlong era, contributions from the Tianjin salt merchants who used the river to sell their salt were used to pay for these works. Later, and in particular after 1766, Manchu officials involved in the salt trade and administration gradually acquired greater influence over flood control policies, and became important political actors.[20]

Paddy Field Development Projects during the Yongzheng Era

In addition to the infrastructure improvements that primarily focused on flood controls discussed earlier, irrigation development projects known as *Jifu yingtian* were also conducted during the Yongzheng era. Prince Yi (1686–1730), the younger brother of the Yongzheng Emperor, started a redevelopment project for the areas surrounding the capital in 1725. Irrigation facilities were built, and efforts were made to develop paddy fields, in an attempt to increase the productivity of a region that was then a dryland farming area. There had previously been multiple debates over the issue, with discussions during the periods of crisis at the end of both the Yuan and Ming dynasties over whether to increase agricultural production in the Jifu Region to lessen the burden of transporting grains from the south to the north. However, the aim behind developing the region in the eighteenth century was to improve its productivity, while maintaining the grain tribute from south to north, and it may have involved the application of a type of labor-intensive rice paddy cultivation in northern China that was becoming increasingly popular in the Jiangnan province and Japan at the time.

From 1727 to 1730 a special government office *(shuili yingtian fu)* led by Prince Yi as its commissioner divided Zhili province into four jurisdictions to develop the rice paddies. Experienced farmers from the south were invited to provide technical guidance, while the government provided funds, and gave awards to supportive farmers. The government spent several million taels over three years to develop seven thousand *qing* (420 km²), and private citizens developed a similar-sized area. Liangji Hong (1746–1809), known as the Malthus of China, made a calculation that it contributed the amount of food needed for approximately three hundred thousand more people, assuming that the amount of space needed for one person for one year was 4 *mu* (twenty-four hundred m²).[21]

According to government records, the development project was successful for a time, but in the years following the death of Prince Yi in 1730, with few exceptions, most of the paddy fields were abandoned. Several factors, including environmental factors, were responsible. They included an unstable water supply, very hard sediment, the unsuitability of the soil for rice farming, the technological limitations of rice paddy farming in the Jifu Region, differences in eating habits between the northerners (who preferred wheat) and the southerners (who preferred rice), and resistance from local students *(shengyuan)* and elites *(jiansheng)* who feared tax hikes. Following the death of the Yongzheng Emperor in 1735, the Qianlong Emperor assumed power and immediately abolished the special government office, thereby abandoning the central government-led development of rice paddies in the Jifu Region, and instead focusing on flood control policies.

The Shapeless Treasury (Wuxing Zhi Tangcang)

There were both successes and failures among the numerous public works projects conducted in the Jifu Region by the Qing in the eighteenth century. The phrases *yigong daizhen* (以工代賑) and *gongzhen* (工賑) (i.e., providing work to relieve poverty) were frequently employed as a way of illustrating the worthiness of the government's expenditures on these projects. This was a smart twofold method of employing citizens to work on projects that tackled disasters and paying them wages for their efforts as a form of disaster relief.

In implementing the disaster relief plans, a crucial issue was having an adequate supply of small denomination copper coins available to pay the wages of those who were hired to do such work. In contemporary China, silver was generally used for paying taxes and in larger transactions, and copper was used in everyday life. However in the Jifu Region, copper was more customarily used than silver. As the population grew, the demand for small coin denominations increased, but a fall in the imports of Japanese copper led to an insufficient copper supply, and caused problems for the government. Around 1740, the Qing government was taking three thousand tons of the copper produced each year at the copper mines in Yunnan province. It was transported on a nine-month journey down the Yangtze River and used for public works, rather than as a basis for commercial trade. It was taken north to the two mints in Beijing where up to 1.5 billion copper coins were produced each year[22] that were used to pay the wages of construction workers. Wages for earthworks per day were one *sheng* (around one litre) of rice and eight *wen* (eight copper coins) for food, handling *fang* (approximately 3.3 m³, four to six tons) of soil. This meant that a large number of copper coins were kept in stock in the Jifu Region for currency, which contributed to growth in the region's economy. However, *yigong daizhen* ultimately remained a countermeasure against disasters, and its critics pointed to its inefficiencies.

In 1744, the censor Chao-sheng Zhai[23] became concerned about the policies being implemented to deal with that year's water damage. He therefore went to see the emperor, who was a passionate advocate of the need for irrigation projects in Jifu, to emphasize the serious inefficiency of *yigong daizhen,* and to argue that the civil service should mediate these policies. He argued that instead of paying out large sums of money in relief when a disaster occurred, it would be better to plan irrigation projects in advance, and invest in public works to provide irrigation facilities that would provide "relief that is not abused" (*wubi zhi zhenxu* 無弊之賑恤). Moreover, he argued that instead of stockpiling grain to counteract increases in the price of rice, the government should instead build rice paddies to improve the harvest and so create "never-emptying granaries" (*bujie zhi changping* 不竭之常平). He also argued that instead of providing incentives for wealthy citizens in the capital, the government should revive work on irrigation projects to create a "shapeless treasury" (*wuxing zhi tangcang* 無形之帑藏).[24] This specific term symbolized his argument that developing arable land would have the same effect on coping with famine and poverty as maintaining a treasury or granaries for poor and famine relief. In other words, the term "shapeless treasury" or "never-emptying granaries" in those days implied the sense of "social infrastructure" in a contemporary meaning.

These propositions were an attempt to go beyond the traditional methods based on "famine relief" (huangzheng), and by extension yigong daizhen, that had been used in the past to temporarily deal with disasters and famines. In other words, the Qing should put all its efforts into improving its infrastructure (such as maintaining embankments, improving irrigation facilities, and promoting the cultivation of paddy rice) to improve productive capacity and increase peoples' welfare.

These ideas were disseminated among the administrative organs at each level of the Qing, and resulted in the implementation of various construction projects funded by government finances at both the central and the regional levels in the eighteenth century. They were subsequently also maintained. For example, data from Ningbo, Zhejiang province, shows that water damage clearly lessened between 1751 and 1800, during the reign of the Qianlong Emperor. This information provides one measure of the efficacy of the Qing's infrastructure improvements.[25]

In June 1801, heavy rains caused widespread water damage in the Jifu Region, leading the Jiaqing Emperor (1796–1820) to expend large sums for gongzhen. This achievement was proudly recorded by the Qing in the Chronicle of Public Works and Relief Activities (Qinding Xinyou Gongzhen Jishi), but, in reality, the power of the central government to carry out the improvements of social infrastructures ebbed during the nineteenth century, and this act illustrates that the government was now limited to implementing temporary relief measures through gongzhen.

OTHER PUBLIC WORKS IN THE JIFU PROVINCE DURING THE EIGHTEENTH CENTURY

Various other public works were implemented by the central government in the Jifu Region during the prosperous eighteenth century, as it tried to strengthen social infrastructure and absorb the growing population. These initiatives included Guancheng Fang's decision to build a public granary to hold the fruits of the flood control of the Yongding River,[26] the establishment of a foundling home,[27] relief work for the poor, and the promotion of cotton cultivation.[28]

"Famine relief" (huangzheng)—a custom of providing temporary relief at times of disaster—had existed in China since the time of the ancient emperors, as had flood control projects for the Yong-Ding River and flood control of the Yellow River. There was therefore a close relationship between these traditions and the traditional civil service, and they continued to be practiced at least to some extent until the end of the dynasty. However, several things did not continue: the development of rice paddies, which were ill-suited to the soil and land conditions and required the constant toil of farmers; the public granary, managed autonomously by local power holders; and the foundling homes, based in Buddhist temples. The government's attempt to uplift all sections of society across the region did not last, and private society in the Jifu Region lacked the power to support these efforts by itself. Meanwhile, self-government in Jiangnan was left to the local elite class, of which the Benevolent Societies *(shanhui)* and Benevolent Halls *(shantang)* are examples.[29]

In the early years of the Qianlong Emperor Zhili province was developing its "shapeless treasury," or, in other words, improving its social infrastructure and the region's redevelopment. At the same time, it was guarded by a systematic framework structured by the strong leadership of the emperor, intelligent agenda-setting by the governor general and governor, an embankment maintenance management system funded through focused public investment (which led to an expansion in inhabitable and cultivatable land), and success in absorbing the growing population. Flood control and irrigation projects also served to guarantee employment. The well-thought-out *yigong daizhen* policy, which involved flood control and minting vast quantities of copper coins in Beijing, based on an effective transportation system for moving copper from Yunnan, helped the region transition to a currency-based society, which in turn played an important part in stimulating the province's economy. The favorable economic conditions of the time made these policies possible, and the redistribution of wealth that occurred under these conditions allowed the Qing's authority and sovereignty to impact each member of society in a rather striking way, by stabilizing society and arguably creating a form of commonality.

Qing authority waned as it entered the nineteenth century, and it became difficult for the regional government to carry out public works in the Jiangnan region. Consequently the further implementation of these works was increasingly left up to the local elite. The responsibility for public works in northern China shifted from the central and provincial governments to local magistrates at the county level, but a lack of funds and an inability to oppose the influence of Manchu officials meant infrastructure improvements became patchy.

Under the favorable conditions of a strong economy, population growth, and the authority of wise rulers, eighteenth-century China (albeit limited to the regions around the capital) made several attempts to transcend the framework of a limited government, which had been based on the tax collection contract, minimal maintenance of public order, and the distribution of benevolent relief when disaster struck, through being engaged in the improvement of the social infrastructure that might deserve the concept of welfare state. However, limits to governance, coupled with the technological and social limits characteristic of the time, made it impossible for this new state to continue. As China entered the nineteenth century, the favorable conditions it had enjoyed in the eighteenth century were no longer present, and responsibilities for developing and maintaining infrastructure were decentralized, according to the conditions in each region.

NOTES

1. See Mancall 1984.
2. See Bartlett 1991.
3. Kishimoto-Nakayama 1984.
4. For research summarizing eighteenth-century China from a comprehensive political, cultural, economic, and regional perspective, see Naquin and Rawski 1987.
5. See Ni 2013.
6. Wang 1973.
7. Skinner 1985.
8. See Chi 1936.
9. Ho 1959.
10. See Perkins 1969.
11. See Huang 1985.
12. See Ch'u 1962.
13. See Ho 1962.
14. 1 tael was worth 37.301 g of silver according to the official standard *(ku-ping liang)* for the collection of tax.
15. Sun, Jiagan, *Sun Wen Ding Gong Zoushu* (Collected Memorials of Sun Jiagan), 7, ca. 1800.
16. Both his grandfather and father were exiled during the Literary Inquisition, so he was unable to join the government school during his youth or to earn a high grade in the civil service examinations, but he was raised in the home of a scholarly official, and therefore had a good education, and was a famous poet.
17. See Will 1990.
18. Hong Li, (Qian-long Emperor), *Yuzhishi Siji* (Forth Collection of Qianlong's poems), 59, 1782.
19. *Dong'an xian zhi* (Gazetteer of Dong'an County), 15, 1750. Other questions included "Would it be possible to try and wash away the sediment build-up in cloudy rivers where it is prevalent using rivers with little sediment?" "Are there not unnecessary officials stationed here?" "Would it be possible to install a sluice gate on both banks of the Yongding River to irrigate it?" "Why do some people want the government to buy out the land where it floods downstream, and some who do not?"
20. See To 2011.
21. Hong, Liang-ji, *Juan Shi Ge Wen Jia Ji* (Collected Essays from the Juan-shi Hall), 1, 1795 .
22. The value of this in silver at the time was approximately 1.2 million taels.
23. The Censor was an official of low rank, but had the sole right to ask the emperor about individual political problems.
24. Pan, Xi'en, *Jifu Shuili Sian* (Four Collected Records on the Investment in Beijing Metropolitan Region), 3, 1823.
25. Oka 2012.
26. Fang, Guancheng, *Ji-fu Yicang Tu* (Maps of the Public Granary in Zhili Province), 1753. According to these maps, 1,005 public granaries were built in 144 counties in Zhili province, for which detailed management plans were drawn up and self-managed by the villages. However, they were largely disused after several decades.
27. See Li 2007.
28. Fang, Guancheng, *Mian Hua Tu* (Pictures of Raw Cotton), 1765. Sixteen drawings were made beginning with the cultivation of raw cotton, and ending with the production of cotton textiles, with

explanations by Guan-cheng Fang added. The Qianlong Emperor has attached a poem to the complete works.

29. See Fuma 1997.

REFERENCES

Bartlett, Beatrice S. (1991). *Monarchs and Ministers: The Grand Council in Mid-Chi'ng China, 1723–1820.* Berkeley, University of California Press.

Chi, Ch'ao-ting (1936). *Key Economic Areas in Chinese History: As Revealed in the Development of Public Works for Water-Control.* London, George Allen and Unwin.

Ch'u, T'ung-tsu (1962). *Local Government in China under the Chi'ng.* Cambridge, MA, Harvard University Press.

Fuma, Susumu (1997). *Chūgoku Zenkai Zendōshi Kenkyū* (A Study of Benevolent Societies and Benevolent Halls in China). Kyoto, Dōhōsha.

Ho, Ping-ti (1959). *Studies on the Population of China, 1368–1953.* Cambridge, MA, Harvard University Press.

——— (1962). *The Ladder of Success in Imperial China, Aspects of Social Mobility, 1368–1911.* New York, Columbia University Press.

Huang, Philip C.C. (1985). *The Peasant Economy and Social Change in North China.* Stanford, Stanford University Press.

Kishimoto-Nakayama, Mio (1984). "The Kangsi Depression and Early Qing Local Markets." *Modern China* 10 (2): 227–256.

Li, Lillian M. (2007). *Fighting Famine in North China: State, Market, and Environmental Decline, 1690s–1990s.* Stanford, Stanford University Press.

Mancall, Mark (1984). *China at the Center: 300 Years of Foreign Policy.* New York, Free Press.

Naquin, Susan, and Evelyn S. Rawski (1987). *Chinese Society in the Eighteenth Century.* New Haven, Yale University Press.

Ni, Yuping (2013), *Research on Finance and Society in the Jiaqing and Daoguang Reigns of the Qing Dynasty.* Beijing, Commercial Press.

Oka, Motoji (2012). *Sōdai Enkai Chiiki Shakaishi Kenkyū: Network to Chiikibunka* (Study on the Social History of Coastal Regions during the Song Dynasty). Tokyo, Kyūko Shoin.

Perkins, Dwight H. (1969). *Agricultural Development in China, 1368–1968.* Chicago, Aldine.

Skinner, G. William (1985). "Presidential Address: The Structure of Chinese History." *Journal of Asian Studies* 44 (2): 271–292.

To, Takehiko (2011). *Shindai Keizaiseisakushi no Kenkyū* (The History of Economic Policy in the Qing Dynasty). Tokyo, Kyūko Shoin.

Wang, Yeh-chien (1973). *Land Taxation in Imperial China, 1750–1911.* Cambridge, MA, Harvard University Press.

Will, Pierre-Etienne (1990). *Bureaucracy and Famine in Eighteenth-Century China.* Translated by Elborg Forster. Stanford, Stanford University Press.

Provided for Public Welfare

Traffic Infrastructure and "The Bonum Commune *Topos"*
with Examples from Fifteenth- and
Sixteenth-Century Brandenburg Electorate

Sascha Bütow

Traffic is a global phenomenon. Generally it can be defined as a movement form a point A to point B. In many cases the outcomes of this are repeating traffic conditions and relations between different people with varied needs. Therefore traffic is way to meet these demands. Moreover traffic is a basic condition for trading, market transactions, and economy itself. This term allows us to research the repeating process of exchange and communication, the conditions of local and long-distance traffic, and the development of transport networks and road systems. Mostly categories like centrality or periphery depend on the existence or absence of such traffic relations.

Today the roads and the transport infrastructure as fundaments for traffic are provided and organized by the state with its central institutions. Using the example of waterways the basic law for the Federal Republic of Germany states the following: "The Federation shall be the owner of the former Reich waterways." Furthermore "the Federation shall administer the federal waterways through its own authorities. It shall exercise those state functions relating to inland shipping, which extend beyond the territory of a single Land, and those functions relating to maritime shipping, which are conferred on it by a law. Insofar as federal waterways lie within the territory of a single Land, the Federation on its application may delegate their administration to that Land on federal commission. If a waterway touches the territory of several Länder, the Federation may commission that Land that is designated by the affected Länder."[1]

These regulations received favorable comments by German historians of law like Albrecht Friesecke. He points out: "die vom Grundgesetz gewählte Lösung einer zentralen Verwaltung der Bundeswasserstraßen [bedeutet] den Abschluß einer langen historischen Entwicklung" (Friesecke 1962, 13). In this point of view

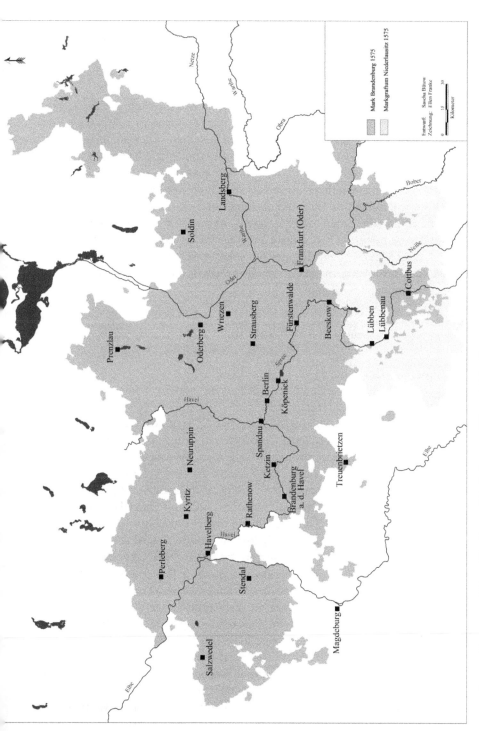

MAP 4. Range of Important Cities of Trading and Traffic between Elbe and Oder River

Source: Drawing by Ellen Franke, MA, Berlin.

only the central state seems to be destined to guarantee the administration and the function of the traffic and its infrastructure. For this reason the state is also the provider of common good and public welfare. According to this Heinrich Geffcken advised against minority interests in his own time using a view to the history of the German water right. He verified: "Auch die künftige Gesetzgebung wird daher, wie ich glaube, gut daran thun, für die öffentlichen Flüsse an dieser Auffassung festzuhalten oder zu ihr zurückzukehren: das Strombett steht im öffentlichen Eigenthume, nicht anders wie die vom Staat erbaute und unterhaltene Landstraße" (Geffcken 1900, 200; for more examples, see 216–217). Today it is widely recognized that these sentiments affects some serious problems especially for historical studies. As Masayuki Tanimoto stresses, "one of the main questions will be about who provides public goods. Although a central government can naturally be nominated as a main provider under the modern state system." But it is also known that "this was not the case before the twentieth century."[2] Nevertheless the modern state serves very often as a rule for good government, security, and public welfare.

MEDIEVAL TRAFFIC IN RESEARCH: POINT OF DEPARTURE

Against this background the traffic in medieval times is usually discussed in a very demoting way. For example in Neil MacFarlane's and Yuen Foong Khong's view medieval Europe was characterized by chaos and permanent conflicts. Hence they speak about "dark" ages with the following result: "Transport systems broke down and the Roman economy collapsed into localized fragments. Since the state as we understand it did not exist during the Dark Ages, the idea of loyalty to the state, or giving the ends of the state a priority greater than that accorded to those of the individual or group, was weak, if it existed at all" (MacFarlane and Khong 2006, 30). The well-known German traffic historian Otto Most pointed out that there is almost nothing good to tell about medieval traffic (Most 1950/1951, 1). This is due to the weak government in the Holy Roman Empire. Referring to the daily life in the Middle Ages Paul B. Newman also stated that the "road building generally stopped with the collapse of the Roman Empire since there was no longer a powerful central authority to plan and direct such projects and raise the taxes to pay for them" (Newman 2001, 84). Therefore many historians refer to the ancient road system as a "pinnacle" in the history of the roads (Lay 1992, 52–56). In contrast the roads in the Middle Ages seemed to be in decline (Lay 1992, 57). Many historians hold local landlords and cities and their self-interest responsible for that situation. In Norbert Ohler's opinion these local rulers seemed to shown no interest in building new roads, bridges, or tunnels (Ohler 2009, 19). Referring to the water transport, Detlev Ellmers regards the inland navigation in medieval times as a cow, which everyone wants to milk but nobody wants to feed (Ellmers 1985, 244).

Based on these statements its questionable whether public welfare, referring to medieval traffic, existed at all.

Of course the medieval traffic history is full of examples of maintaining roads and traffic infrastructure influenced not only by personal interest. So we can notice many efforts to keep roads and waterways in good and passable condition. For example, James Westfall Thompson refers to monks of the Cistercian order "who established themselves in out-of-the-way districts, [and] turned their industrious hands to the building and maintenance of roads" (Thompson 1931, 293). Very often the residents and communities along the roads were requested to keep several parts of them in good condition. In many cases even individual merchants took the building and maintaining of roads into their own hands, as Peter Spufford illustrates (Spufford 2002, 190–191). In this context he talks about a road revolution during the fourteenth century, similar to what Thomas Szabó recognizes a "Discovery" of the road in the thirteenth century (Szabó 1994, 913–929). (See map 4.)

A further reason for those interpretations is the fact that the road and its infrastructure became a more and more important task for medieval governments, as is clearly shown by the communities in northern Italy. Very often these powerful city-states organized the construction and maintenance of roads. For example, they took care of traffic infrastructure like bridges, dams, fountains, and roadhouses. These infrastructural elements were regarded as collective goods. Concerning this matter the several governments considered themselves as guarantors of "human security" and public welfare, as Gerrit Jasper Schenk found out (Schenk 2010, 209–233). The famous frescoes in the town hall of the former Republic of Siena painted by Ambrogio Lorenzetti around 1338/1939 illustrate this self-image in a very concrete way. In minutest details we see here a cultural landscape formed by humans. For instance, there are a lot of infrastructural buildings like a bridge or a mill. In the foreground we can see many people building a road. In the picture the wealthy as well as the poor find their place in community. In the words of Schenk, we can see here "an extremely complex allegory of good government or social peace" (Schenk 2010, 211). Ambrogio's frescos are therefore an impressive example for the importance of the *bonum comune* topos in the late Middle Ages, also in connection with traffic and traffic infrastructure. During this period there was a very pragmatic perception of the common good, as several researchers proved (Gailing, Moss, and Röhring 2009, 51–73, Moss, Gudermann, and Röhring, 2009, 31–49). Thus the *bonum commune* became a main term in the political and social language in medieval times (Simon 2012, here 90).

Against this background the following article concerns the use of this *bonum commune* topos in connection with traffic infrastructure, especially in the fifteenth- and sixteenth-century Brandenburg electorate. In comparison to Italy we have here no impressive frescoes or similarly complex allegories of the *bonum commune*. In fact the main sources are documents and several files published by the elector himself and the three orders. One leading question will be about the building of traffic infrastructure and the maintenance of bridges, paved roads, and locks. Another concern is the way this infrastructure became important collective goods. However, first it is necessary to give a short definition of the *bonum commune* topos in medieval times.

THE *BONUM COMMUNE* TOPOS

Starting in the late Middle Ages providing the *bonum commune* increasingly became an integral part of the political thought of kings, princes, landlords, communities, and other potentates in the Holy Roman Empire (Hibst 1991). This progress is shown, for example, in the King's Peace of this time. For instance, in 1442 king Frederic III founded a "Reichslandfrieden" regarding robbery, murder, and malicious arson, which affected public welfare. Therefore he argued with the *bonum commune* ("gemainer nucz"). Moreover, his subjects were requested to help him enforce the peace as his document proves: "und ermonen auch ew all und yeglich unser und des heiligen reichs undertan, in welhen wirden stat oder wesen ir seit, solher trew und phlicht, als ir gote, dem heiligen rieche, auch uns als ainem Romischen kunige, ewerm obristen herren, gemainem nucze und ew selbst schuldig philichtig und gebunden seit" (Herre and Quidde 1928, No. 209, 402). In this argumentation, providing the public welfare plays a decisive role. As Otto Gerhard Oexle shows, this pragmatic use of the *bonum commune* topos originates from early formations of groups and communities in medieval times (Oexle 2001, 65–83). Daily problems like ensuring safety and protection, providing peace and security, and holding autonomy and identity are references of the *bonum commune* topos used by these communities in fourteenth and fifteenth century. It becomes much more obvious with the building and providing of infrastructure in connection with maintaining traffic and its roads. For instance, in 1469 the city council of Heilbronn concluded a contract with the Count Palatine of the Rhine and the Counts of Württemberg. All parties obligated themselves to make the Murr, a tributary of the Neckar River, navigable. They legitimized that with a reference to "merglichen und gemeinen nuetze" (Knupfer 1904, No. 862, 484). Once again we meet here the *bonum commune* topos used not only by a community or city but also by several rulers. Already in this case, it can be shown that these potentates used the common good as a legitimation for their actions often in the fifteenth century and sixteenth century. Therefore Peter Blickle speaks about a kind of "nationalization" of the *bonum commune* topos during this period (Blickle 2001, 95, 99). Consequently the regulations ("Willkühr") for the city of Löbejün, situated in the territory of the Archbishopric of Magdeburg, are formed by the administrator in 1593 and legitimized by "Gottes Ehre vndt gemeiner Nutz" (Anonymous 1839, here 75). Here the administrator himself became a provider of public welfare.

THE ORIGINS OF THE *BONUM COMMUNE* TOPOS IN BRANDENBURG

In this regard, the electors of Brandenburg are no exception, although the maintenance of roads and traffic was one of the traditional responsibilities of the local cities and communities. They acquired a high grade of autonomy during the fourteenth century (Winkelmann 2011, 167–179). Here we can also find the origins of the common good topos in Brandenburg. For instance, in 1340 the city council of Beeskow arranged a constitution for the guild of tailors. This act was legitimized by "nuttze vnd . . . vromen derselbin stat" (Riedel 1838–1869, Vol. 1, 20, No. VII, 344). Nearly eight years later the council founded another constitution for the guild of butchers. This time the councilmen referred themselves to "groseren nuczen vnd vromen der vorgesprochenen stat." Moreover, two of the councilmen were present at the congregations of the guild. In doing so, they supervised the keeping of the regulations and the common good: "daz si der stat nuczse syn vnd bequeme" (Riedel 1838–1869, Vol. 1, 20, No. XIII, 348–349, here 349). Here and elsewhere recurring terms like "nutz" or "vromen" refers to the "*bonum comune* topos."

They often were used in many contexts, as the Magdeburger Schöppenchronik from the fourteenth century shows. The author wrote a considerable preface, which offers several insights into his intentions. One of them refers to the reader himself, who should learn from history by reading the chronical. In his own words he intended to save his contemporary and the future inhabitants of Magdeburg from any loss by presenting and explaining to them the former legal situations.[3] In this connection the authors aim was the public benefit of his hometown, as he self explains: "Godde to eyneme loue vnd to eren, mynen leuen heren den schepen der stad to magdeborch to leue vnd dersuluen Stadt to vromen" (Riedel 1838–1869, Vol. 4, 1, No. IV, 168). The self-conception of the councilmen in medieval cities is clearly reflected in these and similar phrases, which we can find a lot in documents of Beeskow, Magdeburg, and other communities. All these city councils have used "the common good" and "public welfare" as popular terms to legitimize their political actions since the fourteenth century.

Expectedly trade, traffic, infrastructure, and the conservation and maintenance of cultivated landscape were important reference points of good governance. For instance in 1442 the city of Oderberg had got the authority to cast for fish in the waters of the castle of the elector. This privilege was legitimized by the "Fromen" and "Nucze" of the city of Oderberg (Zimmermann 1838, 183–184, here 183). A similar situation obtained in Prenzlau. Starting in 1448 the local councilmen were entitled to dig lime scale and brick earth out of the fields around the city. The elector who had given this privilege emphasized in his document that he aimed at the "Stadt Nutz und frommen" by doing so (Riedel 1838–1869, Vol. 1,21, No. CCCXVII, 359–360, here 360). In another document from 1515 the councilmen of Prenzlau were also authorized to hold a free cattle market that coincided with

"Nativitatis Marie" (September 16). In order to guarantee the traffic to the Prenzlau market the citizenry was requested to keep the roadways and bridges in good condition. Therefore the council of Prenzlau was free to take a toll *(Deichselpfennig)* from foreign merchants. These takings were intended for the city's and its inhabitant's good and nothing else: "der Stadt gemeinen Nutz vnd sonst nirgend anders hinkehren" (Riedel 1838–1869, Vol. 1, 18, No. XCV, 438). Also the city of Wriezen was allowed to demand a toll from travelers on the roads around the town. The well-known legitimation for that was the city's welfare. In return the community had to maintain these streets with several building materials, such as stone, timber, and sand. In case of need they were admonished to build new roadways. The same applies for Treuenbrietzen. This city was situated on a highly frequented medieval street between the trade fair town of Leipzig and Berlin (Bütow 2015a, 285–286). For that reason road construction became an important element for effective trading. This is documented by two more tolls: one in Beelitz and another in Saarmund. Both cities were also situated on the road between Leipzig and Berlin. Like Treuenbrietzen, they had to provide for the traffic by maintaining the roads and infrastructure, which were used by passengers as well as the merchants with their takings.

Many similar examples could be quoted. Nevertheless these cases are enough to show that the local cities and communities had borne responsibility for traffic and road construction. Moreover, they took care of the traffic infrastructure such as bridges and causeways. There was no "state" for realizing such duties. Instead the elector himself granted several privileges to the cities for financing these important building measures. In all these cases the *bonum commune* topos shows up in several documents, illustrating the activities of the cities in relation to the collective good. In many respects this should increase the value of building roads, bridges, and other infrastructure. The same applies to the municipal administration itself. To provide financing for infrastructure projects, the communities often were allowed to levy a toll on the passing traffic. Many modern historians view those medieval tolls as impediments to traffic flow.[4] Other authors, which we follow here, began to reassess the role of the tolls in the Middle Ages. According to Max Baumann, we can see that under no circumstances did the medieval tolls completely encumber the traffic in a technical or in an organizational way (Baumann 1992, 86). In contrast tolls always act as an indicator for traffic and its infrastructure (Bütow 2015b, 48). Furthermore the *bonum commune* topos was associated with significant social aspects, which are mentioned in the following chapter.

THE HAVES AND THE HAVE-NOTS

Modern historical infrastructure research considers humans as an essential factor (Engels and Schenk 2015, 32). As Birte Förster and Martin Bauch pointed out, infrastructure always has the potential to facilitate social integration (Förster and

Bauch 2015, 18). Felicitous examples of this can be found beginning in ancient times. For instance, providers of infrastructure often used arguments about facilitating public welfare and social health, as Helmuth Schneider proves using the example of building a water pipeline in the city of Sinope at the beginning of the second century. Therefore the roman governor of Pontus and Bithynia Plinius mentioned that a water pipeline could be feed *salubritas* and *voluptas* (Schneider 2015, 90). Astrid Möller states that the water supply in archaic Greek was a collective achievement although single aristocrats exceled in this occasion (Möller 2015). However, infrastructure could even force or document social segregation (Förster and Bauch 2015, 18). For instance, Jaroslav Jásek describes several systems of water distribution in medieval Prague (Jásek 2015, 60–64). One of the oldest systems can be found in the area of Vyšehrad. Established in the twelfth century, this water supply was designated for the king and his court. The general public got water in other places. The first communal water main existed in today's Havelské marketplace of the Old Town of Prague. Examples like this are useful in illustrating that the research needs to go beyond conventional technical descriptions of infrastructural systems (Schröder 2014, 11).

This finding can be confirmed in the medieval Brandenburg electorate. As we saw traffic infrastructure, road construction, and municipal buildings or properties are favored references for the public welfare. The regulations of Soldin from 1511 offer a kind of summary of these important common goods, including interests, benefits, contributions (including traffic and trade), customs, waters, fishery, woods, grasslands, brick manufacture, the cellar of the town, and other possessions of the community (Riedel 1838–1869, Vol. 1, 18, No. XCIX, 509–512, here 509). Many users had access to these public goods, which were often administrated by the councilmen. Their governance was commendable if the council preferred no single group but all groups of the citizenship, the haves and have-nots. Therefore the reference to the rich and poor people became an important issue of good governance. In many cases rulers used these terms in connection with the *bonum commune* topos. For instance, in 1343 bishop Otto II of Würzburg passed a new order for his city and its inhabitants. According to the text of this regulation Bishop Otto intended to facilitate the common good concerning the rich and the poor people "in der stat zuo Wirtzebug" (Hoffmann 1955, No. 10, 43). Moreover, in 1474 King Matthias of Bohemia permitted his city of Bautzen to put up a cellar of the town regarding the public welfare and the rich's and poor's good. Back to the medieval Brandenburg electorate, the margravine Agnes authorized the two cities, Berlin and Cologne, to export their excessive grain to Hamburg and elsewhere. That applied to the rich and the poor people of both cities, as we can see in a document of the year 1320: "volumus eciam, quod pauperes Ciues Ciuitatum premissarum cum suo frumento non minus quam diuites . . . Ciuitatem Honbusch [Hamburg] ac reliquas Ciuitates frequentent nauigando" (Voigt 1869, No. L, 35–37, here 36). As a last example, we consider the regulations of the city of Landsberg from 1511, which accentuated that the city council was committed to supervise the measures and weights in the city's taverns. Once more this authority should be used within the meaning of public welfare treating rich and poor with equal dedication: "damit dem gemeinen nutz, dem armen als den Reichen, vor das sein gleich geschee" (Riedel 1838–1869, Vol. 1, 18, No. LXXXIX, 432–434, here 433). All these expressions and phrases provided the opportunity to encompass all persons and groups in a single city, area, or territory, making clear that the regulations, arrangements, or laws applied to them all without any exception.

AVOIDING ANY SELF-INTEREST

Administrating common goods means avoiding the preference of someone's self-interests. As the councilmen of Prenzlau 1515 pointed out: nobody should make any individual profit by using the city's common goods (Riedel 1838–1869, Vol. 1, 21, No. CCCXLIV, 383–388, here 383). Therefore, tolerating personal gain was a characteristic trait of bad governance. Cities very often used that as an argument to put several opponents in a bad light. For instance, in 1562 the community of Lübben were involved in a legal dispute with the lord-high-constable Sigmund von Tschammer of Lübben about a dam in the Spree River. This dam had been constructed a few months before at the village of Schlepzig to avoid the flooding of the constable's possessions.[5] The territory of the city of Lübben was situated on the other side of this dam. Because of the new infrastructural building, the fields, grassland, and range lands owned by the citizenship were very often overflowed. For this reason, the councilmen of Lübben wrote to the governor of the March of the Lower Lusatia. In this letter the councilmen criticized their opponent, Sigismund von Tschammer, by bringing out his personal and individual interests against public welfare. They mentioned "das mhan recht haben wollte, den gantzen waldt vnd pusch ßeins eigenen Nutzens vnd gefallens zuvortemmen."[6] To foreclose someone's selfishness city councils very often supervised their deputies and municipal officers, who became fixed in corresponding regulations and directives. Moreover, the councilmen controlled one another. For example, the regulations of the city of Soldin pledged every single councilman to account for his earnings and spending habits in public and private (Riedel 1838–1869, Vol. 1, 18, No. XCIX, 509–512, here 509). Thereby any misuse of authority could be specifically prohibited.

FROM CITY'S GOOD TO PUBLIC WELFARE

In all these cases a community was anxious to procure its common good. Councilmen very often used not only the single community's good but also the public welfare as arguments for legitimation. Beyond city limits they wanted to confirm that they care for the general public's good. Infrastructure was an excellent subject for verifying that. For example, in the early sixteenth century the community of Soldin rebuilt their ruined brick-kiln together with the brick-barn by referring to the city's and public's profit.[7] Nearly at the same time, the city of Lenzen was allowed to publish a new fire protection regulation *(Willkür)* providing for the city's good and the public welfare (Raumer 1831–1833, Vol. 2, No. VI, 210). Like other communities in the Middle Ages, the city of Treuenbrietzen was an owner of woodland *(Holtzung)* situated in the municipal area. A document from 1525 confirms that the citizens were requested to keep their woodlands in good condition in order to supply the city's and general public's good (Raumer 1831–1833, Vol. 2, No. LXXL, 286–289, here 287). As we can see in these cases, there seems to be a significant compatibility between the common good of a city, on the one hand, and the public welfare, on the other hand. This was a typical phenomenon in the Middle Ages, as Peter Blickle remarks (Blickle 2001, 87–88). Under these terms the *bonum commune* topos expanded into the chancellery of the elector of Brandenburg in the late Middle Ages. Our final question will be about the transfer levels and the transmitters in the context of this development.

It is safe to say that the unifications of the cities in the fourteenth century assumed an increased significance for this gradual change in using the *bonum commune* topos. For instance, in 1348 the cities of Prenzlau, Pasewalk, Angermünde, and Tempin formed an alliance for mutual protection. Later in the document of this unification, they declared that this alliance was formed to promote their lord's and the land's good (Riedel 1838–1869, Vol. 1, 21, No. XCVI, 161). Beyond individual interests of one single member we can recognize here a superior concern for the general public and its welfare. The same goes for another unification of several cities of the Mittelmark in 1399.[8] Their members referred also to the margrave of Brandenburg and the common good in the electorate.[9] The main basis for this was a well-known principle expressed in the unification document: the problems that face one member of the union concern the others.[10] At this period the elector himself began to use the *bonum commune* topos several times, having probably been affected by his cities. For example, in 1369 some of them together were anxious to get control of the mint, which was situated in Berlin. Elector Otto of Wittelsbach permitted this because of the general public's profit and good. This term seemed to originate from the cities. They had called the elector's attention to their hardship with the value and weight of the coins.[11] It is likely that they had called on the common good argument as a legitimation for their petition. However, they exactly argued in all mentioned cases that the unifications between serval communities in Brandenburg and the legitimation for these acts had contributed to the expansion of the public welfare terms into the elector's environment. Nevertheless, we have to notice that the common good terms were no integral part of the legitimation strategy for the unifications between the cities, because in many cases the *bonum commune* topos is absent in the several texts of the unification documents.

Therefore there must be other possibilities for transferring the topos. That applies to the diets ("Land- und Herrentage") in the late Middle Ages and early modern times. For instance, in 1518 the elector of Brandenburg assembled the estates of his territory to discuss his outstanding debts and ways of resolving them. In return he met several requirements of the estates regarding the mintage, the day's wages, the banking out of the farmers, shooting with rifled guns, and other subjects. On this account the elector promulgated a series of regulations concerning all these topics. Accepting his estate's advice, he pronounced that he was willing to strengthen the common good for his whole territory. So he mentioned in the resolution's text: "unnser Lande und underthan gemeinen nutz zu befordern" (Raumer 1831–1833, Vol. 2, No. XVI, 224–226, here 224). First this intention referred to trading. Therefore the elector decided to stop the production of new coins for a while in order to avoid a price decline. To legitimize this proposal, he referred once more to the common good in his territory. Here we can see a systematic use of the *bonum commune* topos practiced by the elector himself. In this case the public welfare is an important term in the political and social language at the beginning of the sixteenth century. Since this period the elector became more and more a provider of public welfare by caring for trade and building traffic infrastructure such as bridges, paved roads, and locks. For instance in 1523 Elector Joachim I of Brandenburg assembled the prelates, the gentry, and the communities of his territory to discuss the export of the grain. Much to his surprise, he found that many of the invitees did not show up. That applied especially to the gentry. Together with the remainder of the estates, he made the decision to forbid the illegal export of grain, which was often practiced by the gentry. Joachim confirmed this prohibition by referring to the general public's good: "solich verbot gemeinen nutz und dem armut zum Besten geschicht, thewrung zuvorkommen" (Raumer 1831–1833, Vol. 2, No. XVII, 227–232, here 228). We can see here that this request included the poor people as an essential legitimation for this important act. Moreover, the elector wanted to substantiate that this resolution concerns all of his subjects, although many of them had not come to the diet. Therefore he used also the *bonum commune* topos. Against this background it makes good sense that the diets were a fundamental background for transferring this topos into the chancellery of the elector. By exchanging information and communicating between the elector and his subjects in the context of the diets, the common good terms began to stabilize. For both parts, it was an essential term for legitimizing their positions. To look at the whole topic from a higher point of view, we can assert that the rulers and their estates together were constituent parts within the development of the constitution in the Holy Roman Empire. Jointly but also against one another, they had a major impact upon the social and national modernization in Germany in medieval times, as Kesten Krüger mentions (Krüger 2003, 30).

Also in this period infrastructure and traffic were favored reference objects for the public welfare topos used by the elector of Brandenburg. For instance, in 1459 Elector Frederick II planned to build a bridge in Plaue, near to the city of Brandenburg. At that time a ferry boat had to be used to pass the Lake of Plaue.

Frederick executed an instrument in which he declared that he considered his chamber-master, Georg von Weidenfels, responsible for the construction of the bridge. In the arrenga of this document the elector set out his personal view by using the common good terms as a demonstration of political virtue. Therefore, he insisted that he is willing to achieve his subject's and territory's good. Moreover, he pointed out that this is one of his urgent duties as a ruler and elector of Brandenburg.[12] In this connection the construction of the bridge in Plaue was a central element of providing public welfare by the elector. In his argumentation and acting, Frederick II followed those of the communities in fourteenth-century Brandenburg. His successor, Margrave Johann Cicero, did similar things while building important infrastructural facilities.[13] For example, in 1480 he established saltworks in the town of Saarmund, near Berlin. The intention for this building was the general public's good and profit, as Johann himself mentioned: "umb besserung und zunehmunge willen disses kurfurstentumbs der Marck zu Brandenburg" (Raumer 1831–1833, Vol. 1, No. XLVIII, 45–46, here 45). But building the saltworks seemed to be a result of communication between the elector and his estates. So Johann noted that several of his subjects had asked for such saltworks by sending him numerous requests. It seems clear that these subjects had used the *bonum commune* topos as an argument to enforce their requirements. Thus the common good term found its way into the document of the elector.

In summary we can assert that under the rule of Johann Cicero and later under his son and successor, Joachim I, the common good terms became an integral part of legitimizing their political actions as electors of Brandenburg. They both left no doubt about their role as guarantors of public welfare. For instance, Johann Cicero presented himself as an overlord and a sovereign who provides the general good for all his subjects, as is articulated in several documents (Riedel 1838–1869, Vol. 1, 9, No. CCCXIV, 241–242, here 241). Elector Joachim I for his part used the common good terms in a very systematic way. To cite an example, the city regulations of Soldin (1502), Frankfurt (1505), Landsberg (1511), Prenzlau (1515), Strasburg (1515), and Treuenbrietzen (1525) have nearly the same wording. As the initiator of this order, the elector referred to "der Stat vnd dem gemeinen nutz" in all cases (Riedel 1838–1869, Vol. 1, 23, No. CCCLXXVI, 319–322, here 319). In order to retain his interests in three rivers, the Oder, the Spree, and the Havel, and their use as traffic routes, Joachim concluded individual contracts with the cities Frankfurt, Berlin, and Brandenburg. Similar to the city regulations, all the contracts follow the same wording with the exception of the names of the different rivers. Expectedly Joachim I legitimized his declared intention with terms about providing the common good. Regarding this, we can agree with Winfried Eberhard, who pointed out that the ruler himself had the right and also the duty to make decisions about the public welfare by interpreting and representing it (Eberhardt 1986, 246). Nevertheless we should not forget the role of the estates, which called for the common good in many situations. According to this, the public welfare could not have been realized without their help. Finally, also in the sixteenth century the communities still show responsibility for the common good. For instance, with the elector's acceptance the councilmen in the cities were in charge of a righteous regiment willing to realize the public welfare by defining new regulations and exercising the police powers as they did centuries before.[14] In certain circumstances they acted together with the elector in order to avoid mischief. For example, in a diet in the late fifteenth century both parts turned against illegal shipping on the river Elde at the border between Brandenburg and Mecklenburg. In this situation Johann Cicero made clear that he would not come to any decision without the advice of his estates. He justified his intention with the common good term and the security in his territory. Joachim I for his part took care to preserve his freedom of action upon controlling traffic and its infrastructure and other important objects. For instance, toward the three communities of Berlin, Brandenburg, and Frankfurt, he stipulated that the Spree, Oder, and Havel are rivers under his control. As he mentioned, all conflicts about any alteration in the course of these rivers or problems with navigation should arranged by him (Raumer 1831–1833, Vol. 2, No. XXII, 234–235, here 235).

Nevertheless, the estates and especially the communities had not lost their meaning. We can demonstrate this by using the example of Elector Joachim II. Under his rule a number of locks were constructed in the cities of Rathenow, Brandenburg, Berlin, and Fürstenwalde. Using the example of the lock in Rathenow, which was built since 1548, Joachim II pointed out that this infrastructural building would enforce the public welfare in his hole territory. Moreover he praised it in extravagant terms of usefulness and welfare: "zu vnsern vnnd vnsers freuntlichen lieben sons des Erz Bisschofs zu Magdeburgk beiderseitz Landenn, Algemeinen Nutz aufnhemen und wollfardt, Dasz hochnützliche werck die Schleuse bei Inen Im Bau vorlegt vnd geforderdt" (Riedel 1838–1869, Vol. 1, 7, No. LXV, 453–454, here 453). Even though Joachim was the builder-owner of this lock, he could not finance it alone. He depended on the community of Rathenow, which had spent a lot of money in 1548 to dig a "Schutgraben" (Riedel 1838–1869, No. LXI, 449–450, here 449). In return the elector promised to reimburse these expenses. Despite this, the city of Rathenow had a share in providing the territory's welfare. In the same way the councilmen were responsible for the functioning and maintenance of the lock. Therefore they were allowed to keep half of the lockage to use for repair (Riedel 1838–1869, No. LXIII, 451–452). This is more proof that the estates of Brandenburg took a lot of responsibility for providing public goods.

Between fifteenth and sixteenth century the *bonum commune* became an important part of the political thought in the Holy Roman Empire. In this time, providing the public welfare was a major concern of the king and other rulers in the empire. An important proof of this welfare thinking on a high level of the Holy

Roman Empire is the Reichspoliceyordnung, published in 1548. This document contains a multitude of references to the common good topos and the public welfare ideology, as Wolfgang Reinhard confirms (Reinhard 2001, 197). But that was not the beginning of arguing with this topos. Centuries before, communities had used several common good terms as legitimations for their ruling. Traffic and infrastructure were especially popular reference objects for the *bonum commune* topos.

The same counts for medieval Brandenburg, where the maintenance of roads and traffic was one of the traditional responsibilities of the communities. But at the beginning of early modern times things changed gradually. The elector himself became a provider of public welfare by building traffic infrastructure such as bridges, paved roads, and locks. By this time the common good terms had found their way into the elector's chancellery. The unifications between several cities in the fourteenth century, on the one hand, and the communications between the elector and his estates in the context of the diets in the late fifteenth century, on the other hand, were important interfaces for this transfer of the topos. Moreover the elector uses the *bonum commune* topos to legitimize his ruling and his actions. On this account the infrastructure itself became an important public good. Elector Joachim I for his part used the public welfare terms in a systematic way. That represents a significant feature of his ruling. However, under his and his son's rule this conception could not have been realized without the help of the cities. Also in the sixteenth century they still show responsibility for the common good as they did centuries before. Through the time of change between the Middle Ages and early modern times, this indicates some sort of often overlooked continuity.

NOTES

1. Basic Law for the Federal Republic of Germany in the revised version published in the Federal Law Gazette, Part III, classification number 100–1, as last amended by the Act of 11 July 2012 (Federal Law Gazette I, 1478), Art. 89, 1, 2. www.gesetze-im-internet.de/englisch_gg/englisch_gg.html#p0475.

2. For details of these aspects see the overview by Masayuki Tanimoto in this volume, chapter 2.

3. "vppe dat me by den dinghen, de scheen sind, schaden bewaren moge." Riedel (1838–1869), Vol. 4, 1, No. IV, 168.

4. For example, according to *East Central Europe in the Middle Ages* Jean W. Sedlar pointed out that "tariffs and internal tolls diminished the total quantity of trade in the interest of benefiting the royal treasury or powerful individual lords." Sedlar 1994, 360.

5. Until today this document was not edited. See Brandenburgisches Landeshauptarchiv, Rep. 8 Lübben, No. 12/1, fol. 237v–241r.

6. Brandenburgisches Landeshauptarchiv, Rep. 8 Lübben, No. 12/1, fol. 241.

7. Riedel (1838–1869), Vol. 1, 18, No. XCIX, 510: "der Stadt unnd gemeinen nutz zum besten."

8. The Mittelmark was the core territory of the Margrave of Brandenburg. Many important cities like Brandenburg (Oldtown and Newtown), Berlin-Cölln, Frankfurt, Strausberg, Bernau, and Eberswalde were situated in this region. For more details and information, see Schich 2008.

9. "vnsen gnedighen heren vnde syne lande to ghude." Riedel (1838–1869), Vol. 1, 24, No. XCVI, 393–394.

10. Riedel (1838–1869), Vol.1, 24, No. XCVI, 393: "wat eyner stad angheyet, dat schal vns allen steden med eyn andern anghan vnde schullen dar by blyuen."

11. Riedel (1838–1869), Vol. 1, 12, No. XXVII, 501–503. They mentioned: "an desse kegenwortige tzyd von der Muntze wegen doselves besweret und bekummert geweset syn, und durch das sy dicke grocze nod und treflichen scaden genomen und gemeynlichen geleden haben" (501).

12. "Als wir alltzeit geneyget und auch dortzu von unsers Stats wegen verpflichtet und schuldig sein, unnsrer land und leut bests und besserung In unnserm Curfurstenthum der Margk zu Brandburg und anndderswo zu betrachtenn und furzunemen." Riedel 1838–1896, Vol. 1, 10, No. XV, 23–25, here 23.

13. For more information about Margrave Johann the later Elector of Brandenburg, see Fischbacher 2015.

14. Referring to the councilmen Elector Joachim I noted: "bey Irn mitburgern In allem regiment ein rechte pollicej dem gemeinen nutz zu gut verordnen und hanthaben, wie sie von alters gehabt und gebraucht haben." Raumer (1831–1833), Vol. 2, No. XXVII, 240. As Tomas Simon states the common good topos was frequently used in the context of legislation: Simon 2012, 91.

REFERENCES

Anonymous (1839). *Neue Mitteilungen aus dem Gebiet historisch-antiquarischer Forschung* 4 (4): 75–81.

Baumann, Max (1992). "Flüsse als europäische Verkehrsadern: Eine Skizze am Beispiel des Hochrheins." In *Mundo Multa Miracula*, edited by H. Berger, C. H. Brunner, and O. Sigg, 82–96. Zürich, Verlag Neue Zürcher Zeitung.

Blickle, Peter (2001). "Der Gemeine Nutzen: Ein kommunaler Wert und seine politische Karriere." In *Gemeinwohl und Gemeinsinn: Historische Semantiken politischer Leitbegriffe*, edited by H. Münkler and H. Bluhm, 85–107. Berlin, Akademie.

Bütow, Sascha (2015a). "Verkehrsraum in überlandschaftlichen Konturen: Spätmittelalterliche Wegelenkung, Straßenbaumaßnahmen und historische Kartographie." *Blätter für deutsche Landesgeschichte* 151:275–290.

——— (2015b). *Straßen im Fluss: Schifffahrt, Flussnutzung und der lange Wandel der Verkehrsinfrastruktur in der Mark Brandenburg und der Niederlausitz vom 13. bis zum 16. Jahrhundert*. Berlin, Lukas.

Eberhard, Winfried (1986). "Der Legitimationsbegriff des 'Gemeinen Nutzens' im Streit zwischen Herrschaft und Genossenschaft im Spätmittelalter." In *Zusammenhänge, Einflüsse, Wirkungen: Kongreßakten zum ersten Symposium des Mediävistenverbandes in Tübingen 1984*, edited by J. O. Fichte, K. H. Göller Heinz, and B. Schimmelpfennig, 241–254. Berlin and New York, De Gruyter.

Ellmers, Detlev (1985). "Wege und Transport: Wasser." In *Stadt im Wandel: Kunst und Kultur des Bürgertums in Norddeutschland, 1150–1650*, vol. 3, edited by C. Meckseper, 243–255. Stuttgart and Bad Canstatt, Edition Cantz.

Engels, Jens Ivo, and Gerrit Jasper Schenk (2015). "Infrastrukturen der Macht—Macht der Infrastrukturen: Überlegungen zu einem Forschungsfeld." In *Wasserinfrastrukturen und Macht von der Antike bis zur Gegenwart*, edited by B. Förster and M. Bauch, 22–58. Berlin, München and Boston, De Gruyter Oldenbourg.

Fischbacher, Thomas (2015). "Kurfürst Johann: Ein Leben nach dem Tod." In *Die Hohenzollern in Brandenburg: Gesichter einer Herrschaft*, edited by T. Fischbacher, 48–59. Regensburg, Pustet.

Förster, Birte, and Martin Bauch (2015). "Einführung: Wasserinfrastrukturen und Macht: Politisch-soziale Dimensionen technischer Systeme." In *Wasserinfrastrukturen und Macht von der Antike bis zur Gegenwart,* edited by B. Förster and M. Bauch, 9–21. Berlin, Munich, and Boston, De Gruyter Oldenbourg.

Friesecke, Albrecht (1962). *Recht der Bundeswasserstraßen.* Cologne, Berlin, Bonn, and München, Heymann.

Gailing, Ludger, Timothy Moss, and Andreas Röhring (2009). "Infrastruktursysteme und Kulturlandschaften—Gemeinschaftsgut- und Gemeinwohlfunktionen." In *Im Interesse des Gemeinwohls: Regionale Gemeinschaftsgüter in Geschichte, Politik und Planung,* edited by C. Bernhardt, H. Kilper, and T. Moss, 51–73. Frankfurt am Main and New York, Campus.

Geffcken, Heinrich (1900). "Zur Geschichte des deutschen Wasserrechts." *Zeitschrift der Savigny-Stiftung für Rechtsgeschichte: Germanistische Abtheilung* 21:173–217.

Herre, Hermann, and Ludwig Quidde, eds. (1928). *Deutsche Reichstagsakten: Ältere Reihe.* Vol. 16, *1441–1442,* 1. half, 2. half, bk. 16, Stuttgart and Gotha, Vandenhoeck & Ruprecht.

Hibst, Peter (1991). *Ultilitas Publica—Gemeiner Nutz—Gemeinwohl: Untersuchungen zur Idee eines politischen Leitbegriffs von der Antike bis zum späten Mittelalter.* Frankfurt am Main, Bern, New York, and Paris, Peter Lang.

Hoffmann, Hermann, ed. (1955). *Würzburger Polizeisätze: Gebote und Ordnungen des Mittelalters, 1125–1495.* Würzburg, Schöningh.

Jásek, Jaroslav (2015). "An Attempt at an Outline Oft the Historical Development of Water Supply and Sewerage of Medieval Settlements in the Czech Lands." In *Wassermühlen und Wassernutzung im mittelalterlichen Ostmitteleuropa,* edited by Martinan Maříková and C. Zschieschang. Stuttgart, Franz Steiner.

Knupfer, Eugen, ed. (1904). *Urkundenbuch der Stadt Heilbronn 1.* Stuttgart, Kohlhammer.

Krüger, Kesten (2003). *Die landständische Verfassung.* Munich, Oldenbourg.

Lay, Maxwell G. (1992). *Ways of the World: A History of the Worlds's Roads and of the Vehicles That Used Them.* New Brunswick, NJ, Rutgers University Press.

MacFarlane, Neil, and Yuen Foong Khong (2006). *Human Security and the UN: A Critical History.* Bloomington and Indianapolis, Indiana University Press.

Möller, Astrid (2015). "Zwischen Agonalität und Kollektivität: Wasserversorgung im archaischen Griechenland." In *Wasser: Alltagsbedarf, Ingenieurskunst und Repräsentation zwischen Antike und Neuzeit,* edited by S. von Reden and C. Wieland, 27–47. Göttingen and Bristol, Vandenhoeck & Ruprecht.

Moss, Timothy, Rita Gudermann, and Andreas Röhring (2009). "Zur Renaissance der Gemeinschaftsgut- und Gemeinwohlforschung." In *Im Interesse des Gemeinwohls: Regionale Gemeinschaftsgüter in Geschichte, Politik und Planung,* edited by C. Bernhardt, H. Kilper, and Timothy Moss, 31–49. Frankfurt am Main and New York, Campus.

Most, Otto (1950/1951). "Land- und Wasserwege in der deutschen Staatengeschichte." *Zeitschrift für Verkehrsgeschichte* 21:1–33.

Newman, Paul B. (2001). *Daily Life in the Middle Ages.* Jefferson, McFarland.

Oexle, Otto Gerhard (2001). "Konflikt und Konsens: Über gemeinschaftsrelevantes Handeln in der vormodernen Gesellschaft." In *Gemeinwohl und Gemeinsinn: Historische Semantiken politischer Leitbegriffe,* edited by H. Münkler and Harald Bluhm, 65–83. Berlin, Akademie.

Ohler, Norbert (2009). *Reisen im Mittelalter.* Darmstadt, Wissenschaftliche Buchgesellschaft.

Raumer, Georg Wilhelm v., ed. (1831–1833). *Codex Diplomaticus Brandenburgensis Continuatus*, 1–2. Berlin, Stettin, and Elbing, Nicolai.

Reinhard, Wolfgang (2001). *Probleme der deutschen Geschichte, 1495–1806: Reichsreform und Reformation, 1495–1555*. Stuttgart, Klett-Cotta.

Riedel, Friedrich Adolph, ed. (1838–1869). *Codex Diplomaticus Brandenburgensis: Sammlung der Urkunden, Chroniken und sonstigen Quellenschriften für die Geschichte der Mark Brandenburg und ihre Regenden*, 1–41. Berlin, Morin.

Schenk, Gerrit Jasper (2010). "Human Security in the Renaissance? Securitas, Infrastructure, Collective Goods and Natural Hazards in Tuscany and the Upper Rhine Vallay." *Historical Research* 134 (35): 209–233.

Schich, Winfried (2008). "Veränderungen im Verhältnis von Zentrum und Peripherie innerhalb der Germania Slavica durch den hochmittelalterlichen Landesausbau: Mit besonderer Berücksichtigung der brandenburgischen Mittelmark." In *Zentrum und Peripherie in der Germania Slavica*, edited by D. Buchlach and M. Hardt, 13–37. Stuttgart, Franz Steiner.

Schneider, Helmuth (2015). "Macht und Wohlfahrt: Wasser und Infrastruktur im Imperium Romanum." In *Wasserinfrastrukturen und Macht von der Antike bis zur Gegenwart*, edited by B. Förster and M. Bauch, 82–104. Berlin, Munich, and Boston, De Gruyter Oldenbourg.

Schröder, Lina (2014). "Infrastruktur-Geschichte und Landesgeschichte." *Niederrhein-Magazin* 18:9–14.

Sedlar, Jean W. (1994). *East Central Europe in the Middle Ages, 1000–1500*. Seattle, University of Washington Press.

Simon, Thomas (2012). "Gemeinwohl." In *Handwörterbuch zur deutschen Rechtsgeschichte*, vol. 2, edited by A. Cordes, 90–94. Berlin, Erich Schmidt.

Spufford, Peter (2002). *Power and Profit: The Merchant in Medieval Europe*. New York, Thames & Hudson.

Szabó, Thomas (1994). "Die Entdeckung der Straße im 12. Jahrhundert." In *Società, Instituzioni, Spiritualità: Studi in onore di Cinzio Violante*, vol. 2. Spoleto, Centro italiano di studi sull'alto Medioevo.

Thompson, James Westfall (1931). *History of the Middle Ages, 300–1500*. New York, W. W. Norton.

Voigt, Ferdinand, ed. (1869). *Urkunden-Buch zur Berlinischen Chronik*. Berlin, Decker.

Winkelmann, Jan (2011). *Die Mark Brandenburg des 14. Jahrhunderts: Markgräfliche Herrschaft zwischen "Ferne" und politischer "Krise."* Berlin, Lukas.

Zimmermann, August, ed. (1838). *Versuch einer historischen Entwickelung der märkischen Städteverfassung*, vol. 2, *Urkundenbuch*. Berlin, Dümmler.

PART IV

Managing the Forest

DURING THE EARLY MODERN periods and even later, the lives of people worldwide depended on woodlands. Woodlands satisfied the basic needs of local inhabitants in various ways. They provided timber for building houses, barns, stables, and workshops, as well as firewood, which was an indispensable fuel for households and industries. In addition, woodlands supplied various foodstuffs and served agro-pastoral needs for pasturage, fodder, and fertilizer.

Because of these multiple uses, various users felt a sense of entitlement to a single woodland, which was either common to a community or owned by a single party, who granted usufruct to the local people for a moderate fee. Since woodlands were lifelines, forest owners often found it difficult to exclude the surrounding populace from using their forest. From a "market economy" perspective, forest owners were interested in selling their products to well-off consumers who offered the highest purchasing-price, regardless of whether they were local or not. However, from a "moral economy" perspective, forest owners often had to consider the demands of the locals in need.

The frequent occurrence of freeriding users, or "thieves," in the forests could be explained by the difficulties in monitoring forest use. The larger and denser the forest, the more difficult it was to levy a proper fee on forest use or to catch and punish wood thieves. Thus, forests could be regarded as nonexcludable "public goods," if not nonrivalrous.

Part 4 of this volume focuses on forests owned by or reserved for the state in Prussia, Japan, and China in the early modern and modern periods, and discusses to what extent and in which ways they contributed to meeting basic needs of the local populace. We begin our discussion with the Prussian case because Japanese modern government explicitly based its approach to forestry management on the German model. However, it is revealed that the state forestry in Japan did not follow the German way. This Japanese trajectory clearly reflects the diverse possibilities in the way of managing the forest and meeting people's needs among societies.

As shown in Takashi Iida's chapter (chapter 13), traditionally the major revenue of the Prussian kingdom was generated from the direct management of royal domains and forests. Specifically, from the mid-eighteenth to the mid-nineteenth century, state authorities intensively created and expanded fast-growing coniferous stands to improve timber and firewood production and sale, while granting the domain subjects (mainly peasant farmers) the entitlement to obtain timber, firewood, pasturage, and litter in the royal forests for domestic use but never for sale. After experiencing various conflicts between the forestry and the subjects' forest use, the authorities redeemed the subjects' entitlements by 1870s and 1780s by paying the compensation that they elaborately assessed. Through the redemption, the authorities created sufficient latitude to widely and flexibly accept the previously unentitled parties from a growing landless class and from outside the domains, who were in real need of forest use, without burdening the forestry. Thus, the authorities consistently controlled the people's forest use, while achieving the profitable forestry for improving the state budget.

In spite of the adoption of Prussian or German model, Japanese modern state forestry, as Takeshi Aoki (in chapter 14) discusses, developed more path-dependently, adopting the practice of domain lord forestry in the Tokugawa period. Unlike the Prussian system in which the authorities grasped and regulated the locals' forest use directly, Japanese local villagers retained self-governed access in domain and state forests to fulfill their basic needs, which the domain and state authorities consistently tolerated and saw no reason to redeem. In addition, villagers played an active role in managing domain and state forests, sometimes even profiting from activities such as charcoal making and the grazing of animals; villagers checked the excessive expansion of artificial conifer stands, leaving diverse tree species that they needed for various purposes. Thus, unlike with German forest authorities, in the Japanese domain and state forestry, the ruler placed more importance on granting people the opportunity to self-govern and earn their own living.

In early modern China, unlike Prussia and Japan, forestry for timber production and sale was mostly in private hands; the government was rarely involved in it, except in Northeastern areas of Qing-China. For nonmarket provision of wood resources, such as firewood, only insufficient records are available. However, as Yoshiyuki Aihara (in chapter 15) clarifies, the areas designated as "government mountains" contributed to such nonmarket provision, at least in the relatively mountainous areas of Southern China. These areas could not be owned by individuals for profit-making purposes. Instead, they served as "commons for the poor," and were often wasteland or grassland.

Both Prussian and Japanese state forestry operated profit-making activities while meeting the needs of the locals. In Japan, however, unlike Prussia, the local village communities significantly undertook the management of state forests, demonstrating the specific character of the Japanese historical path. In China, although the forestry business was mostly operated by private individuals, the state reserved "government mountains" that functioned as common areas for the poor.

Takashi Iida

Lords' Forestry for People's Basic Needs

Evidence from Prussia's Royal Domains and Forests during the Eighteenth and Nineteenth Centuries

Takashi Iida

In early modern Brandenburg-Prussia, the Hohenzollern monarchs were not only sovereigns of the electorate of Brandenburg or the Prussian kingdom but also lords of their domain estates, just as nobles were lords of their noble estates. Like noble lords, the sovereign lords owned domain estates as landed property, which included their demesne farms and their forests, as well as the peasant farms that they lent to their domain subjects in hereditary or leasehold tenure. Tenant peasants were obligated to render labor for the lords' demesne farms and forests as well as to pay feudal rent in cash or kind. Conversely, the lords were also obligated to supply their subjects with many of life's necessities, especially from their forests, because most of subject peasant communities lacked woodland.[1] In general, demesne lords had an obligation to grant the necessary timber for construction free of charge to subject peasants who held farmsteads in leasehold tenure. This obligation was owed, because the lords owned the farmsteads exclusively and, thus, were solely responsible to (re)build and repair the farm buildings.[2] Otherwise, demesne lords were obligated to allow their subjects access to their forests to gather fallen dead wood as firewood, graze livestock, collect litters, and so on. Accordingly, while the royal authorities managed their forests for profit, they were obligated to meet the basic needs of royal domain subjects.

In 1713, however, King Friedrich Wilhelm I transferred all domains, including the forests, to the state budget and reserved only a specific amount for the royal family and the court. Owing to this development, the Prussian General Legal Code (*Allgemeines Landrecht für die preußischen Staaten*) of 1794 declared the domains to be the property of the state.[3] Consequently, the royal authorities had to allow not only domain subjects but also the other state's population to use the royal forests. During the eighteenth century, the Prussian state rose to become one of the great European powers through the expansion of its army. To secure army personnel, the state was very eager to increase the state's population. As a result, an increasing population of cottage residents emerged, among which the lodgers were not domain subjects but joined in the use of the royal forests.[4] Furthermore, King Friedrich II, with his remarkable sense of right and wrong, began allowing subjects of noble lords to use the royal forests just as his domain subjects.[5] Thus, while the exploiting pressure on the royal forests increased, Friedrich II started the project of afforestation and established the system of sustainable forestry in the royal forests.[6]

This chapter examines how and to what extent the royal authorities met the demands of the growing population both inside and outside domain estates for wood resources in the royal forests while advancing the forestry. Prussia's royal domains and forests in Brandenburg during the eighteenth and nineteenth centuries will be explicitly focused on. While surveying the general developments in Brandenburg, this chapter details the case of the royal domain and forest district of Alt-Ruppin *(das königliche Domänenamt und Forstrevier Alt-Ruppin)*. Delving into this case will help reveal the realities that a survey of Brandenburg alone cannot.

ROYAL DOMAIN(S) AND FOREST(S) IN BRANDENBURG AND ALT-RUPPIN

The royal domain and royal forest district of Alt-Ruppin traditionally belonged to the Kurmark Brandenburg (the greater part of Brandenburg comprising the Altmark west of the Elbe River and the East Elbian areas to the Oder River surrounding Berlin and Potsdam). In 1815, after ceding the Altmark in 1807, the Kurmark area roughly became the governorate district of Potsdam *(Regierungsbezirk Potsdam)*, the western part of the Prussian province of Brandenburg.

Traditionally, the Kurmark had a higher density of sovereign lordship than other Prussian territories. At the end of the eighteenth century, it included fifty-four royal domains, encompassing 40% of all peasants in the East Elbian area.[7] Throughout the eighteenth and nineteenth centuries, approximately one-third of Brandenburg was covered in forests.[8] In the Kurmark around 1800, the crown owned seventy-two royal forest districts covering approximately 58% of the total woodland, while the nobility and peasants owned 28%, and the cities and towns owned 14%. This calculation, however, did not include at least 134 other forested areas belonging to nobles and peasants because no records were available for these areas.[9] Data regarding the share of peasant' ownership is available in the Ruppin district *(Kreis Ruppin)* of the Kurmark. This data shows that peasants owned only 4% of the forests while 75% belonged to royal families and 13% to noble lords and private owners.[10] Peasants or peasant communities often had meager or no wood-lots, making their entitlement to the lords' forests indispensable.

Both the royal domain of Alt-Ruppin and the royal forest district of Alt-Ruppin had their headquarters in or around the town of Alt-Ruppin, which lay approximately sixty kilometers northwest of Berlin. The domain and forest authorities cooperated in the exercise of royal lordship over the agricultural lands in the domain as well as the woodlands in the forest district.[11] As a result of incorporating a part of the domain of Lindow in 1764, the royal domain of Alt-Ruppin became comparatively sizable among the royal domains in the Kurmark. Around the year 1800, the domain included the two towns of Alt-Ruppin and Lindow, two royal demesne farms in the town of Alt-Ruppin and the village of Dabergotz, twenty-six villages, and new settlements such as eight colonies (one of them was a colonist village) and two *Büdner-etablissements*. Some of the new settlements were constructed by a tar oven, a glasswork, or a farm hereditarily leased to a nobleman. While the towns and the villages had long been established mostly since the Middle Ages, the construction of the new settlements occurred only in and around the 1750s. The royal authorities settled these new settlements with "foreigners" and retired soldiers.[12]

Table 8 presents the development of the social structure in the rural settlements that belonged to the royal domain of Alt-Ruppin in the year of 1800. Farms of peasants (*Bauern* and *Kossäten*) existed only in villages and towns. Due to limits on arable land and the impartibility of individual farms, the number of peasant farms was mostly constant except for the devastation caused by the Thirty Years' War. Conversely, the number of cottages increased drastically beginning in the early eighteenth century. The cottages were built not only in old villages but in new settlements also. An increasing number of disinherited children of peasant farmers and offspring of cottage residents were repeatedly permitted to own and lease cottages as cottagers (*Büdner*) and lodgers (*Einlieger*), respectively.

In 1798, the forest district of Alt-Ruppin included a total area of more than thirty-five thousand *Morgen* (one *Morgen* is approximately 0.26 hectares), a comparatively large area among the royal forest districts in the Kurmark.[13] In 1820, it incorporated a part of the neighboring forest district of Zühlen, and this amounted to a sizable district of more than forty thousand *Morgen*, which consisted of the seven subdistricts of Klausheide, Lietze, Krangenbrück, Hohenheide, Pfefferteich, Glienicke, and Rägelin. This size proved to be uneconomic in many regards. In 1843, as the new forest district of Neu-Glienicke was founded, the two subdistricts of Glienicke and Rägelin were transferred to it. As a result, the Alt-Ruppin forest district was reduced to about twenty-six thousand *Morgen*, a size more conducive to protection and administration.[14]

According to an investigation in 1825, six-sevenths of the forest district of Alt-Ruppin consisted of pine stands. Considering the dominance of pine trees, it is no wonder that in the forest district of Alt-Ruppin, high forest management with 100- or 120-year cutting cycles was practiced. Here, even broad-leaf trees formed exclusively high forests, leaving no room for coppice. Thus, the subjects and locals

TABLE 8. Development of the Social Structure of Rural Settlements That in 1800 Belonged to the Royal Domain of Alt-Ruppin, 1687–1831

	1687	1757/64	1800	1831
Large peasants *(Bauern)*	347 (97)	420 (1)	420	412
Small peasants *(Kossäten)*	98 (21)	110	105	94
Cottagers *(Büdner)*	0	124	124	359
Lodgers *(Einlieger)*	18	135	322	682

SOURCES: Iida 2010, 43; for 1831, BLHA, Rep. 7, Amt Alt-Ruppin, 283.
NOTES: (1) A fishing village was not considered. (2) The number of devastated farms in parentheses.

were permitted to gather fallen dead wood as fuel and to graze their livestock under the high trees.[15]

FEUDAL ERA TO 1811

After the end of Thirty Years' War in 1648, it took more than half a century to resettle the peasant farms devastated and abandoned during the war. In the Alt-Ruppin domain, one-fourth of the peasant farms were still not yet resettled even forty years after the war (Table 8). During the postwar depopulation, the woodlands increased.[16] In 1688, however, the annual income of the electorate of Brandenburg from the electoral forest was only about sixty-one thousand Reichstaler (rt), while that from the electoral domains (which consisted mainly of farmland) amounted to more than one million rt. As Otto Behre noted, this meager income from the electoral forest was in striking contrast to its immense size. After deducting the salaries of forestry and hunting officials, the surplus that the electorate of Brandenburg could earn from his immense forest did not reach even seven thousand rt.[17] At that time, based on the wood ordinances of 1590, 1593, and 1622, peasants of the electoral domains were entitled to obtain the necessary timber for maintaining and constructing farm buildings by paying half of the cost.[18]

While Elector Friedrich III (1688–1713, King Friedrich I beginning in 1701) only minimally improved the electoral or royal forests, King Friedrich Wilhelm I (1713–1740) succeeded in increasing the revenue from the forests mainly through an intensive ship timber trade with foreign countries as well as by putting the forest accounting system in good order. The monetary budget of the royal forests in the Kurmark in the fiscal year 1731/1732 was 108,017 rt in revenue and only 6,057 rt in expenditure.[19] However, Friedrich Wilhelm I was more interested in improving agriculture on domain lands than in improving the forestry. Thus, the king lowered the price of timber for his peasants. Even after the farms were completely resettled in the early eighteenth century, royal authorities still faced the problem that buildings on usufructuary peasant farms were mostly dilapidated because the peasants could not afford to pay for the timber. Such conditions made the farms susceptible to fires, collapse, or total abandonment. To remedy this problem, King

Friedrich Wilhelm I released a patent on April 25, 1729, in which he declared that all timber, regardless of whether it was necessary for new constructions or maintenance, would be given from his forests to non-farm-owning peasants in the royal domains free of charge. According to the investigations in 1747 and 1748, about 53% of all peasants (5,774 out of 10,898) in the royal domains in the Kurmark were non-farm-owners. Additionally, the king declared that timber granted to his farm-owning peasants for new constructions and repairs would only require payment of one-third of the total cost. In this way, the domain peasants' entitlement to timber reached its peak in 1729.[20]

King Friedrich II (1740–1786) further increased the revenue from his forests through timber trade with foreign countries. The revenue from the royal forests in the Kurmark amounted to 215,044 rt in the fiscal year 1747/1748 and 233,046 rt in the fiscal year 1756/1757.[21] He was the first monarch who thoroughly engaged in afforestation, which, however, did not advance without difficulty. The Seven Years' War (1756–1763) interrupted his forestry endeavors and caused devastation to the royal forests, from which they recovered only over a long period.[22] Furthermore, the king's forestry endeavors clashed with his other central policy of populating his kingdom.[23]

In the royal domains in the northern districts of Brandenburg like Prignitz, Ruppin, and Uckermark, the building of new settlements concentrated within a few years around 1750.[24] Within the Alt-Ruppin domain alone, at least eight colonies and two *Büdner-etablissements* were established in and around the 1750s. Some of these, such as Frankendorf, Woltersdorfer Baum, and Wüsten-Rägelin, were founded within the royal forest district of Alt-Ruppin.[25] Thus, colonization increased exploitation on the royal forests.

While new establishments increased the demand for building timber from the royal forests, the authorities took measures to prevent the waste of timber grants, which was likely to occur, especially in cases of non-farm-owning peasants who were entitled to free timber. In 1784, the General Forest Department created a draft of a building code. Domain and construction officials from the Altmark and the Prignitz were commissioned to provide expert reports if the code would apply to their areas. According to the draft, the necessity for a new building and its size were determined by the building's master carpenter and peasants, which often resulted in excess timber being granted. To remedy this problem, the draft proposed that a construction official should visit the construction site to determine whether or not a repair would be sufficient and to estimate the size and amount of timber needed for the new building on the basis of model drawings (clauses 1, 2, and 6 of the proposed code). This proposal had, as expert reports revealed, already been put into practice in several domains and then was generally applied during the 1780s. In fact, in 1840, an official named Wittchow, of the governorate of Potsdam, reported for the Alt-Ruppin domain that buildings that were more than sixty or eighty years of age had been built with superior timber and had greater longevity than newer buildings.[26]

Specifically in the Alt-Ruppin domain, the timber economy advanced in another way. In 1763 and 1764, as the royal domain of Lindow was dissolved and incorporated into the neighboring domains, including Alt-Ruppin, the authorities offered farm ownership to the usufructuary peasants in these domains. Approximately 240 usufructuary peasants from sixteen villages in the expanded domain of Alt-Ruppin accepted this offer by agreeing to pay one-third of future timber costs, while approximately 260 peasants from ten other villages did not accept the offer due to concerns with losing the provision of free timber. Consequently, the authorities not only improved the royal forest revenue but could certainly economize on timber grants as well, because the farm owners used to refrain from demanding unnecessary timber due to the one-third payment, as expert reports on the draft of the building code of 1784 explained.[27]

One reason why many peasants in the Alt-Ruppin domain gave up free timber is illustrated by the case of the village of Grieben (which belonged to Lindow domain until 1764, then to Friedrichsthal, then to Alt-Ruppin after 1819). Here, only eight peasants accepted farm ownership while the other twelve refused it. Starting in 1765, however, even the twelve usufructuaries paid one-third of the costs for granted timber, the same as the farm owners, a choice that was influenced by the threat of eviction. Being replaced by other tenants who were willing and able to pay more for timber was no longer an unrealistic fear. It might have been out of such a fear that all of the peasants in each of the sixteen villages fell into line with accepting farm ownership by giving up free timber.[28] Rivalry over the limited number of impartible farms intensified in the agrarian boom during the latter third of the eighteenth century, as farms enjoyed an increasing demand for grain from growing populations in rural Brandenburg and Berlin as well as from industrializing England.[29]

While economizing on timber grants, the authorities improved the royal forestry to increase wood production. In 1764, King Friedrich II prohibited selection cutting and introduced compartment cutting, which made artificial planting in each compartment possible.[30] On the basis of this development, the authorities began to mobilize the labor of subjects toward afforestation works. On January 17, 1785, it was declared that each subject who was entitled to receive timber from royal forests should work to improve the forests. This consisted of ploughing, harrowing, and raking forest lands as well as gathering and delivering pinecones to the authorities, who used them for artificial regeneration.[31] In the late eighteenth century, as the afforestation of the royal forests advanced, the authorities no longer permitted new settlements in the royal forests to conserve wooded areas.[32]

Traditionally, the royal authorities not only provided domain subjects with timber but also firewood. While the authorities collected the larger cordwood to be sold, the subjects were typically permitted to gather only the thinner fallen dead wood *(Raff- und Leseholz)* for domestic use "but never for sale."[33] To make this division effective, authorities forbade subjects to bring axes or hatchets into the royal forests and specified an upper limit of wood to be gathered. These regulations, however, were often met with resistance as the fallen dead wood became insufficient for the growing population, especially from the mid-eighteenth century.[34]

According to the oldest available register, from 1809/1810,[35] 243 inhabitants of nineteen surrounding settlements were entitled to gather fallen dead wood in the royal forest district of Alt-Ruppin. Most were subjects and preachers in the villages and colonies belonging to the royal domain of Alt-Ruppin. Three of the registered settlements, however, belonged to the noble or princely estates, from which the lords' demesne farms and their subjects were entitled to the fallen dead wood. A peasant farmer or a preacher was entitled to gather fallen dead wood with a two-horse-drawn wagon by paying four Scheffel oats or twenty-four to thirty-two *Groschen* (gr) for two days a week, while a cottager was entitled to bring only a handcart and paid eight gr. The register included 227 wagon users, from which seven were allocated to two noble demesne farms, and sixteen handcart users.

It should be noted that among the nineteen registered settlements, at least five (Pfalzheim, Frankendorf, Stendenitz, Gühlen, and Woltersdorf) were only established in and around the 1750s. They joined with nineteen wagon users and ten handcart users in the practice of gathering fallen dead wood. Additionally, as reported in the late eighteenth century, there were a large number of *freiwillige Heidemieter,* who apparently entered the forest for firewood without entitlement. This was probably due to the fact that the lodgers, who increased most rapidly in number (table 8), were not included in the register of the entitled inhabitants. With this increasing rivalry, authorities were compelled around the year 1800 to raise the maximum thickness limit of fallen dead wood that subjects could gather, namely, from 2.5 to 3 *Zoll*. Furthermore, since the royal forestry shifted from selection cutting to compartment cutting in 1764, pure pine stands became dominant, which caused frequent insect damage, because pure stands were more vulnerable to insects. Especially in the years following insect or wind damage, subjects could enjoy an abundance of fallen dead wood without strict controls by the royal authorities.[36]

The royal forests were not only the place of timber and fuel-wood production but offered pasturing areas as well. In the seventeenth century, the forest orders did not yet care about the damage of unrestricted pasturage in the royal forests, because the livestock were few at that time.[37] Population growth during the eighteenth century, however, resulted in an increase of livestock and, thus, grazing pressure on the royal forests. According to the first available list of 1812,[38] twenty-six settlements were entitled to pasture a fixed number of livestock in the forest district of Alt-Ruppin. Most of these settlements belonged to the royal domains, but a few were subject to surrounding noble estates. Out of the twenty-six registered settlements, at least three farms hereditarily leased to nobles (Woltersdorf, Frankendorf, and Gühlen) and three colonies (Bienenwalde, Stendenitz, and Pfalzheim) were established in the royal domain of Alt-Ruppin between 1747 and 1755 and joined in the pasturage of the forest district of Alt-Ruppin.

While the number of pasturing parties increased, the pasturing area in the royal forests narrowed because, for successful afforestation, the authorities enlarged the area preserved from the grazing animals. As a result, the forest-grazing parties were not in harmony. A report from 1797 mentioned "countless numbers of conflicts" in the Pfefferteich subdistrict. At that time, livestock from Darritz, Frankendorf, Storbeck, Woltersdorf, and Katerbow grazed there collectively. Since no party had a specified territory, they constantly felt intruded upon and were at odds with one another. Parties who advanced their interests by force gained the upper hand. In this respect, Storbeck stood out. Around 1797, Storbeck seized the animals that the villagers of Darritz pastured in an area called Hasche, denying them their rights to pasture there without reason.[39] In any case, such rivalry functioned as mutual regulation of the number of animals pastured in the forest.[40]

To support forest-grazing villages, the authorities offered them additional pastoral use of the forest. In 1796, the villagers of Storbeck petitioned the authorities to permit them to continue raking moss and pine needles in the Alt-Ruppin forest. They could not spare these forest by-products for supplementing the litter that they lacked because of insufficient hay and straw yields. On this occasion, the forest official of Alt-Ruppin not only accepted Storbeck's demand, but also offered the same permission to other villages like Darritz, Pfalzheim, and Nietwerder, who were experiencing the same or an even more severe litter shortage. Ultimately, the four villages were allowed to rake moss and pine needles only on a predetermined day every week during the winter half-year in a place specified by the forest officials.[41] As discussed in the annual economic report for 1802 on the district of Ruppin (*Kreis Ruppin*), to which the Alt-Ruppin domain and forest belonged, raked moss and pine needles helped peasants to keep up with the general intensification of manure production at that time, which notably resulted in intensive potato cultivation on fallow lands. The potatoes and their waste served as livestock feed.[42]

The peasants' gain from the forest was, of course, combined with their obligations to the forest owner. In return for being permitted to rake moss and pine needles, the peasants were obligated to deliver a certain quantity of pine cones to the forest authorities. This obligation was due to an ordinance from 1788, with which the authorities had increased their opportunities to extend their subjects' labor into afforestation.[43]

REFORM LEGISLATION OF 1811 AND THE FOLLOWING HALF CENTURY

After the defeat of Prussia by Napoleonic France in 1806, Prussia launched a reform to dissolve the relationship between lords and subjects. The reform legislation (such as the 1811 *Regulierungsedikt* and the 1821 *Ablösungsordnung*) prescribed how to redeem the rights of lords and subjects, including the subjects' entitlements to the lords' forests. However, these entitlements were often long maintained because they were excluded from settlements where relationships between lords and subjects were dissolved.

Even before the legislation, royal authorities watched for an opportunity to negate subjects' rights to free timber. They found such an opportunity in 1799, as they offered freedom from labor obligations and farm ownership to those peasants in the royal domains who did not enjoy these.[44] In the domain of Alt-Ruppin, negotiations began in 1803 with four villages (Dabergotz, Molchow, Nietwerder, and Wuthenow) where the peasants were mostly usufructuary farm holders and saddled with labor obligations for the royal demesne farms. For freedom from labor and farm ownership, the authorities enforced rigid conditions, including that peasants should surrender their entitlements to free timber without any compensation. The peasants eventually accepted such conditions by 1818 because their greatest concern was emancipation from labor services.

In the royal domain of Alt-Ruppin, however, peasants saddled with labor obligations for the royal demesne farms were in the minority. Besides the four villages referenced earlier, there were six villages dominated by usufructuaries that were already exempt from labor obligations. Without the inducement of freedom from labor obligations, they could take the time to fight against the abolishment of their entitlement to free timber. Eventually, the royal authorities redeemed the entitlement in the form of rent by the mid-nineteenth century. Furthermore, the domain included sixteen to nineteen villages comprising mostly farm-owning peasants without labor obligations for the demesne farms, who were entitled to timber for a one-third payment. The authorities proposed to redeem their entitlements through rent. In most cases, the negotiations only began around 1840. As a result of the determined opposition of the majority of the farm-owning peasants, however, the authorities found no alternative but to continue granting them timber until the 1860s and 1870s when, eventually, their rights were redeemed. Until then, the authorities had to meet their increased timber needs for enlarging or increasing their stables and barns to handle concurrent advancements in agriculture, in accordance with Clause 210, Title 22, Part I of the Prussian General Legal Code of 1794.[45]

In contrast to the situation regarding timber, the royal authorities left the subjects' rights to fallen dead wood and forest pasturage untouched for half a century after the reform legislation of 1811. In his guidebook for redeeming rights to forests from 1829, Georg Ludwig Hartig, the chief forester of the Prussian kingdom, argued that it was unwise for forest owners to redeem entitlements to fallen dead wood and forest pasturage. Fallen dead wood, which satisfied the necessity of subjects, was of little or no value for the authorities because it was unsaleable and cost time and labor to collect piecemeal. Pasturing animals caused no noticeable harm to the forest, as long as they were kept from preserved areas. It was not prudent to abolish forest grazing because the rich undergrowth would then die uselessly.[46]

For regulating the surviving entitlements to the forests, the authorities relied on the 1811 *Landeskulturedikt,* which promoted the cultivation of land. Concerning forestlands, the *Landeskulturedikt* stated that, for silviculture, entitlements to pasturage and gathering firewood were, per se, not harmful unless there were abuses. Based on this perception, the edict ordered that each forest owner should be authorized to limit the fallen dead wood collected by an entitled person to necessary purposes only, by permitting the gathering of wood only on fixed days under a forest official's supervision (§26). Preservation areas were to be made as large as necessary to enable regenerative silviculture (§28). If, however, the indispensable forest pasturage suffered from the unrestricted application of this rule, a fair restriction would be put in place by an arbitrator (§29). Thus, the edict aimed to make sustainable forestry and indispensable forest use somehow compatible.[47]

In the Alt-Ruppin forest district, the authorities not only retained entitlements to fallen dead wood but also even permitted unentitled parties to gather it. As reported in the Description and Management Plan of the forest district in 1825:

> Besides (the entitled parties), still many unentitled individuals enter the forest for fallen dead wood. They cannot be removed because they were living in the forest and very poor. They, however, had to pay a higher access fee than the entitled.[48]

In 1846/1847, while 270 wagon users and twenty-eight handcart users were entitled to gather fallen dead wood in the royal forest district of Alt-Ruppin, the authorities allowed two wagon users and 159 handcart users to do so, not by entitlement but by granting formal permission. Thus, the authorities accepted the previously unentitled parties mostly from the growing lower-class population living in cottages. This increased openness was based on the increasing volume of wood as a result of advancing afforestation.[49]

While fallen dead wood increased with advancing afforestation, forest-grazing areas narrowed as a result. In 1820, in the Alt-Ruppin forest district, the authorities planned to afforest all existing clearings of 4,523 *Morgen* by 1839. In fact, between 1825 and 1846, clearings were reduced from 4,145 *Morgen* to 572 *Morgen* or from 10.2% to 2.2% of the total district area.[50] To afforest the clearings, additional areas had to be continuously preserved to prohibit grazing animals. Meanwhile, however, the authorities kept the people's entitlements to forest pasturage intact. To make forestry and pasturage somehow compatible, the authorities carefully investigated each preserve, focusing on when it could be reopened for pasturing.[51] Starting in the 1840s, the forest authorities spoke of the "permissible extent of preserved areas," which was, on the whole, limited to one-fifth of the total pasturing area.[52]

Obviously, the forest-grazing parties did not fully exercise their entitlements. As reported in the Description and Management Plan of 1825, "although many villages were entitled to pasture horses, they did not exercise these rights any more at all."[53] This was the result of their efforts to shift from pasturage to the feeding of horses by stalls.[54] Nevertheless, the pasture in the forest district seemed to be

TABLE 9. Number of Livestock Pastured in the Royal Forest District of Alt-Ruppin, 1847–1854

	Horses	Oxen	Cows	Calves	Sheep	Pigs	Calculated as cows
1847	15	51	398	71.3	8,188	343	1,383
1848		55	289	35	9,847	300	1,402
1849	10	55	313	54	7,133	327	1,181
1851	14	10	320	44	8,534	390	1,276
1852	16	10	358	53.7	7,910	321	1,251
1854		4.7	215	21.5	6,290	171	882

Source: BLHA, Rep. 2A, Regierung Potsdam, III F, no. 4288, 263–283.
Notes: (1) One cow = 3/4 horse = 3/4 ox = two calves = ten sheep = eight pigs. (2) The values of 1850 and 1853 are not presented, because for both years the data is incomplete. (3) Numbers of geese, which were very few, were not considered.

insufficient for the livestock pastured. As the forest and domain officials of Alt-Ruppin in 1829 reported, even during the summer months, the forest pasturage could not support the livestock without supplementary fodder.[55]

From 1847 to 1854, the numbers pastured in the forest district of Alt-Ruppin were recorded. For each year, the forest official counted and recorded the numbers of livestock pastured by each party. The total number of animals pastured in the forest district of Alt-Ruppin was between 882 and 1,402 in cows (table 9). Even the smallest number significantly exceeded the capacity of the district's pastures, which, in the assessment of 1856, worked out at 661.9 cows.[56]

Excess grazing animals had significant consequences, especially in the 1840s. In 1842, most areas of the Prussian state were struck by an unprecedented drought, causing a severe lack of livestock feed, primarily because the meadows and pastures became arid. On September 1, the central authority in Berlin proposed to permit suffering peasants, even if unentitled, to graze their livestock in the royal forests, which, because of the shade, still afforded some pastures. To this proposal, the domain of Alt-Ruppin replied that it would be no use, because a large number of peasants were already entitled to pasturage in the Alt-Ruppin forest and, therefore, would never admit the unentitled parties. The domain proposed that peasants lacking straw and hay be given extraordinary permission to gather litter in the forest. This counterproposal was, eventually, supported by the forest inspector of Rheinsberg, von Schaltzen. He initially remarked that a forester always wanted to see his forest as free as possible from litter exploitation because it hindered the growth of trees.[57] Ultimately, he gave priority to the general interest over special forestry interests.[58]

The excessive quantity of grazing animals also damaged the foresters' meadows and surrounding stands in the forest district. In 1847, the senior forester (Oberförster) of the Alt-Ruppin forest district petitioned the governorate of Potsdam to redeem the pasture rights on the meadows of all foresters in the district. The meadows were pastured by many entitled parties in spring and autumn. Consequently, they deteriorated constantly, and their productivity levels were deficient because there was no opportunity to improve them. For years, all foresters had requested this redemption without success. In 1847, they could no longer endure as their meadows were deteriorating at a greater rate than ever because hungry animals could find "no fodder" in the forest and, thus, depended almost exclusively on the meadows.[59]

In his petition, the senior forester indicated the merit of stopping spring and autumn pasturage on Eggersdorf meadow for the benefit of the forest surrounding it. If ceased, the animals would also leave the royal forest in spring and autumn because the forest alone could hardly feed them during these seasons. For the forest, the pasturage in early spring was most dangerous because the grass was lacking: therefore, woody plants necessarily served as fodder and suffered. As this meadow was narrow and long, the pasturage on it continuously and inevitably damaged the neighboring forest preserve. It was all the more sensitive as the bordering forest grounds were mostly designated for growing beech trees.[60]

In fact, in 1847 and 1848, the number of livestock pastured in the forest was remarkably large (table 9). This situation might have resulted from a severe potato failure that prevailed in Brandenburg during the 1840s, most seriously in the middle of the decade. It meant a decrease in feed, which made the livestock more dependent on the wood pastures than usual.[61] Also, 1848 was the year of revolutions, in which the populace overused the royal forests in various ways.[62]

THE REDEMPTION OF THE
ENTITLEMENTS TO FOREST

In 1849, the budget of the royal forests in the governorate district of Potsdam was approximately 504,289 rt in revenue and 202,289 rt in expenditures. The revenue was more than twice that of the Kurmark a century earlier, when King Friedrich II began afforestation activities, and approximately 452,660 rt (90%) were generated from the sale of timber and firewood.[63] During this century-long forestry improvement scheme, subject's and local's traditional use of royal forests was, as shown, intensified as a result of population growth. This use survived for a substantial period even after the reform legislation of 1811.

In Alt-Ruppin, it was only in 1856 that the values of all the people's entitlements to the forest district were thoroughly estimated by Marot, an official of the Potsdam governorate. His task was to calculate the cost of redemption and to examine whether it was practicable and profitable. According to this assessment, the total annual yield of the forest district was 21,606 rt, of which 6,634 rt (30.7%) went to the local populace.[64]

While the redemption of timber entitlements had long been pursued and partly realized, Marot's report in 1856 was the first official report that recommended the authorities redeem the entitlements to fallen dead wood and forest pasturage by paying an assessed amount.

Marot considered that it would be profitable to the authorities to redeem the entitlements to fallen dead wood as soon as possible, and with good reasons. First, the entitlement holders obtained 195,482 *Kubikfuß* from the forest while they were legally able to obtain only 128,314 *Kubikfuß*. Thus, the authorities lost 67,168 *Kubikfuß* because it was impossible to monitor firewood gatherers thoroughly. After the redemption, they would be free from this loss because they would then pay compensation rent only for the lesser legal amount. Second, as silviculture and forest monitoring improved, the volume of wood and fallen dead wood (which entitled subjects and locals could gather) increased. Therefore, the authorities could redeem entitlements by paying lower rent sooner than at some future point. Third, with this redemption, Marot did not intend to stop the widespread practice of gathering firewood entirely. Instead of entitled parties who were mainly from the farm-owning class and had their wagons, he planned to accept more of the unentitled parties, which consisted mainly of lower-class people with handcarts, for a particular access fee. The fee would then help to cover the redemption rent paid to entitled parties, which he estimated at 1,046 rt. Marot also expected that a significant number of the people committing wood theft would prefer the honest way if they were given an opportunity to obtain fallen dead wood for a moderate fee, which would profit the public interest as well as the interest of forest owners.[65]

Marot reported that the authorities should redeem pasturing rights by paying 1,631 rt as annual compensation. His reason was that the forestry needs for the preserved areas, which at that time exceeded the permissible limit of 20% of the total pasturing area, could not be satisfied without redeeming the existing rights to forest pasturage. Even with his redemption plan, however, Marot never intended to drive the grazing practice itself out of the forest but to lease the woodlands for pasturage once they were free from the pasturing rights, under conditions better fitting forestry needs. He expected that the rent obtained by the leases would cover the bulk of the compensation.[66]

Marot's plan seems to have been based on the general policy of the Potsdam governorate for leasing forest pastures. In 1853, the governorate declared that, when necessary, even livestock owners who were not entitled to forest pasturage should "always" be permitted to exercise such by paying a pasture fee according to a tariff schedule. Following this declaration, each royal forest district within the governorate's jurisdiction had drafted a tariff schedule according to animal types.[67]

It was primarily in the 1870s and 1880s that the redemption plan was put into practice. At the end of the 1880s, only the town of Alt-Ruppin and some other parties maintained the rights to pasture livestock equivalent to 292 cows. Through the redemptions, the Alt-Ruppin forest district created sufficient latitude to provide the surrounding livestock owners with pastures according to their needs, especially in cases of severe hay and straw shortages.[68]

This research has proven that the royal forestry improved its wood production during the eighteenth and nineteenth century, especially after Friedrich II introduced afforestation practices. Meanwhile, however, the royal forests provided for the basic needs of subjects and locals. The entitlements of domain subjects to the royal forests were enlarged as a result of the establishment of new settlements in the domain in the mid-eighteenth century; they substantially survived reform legislation in the early nineteenth century; and, in most cases, they were only redeemed between the 1860s and 1880s. Additionally, the royal forest had to permit unentitled parties from the growing landless class and individuals from outside the domains access to the royal forests. The continuing and intensifying forest use of the subjects and locals was a burden on the royal forestry. There were many free riders among the *Heidemieter*. In particular, forest pasturage clashed with the enlargement of preserved areas for successful afforestation and collecting litters impoverished the soil of the woods.

From the 1860s to the 1880s, almost all the entitlements to the royal forest were finally redeemed. After redeeming peasant farmers' entitlements to gather fallen dead wood, lower-class people were permitted to continue to do so in the form of flexible contracts in higher numbers than before. Thus, the authorities provided latitude to accept firewood theft honestly. Through the redemptions of the entitlements to wood pastures, forest authorities created sufficient latitude to widely and flexibly provide the surrounding livestock owners with grazing according to their needs, especially in cases of severe hay and straw shortages. Through such flexible provision, forest use practices could be made more compatible with forestry practices than before.

NOTES

1. Hasel 1974, 6, Hasel and Schwartz 2006, 100–102.
2. Eisenberg and Stengel 1796, 10–11.
3. Hasel and Schwartz 2006, 83.
4. See chapter 7 in this volume.
5. Pfeil 1839/2009, 87.
6. Stadelmann 1882, 139–145, Rubner 1967, 68–70, Asche 2015, 70–74.
7. Müller 1965, 152.
8. Materna and Ribbe 1995, 21.
9. Bratring 1804–1809/1968, 25, 119–123.
10. Bratring 1799, 40–48.
11. Bratring 1799, 390–395.
12. Schulze 1935, 52–57, Iida 2010, 49.
13. Bratring 1804–1809/1968, 122.

14. Brandenburgisches Landeshauptarchiv, Potsdam, Germany (hereafter: BLHA), Rep. 2A, Regierung Potsdam, III F, no. 4286, fol. 266, 285, No. 4524–4529.

15. BLHA, Rep. 2A, Regierung Potsdam, III F, no. 4285, fol. 4, 52, no. 4295.

16. Pfeil 1839/2009, 61.

17. Behre 1905, 85.

18. Christian Otto Mylius, ed., *Corpus Constitutionum Marchicarum oder Königlich Preußische und Churfürstlich Brandenburgische in der Chur- und Marck Brandenburg, auch incorporirten Landen publicirte und ergangene Ordnungen, Edicta, Mandata, Rescripta etc.* Berlin 1737–1751, IV. Theil, I. Abtheilung, II. Cap., Sp. 501, 515, 537, Pfeil 1839/2009, 54.

19. Pfeil 1839/2009, 135.

20. Iida 2013, 506–11.

21. Pfeil 1839/2009, 175–176.

22. Stadelmann 1882, 140–141, Koser 1903, 113.

23. Stadelmann 1882, 144; Asche 2015, 70–71.

24. Asche 2015, 70.

25. Iida 2010, 48–9, Bratring 1799, 452, 454–455.

26. Iida 2013, 514–515.

27. Iida 2013, 515–516.

28. Iida 2010, 104, 121–123.

29. Harnisch 1984, 43–45, Harnisch 1986.

30. Rubner 1967, 69–70.

31. Novum corpus constitutionum Prussico-Brandenburgensium Praecipue Marchicarum, Oder Neue Sammlung Königl. Preuß. und Churfürstl. Brandenburgischer, sonderlich in der Chur- und Marck-Brandenburg, Wie auch anderen Provintzien, publicirten und ergangenen Ordnungen, Edicta, Mandaten, Rescripten etc, Berlin 1751–1803, vol. 7, colum 3009–14.

32. Iida 2013, 514.

33. Mylius, ed., *Corpus Constitutionum Marchicarum,* IV. Theil, I. Abtheilung, II. Cap., Sp. 692.

34. Iida 2014, 46–54.

35. BLHA, Rep. 2A, Regierung Potsdam, III F, no. 1836, fol. 64–67.

36. Iida 2014, 46–54.

37. Pfeil 1839/2009, 49.

38. BLHA, Rep. 2A, Regierung Potsdam, III F no. 4286, fol. 518–521.

39. BLHA, Rep. 7, Amt Alt-Ruppin, no. 115, fol. 106–107.

40. See Warde 2009, 75–76.

41. BLHA, Rep. 2A, Regierung Potsdam, III F, no. 1871, fol. 1–7, BLHA, Rep. 7, Amt Alt-Ruppin, no. 115, fol. 92.

42. BLHA, Rep. 2, Kurmärkische Kriegs- und Domänenkammer, no. D.39, fol. 98–99.

43. BLHA, Rep. 2A, Regierung Potsdam, III F, no. 1871, fol. 1–7, No. 1836, fol. 65–66.

44. Knapp 1887/1927, 1:96.

45. BLHA, Rep. 2A, Regierung Potsdam, III F, Nr. 4288, 96–97, Iida 2013, 517–520.

46. Hartig 1829, 19, 62–63.

47. *Gesetz-Sammlung für die Königlichen Preußischen Staaten,* 1811, 306–307, Hasel 1974, 25–26.

48. BLHA, Rep. 2A, Regierung Potsdam, III F, Nr. 4285, fol. 6.

49. Iida 2014, 58–59, 61.

50. BLHA, Rep. 2A, Regierung Potsdam, III F, no. 4285, fol. 52, no. 4286, fol. 66.

51. BLHA, Rep. 2A, Regierung Potsdam, III F, no. 4524.

52. BLHA, Rep. 2A, Regierung Potsdam, III F, no. 4286, fol. 409–427, 517.

53. BLHA, Rep. 2A, Regierung Potsdam, III F, no. 4285, fol. 6.

54. BLHA, Rep. 7, Amt Alt-Ruppin, no. 283.

55. BLHA, Rep. 2A, Regierung Potsdam, III F, no. 4535.

56. BLHA, Rep. 2A, Regierung Potsdam, III F, no. 4288, fol. 45, 233.

57. For far more devastating and lasting damage by exploiting litters to the forest soils than by forest pasturage, see Hasel and Schwartz 2006, 204–206.

58. BLHA, Rep. 2A, Regierung Potsdam, III F, no. 563.

59. BLHA, Rep. 2A, Regierung Potsdam, III F, no. 4536.

60. BLHA, Rep. 2A, Regierung Potsdam, III F, no. 4536.

61. BLHA, Rep. 2A, Regierung Potsdam, III F, no. 4536. For potato failure in Brandenburg, Materna and Ribbe 1995, 427.

62. Iida 2014, 60, see also Radkau 2012,188.

63. Rönne 1854, supplement to, 66.

64. BLHA, Rep. 2A, Regierung Potsdam, III F, no. 4288, 89.

65. Iida 2014, 60–63.

66. BLHA, Rep. 2A, Regierung Potsdam, III F, no. 4288, 91–96.

67. BLHA, Rep. 2A, Regierung Potsdam, III F, no. 3361.

68. BLHA, Rep. 2A, Regierung Potsdam, III F, no. 4302, fol. 176–177.

REFERENCES

Asche, Matthias (2015). "Von Waldglashütten, Teeröfen und anderen Formen traditioneller Holznutzung: Brandenburg-preußische Staatswirtschaft im Spannungsfeld von Nachhaltigkeitsdenken und Ressorcenbegrenzung, Landesausbau und Peuplierungspolitik vom 17. bis zum frühen 19. Jahrhundert." In *Wirtschaft und Umwelt vom Spätmittelalter bis zur Gegenwart: Auf dem Weg zu Nachhaltigkeit?*, edited by G. Schulz and R. Reith. Stuttgart, Franz Steiner.

Behre, Otto (1905). *Geschichte der Statistik in Brandenburg-Preussen bis zur Gründung des Königlichen Statistischen Bureaus.* Berlin, Carl Heymanns.

Bratring, Friedrich Wilhelm August (1799). *Die Grafschaft Ruppin in historischer, statistischer und geographischer Hinsicht: Ein Beitrag zur Kunde der Mark Brandenburg.* Berlin, Gottfried Hayn.

——— (1804–1809/1968). *Statistisch-Topographische Beschreibung der gesamten Mark Brandenburg.* Berlin, Walter de Gruyter.

Eisenberg, F. P., and C. L. Stengel (1796). *Beiträge zur Kenntniß der Justizverfassung und juristischen Literatur in den Preußischen Staaten.* Vol. 2. Berlin, G. C. Nauk.

Harnisch, Hartmut (1984). *Kapitalistische Agrarreform und industrielle Revolution: Agrarhistorische Untersuchungen über das ostelbische Preußen zwischen Spätfeudalismus und bürgerlich-demokratischer Revolution von 1848/49 unter besonderer Berücksichtigung der Provinz Brandenburg.* Weimar, Hermann Böhlaus Nachfolger.

——— (1986). "Peasants and Markets: The Background to the Agrarian Reforms in Feudal Prussia East of the Elbe, 1760–1807." In *The German Peasantry: Conflict and Community in Rural Society from the Eighteenth to the Twentieth Centuries,* edited by Richard J. Evans and W. R. Lee. New York, St. Martin's.

Hartig, Georg Ludwig (1829). *Beitrag zur Lehre von Ablösung der Holz-, Streu- und Weideservituten.* Berlin, Duncker & Humblot.

Hasel, Karl (1974). *Zur Geschichte der Forstgesetzgebung in Preußen.* Frankfurt am Main, J. D. Sauerländer.

Hasel, Karl, and Ekkehard Schwartz (2006). *Forstgeschichte: Ein Grundriss für Studium und Praxis.* 3rd ed. Remagen, Dr. Kessel.

Iida, Takashi (2010). *Ruppiner Bauernleben, 1648–1806: Sozial- und wirtschaftsgeschichtliche Untersuchungen einer ländlichen Gegend Ostelbiens.* Berlin, Lukas.

—— (2013). "The Practice of Timber Granting from Lords to Peasants: A Forest-Historical Perspective of the *Gutsherrschaft* in Brandenburg-Prussia from 1650 to 1850." *Agricultural History* 87.

—— (2014). "Raff- und Leseholzholende und königliche Forstobrigkeit: Die Verhandlungen um Interessenausgleich im Alt-Ruppiner Forstrevier (Brandenburg) von ca. 1750 bis 1890." *Jahrbuch für die Geschichte Mittel- und Ostdeutschlands* 60.

Knapp, Georg Friedrich (1887/1927). *Die Bauernbefreiung und der Ursprung der Landarbeiter in den älteren Theilen Preußens.* 2 vols. Munich, Duncker & Humblot.

Koser, Reinhold (1903). "Die preußischen Finanzen von 1763 bis 1786." *Forschungen zur Brandenburgischen und Preußischen Geschichte* 16.

Materna, Ingo, and Wolfgang Ribbe, eds (1995). *Brandenburgische Geschichte.* Berlin, Akademie.

Müller, Hans-Heinrich (1965). "Domänen und Domänenpächter in Brandenburg-Preußen im 18. Jahrhundert." *Jahrbuch für Wirtschaftsgeschichte* (1965): pt. 4.

Pfeil, Wilhelm (1839/2009). *Die Forstgeschichte Preußens bis zum Jahre 1806.* Remagen, Kessel.

Radkau, Joachim (2012). *Wood: A History.* Cambridge, Polity.

Rönne, L. von (1854). *Das Domainen-, Forst- und Jagdwesen des preußischen Staates.* Berlin, Veit & Comp.

Rubner, Heinrich (1967). *Forstgeschichte im Zeitalter der industriellen Revolution.* Berlin, Duncker & Humblot.

Schulze, Berthold (1935). *Besitz- und siedlungsgeschichtliche Statistik der brandenburgischen Ämter und Städte 1540–1800.* Berlin, Kommissionsverlag von Gsellius.

Stadelmann, Rudolph (1882). *Preußens Könige in ihrer Thätigkeit für die Landescultur. Zweiter Theil, Friedrich der Große.* Leipzig, Verlag von S. Hirzel.

Warde, Paul (2009). "The Environmental History of Pre-Industrial Agriculture in Europe." In *Nature's End: History and the Environment,* edited by S. Sörlin and P. Warde. Basingstoke, UK, Palgrave Macmillan.

The Role of Villagers in Domain and State Forest Management

Japan's Path from Tokugawa Period to the Early Twentieth Century

Takeshi Aoki

This chapter investigates to what extent and in which ways Japanese villagers took initiative in forest management from the Tokugawa period to the early twentieth century, focusing on the path-dependent process of the modernization of forest management.

Early efforts at forest management in Japan can be traced to the Tokugawa period,[1] when villagers and local notables began to share their knowledge of forest management techniques. This pattern of development stands in contrast to what we see in Germany, which has long been regarded as the leader in forest management.

Japanese forestry administration is often thought to have had similar characteristics to Germany's, in that both tend to have a top-down structure.[2] This view is seemingly understandable because Meiji Government was also eager to adopt the German style of state forestry.

In fact, in Germany, the intensification of agricultural and forest land use was usually initiated by the officials of lords and state authorities from the early modern period onward. They established guiding principles for intensified land management that annually contributed to the lords' and state's finance.[3] Therefore, the forestry administration in Germany of the same period as Tokugawa Japan had the literally top-down characteristics. The strong linkage between forest management and power also facilitated the juridification of forest usages that enabled various users, irrespective of the rulers and the ruled, to struggle over forest rights by legal means. In juridical processes, the ruled were often able to ward off encroachments on their forest-use rights from the authorities that tried to regulate and restrict customary forest use for intensified land management.[4]

The local domains in Tokugawa Japan also introduced sustainable forestry methods such as rotation cutting, which had been practiced in Germany. To draft wood-cutting plans, the domains' officers drew forest maps and quantified tree volume.[5] Thus, the Japanese domains were seemingly oriented toward top-down regulation of forest use. However, in Tokugawa Japan, it was villagers or local notables that accumulated and disseminated experience in on-site forest management, such as tree planting and nurture. A good example of this is the publication of the books on agro-forestry by villagers or local notables that also provided the know-how to practice silviculture as subsidiary work in off-season for farmers.[6] The villagers deeply involved in silviculture planted trees not only in their own fields, but also in the lords' forest lands, free from prior approval or monitoring by the authorities. The villagers' forestation activities often competed with communal forest use, such as cutting brushwood or procuring grass as green manure. In such cases, the struggles between different forest usage also in the lords' forest lands took the form of the disputes between fellow villagers or several villages. Japanese scholars have long discussed how local disputes among the different forest uses often broke out among villagers in Japan and how disputes were settled out of court. Villagers frequently achieved the local consensus on what kinds of forest use they considered suitable, free from interference by domains' authorities.[7] This is because the authorities did not aspire to grasp the full extent of daily use of their forest lands to manage them directly. Accordingly, the domains in Tokugawa Japan could turn forest regulations into a reality only if villagers participated in the governance of forest use. What mattered for villagers' forest use in Japan was "informal institutions, unwritten law, and collective patterns of behavior established by long-standing custom."[8]

Japan and Germany followed different paths in regard to who accumulated and passed on silvicultural experience and in what manner. This difference persisted into the first half of the twentieth century: the primary actors in Japanese forest management continued to be villagers and rural communities, while in German forestry, forestry officials were the leading actors. This chapter considers the consistent characteristics of villagers' role in forest management from the Tokugawa period to the early twentieth century.

VILLAGERS' ROLES IN DOMAIN FORESTRY IN TOKUGAWA JAPAN

Tokugawa Japan consumed an enormous volume of timber in building its castle towns, particularly during the first half of the seventeenth century. The construction of these towns required considerable timber, not only for the lords' residences but also to house the common people who served the lords and their retainers. Urbanization also created a demand for fuel wood for domestic heating. Additionally, domestic monetization and the growth of metal exports in Tokugawa

Japan required the development of metal ore mines and nearby forests for fire-wood. Accordingly, lords especially in northeast Japan during the Tokugawa period often laid claim to entire timber forests or valuable forest products on their domains, prohibiting the unauthorized logging of certain valuable trees or declaring certain timber and firewood forests off-limits to villagers.[9]

However, most Japanese lords did not aspire to direct forest management to the extent of actually conducting activities such as tree nurture and lumbering, which were instead managed by the neighboring village communities. In most cases in northeast Japan during the Tokugawa period, forestry was implemented as natural regeneration. Villagers were authorized to cut and collect firewood or grass in lords' reserved forests to procure fuel for cooking and heating, or to collect green manure. In return, they took charge of patrolling timber forests, and participated in timber-cutting operations at the lords' request. In relation to natural regenerative forestry, the lords' claiming of timbers, including conifers, together with daily forest use by villagers, such as cutting brushwood and grass, significantly contributed to timber growth in the lords' forests: brushwood and grass grow more robustly than young conifers, especially in northeast Japan, and the young conifers tend to fail, if not given some assistance in their early years. In other words, forest use by villagers encouraged the growth of young conifers by removing competing vegetation that would otherwise have crowded out the young conifers. Valuable timber forests, including Japanese cedar *(sugi)* forests in the Akita domain in northeast Japan, resulted from intensive salvage-cutting by villagers during Tokugawa period.[10]

Therefore, the protection of timber forests that the lords in Tokugawa Japan considered important succeeded only if local villagers actively participated in the lords' forestry administration. A typical case can be found in the coppice forests near the castle town of the Akita domain.[11] The coppice forests had supplied the lords' vassals of the castle town with fuel wood, and the nearby villagers' living, including charcoal making, also depended on raw materials provided by the forests. During the second half of Tokugawa period, the coppice forests supplied the castle town with more and more fuel wood. For example, from 1792 to 1835, the volume of charcoal that the branch family of the lord received increased from twenty *hyo* to eighty *hyo*.[12] The domain's official and the village leaders had reported that most coppices in the forests were cut down, and more and more conifer trees, such as the Japanese cedar, grew in the cutover area, partly due to the prohibitions of illegal cutting of conifers. Thick-grown conifers interfered with the growth of brushwood and grass; they hindered villagers' charcoal making, so the villagers or the minor forestry officials requested permission from the high domain officers to remove crooked or poorly developed conifer trees to create space for the regrowth of shrubbery, even if the logging of these trees was banned.[13]

The lords or their officers understood the symbiosis between their forest protection and villagers' forest use, and they always tried to keep open the space where villagers could collect or cut grass and brushwood at their discretion.[14] The lords did not interfere with self-governance of villagers' forest access, and they did not usually investigate the actual conditions of villagers' forest use unless illegal cutting of valuable conifers was reported. This toleration policy toward the use of the lords' forest was a major factor blocking German-style top-down forestry administration that compiled information on all the usage of their forest lands to regulate villagers' forest use for intensified and rationalized land management.[15]

In addition to natural regeneration, another means of forest management was artificial forestation. Again, it was the villagers rather than the lords who played the central role in this process. While the lords' functionaries did not play an active role in forestation, tree planting by villagers in their lords' forests was officially recognized and promoted throughout the eighteenth and nineteenth centuries. When the trees were fully grown, the proceeds of mature trees in the form of logs or cash were shared among the lords and the villagers. These sharing agreements related to forest management were adopted by some lords in northeast and southwest Japan.[16]

A typical case can be found in the Akita domain in northeast Japan. By the early eighteenth century, there were already a number of informal examples of the sharing of proceeds, in which the lords and the villagers shared the proceeds of mature trees in a ratio of 7:3. Thereafter, the lord in this case came to recognize that villagers were reluctant to plant and nurture trees without being given a greater incentive to engage in forestation, which led the lord to authorize the sharing of proceeds with the villagers in a ratio of 5:5 in 1712. This sharing ratio remained fixed for more than a century. However, villagers excessively used the domain's forest to procure basic necessities during the years of the famines in the last quarter of the eighteenth century. To restore the degraded forest lands to health, the domain's authorities decided to promote villagers' forestation activities by further enhancing villagers' incentive, so they increased the villagers' share from one-half to seven-tenths of the total in 1811.[17] But, according to the analysis of the forestry official in the Akita domain, only two-tenths of trees planted by villagers there from 1819 to 1823 completed their growth.[18]

The poor achievements from the viewpoint of the domains' officers notwithstanding, villagers' planting activities in the lords' forests certainly worked to their advantage: they would like to secure access also to the lords' reserved forests to gather their forest outgrowth (lower branches, weeds, and the like) rather than to claim a share of the plantation's profits. In other words, artificial forestation by villagers, who were compensated for their work by receiving extensive forest access, seems to have been one of the bottom-up means to secure communal use area.[19]

In consequence, the retention of some valuable forests during the Tokugawa period resulted from the tense and symbiotic relationship between the lords and the villagers over forest use.

APPLICATION OF GERMAN FORESTRY METHODS IN
MEIJI JAPAN

Forestry administration in the Tokugawa period was oriented toward the sustainability of their forest resources. However, lords and their functionaries did not play a proactive role in on-site forest management, so the enforcement of forest regulation depended mainly on villagers' cooperation. In addition, when Meiji government took over political control of the lands and their subjects from the lords in 1869, the domains' forestry officers did not usually transfer to positions as government officials. Instead, the experiences in on-site forest management, such as drafting of rotation cutting plans, had accumulated in the village communities in the former Akita and other domains.[20] For these reasons, the new Japanese government was less inclined to engage in direct forest management. Furthermore, the government considered the forest lands taken from the lords as the areas proposed for the former samurais' returning to the farming, and as financial sources to fund the early industrialization policy. First, the new government decreed the ordinance of land reclamation in 1870, and the forest lands suitable for clearing were assessed at two hundred thousand ha by the authorities. After that, in 1872, the new government tried to auction off all the forest areas.[21]

However, the Japanese government began to reconsider earlier practices as it became familiar with central Europe's experiences in the reform of forestry administration. For example, Toshimichi Ōkubo, a member of a high-ranking mission, traveled to America and Europe to seek the renegotiation of existing commercial treaties in the first half of the 1870s. During his stay in Berlin, he heard a lecture on the superiority of German forestry by Hazama (Kan) Matsuno, who had studied in Germany with funding from the Japanese government. After hearing this lecture, Ōkubo became a leading advocate for the establishment of modern forestry administration, and he influenced the government's decision in 1873 to stop selling forest lands. In 1882, after the government decided to model its modern forestry administration after that of Germany, it founded a governmental forestry school (Tokyo Sanrin Gakkō) in Tokyo. The faculty's first head teacher was Matsuno, who had returned from Germany in 1875 and who would train budding foresters to be well versed in German methods.[22]

In contrast to Japanese lords, Germany's lords and their functionaries seemed to have accumulated experience in on-site forest management. During the nineteenth century, they advanced significantly toward developing a direct forest management system. This process often corresponded with the modernization of the forestry administration. Essential steps in the process were the nationalization of the lords' forests and the redemption of forest-use rights exercised by villagers.[23]

To redeem forest-use rights, forestry authorities in Germany engaged in tough bargaining with other claimants. After long negotiations, the state redeemed villagers' rights in return for parceling out forests or providing fixed-benefit pension plans. Through this step, the roles of the government and villagers in forest management became fundamentally separated in Germany in the course of the nineteenth century.[24]

DIVISION OF FOREST OWNERSHIP IN MODERN JAPAN

As graduates from forestry schools in Japan attempted to put the German style of forestry into practice, they were challenged by the necessity of establishing a direct forest management system from scratch. As a first step in that direction, the Japanese government, beginning in the 1870s, set about dividing forests between the government and villagers while training its forestry officers.

In Germany, the division of forests meant eliminating or limiting villager access to state forests by formally redeeming forest-use rights. However, the Japanese government avoided being drawn into potentially interminable negotiations over forest-use rights. Instead, it placed the burden of proof of forest ownership on villagers. To present evidence of forest ownership, they were obliged to prove that they had spent a certain amount of money and labor in managing the forest they asserted their claim to. Between the 1870s and the 1890s, the government nationalized forests for which villagers could not present proof of ownership. This procedure created state-owned and imperial forest lands covering about nine million ha, or nearly one-third of the total forest area of Japan. The procedure of dividing forests created two types of regions.

In the first type of region, such as the Kinki, Chūgoku, and Chūbu regions, villagers' historical control of forests was relatively entrenched. In the Kinki region, the villagers in the Tokugawa period engaged in timber-planting and lumbering to bring forest products to the neighboring metropolitan markets, such as that of Osaka.[25] In the Chūgoku region in the pre-Meiji period, villagers in the hills managed the thickets and pine woodlands to supply the fuel for salt making in the coastal areas of the Inland Sea.[26] Accordingly, they were able to establish their claims to and retain their ownership of the forests they had managed. Thus, the percentages of the forest lands owned by the government as of 1936 were almost negligible in the Kinki and Chūgoku regions.[27]

In Yamanashi prefecture, in the Chūbu region, grasses and trees in communal forest lands were used for fattening horses and wooden handicrafts. Local communities in Yamanashi Prefecture also asserted their claims to the forest lands, but they failed to present proof of ownership. The former communal forest lands were nationalized and later transferred to the imperial estate. Village communities resolutely petitioned the Imperial Property Office for the return of the converted forest lands. Furthermore, they pressured the imperial authorities to accept the petitions through illegal felling of trees, setting fires, or unauthorized grazing on the imperial forest lands. After these struggles against the Imperial Property Office, the imperial authorities decided to hand over the ownership of the former communal forest lands to the prefectural authorities in Yamanashi in 1911. The relevant bureau in Yamanashi came to manage the forest lands, taking note of the local communities' needs.[28] The subtotal percentage of government and imperial forest lands in the Chubu region as of 1936 was 22%, so this region belonged to the first type of region, where the subtotal percentage of government and imperial forest lands was relatively low.[29]

In the second type of region, where the lords had reserved control over extensive forests or valuable trees within their domains during the Tokugawa period, power relations in forest management favored a quick takeover of forest ownership by the state. Furthermore, the orientation of villagers toward securing forest ownership for communal use was relatively weaker, because they expected to be granted tax-free use of the underbrush and thinnings from the government's forest lands. This type of province was concentrated in northeast Japan, where the subtotal percentage of government and imperial forest lands was 47%.

THE CONFLICTS OVER POLICY DIRECTION ON
NEW STATE FORESTRY IN JAPAN

Following the introduction of German state forestry methods in Meiji Japan, there were many who questioned the suitability of the new methods in the Japanese context.[30]

When Zentarou Kawase, a Japanese forestry student a generation younger than Matsuno, visited Germany in the late nineteenth century, that nation had already advanced to a final stage in its modernization of the administration of forestry. According to Kawase's observations, German state forests were managed in conformity with officially drafted management plans, the goal of which was to assure regular harvests, and thus incomes, in perpetuity. Plans drafted in the nineteenth century were generally based on the scientific concept of the "Normal Forest," which favored setting out each high forest of even-aged conifer trees, with long cutting periods. Furthermore, operations in state forests, from tree planting to lumbering, were conducted under vertical integration only by the government sector. As for labor management, forestry authorities directly employed regular workmen, thus providing them with opportunities for life and pension insurance.[31]

During Kawase's stay in Germany, opinion became widespread in Japan that the complete separation of the roles of government and villagers in forest management would deviate from Japanese tradition, in which both actors worked together to manage and share proceeds from forests owned in common. Kaneko Kentaro, a current undersecretary of the Ministry of Agriculture and Commerce in 1893, who had once helped Ito Hirobumi with making the draft Meiji Constitution modeled on that of Germany, agreed with this opinion. According to this opinion, extensive forest access for villagers to procure essential goods, along with their responsibility for patrolling forests and undertaking operations such as timber planting or lumbering, contributed to sustainable forest management.[32]

In an article he submitted to a magazine well known in Japanese forestry circles, Kawase refuted this opinion, emphasizing that only the governments, as champions of the concept of "Normal Forest," could manage forests sustainably. Because German forestry theory, which he studied, deemed villager participation detrimental to the performance of state forestry, he also took little notice of the roles of villagers in forest management during the Tokugawa period.[33] After returning from Germany, he, who had once served as an expert at the Forestry Bureau of the Ministry of Agriculture and Commerce, became the first professor of forestry at the College of Agriculture, University of Tokyo, and trained many budding forestry officers.[34] But the modernization of forestry administration in Japan, which Kawase's former students promoted, would follow a path-dependent process different from its development in Germany.

In 1896, the Japanese government presented the Forest Bill to the Imperial Diet session. The bill included sections on state forest policing and administrative supervision of private forest management. However, it aroused fierce opposition among members of the House of Representatives, most of whom raised the question of whether the earlier division of forest ownership between the government and the villagers had been a suitable method of creating an area of state forestry in modernizing Japan.

Yaroku Nakamura, who had been a forestry teacher at Tokyo Sanrin Gakkō in the 1880s and was later elected to the House of Representatives, insisted that the method the government had adopted to divide forest ownership was inappropriate. According to Nakamura, the government had not conducted a German-style redemption of forest-use rights and hence failed to create state forests from which villagers' access was eliminated. The German-style redemption of villagers' rights may have taken the form of parceling out extensive bushlands suitable for producing fuel wood and low-grade timber to villagers. This redemption process would also enable the division of roles between state and private forestry, allowing the government to concentrate its funds and personnel in the management of the protected forest areas beyond the capacity of other business entities. His opinion was a result of a realization that the government had insufficient funds and personnel to manage the forests it had previously taken over. In other words, he questioned what the purpose of state forestry would be and how much forest land the government needed to achieve its goals.

In addition to discussions of Nakamura's expert viewpoint, others spoke out about local residents' complaints regarding the results of the division of forest ownership between the 1870s and the 1890s. Yukimoto Kudō, a member of the House of Representatives from the Aomori prefecture in northeast Japan, argued that valuable state forests in the Aomori prefecture had been created by the tree planting and nurturing activities by villagers during the Tokugawa period. According to Kudō, villagers in the Aomori domain not only were granted extensive access to the lords' forests to procure basic necessities, but also shared profits from forest products with the lord as a reward for their forestation labor. Accordingly, he lamented the fact that the villagers in the Aomori prefecture who ought to have retained the ownership of forests they used had been unable to present positive proof of forest ownership in the earlier procedure of the division of forests. He complained that they had been extremely restricted in their traditional use of state forests after the division of forests, arguing that the government should revise the division of forest ownership so that more villager ownership of forest could be recognized.

Despite these discussions, the government at that time was not deeply involved in discussions regarding the appropriateness of the previously conducted division of forest ownership. All that the government did was to present a bill separate from the Forest Bill. This bill allowed those unsatisfied with the earlier division of forest ownership to petition the forestry administration for the return of forests under dispute on a case-by-case basis. Despite the strong opposition to the bill among some representatives, it passed in 1899.

Following criticism by those representatives versed in forestry, such as Nakamura, the government also presented a National Forest Bill to the Diet in 1899. However, the bill included only the procedures for the administration of national forest lands and clarified neither the division of roles between state and private forestry nor the purpose of state forestry. Interestingly, it included clauses recognizing the roles of villagers in state forest management, which aroused fierce opposition among some members of the House of Peers, including Takei Morimasa, an ex-bureaucrat who had once served as chief at the Forestry Bureau of the Ministry of Agriculture and Commerce. He supported the idea that forest management should be the special domain of the state and its forestry officers and that state forestry should make a sustainable amount of profit, contributing annually to its general account. Accordingly, he opposed the arguments in the House of Representatives that state forestry should limit itself to unprofitable activities such as management of protected forest areas. However, among the other members of the House of Peers, who rather appreciated the achievement of villagers' forest management, there were discussions supporting the clauses that recognized the roles of villagers in state forest management. In deliberations over the bill in sessions of the House of Peers, it was made clear that the government and most members of the House of Peers did not regard villagers' continuing access to state forests and their engagement with state forestry as problematic. Although the discussions on the purpose of state forestry remained unresolved, the National Forest Bill also passed in the 1899 Diet.

MODERN STATE FOREST MANAGEMENT IN JAPAN

Overview of State Forestry in Modern Japan

On June 30, 1900, the Japanese government officially closed petitions for the return of forests in accordance with the law of 1899. Petitions for the return of forests encompassed a total area of about two million ha. However, only an area of about three hundred thousand ha was authorized for return to the petitioners. The geographical distribution of state forest lands created by the division of forests between the 1870s and the 1890s was rarely changed through the procedures put into place by the law of 1899.[35]

State forest lands in Japan consisted mainly of broadleaved trees. According to statistics from 1915 that described the composition of Japan's forest lands for the first time, total forest lands consisted of unforested fields of 3,638,887 ha, bamboo thickets of 121,895 ha, coniferous forests of 3,989,628 ha, broadleaved forests of 6,933,581 ha, and mixed forests of conifers and broadleaves of 7,645,770 ha. In comparison, the state-owned proportion of the total consisted of unforested fields of 491,761 ha, bamboo thickets of 344 ha, coniferous forests of 820,864 ha, broadleaved forests of 3,361,204 ha, and mixed forests of conifers and broadleaves of 3,147,237 ha. In view of these statistics, the composition of state forest lands of about eight million ha was rather broadleaved and natural, and broadleaved forests in state forest lands were located more in remote mountain zones than on level ground.[36]

How did the forestry authorities in Japan try to change the existing composition of state forest lands? They began to draft a management plan for state forest lands in 1899 and finished drawing up the plan for the total area of about four million ha, except the nonmanaged woodlands, until 1921. According to the authorized management plan for an area of 4.13 million ha until 1924, 61% of the total area was left to the management of high forest, including conifers.[37]

Forestation activities in state forest lands consisted of the afforestation of treeless wastelands in mountains near human settlements, and changeover forestation in remote mountain zones, from natural forest areas to artificial plantations. Between 1899 and 1921, these operations advanced in parallel. The proportion of annual forestation area to that of the total state forest lands hovered around 0.9%. However, after 1922 forestation activity was limited to the changeover forestation from natural forest areas to artificial plantations. Hereafter, the pace of forestation slowed. The proportions of annual forestation areas from 1922 to 1935 ranged between 0.38% and 0.24%. This slow pace of replanting was partly due to the lack of good markets for the broadleaved trees from the mountainous state forest lands; as a result, proceeds from sales did not cover the government's expenses in cutting, processing, and transporting. The reduced market for broadleaved trees at that time hampered their cutting and the replanting of the cutover area with conifers.[38]

This lack of adequate marketability of state forest products, including broad-leaved trees, led to a low level of government logging of trees in terms of the pro-portions of the volume of governmental logging to total cut volume in state forest lands. Governmental logging began only after the beginning of the twentieth cen-tury, and the government focused on logging timber forests.[39] Indeed, the percent-age of timber volume cut by governmental logging increased steadily from 16% in 1905 to 61% in 1935. However, the percentage of fuel-wood volume by govern-mental logging increased modestly from 1% in 1907 to 15% in 1935.[40] This low level of governmental logging is explained partially by the low cost-bearing capacity of broadleaved trees that had no use other than as fuel.

Another important feature of Japanese state forest management, in compari-son with Germany's, is embodied in the structure of the organs of actual for-est management. Regional and district forest offices in Japan were responsible for a much more extensive area of jurisdiction than their German counterparts. In Japan, during the interval between the two world wars, the average regional forest office in the home islands was in charge of a forest area of about seven hundred thousand ha, and the average district forest office was in charge of a maximum forest area of twenty-five thousand ha. In comparison, in Germany, a regional forest office was, on average, responsible for an area of about one hun-dred thousand ha and a district office was in charge of four thousand ha. This contrast also seems to explain Japan's low level of modern state forestry com-pared to Germany.[41]

As discussed in detail later, the slow pace of the governmental logging and for-estation in Japan's state forest lands resulted mainly from villagers' continuous par-ticipation in forest management.

Villagers' Forest Use in State Forests

High rates of state ownership of forest lands in northeast Japan resulted from the relative weakness of the ownership claims presented by villagers or communities. Despite this weakness, villagers did not give up traditional forest use in state forests, and the government also took over the former lords' policy of tolerating villagers' self-governance of communal forest use.[42] Thus, high rates of state forest lands, particularly in northeast Japan, coexisted with villager retention of extensive access to state forests.

Table 10 shows the areas of state forest lands in which traditional forest uses were officially recognized during the early twentieth century. The dedicated cat-egories of traditional uses consisted mainly of forests with sharing of proceeds, grass-collecting areas, pasturing areas, and fuel-wood supply forests.

First, the institution of forests with sharing of proceeds dates back to the Tokugawa period. The modern Japanese government inherited the institution of the sharing of proceeds to promote artificial forestation by villagers in state forests. During the Tokugawa period, villagers in the domains of northeast Japan engaged

TABLE 10. Areas of State Forest in Traditional Use in 1935

Region		Total of State Forest Lands (ha)	Nontraditional Use Area (ha)	Traditional Use Areas			
				Proceeds-Sharing Forests (ha)	Pasturing Areas (ha)	Grass-Collecting Areas (ha)	Fuel-Wood Supply Forests (ha)
Northeast Japan	Tōhoku	2,224,182	1,136,598	7,177	100,046	68,944	911,417
		100.00%	51.1%	0.3%	4.5%	3.1%	41.0%
	Kantō	408,730	324,188	6,730	6,802	17,562	53,448
		100.00%	79.3%	1.6%	1.7%	4.3%	13.1%
	Chūbu	663,132	576,151	2,457	878	22,056	61,590
		100.00%	86.9%	0.4%	0.1%	3.3%	9.3%
Central Japan	Kinki	58,849	53,011	46	0	5,127	665
		100.00%	90.1%	0.1%	0.0%	8.7%	1.1%
	Chūgoku	112,575	98,196	12	6,577	6,137	1,653
		100.00%	87.2%	0.0%	5.8%	5.5%	1.5%
	Shikoku	176,727	157,166	1,449	116	14,645	3,351
		100.00%	88.9%	0.8%	0.1%	8.3%	1.9%
Southwest Japan	Kyūshū	537,130	454,211	24,465	4,522	17,045	36,887
		100.00%	84.5%	4.6%	0.8%	3.2%	6.9%

SOURCE: Nourin-shō Sanrin Kyoku 1937b.
NOTE: This table is drawn up on the assumption that 1 cho equals 1 ha.

in a certain amount of forestation activities under agreements for the sharing of proceeds with lords. The villagers practiced selective-cutting operations in forests under such agreements, so the composition of such forests was rather uneven in age. However, the government recognized only forests of even-aged conifer trees created by clear-cutting operations as subject to legitimate agreements for sharing of proceeds, so it disregarded most of the villagers' tree planting achievements.[43] Therefore, villagers were less and less inclined to continue planting trees under agreements for the sharing of proceeds from the time of the Meiji Restoration.[44]

In modern Japan, a relatively successful case of the institution of the sharing of proceeds is found in Miyazaki prefecture in the Kyūshū Region, which had a relatively large area of state forest lands under a proceeds-sharing agreement between villagers and district forest offices (see table 10). For example, the Obi district forest office in Miyazaki Prefecture had jurisdiction over a state forest area of approximately 22,350 ha as of 1921, which amounted to 66% of the total forest lands in the district. In Obi district, there was an established custom whereby villagers gained access to the lord's forest and planted trees on the basis that the villagers received two-thirds or four-fifths of the total proceeds. Accordingly, they complained about the state's takeover of extensive forests at the time of the division of the forest. To mitigate their complaints, the Obi district forest office drafted a local management plan as of 1922 that designated 49% of the total state forest area as subject to agreements for the sharing of proceeds with villagers. Villagers planted *sugi* (Japanese cedar) sets in state forests under the agreements and set out forests suitable for the logging of ship-building timbers. The total area of forested lands in Obi district between 1923 and 1942 was 4,363 ha, a little less than three-fourths of which was areas forested by villagers. Judging from this case, the allowance of villagers' relevant access to state forests enabled them to participate in high forest management, which the German state forestry model considered to be the sole responsibility of forestry officers.[45]

Second, the designation of pasturing and grass-collecting forests meant that state forest lands were left only to pasture and grass collection, particularly for animal husbandry. The lords in the Tokugawa period tacitly permitted their villagers to use their forest lands for animal breeding and husbandry. The villagers managed the pasturing and grass-collecting area communally, so they practiced also the controlled burning of a field for protection against the growth of thorny plants, as part of their work for sustainable use of fields as grassland.[46] But the afforestation activities of the treeless areas in state forest lands from 1899 tended to shrink the former pasturing and grass-collecting area unless there were protest movements by the local stock farmers. According to table 10, the Tōhoku region, a famous breeding center for horses and other animals, had a relatively large area of state forest land left to pasture and grass collection. This designation of pasturing and grass-collecting area was a result partly of a request by the Army Ministry of Japan, which had placed a premium on the production of warhorses after the Russo-Japanese War.[47] This is also because the regional authorities of state forestry faced difficulties from the intentional and unauthorized burning of state forest lands by villagers and they accepted the villagers' petitions for protection of customary use for horse breeding and husbandry. Thus, in the Aomori regional forest office's jurisdiction, the villagers participating in horse breeding and husbandry could maintain a designated area almost as large as the customary use area.[48]

Finally, the largest category of traditional use was for supplying fuel wood for villagers' domestic heating and cooking or producing charcoal for sale. In a state forest designated for the supply of fuel wood, the forestry authorities did not sell self-logged wood, but specified the places where villagers themselves could fell standing trees. Villagers bought the standing trees in the specified places. This sales method enabled villagers to receive relevant forest access to cut some firewood and make charcoal as commodities. The merit of this method for forestry authorities lay in the fact that the villagers cut down aged broadleaved trees at their own cost. But the forestry authorities were also obliged to keep open a certain area of broadleaved forests where villagers could get access to fuel wood.[49]

In northeast Japan, the composition of state forest lands was more broadleaved. For example, in 1915, state forest lands there consisted of unforested fields of 136,365 ha, bamboo thickets of eight ha, coniferous forests of 214,010 ha, broadleaved forests of 1,291,751 ha, and mixed forests of conifers and broadleaves of 639,172 ha. Full-scale use of these extensive broadleaved forests began after the construction of a national network of railways in the 1890s that could transport the charcoal from rural areas to metropolitan markets like Tokyo.[50] As table 10 shows, fuel-wood supply forests amounted to 41% of the state forest lands of 2,224,182 ha in northeast Japan. In the jurisdictions of the Aomori and Akita regional forest offices in the Tōhoku Region, the supply of fuel wood to a large extent took the form of sales of standing trees. For example, as of 1920, the percentage of sales of standing trees that were for fuel wood was 96.2% in the area under the Aomori regional forest office and 90.3% in Akita.[51] Furthermore, under the Aomori regional forest office's jurisdiction, most fuel wood was sold under private contract at a special price lower than the competitive contract price. This private contract price applied to sales of fuel wood both for domestic use and for villagers' production activities such as charcoal making. If the German experience is used as a model of state forestry, selling forest products at an uncompetitive price might not be seen as an ordinary practice. This is because German state forestry tried to transfer its proceeds to the general state account and reduce tax burdens by selling forest products at an increased profit.[52] However, in Japan, the allotment of fuel-wood supply forests and this sales method guaranteed villagers' rights to participate in and profit from production activities in state forests, particularly during the charcoal booms after the First World War.[53]

Villagers' Organization of Labor in State Forests

Japanese forestry authorities used the allotment of forests for traditional use as a lever to organize two types of villagers' units to engage in forestation-related operations such as nurturing trees or patrolling state forest lands. The first type of organization was the labor units, taking on regular patrols of state forest lands while being compensated for their work by receiving forest access to gather forest outgrowth, such as lower branches, weeds, mushrooms, and edible wild plants. The second type of organization was that of units engaged in tree planting and nurturing operations while being granted free cutting of fuel wood for domestic use.

A typical case in the first type of organization can be found in the Aomori regional forest office.[54] The Aomori regional forest office began to use the grant of free use of forest outgrowth as a lever to prompt villagers to patrol state forest lands as early as 1910. In the Aomori regional forest office's jurisdiction, which as of 1937 included 313 municipalities containing state forest lands, there were 522 labor units to which the forest offices subcontracted the operations in 1933. These data suggest that one or more units were organized in each municipality. These labor units, as a whole, took charge of most of a state forest area under the jurisdiction of the Aomori regional forest office.[55]

A good example of the second type of organization can be found in the Akita regional forest office. In the Akita office's jurisdiction, from the early 1920s, the weight of forestation activities had begun to shift away from the afforestation of wasteland in mountain zones near human settlement to changeover forestation in remote mountain zones, from natural forest areas to artificial plantations. This shift in forestation activities would only work if the forestry authorities could secure more industrious laborers for forestation operations at much lower wages. Accordingly, the authorities organized villagers' units, which would take collective responsibility for working on state forest operations. In the jurisdiction of the Akita regional forest office, which as of 1937 included 224 municipalities containing state forest lands, there were ninety-nine municipalities where villagers' units were placed, or about one villagers' unit for every other municipality.[56]

One illustrative example of the forestation labor units can be found in the state forest within the Noshiro district, under the jurisdiction of the Akita regional forest office *(Nibuna Kokuyū-rin)*. This state forest covered approximately thirty-six hundred ha. In 1918, tree planting was conducted on approximately 133 ha, with tree nurturing being conducted on 341 ha and logging being conducted on 78 ha. Subcontracting units employed 243 workmen, who were local inhabitants either serving as full-time forestry laborers or working in state forests as a side job. There were 662 households in the communities, so the ratio of state forest workmen to local households was approximately 1:3. In return for engaging in these operations, full-time forestry laborers were supplied with timber at a specially reduced price; temporary workmen received fuel wood in the same way.[57]

At the beginning of Meiji period, the Japanese government decided to model its state forestry after that of Germany. In fact, the existing tradition of forestry administration in Japan was already similar to that of Germany. As with the German method by lords' authorities, Japanese domain lords during the Tokugawa period often laid claim to timber forests or valuable trees on their domains, intending to use them for their own use and for their timber dealing business in the metropolitan markets, such as those of Edo and Osaka.

However, generally, the domain lords and their forestry officials in Tokugawa Japan were not directly involved in domain forest management, leaving substantial activities such as timber nurture and lumbering to local villagers' initiatives. Villagers' active roles in domain forestry often led them to check the excessive expansion of conifers in the lords' forests, and they tried to secure the coppiced area subject to their communal use. The villagers' forest access was regulated by customary laws that had been updated through many intravillage or intervillage disputes, and their informal settlement, free from lords' interference. The lords' toleration of villagers' self-governance of informal communal forest use, however, not only eliminated the chance of villagers' legally protecting their forest usage, but also decreased the opportunities for forestry officials to regulate villagers' usage for rationalized land management. Thus, the state forestry that took over the domain lords' forests followed a historically path-dependent process different from that of Germany.

First, the Japanese government left the neighboring villagers' access to state forests intact. After taking over domain lords' forests, the government incorporated those forests for which villagers could not present proof of ownership into the state forests. During the 1899 Diet's deliberation on the National Forest Bill and other matters, some representatives who were experts in forestry insisted that the government had failed to create state forests from which villagers' access was eliminated because it had neglected the redemption of forest-use rights as accomplished in Germany. However, the government that had ended up taking over the lords' toleration policy toward communal forest use strongly denied the necessity of redeeming villagers' forest access. Thus, the government did not regard villagers' continuous access to state forests as problematic.

Second, the government, which had learned to apprehend the established symbiosis between forest management and villagers' forest use, recognized the neighboring villagers' involvement in state forest management. As the case of the regional forest office in northeast Japan shows, the fuel-wood sales method in state forests was generally stumpage sale, which allowed villagers to cut standing trees in state forest areas themselves. It enabled villagers not only to meet their basic daily needs but also to participate in and profit from production activities such as charcoal making. The merit of this method for forestry authorities lay in the fact that the villagers cut down aged broadleaved trees at their own cost. However, this method obliged the authorities to leave a certain proportion of the cutover area open for the regrowth of broadleaved forests where villagers could get access to fuel wood again. This is a basic reason why broadleaved and natural woodlands remained dominant in the Japanese modern state forest lands. In addition, as the records of a proceeds-sharing arrangement in southwest Japan show, allowing villagers to plant and nurture saplings in state forests could contribute directly toward the creation of high forest management, which the German state forestry model considered to be the sole responsibility of forestry officials. Japan's modern forestry authorities used the allotment of forests for these traditional uses as a lever to secure villagers' labor units that were engaged in forestation-related operations such as nurturing trees or patrolling state forest lands. The villagers' labor organizations enabled the authorities to manage a much more extensive area of jurisdiction.

In sum, the development of modern forestry in Japanese state forests should be considered as a history of the ongoing interaction of villagers' forest use with the tradition of forestry administration that tried to use the granting of forest access as a lever to keep order in forest management.

NOTES

1. Totman 1998, Diamond 2006, 294–295.
2. Caradonna 2014, 32–46.
3. Bennett 2015, 25.
4. Radkau 2008, 187, Radkau 2012, 324–325.
5. The illustrative case of rotation cutting can be found in the Akita domain starting in the mid-eighteenth century. For more details, see Iwasaki 1939, 112–121, 257, Tsutsui 1987, 48–51.
6. Bennett 2015, 28.
7. Tsuji 1978, Tsutsui 1973, 407–444, Nishikawa 1978, Watanabe 2017.
8. Radkau 2008, 185.
9. Nishikawa 1978, 3–4.
10. Totman 1985, 36–37.
11. Tsukii 1905, 72–91.
12. Tsukii 1905, 83.
13. Iwasaki 1939, 329–334, 370–371. For a similar case of Japanese cypress, see Endō 1938, 132–133. The officers in the Akita domain observed a negative correlation between thick-grown timber forests and shrub vegetation also in the case of management of copper mine and nearby forests for fuelwood. See Haga 2011.
14. In the closing days of the Tokugawa period, an officer of the Sendai domain (the Akita's nearby domain) still put importance on the various uses of coppices, so he insisted that the excessive expansion of timber forests should be checked also in the lord's forests. For details, see Endō 1938, 123–124.
15. Bennett 2015, 24–29.
16. Saito 2009, 2014, Shioya 1959.
17. Hattori 1967, 120–165, Totman 1985, 50–53.
18. See Akita-ken 1973, 201.
19. Sugimoto 1976, 134, Nishikawa 1978, 407–411.
20. Haga and Kato 2012, 23.
21. Arimoto 1968, 301–310.

22. Tezuka 1987, 7–18, 32–39.
23. Iida 2013.
24. Kawase 1912.
25. Kasai 1978, 173–180, Fujita 1995.
26. Chiba 1956, 146–175, Arimoto 1968, 345–368.
27. Rinya-chō 1971.
28. Ringyō Hattatsushi Chōsakai 1960, 118–125, Totman 2007, 43–56.
29. Rinya-Chō 1971.
30. For the source of the description of the sessions of the Imperial Diet in this section, see Aoki 2014.
31. Kawase 1893, 51–52.
32. Kaneko 1893a/1893b.
33. Kawase 1893, 51.
34. Tezuka 1987, 121.
35. Akiyama 1960, 77.
36. Akiyama 1960, 198–208, Rinya-Chō 1971.
37. Akiyama 1960, 108.
38. Akiyama 1960, 237–238.
39. Hattori 1967, 5–10.
40. Rinya-Chō 1969, 9.
41. Akiyama 1960, 229–231.
42. Nishio 1988, 89–111.
43. Aomori Dairinku-sho 1919, 46.
44. Shioya 1959, 444–464.
45. Shioya and Washio 1965, 84–89.
46. Aomori Eirinkyoku 1927, 17, 407–411.
47. Dainihon Sanrinkai 1983, 94–99.
48. Aomori Eirinkyoku 1927, 24–26, 223–225.
49. Nourin-shō Sanrinkyoku 1937a, 82–32.
50. Okuchi 1974, 463.
51. Noushōmu-shō Sanrinkyoku 1922.
52. Heske 1938, 84.
53. Dainihon Sanrinkai 1983, 357–376.
54. Aomori Dairinku-sho 1919, 65–69.
55. Aomori Eirinkyoku 1937, 124–125.
56. Nourin-shō Sanrinkyoku 1937b, Kikuma 1976, Dainihon Sanrinkai 1983, 88.
57. Noushōmu-shō Sanrinkyoku 1921, 217–221, 230–231.

REFERENCES

Akita-ken (1973). *Akita-ken Ringyō-shi (jyō)* (History of the Forestry in Akita Prefecture). Vol. 1. Akita, Akita-ken.

Akiyama, Tomohide (1960). *Kokuyū Rin Keiei-shi Ron* (Study of the History of National Forestry in Japan). Tokyo, Nihon Ringyō Chōsa-kai.

Aoki, Takeshi (2014). *Kingendai Nihon niokeru Kyōyūrin to Rinsei* (The Forest Owned in Common and Forestry Administration in Modern Japan). PhD diss. Tokyo, Keio University.

Aomori Dairinku-sho (1919). *Kan-nai Shisetsu Ippan* (Handbook on the Policy of State Forestry in Aomori Regional Forest Office). Aomori, Aomori Dairinku-sho.

Aomori Eirinkyoku (1927). *Hōboku-Saisōchi Bunkatsu-Gentei-shi* (History of the Designation of Pasturing and Grass-Collecting Area). Aomori, Aomori Eirin kyoku.

—— (1937). *Kan-nai Yōran* (Handbook on the State Forestry in Aomori Regional Forest Office). Aomori, Aomori Eirinkyoku.

Arimoto, Masao (1968). *Chiso Kaisei to Nōmin Tousō* (Land Tax Reform and Peasant Revolts). Tokyo, Shinseisha.

Bennett, Brenett M. (2015). *Plantations and Protected Areas: A Global History of Forest Management.* Cambridge, MA, MIT Press.

Caradonna, Jeremy L. (2014). *Sustainability: A History.* New York, Oxford University Press.

Chiba, Tokuji (1956). *Hageyama no Kenkyū* (Study of Denuded Hill). Tokyo, Nourinkyōkai.

Dainihon Sanrinkai (1983). *Nihon Ringyō Hattatsu-shi: Nougyō Kyoukō Senji Tousei-ki no Katei* (History of the Development of Japanese Forestry). Tokyo, Dainihon Sanrinkai.

Diamond, Jared (2006). *Collapse: How Societies Choose to Fail or Succeed.* London, Penguin.

Endō, Yasutarō (1938). *Sanrinshijyō yori Mitaru Tōhoku Bunka no Kenkyū* (Research on the Culture of Northeastern Japan Considering Forest History). Tokyo, Nihon Sanrinshi Kenkyūkai.

Fujita, Yoshihisa (1995). *Nihon Ikusei Ringyō Chiiki Keiseishi-ron* (Study of the Formation of Producing Centers of Regenerative Forestry in Japan). Tokyo, Kokon Shoin.

Haga, Kazuki (2011). "Kinsei Ani Douzan Sumikiyama no Shinrin Keiei Keikaku: Tenpō 14 nen Sumibanyamaguri wo Chūsin ni" (Analysis of the Charcoal Forest Management Plan for Ani Copper Mine in Early Modern Japan; The Case of Sumibanyamaguri in 1843). *Ringyō Keizai* (October 2011): 19–36.

Haga, Kazuki, and Kato, Morihiro (2012). "19 Seiki no Akita-han Rinsei Kaikaku to Kindai he-no Keishō" (A Study of Forest Policy Reformation of the Akita Clan in the 19th Century and it Succession to the Modern Era). *Ringyō Keizai Kenkyū* (March 2012): 14–26.

Hattori, Marenobu (1967). *Ringyō Keizai Kenkyū* (Research on Forestry Economics). Tokyo, Chikyū Shuppan.

Heske, Franz (1938). *German Forestry.* New Haven, Yale University Press.

Iida, Takashi (2013). "The Practice of Timber Granting from Lords to Peasants: A Forest-Historical Perspective of the Gutsherrschaft in Brandenburg-Prussia from 1650 to 1850." *Agricultural History* (Fall 2013): 502–524.

Iwasaki, Naoto (1939). *Akita-ken Noshiro-Kawakami Chihō niokeru Sugibayasi no Seiritsu narabini Kōsin ni Kansuru Kenkyū* (Research on the Growth and Regeneration of Japanese Cedar in the Basin of the Noshiro River in Akita Prefecture). Tokyo, Kourin-kai.

Kaneko, Kentarō (1893a). "Shinrin Seido Nitsuite" (Inquiry into Forestry Administration). *Dainihon Sanrinkai* Hōkoku (June 1893): 33–43.

—— (1893b). "Shinrin Seido Nitsuite (Shōzen)" (Inquiry into Forestry Administration, Continued). *Dainihon Sanrinkai* Hōkoku (July 1893): 1–13.

Kasai, Kyōetsu (1978). *Rinya Seido no Hatten to Sanson Keizai* (Development of the Regime of Forest Lands and Mountain Economy). Tokyo, Ochanomizu Shobō.

Kawase, Zentarō (1893). "Shinrin Seido Nitsuite" (Inquiry into Forestry Administration). *Dainihon Sanrinkai Hōkoku* (October 1893): 38–57.

Kawase, Zentarou (1912). *Kōyu Rin Oyobi Kyoudō-Rineki: Soku Iriai Kankei* (Public Forest and Communal Forest Servitude Considering Communal Use). Tokyo, Miura Shoten.

Kikuma, Mitsuru (1976), "Kokuyū-Rin Keiei Niokeru Zourin Roudō Soshiki to Itaku-Rin Seido: Akita Eirinkyoku Kakunodate Eirinsho nai Niokeru Itakurin Seido wo Taishō Nisite" (Reforestation Labor Organization and Consigned Forest System in the National Forest Management in the Kakunodate District Forest Office in the Akita Regional Forest Office). *Hokkaido Daigaku Nougaku-bu Enshū-rin Kenkyū Hōkoku* (Bulletins of the College Experiment Forests in Hokkaido University). 33 (2): 315–405.

Nishikawa, Zensuke (1978). *Rinya Shoyū no Keisei to Mura no Kōzō* (Formation of the Forest Ownership and Structure of the Villages). Tokyo, Ochanomizu Shobō.

Nishio, Takashi (1988). *Nihon Sinrin Gyōsei-shi no Kenkyū* (Research of the History of Forestry Administration in Japan). Tokyo, Tokyo Daigaku Shuppan.

Nourin-shō Sanrinkyoku (1937a). *Shōwa 9 Nendo Dai 17 Ji Kokuyū Rinya Ippan* (Statistics of Japanese State Forestry). Tokyo, Nourin-shō Sanrinkyoku.

——— (1937b). *Kokuyū Rinya no Shi-Chō-Son Betsu Bunpu oyobi Jimoto Shisetsu* (Distribution of State Forest Lands in Municipalities and Policy toward Local Needs). Tokyo, Nourin-shō Sanrinkyoku.

Noushōmu-shō Sanrin Kyoku (1921). *Honpō ni okeru Ringyō Roudōsha no Jyōkyō* (Situations of the Forestry Laborers in Japan). Tokyo: Noushōmu-shō Sanrin Kyoku.

——— (1922). *Taishō 11 Nen 6 Gatu Dai 3 Kai Kokuyū Rinya Ippan* (Statistics of Japanese State Forestry). Tokyo: Noushōmu-shō Sanrin Kyoku.

Okuchi, Shō (1974). Kokuyūrin ni Okeru Roudō-Soshiki no Keisei to Tenkai 1 (The Organization and Development of Labor Units in State Forests). *Ritsumeikan Keizaigaku* 23 (4): 447–489.

Radkau, Joachim (2008). *Nature and Power: A Global History of the Environment.* Translated by Thomas Dunlap. Washington, DC, Cambridge, New York, German Historical Institute, Cambridge University Press.

——— (2012). *Wood: A History.* Translated by Patrick Camiller. Cambridge, Polity.

Ringyō Hattatsu-shi Chōsa-kai (1960). *Nihon Ringyō Hattatsu-shi* (History of the Development of Japanese Forestry). Tokyo, Rinya-chō.

Rinya-chō (1969). *Kokuyū Rinya Jigyō Ruinen Tōkei Sho* (Annual Statistics of National Forest Service). Tokyo, Rinya-chō.

——— (1971). *Rinya Menseki Ruinen Tōkei* (Annual Statistics of Forest Lands 1880–1965). Tokyo, Rinya-chō.

Saito, Osamu (2009). "Forest History and the Great Divergence, China, Japan, and the West Compared." *Journal of Global History* (April 2009): 379–404.

——— (2014). *Kankyō no Keizai-shi* (Economic History of Environment). Tokyo, Iwanami Shoten.

Shioya Tsutomu (1959). *Bubun-Rin Seido no Shiteki Kenkyū* (Historical Research on the Institution of Proceed-Sharing Forests). Tokyo, Rinya Kyousai-kai.

Shioya Tsutomu and Washio Rhouji (1965). *Obi Ringyō Hattatsu-shi* (History of the Development of Obi Forestry). Miyazaki, Hattori Rinsan Kenkyūjyo.

Sugimoto, Hisashi (1976). *Rinya Shoyūken no Kenkyū* (Research on Forest Land Ownerhip). Osaka, Seibundō Shuppan.

Tezuka, Heizaburō (1987). *Mori no Kitamichi: Meiji kara Showa Nihon Rinsei-shi no Dorama* (Course of Japan's Forest: The Dramas of Japanese Forestry Administration History from the Meiji to Showa Era). Tokyo, Nihon Ringyō Gijyutu-kyōkai.

Totman, Conrad (1985). *The Origins of Japan's Modern Forests: The Case of Akita*. Honolulu, University of Hawaii Press.

——— (1998). *The Green Archipelago, Forestry in Pre-industrial Japan*. Translated by Kumazaki Minoru into Japanese. Tokyo, Tsukiji Shokan.

——— (2007). *Japan's Imperial Forest Goryorin, 1889–1945, with a Supporting Study of the Kan/Min Division of Woodland in Early Meiji Japan, 1871–76*. Folkestone, Global Oriental.

Tsuji Koushū (1897/1978). *Shinrin Seido Kakushin Ron* (Opinions about the Reform of Forestry Administration). Tokyo, Nagasaki Shuppan.

Tsukii Tadahiro (1905). *Akita Han Rinsei Seishi* (Official History of Forestry Administration in Akita Domain). Akita.

Tsutsui, Michio (1973). *Rinya Kyoudōtai no Kenkyū* (Research on Communities of Forest Lands). Tokyo, Nourin Shuppan.

——— (1987). *Nihon Rinsei no Keifu* (Genealogy of Japanese Forest Administration). Tokyo, Chikyūsha.

Watanabe, Takashi (2017). *Edo-Meiji Hyakushō-tachi no Yama Arasoi Saiban* (Disputes over Forest Use Rights among Peasants during the Edo and Meiji Period). Tokyo, Sōshisha.

Forests as Commons in
Early Modern China

An Analysis of Legal Cases

Yoshiyuki Aihara

Today, the relationship between human beings and forests has become increasingly important. Researchers have stressed the role forests play in fulfilling basic needs of local populations for timber and nontimber forest products, and in embodying environmental, recreational, and many other social values.

In this chapter, I will focus on the functions of forests that provide for the basic needs of local residents, and the role of government authorities concerning the provision of forests for their use. We can identify a range of ways for managing forests: in some countries and regions, forests are owned by the government; in other places, the ownership or management falls to local administrations, individuals, or communities. Considering these issues in a historical context, many environmental historians have used theories about the "commons" to approach questions related to forest management. The term "commons" refers to institutions for the collective management and use of natural resources, in addition to the natural resource themselves.[1] Following the publication of Garrett Hardin's famous article "The Tragedy of the Commons" in 1968—which concluded that the use of resource areas as commons would inevitably generate major problems through excessive use, ultimately leading to the destruction of the resource—much counterevidence has been provided from regions around the world. This counterevidence offers examples of sustainable cooperative resource use. Moreover, it has been observed that the "tragedy of commons" of which Hardin forewarned was actually the "tragedy of open access"—that the problem is not "commons" but lack of rules about how the commons can be used. Scholars have identified the kinds of conditions that lead to sustainability, such as membership, scale, property, management, the kind of resources, and the legitimacy of governance.[2]

Regarding the commons in China, scholars have questioned the strength of community ties in rural China. However, most of the research concerning this topic is based on studies of customary law in rural North China during the late 1930s and early 1940s, conducted by Japanese researchers, or based on the collection of customary laws that were investigated by Chinese administrative powers in the early twentieth century.[3] The most frequently cited example is the custom of *kai yezi* (open leaves), a custom that allowed anyone to enter the fields and collect sorghum leaves during a fixed period just before the sorghum matures. Since the right to pick up leaves was not restricted to village members, many researchers consider this to indicate a lack of strong communal ties in North China villages.[4] In recent years, some studies about the management of natural resources in China have been undertaken, inevitably taking into consideration the concept of commons.[5]

However, these articles are mostly based on research that took place in the first half of the twentieth century, or they only regard lineage land as commons. Consequently, there has been little study of how people in the Qing era used and managed the land itself, or how and by whom the legitimacy of that utilization was granted.

ABOUT THE MATERIALS

In this chapter, I extract examples from the archives called Xingke Tiben (routine memorials or reports to the Ministry of Justice, hereafter "XKTB"). In Qing China, cases where defendants faced the death penalty were reported from lower-level government offices to higher government offices. XKTB is the final one: reports from high-level officers to the emperor to decide the judgment.

XKTB reports include many statements regarding the suspect(s) and the person(s) concerned, as they comprise the important evidence used in making judgments and sentencing decisions in criminal courts. A variety of data can be extracted from the testimonies and can be used in studying social history.[6]

In this chapter, I extract and analyze examples of the use and management of forest resources from descriptions of mountains, forests, wild lands, and trees included in these archives. I will examine how ordinary people used natural resources in the mountains, particularly through the observation of descriptions of "public mountains" *(gong shan)* and "government mountains" *(guan shan),* and will discuss the role of local commons in rural China. Furthermore, I will demonstrate how the administrative power approved people's acquisition of resources that would meet their basic needs.

XKTB is held in the First Historical Archives of China in Beijing and in the Institute of History and Philology, Academia Sinica, in Taipei, and several reprints have been published. In this article, I mainly use the archive held by Academia Sinica (hereafter "ASX") and the reprinted series *Qing Jiaqing Chao Xingke Tiben*

Shehui Shiliao Jikan ("Sources on Society Excerpted from Routine Memorials of Scrutiny for the Board of Punishments during the Jiaqing Reign (1796–1820)," hereafter "JQX").[7]

THE VARIETY OF ECONOMIC ACTIVITIES IN MOUNTAINS IN XKTB

Common people carried out a variety of activities in forests and extracted various profits from the mountains. The profits can be classified into four types. The first type of profit came from extracting various products from the mountains, usually involving investment in order to extract resources.[8]

The second type of profit was gained by extracting or removing materials from the mountain, but without investment in production.[9]

The third type of profit did not involve extracting materials from the mountain, but rather the continual investment in, or care of, the land. The most frequent examples of this usage are ancestral burials and the maintenance of forests or trees for the purpose of "protecting good geomancy" *(fengshui)*. Although not discussed in depth in this chapter, ancestral graveyards were of great importance and were protected in particular ways.[10]

The last type of profit use also did not extract resources from the mountain, nor did it involve investment. Poor people, unlike the better off, could not invest time and money to maintain their ancestral graveyards, and so they used the mountains for simple burials. In historical documents, this was called *pinmin anzang* (the burial of the poor).

Of course, these four types often overlapped, as multiple benefits were derived from the same mountain land.

FRAMEWORK OF PROPERTY RIGHTS OVER MOUNTAINS IN QING CHINA

Any consideration of commons must include an inquiry into who was regarded as having a legitimate right to use and manage mountains. I begin with a brief survey of the notions of property rights with regard to land in late imperial China. It is well known that the notion of *Wang-tu wang-min* (which appeared in *The Book of Songs* [*Shi Jing*] and means "all land and all people are owned by the sovereign") persisted throughout the imperial period. In essence, regardless of whether it is clearly stated, principally and originally, the owner of all land was the "government" *(guan)*. However, if people established themselves with suitable enterprises and started managing the land (such as by clearing land, residing on it, or opening mines), then they could be granted rights to the land, and it would be reclassified as land under the ownership of "people" *(min)*. The right to gain profit from land was divided into units, which were called *ye*. These units could be sold, mortgaged, or passed down to descendants. The person who owned the unit of profit-making *(ye)* was, for convenience, referred to as the "owner of land" *(zhu)*, and the land itself was regarded as "one's property."[11]

Conversely, when no specific individual had guaranteed property rights over a particular tract of land, it was still assumed to belong to the government and so was called "government land" *(guan di)* or "government property" *(guan ye)*. Hence, "government mountain" *(guan shan)* referred to mountain areas that did not belong to specific individuals.

Lands that were managed jointly by multiple individuals, including families, made up a subcategory known, in the case of mountains, as "public mountain" *(gong shan)* or "public property" *(gong ye)*. These mountains or properties were also "people's property" *(min ye)*, rather than part of "government property."

Not all government mountains were managed in the same way. From examples given in historical records, we can distinguish three patterns of management of government mountains. It is possible to classify the land designated in Qing dynasty historical records as "government mountains" into three types, according to who used and managed it.[12] The first type of "government mountains" were those used and managed by the government or individuals to whom the government gave this authority. Examples include the mountains around Shengjing (Mukden), which provided wood and ginseng for imperial use, the mountains preserved for the Emperor's autumn hunt, and the land used for the imperial tombs.[13] It was necessary to distinguish these activities, particularly from private business, since these advantages were only afforded to the emperor or the imperial family.

Regarding the second type of "government mountains," the government and the common people were forbidden from using resources from these regions. These were mountainous regions that had been the sites of rebellions, or were believed to be likely to be used for such acts, and therefore no one had the right to utilize such areas. This type of mountainous area was also sometimes called "banned mountains" *(fengjin shan)*. We can find some examples in late imperial China, such as the Tongtang Mountains along the border between Fujian and Jiangxi, in addition to certain mines that had been shut down. These were called "government mountains" as a reminder that the use of their resources had been halted at a certain point in time.

The third type of "government mountains" were those that the government did not manage or utilize and where no individuals were given exclusive legitimacy to generate profits. Mountains of this type were mostly located near villages, and as noted later, villagers used these lands daily. Concerning this third type of "government mountain," Noboru Niida noted that there was no individual ownership over these regions and anyone had the right to access them.[14] Akira Morita quoted the description in the Gazetter of Funing (in Fujian province) and claimed that such "government mountains" were open access. He repeatedly emphasized that these mountains were exposed to a wave of privatization, although this was limited because the condition of such lands was poor.[15] Menzies also cited this material and observed that the state's "policy of inclusion" might have been practiced in such mountains.[16]

The term "government" *(guan)* was not only used with "mountain" but also with various natural resources.[17] We can, therefore, observe some indications that these "government mountains" were open access. Consequently, I analyze these mountains' "openness" in detail in comparison with the case of "public mountains," and describe how the forests provided for the basic needs of local people in Qing China, and whether there were any rules for their management.

MANAGEMENT AND USE OF "PUBLIC MOUNTAINS"

As noted earlier, the phrase "public mountain" *(gong shan)* refers to those mountains that were owned in common. Although it was not stated in historical materials that regions were "public," a description such as "this family's (or lineage's) mountain" meant that the mountain was held in common by one family or lineage. I will first analyze the range of coownership. Possession by families of the same surname was the most general and these mountains were also known as "lineage property" *(zu chan)*. There are some examples of coownership by multiple families.

Conversely, in cases where a mountain was owned by a lineage or other group, not all members of the group necessarily had free access to the mountain. We can find examples where a person who had changed his family name and entered the lineage would not receive much profit from the public mountain (JQX, 533). In another case, a husband who entered the family as bridegroom to a widow had no share in the public mountain (Zheng and Xiong 1999, 274). Furthermore, some people may have been restricted from having cultivation rights upon the mountain because of bad behavior (JQX, 906).

There were many examples of mountains owned in "partnership" *(hegu)* rather than by a family; multiple individuals might own a mountain based on joint financing arrangements. Such a case could also be designated as one of a "public mountain." For enterprises with high commercial value, such as timber or charcoal, coowners might establish a rule for dividing the profits. In some cases profits were divided by dividing the land itself (ASX, no. 73818, no. 75002), while in other cases the agreement was based on sharing in the profits (JQX, 60, 534). In Wuning County, Jiangxi province, the Wang family's mountain was rented to Erxian Zhuo, and the rent was for public use (JQX, 1348). In the case of Mao County, Sichuan province, the public mountain was rented to a family of another surname to grow trees timber (JQX, 693) or cultivate maize (JQX, 810).

However, even if the rights were divided among individuals, there were often contrary opinions as to whether owners could sell their shares to others. In a case in Changhua County, Zhejiang province, Jiayou Wu intended to sell a share of the right over "Muzhuping public mountain" and was searching for a buyer. While Jiayou Wu was negotiating a sale, Wu Facheng (of the same lineage) refuted the assertion that the mountain was public, and consequently, no one was able to sell their share (JQX, 60). In another case, in Jiangshan County, Zhejiang province, Shugen Wu sold a public mountain arbitrarily to Jizong Jiang, with Tingcang Wu as a mediator. In court, the seller, the mediator, and the buyer were punished (JQX, 261). Public ownership can be seen to have aroused quarrels easily. In the year Jiaqing 9 (1804), Guangfu Xu of Shangrao County, Jiangxi province, did not wish to buy the Tong Shitang family's private mountain, because it was next to a public mountain and so could easily become involved in quarrels (JQX, 41).

There are many examples of people crossing the boundaries onto a neighboring mountain and then being challenged. It seems that the land boundaries were clear and outsiders were not allowed to enter. Occasionally, a very small quarrel concerning borders triggered armed battles between lineage groups (ASX, no. 197020). Although there were rules about profit sharing with regard to certain products of the mountain, all those who shared the rights to the mountain could freely gather firewood or other products that required no investment. For example, Zonglu Zhang of You County, Hunan province, cut the grass on the public mountain daily (JQX, 496). In the case of Changsha County, Hunan province, the Li lineage and others had a public mountain called "Yanjia Tang," which provided firewood that could be gathered by anyone of the Li lineage. Li Maoqi also had his own trees on the mountain. As Maoqi Li was afraid of his trees being felled by others, he suddenly erected a stele to prohibit firewood gathering. After a violent quarrel, Maoqi Li died from his wounds. In the ruling on this case, the judgment was to "keep these mountains for public use" (ASX, no. 148). In the case of Yongjiang County, Zhejiang province, the Xie lineage and the Wang lineage owned a mountain in common, and it provided for both lineages (ASX, no. 15396, ASX, no. 45653).

There were some examples where a clear statement was made about the mountain in a decision, but this was infrequent, because the matter of utmost importance was to decide on the punishment of the criminal. The decisions dealing with public mountains varied. For example, "All of the firewood in the mountain ought to be prohibited from being cut, so as to stop quarrels" (JQX, 268), and "The public land that Xie Hui and Xie Kai hold must be separated in half and managed separately. A clear boundary must be set up to avoid conflict" (ASX, no. 15396). However, in judgments, magistrates nearly always made rulings based on the stated aim "to stop future disputes." Although this attitude may seem superficial, it was a direct expression of the Qing government's position. In summary, we can say that a "public mountain" was open to insiders or stakeholders, but closed to outsiders. The Qing government almost always preserved the local use of the mountain, except when it led to quarrels.

MANAGEMENT AND USE OF
"GOVERNMENT MOUNTAINS"

"Government mountains" were open-access to anyone, and to engage in an enterprise of one's own on such mountains was generally prohibited, because this obstructed the rights of others. In the year Qianlong 10 (1745), Fake Xie of Haifeng County, Guangdong province, went to the mountain to fell miscellaneous small trees for making charcoal. After he had cut three branches, Junxiang Lai approached hurriedly and sharply admonished him for stealing the pine and cypress trees that he had cultivated. Fake Xie denied this allegation, retorting that the branches he had cut were from miscellaneous small trees on the mountain. The judgment stated: "On the trees on the government mountain, Junxiang Lai is only in charge of the land where he had planted the pine and cypress trees, other miscellaneous trees must be reserved for gathering firewood for the poor. Fake Xie need not return the three branches that he had cut, because they were not from the trees that Junxiang Lai planted" (ASX, no. 13518).

Let us consider another case. In March in Qianlong 12 (1747), Yalong Chen of Lianping District, Guangdong province, designated a piece of grassland in Litong'ou as his property, stating that he intended to cut the grass in the autumn. On August 15, Yalong Chen cut the grass and piled it on the ground. Three days later, Shizong Ou also went to the mountain to cut the grass; however, Yalong Chen claimed that he had already claimed the grass on the mountain as his, so others should not cut it. The judge declared that Litong'ou was a government mountain, so the firewood and grass on the mountain should be reserved for gathering by the poor, and no one had the right to declare those resources as his own in advance (ASX, no. 43620).

In a case in Le'an County, Jiangxi province, in Qianlong 14 (1749), the records show that a government mountain named Niueling was reserved as an area where anyone with any surname could gather firewood. Furthermore, after a quarrel between lineages about cutting trees, the judge ordered each lineage to present a confirmation about the use of the mountain where persons of that family name could undertake firewood collecting, in order to stop quarrels (ASX, no. 50512).

In another case, there was a government mountain named Wushi behind the Ceng family's house. Fulong Ceng found that lime could be extracted from the mountain, so he gathered friends, invested, paid a wage to one, Chaohuai Zhong, and others, and prepared to dig lime out of the mountain. However, a judgment was issued to stop such digging, and it was declared that in order to prevent quarrels, no one could enter that area and dig into the mountain. This judgment was based on the illegality of encroaching on the government area, even for those living nearby (JQX, 133).

From these examples, we can extract some rules and principles regarding government mountains. As a rule, such mountains were open-access to anyone; everyone could use the profits gained from them through gathering firewood and grass. To engage in an enterprise of one's own on such mountains was prohibited, because this obstructed the rights of others. However, in cases where it would not prevent the access rights of others, it could be permitted, subject to certain limits.

FORESTS FOR LIVELIHOOD

It is worth questioning what kinds of people have priority to use common land. Regarding the nature of the hierarchy used in the commons, there are various examples in many regions. For example, Hiroyuki Torigoe claimed that in *Iriai-chi* (village common land) in Japan, the weak were allowed to use more resources than others,[18] whereas Yanagisawa Haruka argued that rich, large-scale farmers who owned abundant farmland also enjoyed great profits from the commons.[19] It is necessary to investigate which type of use better represents the situation in China, or whether the Chinese case was unique.

Many XKTB records describe "gathering firewood in the forest" as a means of livelihood that was related to poverty. We can find many examples that say the needy could satisfy their basic needs from forests. Of course, for the common people, collecting firewood from the mountain around the village as fuel for daily life was performed routinely. However, if people made a living only by gathering and selling firewood, they were seen as poor. We consider some examples later.

Shouer Zhou of Xinyu County, Jiangxi province, made a living by selling firewood. One morning, Zhou attempted to wake his wife, Mrs. Sun. However, she was lazy and talked back to him. Shouer Zhou was so angered by this that he struck his wife. After a struggle in the kitchen, Mrs. Sun died from her wounds. In his testimony in this case, Shouer Zhou said: "my family is poor, so I earn money by gathering firewood," stressing his family's poverty (ASX, no. 71519).

The next example shows that gathering firewood was an activity taken into consideration when making a judgment in court. In Yongfeng County, Jiangxi province, the Wu lineage's mountain and Wang lineage's mountain were close to each other. One day, Sisheng Wu gathered firewood on the Wu lineage's mountain. Xili Wang happened to pass by and, suspecting that Sisheng Wu was collecting firewood on the Wang lineage's mountain, hit Sisheng Wu. After a struggle, Sisheng Wu beat Xili Wang to death. In the court, the magistrate (presiding as the judge) took into consideration the situation that Sisheng Wu was the only adult son of his mother, and whether he was one of the "poor little people who gather firewood" (ASX, no. 50115).

The case later involved a man and his wife from another county who organized a gathering. Chen Shenshan was born in Chengmai County, Guangdong province, and moved to the next county, Ding'an, in Qianlong 1 (1736). One morning, Chen and his wife, Mrs. Li, went to the mountain to gather firewood and returned home in the afternoon (ASX, no. 27934).

Furthermore, the needy relied on their relatives and might ask permission to make a living by gathering firewood on a relative's mountain. Zhenqi Liang lived with his wife, Mrs. Feng, in the house of Shangzhi Pan, who was Liang's second eldest sister's husband. In September of Qianlong 19 (1754), Zhenqi Liang and Mrs. Feng went to the house of Tianjue Xie, Liang's eldest sister's husband, and implored him: "Our family is very needy; please let us move here and make a living by gathering firewood." Tianjue Xie considered his kinship with them and allowed them to live with him. However, unexpectedly, there was no firewood to cut down on the mountain. On October 13 of that year, Liang and Mrs. Feng traveled back to Shangzhi Pan's house (ASX, no. 41692).

These examples show how impoverished people made a living on the mountains. Some even said that they were poor and lived with firewood as a matter of course, and it was not unusual for impoverished people to ask a person close to them to allow them to take firewood from a mountain. It may be risky to assume that mountains and forests always functioned as a safety net for the needy. However, the words "gathering firewood for livelihood" were recorded not only in these legal cases, but also in the historical materials from many other periods. Therefore, the collection of firewood in the mountains by the poor seems to be more common than expected.

Concerning examples from the XKTB, we can conclude that the Qing government is primarily interested in preventing disputes. This was increasingly a problem in the later Qing, as population pressure forced more of the poor into trying to gain things from the mountains. Therefore, the prevention of conflicts helped preserve the place where the poor gathered firewood.

However, it seems that the Qing government had little obvious intent to keep the mountains covered by forests. In fact, forests on government mountains were also vulnerable as their cultivation was not legally prohibited. Since the population increased almost continuously throughout the Qing period, it was important to enlarge cultivated areas and to increase food production.

A PROPOSAL TO PLANT TREES ON "GOVERNMENT MOUNTAINS" IN THE EIGHTEENTH CENTURY

In Qing China, unlike cases in Germany and Japan, the dynasty was less often engaged in long-term silviculture management.[20] Although Qing authorities did not usually engage in silviculture, one mid-eighteenth official did draft a proposal to engage in such activities. His proposal mainly aimed to keep the "government mountains (*guan shan*)" as commons for the local "little people" to gain things from there.

In eighteenth-century China, the population increased approximately threefold, and reclamation of land was progressing incrementally. In 1757, taking the state's condition as background, Pengnan Wu, an Imperial censor in Jiangnan province, presented a memorandum to the Qianlong emperor. The title of the memorandum was "Instruct Bureaucrats in the Empire to Conduct a Policy on Mountain Forests, and Enrich Civilian Use." The memorandum stated the following:[21]

> The peaceful time has lasted long, and the population in our empire has increased; however, goods that are produced are not keeping up with the need of the materials to be used. So, we must undertake politics to improve people's living conditions.
>
> I heard waters are blocked up, ponds dried up, lands and mountains went bald; therefore obtaining everyday goods is gradually getting more difficult and prices have increased remarkably. The price of firewood has doubled, the price of building materials increased threefold, and the price of the mast of a ship increased fivefold.
>
> The reason is as follows: Requirements of [timber materials] increased day by day and more people are felling many trees. However, they are logging only in the "government mountain"; they only seek [timber] and do not pursue arboriculture. Nourishing the trees takes time, but cutting trees takes only one moment. This is the first reason.
>
> Ignorant people not only take branches but also remove trunks and roots. In such a way, people can only obtain a temporary profit, but the tree will never come to life again in the following year. This is the second reason.
>
> And besides, there is a lazy trend. If it is difficult to take away creeping weeds, one can easily remove them by setting fire to mountains. Therefore, in all the towns and countryside, people often burn the forest down. The people are going to reduce a temporary burden and let the neighboring forest be reduced to ashes.

In these sentences, Pengnan Wu highlighted that population increase had caused deforestation, which depleted water sources and caused soil runoff. He also notes that the forest resources, as necessities of life, had become rarer and their prices inflated. Furthermore, Wu argued that the deforestation had increased only on "government mountains," and no trees had been planted there.

Wu repeatedly compared the situation with the "government mountain" to that of "private property":

> I was born in Fujian, where half of the land is high mountains. I always knew how to plant trees there, and I recognized that planting ten thousand young trees only costs thirty or forty teals of silver, and they grow in less than three years so that one can get the capital. The situation is the same in Jiangxi and Lingnan. In Jiangxi, Zhejiang, Henan, and Shandong provinces, it is slightly more difficult to plant trees, but you can still plant ten thousand young trees for less than one hundred teals of silver. However, this only takes place on "private property." No one plants trees on the "government mountain."

This statement should be considered in relation to the following description, which was given in the same period and concerned Wu's native land, Fujian:

> Most of the land in Fujian is "government mountains," with no prohibition on cutting timber. Any branches or twigs that grow are burned or taken away, and people even dig up the roots to use as cooking fuel so that nothing can grow again and the

mountains become barren. However, where the mountain belongs to someone, industrious owners plant pine, *Cunninghamia*, bamboo, tung oil tree, and tea oil tree, earning themselves considerable profits.[22]

This also articulated that with the situation of "open access," with no prohibition on public use, "government mountains" were becoming barren.

We can conclude that Wu recognized that the government mountains were extremely important for local people's lives, and he was also fully aware of the open-access nature of the government mountains and even noted a kind of "tragedy of the commons" (or "tragedy of open access"). Of course, these trends should be considered in the context of population growth and resource shortages. Furthermore, Wu might have realized the need to provide the people with the means to satisfy their basic needs, such as firewood, by planting trees with the authorities' help. Based on the notions earlier, Wu proposed giving incentives to government officials, gentlemen, and common people to plant trees on government mountains. This suggestion gained the approval of the Qianlong emperor; a document was then circulated to each local official through *gongbu* ("the board of construction"), and the actual condition of government mountains was investigated by local officials.

However, responses from the local government officials regarding giving tree-planting incentives were predominantly negative. Not all of the local government officials fully understood the significance of Wu's proposal. The reasons for this negativity can be classified as follows: The most frequent reason was that there was no government mountain on which to plant trees in the district concerned, or the existing government mountains were so barren that no plants could be cultivated. Another frequent reason given was that government mountains were lands that lacked ownership and were used by the poor for gathering firewood or for burial, so it was desirable to leave them untouched. In addition, some officials argued against providing incentives because tree planting was the duty of local officials. Furthermore, some officials suggested that the land should not be maintained as "government mountains," but instead changed to "private properties" to better utilize people's capacity.

After the replies from each local government official had been submitted, and despite their widespread objections, official regulations were introduced to establish incentives for tree planting and these were given to local officials and gentlemen. However, the proposals were vague in their contents and their impact was so slight that we cannot trace evidence of the regulations being subsequently implemented in practice. Wu's aim to keep government mountains covered by forest did not bear fruit.

The mountains in Qing China may be classified into two types: the mountains from which any individual had the right to derive profits, called "private property," and those from which no one had the right to derive profits, called "government mountains." Of the former type, some were owned by individuals, but in many cases, they were owned jointly by various means. These jointly owned mountains were called "public mountains." All members of the coownership could freely gather firewood and pasture on these mountains, which often had boundaries and were closed to the outside world. Therefore, if nonmembers crossed a mountain boundary, the members would attack them. To summarize, these lands were "open" to members, but "closed" to others. The second type of mountain was called "government mountains": essentially, anyone could access them and could gather firewood and bury ancestors freely thereon, provided these activities did not disturb the mountain's use by other people. This type can be classified as an "open" mountain. Both of these types of mountains, though their openness is different, had the function as "commons," and served as a reliable source of people's daily necessities.

Making a living by gathering firewood was considered to be standard practice for the poor and weak. Thus, it may be said that, to some degree, allowing use of the public or government mountains was intended to ensure the survival of the disadvantaged. Both types of mountains could therefore be called a kind of "commons" for the poor in early modern China. On government mountains, the legitimacy of these lands' use was specified by the Qing government, and ultimately by the emperor himself. In these mountains, the Qing government determined policies through directions appropriate not to disturb the people's daily use, but to prohibit ownership by individuals for profit-making purposes. However, it is difficult to deduce to what extent the Qing imperial court took an active role in providing livelihoods for the weak and poor while maintaining the reproduction of sustainable resources. As far as can be discerned from the records, it seems that the prevention of disputes in these mountains was the government's main interest. Even if this deduction is correct, we can conclude that some of the poor's basic needs were nonetheless addressed by these policies. In the eighteenth century some proposed actively prescribing that the forest covering the "commons" must be preserved; however, the actions of the Qing government were too vague to institute changes in the management and use of land on such a large scale.

The findings presented are expected to contribute to a better understanding of commons in China and a basis for comparison with similar examples in other regions. However, there are still many unanswered questions. Most of the evidence in this chapter comes from southern China, where forest resources are relatively abundant. The term "government mountain" appears most frequently in historical records from Jiangxi, Guangdong, and Fujian. Further study is needed to examine differences between the regions. In addition, it will be necessary to consider these issues from the perspective of the non-Han people's customs of forest use, as they have a long history in southern China's mountains.

Disagreements over the use and management of forest resources have become a more urgent subject in modern times, as both officials and the people have become aware of the sparse forest cover in China in comparison to other areas in the world, and afforestation has consequently become an important policy issue. Conflicts have arisen when authorities established national or public forests or disposed of areas that "no one had the legitimacy to possess," which actually were often the areas of people's daily use.

Based on newly established forest laws or regulations in the late nineteenth century and twentieth, many "government mountains" and "government wilderness areas" *(guan huang)* were sold or were lent to common people or local entities, and authorities tried to establish exclusive ownership in forests. However, there were many appeals against these actions, citing such reasons as "the mountain is for people gathering firewood and it is unsuitable for occupation." This indicates that some form of the "forests as commons" still functions as a source of resources for basic needs in contemporary China.

NOTES

1. There are various definitions of "commons" offered by many researchers; this definition of commons is based on Inoue 2004.

2. One well-known study is Ostrom 1990. With regard to developing the study of commons, see Mitsumata 2014.

3. Tanaka 1925, Hatada 1973.

4. Hatada 1973.

5. To give some representative examples, Menzies categorized several kinds of forest and argued about the land management of forests in late imperial China by using various documents as well as reports produced under customary law in China (Menzies 1988, 1994, chap. 5). Perdue claimed that a redefinition of Chinese land property rights was in progress, as a response to new trends of population growth, commercialization, and ecological exploitation in eighteenth-century China (Perdue 2002). Quoting examples of *kai yezi*, Suga Yutaka reached the conclusion that Chinese commons were a result of "passive, defensive cooperation" and were maintained by networks of individual relationships, not by villages with definite boundaries and membership (Suga 2009). Ōta Izuru articulated that some parts of the water surface of near Taihu Lake could be regarded as a form of open-access commons (Ōta 2009). Hirano Yūichirō and Okuda Shin'ich considered forest policy in present-day China, showing people were pressed for various responses with the change of the forest possession policy by the nation (Hirano 2008, Okuda 2014).

6. For further information about XKTB, see Horichi 2012. Osborne and Buoye also investigated land problems using this kind of material (Osborne 2004, Buoye 2000).

7. Du 2008.

8. For example, mulberry trees (an example can be seen in JQX, 22), the cultivation of other trees (JQX, 591; i.e., *Cunninghamia lanceolata*, JQX, 1785), fruit trees (JQX, 1565), *tong cha* (JQX, 1227), cypresses (ASX, no. 119973), the cultivation of bamboo (JQX, 721), the grazing of maize (JQX, 810), selling trees (JQX, 809), cultivation (many references), and plantations of indigo (JQX, 1248).

9. For example, coal mining (JQX, 230), grazing (JQX, 590), gathering bamboo shoots (ASX, no.44535), making charcoal (JQX, 547, 905, 1248), gathering and making lime (JQX, 1248), cutting grass for fertilizer (ASX, no. 1306), cutting grass for raising cattle (ASX, no.89904), and collecting dung

(ASX, no. 73119). The most popular activity of this type was "gathering firewood," which served not only for daily use but also for fertilizing the land and making bricks (ASX, no. 72825).

10. On this type of use, some historians discuss in detail the regulations concerning the sale of graveyards and neighboring land and trees. See Nakajima 2004, Wei 2015.

11. On the notion of *wang-tu wang-min* and *ye*, see Terada 1989 and Kishimoto 2011.

12. This classification is mainly based on Morita 1984.

13. Menzies 1994, chap. 3.

14. Niida 1962.

15. Morita 1976.

16. Menzies 1994, chap. 6.

17. Ōta Izuru based his study on a survey of the fishermen at Taihu Lake, arguing that the surface of the water, called "government lake" *(guan hu)*, was also open access, with no one having exclusive rights to it. Furthermore, he observed that the surface of the water provided materials for the livelihood of "little people" (Ōta 2009).

18. Torigoe 1997.

19. Yanagisawa 2012.

20. Saito 2014.

21. This section is based on Aihara 2007. Wu's memorial was copied by Junji-chu (office of Grand Council of State) and in the collection of *Junji-chu Lufu Zouzhe* no.0978–035, in the First Historical Archives China.

22. *Funing Fu Zhi* (Gazetter of Funing, in Fujian Province), printed in 1762, chap. 32, 24b.

REFERENCES

Aihara, Yoshiyuki (2007). "Qingchao Zhongqi de Senlin Zhengce: Yi Qianlong Ershi Nian-dai de Zhishu Taolun wei Zhongxin" (Forest Policy in the Middle of the Qing Dynasty: An Analysis of Discussion about the Policy on Planting Trees). In *Zhongguo Lishishang Huanjing Yu Shehui*, edited by Wang Lihua. Beijing: Shenghuo Dushu Xinzhi Sanlian Shudian.

Buoye, Thomas M. (2000). *Manslaughter, Markets, and Moral Economy: Violent Disputes over Property Rights in Eighteenth-century China*. Cambridge: Cambridge University Press.

Du, Jiaqi, ed. (2008). *Qing Jiaqing Chao Xingke Tiben Shehui Shiliao Jikan* (Sources on Society Excerpted from Routine Memorials of Scrutiny for the Board of Punishments during the Jiaqing Reign [1796–1820]). Tianjin: Tianjin Guji Chubanshe.

Hatada, Takashi (1973). *Chūgoku Sonraku to Kyōdōtai Riron* (The Chinese Village and the Theory of Community). Tokyo, Iwanami Shoten.

Hirano, Yūichirō (2008). "Mori ga Shigen to Naru Ikutsuka no Michi: Chūgoku no Rekishi to Iu Jirei Kara (Some Ways Where a Forest Becomes the Resources: A Case Study of Chinese History). In *Hitobito no Shigen Ron: Kaihatsu to Kankyō no Sōgō ni Mukete*, edited by Jin Satō. Tokyo, Akashi Shoten.

Horichi, Akira (2012). "Shindai Keika Daihon to Kenryu Jūnen (1745) Sansei Daidō-fu Tenchin-ken Dōshin An" (Routine Memorials or Reports to the Ministry of Justice in Qing Period and the case of relief at Tianzhen County, Datong Fu, Shanxi, 1745). In *Minshū Hanran to Chūka Sekai: Atarashii Chūgoku-shi zō no Kōchiku ni Mukete*, edited by Hiroshi Yoshio. Tokyo, Kyūko Shoin.

Inoue, Makoto (2004). *Komonzu no Shisō wo Motomete: Karimantan no Mori de Kangaeru* (In Search of the Thought of Commons: Thinking in a Forest of Kalimantan). Tokyo, Iwanami Shoten.

Kishimoto, Mio (2011). "Property Rights, Land, and Law in Imperial China." In *Law and Long-Term Economic Change: An Eurasian Perspective,* edited by Debin Ma and Jan Luiten van Zanden. Stanford, Stanford Economics and Finance.

Menzies, Nicholas K. (1988). "A Survey of Customary Law and Control over Trees and Wildlands in China." In *Whose Trees? Proprietary Dimensions of Forestry,* edited by Louise Fortmann and John W. Bruce. Boulder, CO, Westview.

——— (1994). *Forest and Land Management in Imperial China.* New York, St. Martin's.

Mitsumata, Gaku, ed. (2014), *Ekorojī to Komonzu: Kankyō Gabanansu to Chiiki Jiritsu no Shisō* (Ecology and Commons: Governance of Environment and Thoughts of Local Independence). Tokyo, Kōyō Shobō.

Morita, Akira (1976). "Minmatsu Shindai no 'Hōmin' ni Tsuite" (About Shed-People ("pengmin") in late Ming and Qing). *Jinbun Kenkyū* 28–9:1–38.

Morita, Shigemitsu (1984). *Shindai Tochi Shoyūhō Kenkyū* (Survey of Land Ownership Law in Qing Dynasty). Tokyo, Keisō Shuppan.

Nakajima, Gakushō (2004). "Bochi wo Utte wa Ikenai Ka: Tō-Shindai ni Okeru Bochi Baikyaku Kinshi Rei" (Can Graveyards Be Sold or Not? The Legal Ban of Selling Graveyards from Tang to Qing). *Kyūshū Daigaku Tōyōshi Ronshū* 32:66–125.

Niida, Noboru (1962). *Chūgoku Hōseishi Kenkyū: Dorei Nōdo Hō, Kazoku Sonraku Hō* (Study of Chinese Legal History: Laws for Slaves and Serfs, Laws for Families and Villages). Tokyo, Tokyo Daigaku Shuppankai.

Okuda, Shin'ichi, ed. (2014). *Chūgoku no Sinrin wo Meguru Hō Seisaku Kenkyū* (Study of Legal Policy about the Chinese Forest). Tokyo, Seibundō.

Osborne, Anne (2004). "Property, Taxes, and State Protection of Rights." In *Contract and Property in Early Modern China,* edited by Madeleine Zelin, Jonathan K. Ocko, and Robert Gardella. Stanford, Stanford University Press.

Ostrom, Elinor (1990). *Governing the Commons: The Evolution of Institutions for Collective Action.* New York, Cambridge University Press.

Ōta, Izuru (2009). "Chūgoku Tai-ko Ryūiki Gyomin to Nai-suimen Gyogyō: Kenri Kankei no Arikata wo Meguru Shiron" (Fishermen in China's Taihu Lake Basin and Inland Freshwater Fisheries: Unsettled Questions about the Nature of Rights). In *Gurōbaru Jidai no Rōkaru Komonzu.* Kyoto, Mineruva Shobō.

Perdue, Peter C. (2002). "Property Rights on Imperial China's Frontiers." In *Land, Property, and the Environment,* edited by John F. Richards. Oakland, CA, ICS Press.

Saito, Osamu (2014). *Kankyō no Keizai-shi: Shinrin, Shijō, Kokka* (Economic History of Environment: Forests, Markets, and Nation). Tokyo, Iwanami Shoten.

Suga, Yutaka (2009). "Chūgoku no Dentō-Teki Komonzu no Gendai-Teki Gan'i"(Modern Connotation of Chinese Traditional Commons). In *Gurōbaru Jidai no Rōkaru Komonzu.* Kyoto, Mineruva Shobō.

Tanaka, Tadao (1925). *Shina Bukken Kanshūhō* (Customary Property Law in China). Shanghai, Nihondō Shoten.

Terada, Hiroaki (1989). "Chūgoku Kinsei ni Okeru Shizen no Ryōyū" (Possession of Nature in Early Modern China). In *Sirīzu Sekai-shi e no Toi 1: Rekishi ni okeru Shizen.* Tokyo, Iwanami Shoten.

Torigoe, Hiroyuki (1997). "Komonzu no Riken wo Kyōju Suru Mono" (Who Gets the Most from the Commons). *Kankyō Shakaigaku Kenkyū* 3:5–14.

Wei, Yuxin (2015). "Funju wo Meguru hō Chitsujo no Kōchiku (Building of Rules of Law about Tomb trees). *Chūgoku—shakai to Bunka* 30:124–145.

Yanagisawa, Haruka (2012). "Indo no Kyōdō Shigen wo Meguru Mondai eno Shikaku: Kenri, Kanri, Kaisō to Rekishiteki Henka" (Changing Phases of Common Property Resources in India: Rights, Control and Class Conflict). *Rekishigaku-kenkyū* 893:37–44.

Zheng, Qin, and Zhao Xiong, eds. (1999). *Qingdai "Fuzhi" Ming'an: Xingke Tiben Dang'an Xuanbian* (A Selection of Qing Dynasty Homicide Cases Involving Family Members Included in the Mourning System). Beijing, Zhongguo Zhengfa Daxue Chubanshe.

Public Goods and Economy in the Early Modern Era—New Perspectives on Modern Economies and Contemporary Environmental Concerns

R. Bin Wong

This volume of essays has examined the ways in which people and their governments produced and paid for nonmarket goods in both early modern East Asia and Western Europe. We have especially considered the kinds of goods often supplied through nonmarket means at the regional and local levels of society, sometimes but not always far removed from the concerns of the central government. This perspective has allowed us to consider the early modern developments of public goods quite separately from the later crystallization of modern public finance. Early modern European public finance, as we mentioned in the introductory chapter is largely associated with the concept of the fiscal state, which is sometimes called the fiscal-military state because of the intimate relationship between increased government borrowing and taxation with military expenditures. The major expenditure of centralizing European states in the seventeenth and eighteenth centuries was military. State formation in Europe took place as part of the construction of relations among European states competing with one another for power and wealth. This dynamic has had profound impact of the shaping of modern politics through the expansion of European power around the world that included the early modern formation of white settler societies in the Americas, the purchase and export of African slaves to the Americas, and a trade in Asian commodities that expanded the range of products available during Europe's early modern consumer revolution. By the early nineteenth century the early modern American white settler societies had shed their colonial status to become independent countries, and by the late nineteenth century, African and Asian trading partners and their neighbors had largely succumbed to colonial rule by European powers.

Fundamental to the imposition of political authority was the presence, or at least threat, of military violence against which subject populations were largely unable to resist. The European deployment of military violence for a combination of political and economic aims in both nineteenth-century Africa and Asia extended political and economic logics first formulated in the early modern era and most clearly developed by the aptly titled "fiscal state." Yet the phenomena that the term most especially points out all lead to a focus on Great Britain, as Richard Bonney, one of the leading specialists on the subject, makes clear when concluding his introduction to a volume on European fiscal states: "Only one state, Britain, had reached the more advanced stage of a 'fiscal state.' . . . In that sense, perhaps the book should have been entitled *The Rise of a Fiscal State in Europe, c. 1200–1815,* instead of *The Rise of the Fiscal State in Europe, c. 1200–1815*" (Bonney 1999, 14). By locating the fiscal state's formation as the product of successful development of state fiscal capacities in response to military threats, Bonney locates the concept firmly within European history and provides background to Britain's rise to its hegemonic position politically and economically in the nineteenth century.

Britain's fiscal successes supplied the norm for the fiscal state. Its main early modern expenditures, especially dramatic in the rising costs of expanding its eighteenth-century navy, are part of a larger British success story of becoming the first industrial nation and Europe's most successful colonizer of peoples in other world regions. Folding the fiscal state into these larger narratives of capitalism and political power gives the fiscal state a particular prominence that is both more and less than the subject of state expenditures. It is more because the fiscal state is made part of a larger set of changes characterizing European economic and political changes. It is less than state expenditures generally because as the fiscal-military state concept in particular makes clear, it highlights one kind of expenditure, namely, those for military matters.

After the important work on the European fiscal state came subsequent efforts to make a "global" history of the fiscal state in *The Rise of Fiscal States: A Global History, 1500–1914,* edited by Bartolomé Yun-Casalilla and Patrick K. O'Brien. Only five of the seventeen case studies addressed non-European cases—two chapters on China and one each on Japan, India, and the Ottoman Empire. The studies in general assemble a rich trove of information on revenue strategies across Europe and the countries beyond Europe just mentioned earlier. On the expenditure side, military matters loom large in most of the European cases. The early modern European state's need to expand its revenue and become a fiscal state derived largely from the costs of its war making. The fiscal state's public finance has relatively little to do with the provision of goods and services ill suited to market mechanisms other than national defense or, what we might perhaps more accurately call in the context of early modern European war making, a successful "national offense." In his essay in *The Rise of Fiscal States: A Global History, 1500–1914* titled "Taxation in the Habsburg Low Countries and Belgium, 1579–1914," Paul Janssens assembles data supporting his estimate that "Only one-third of the total local and provincial revenue from taxation was used for the government's own ends. Apart from administrative expenditure (salaries and operating costs), only public works constituted a significant item of expenditure. The government's contribution to poor relief was limited. The Church played the dominant role here, as it did in education" (Janssens 2012, 76). While others scholars in this global history of fiscal states do not make as comprehensive a summary regarding the relative size of fiscal expenditures, it is unlikely that officials in many European countries were spending much of their time or energy addressing issues of poverty and famine, infrastructure construction, or forestry management, examples of what we are calling in this volume "public goods" to stress the importance of nonmarket management and provision in all of our cases.

Our intention is hardly to argue that the "fiscal state" concept has been unhelpful to understanding the processes of European state formation. But we do suspect that the process of taking the fiscal state concept to a global scale has followed an intellectual path already well trod by economic historians of diverse dispositions who have evaluated non-European sites according to their differences from European economic practices within their preferred frames of interpretation, be these neoclassical economics, Marxist, or Weberian. One of the costs of such an intellectual strategy regarding public goods and public finance is to miss the production of goods that are in no reasonable sense private because they are not produced for exchange on the market for the mutual benefit of private parties. We have argued that such goods can be considered public goods with "public" referring to far more than only the government. Public goods are created in a social space within which market mechanisms might be present, as well as community-based exchanges and those organized by the state. They are not limited to goods and services produced and allocated by the government. Working with an expanded definition of public goods to include non-market-produced goods and services, we have been able to highlight several areas of early modern economic activity in a new way.

The payoffs from the approach we suggest are several. First, considering the provision of nonmarket goods and services addresses activities fundamental to the economic life of early modern societies that are typically not covered in discussions of the fiscal state. These include in fact activities taking place in England, the model of the fiscal state. Second, the kinds of nonmarket goods and services we discuss have clear similarities to nonmarket goods and services today for which public finance remains important. Infrastructure is perhaps the most salient example, but the provision of disaster relief also spans both publicly and privately mounted campaigns. Looking at early modern public goods and the ways in which they were financed thus offers us a different perspective on our contemporary practices from those encouraged by the fiscal state narrative.

A third benefit comes from recognizing the historical particularities of the modern industrial era through appreciation of the concerns shared by early modern and contemporary societies that the modern industrial era did not take as seriously. From our examination of forest management, for example, we can gain a perspective on issues of natural resource management and the environment. The industrial era was built on the exploitation of fossil fuels and their destructive impacts on climate and environment that have become more fully appreciated only in the past several decades. Resources and their exploitation were assumed to have limits in early modern societies since people had no way to anticipate the technological breakthroughs that would enable people to capture ever-greater amounts of energy and create new sources of power. Early modern management of natural resources thus bore some partial parallels with the approaches taken today when an awareness of limits is much stronger than it was between the mid-nineteenth century and mid-twentieth. Our sampling of approaches to early modern forest management can help identify examples of practices potentially relevant to the policies pondered by analysts seeking to establish some standards for best practice today. Issues of water resource management, which we have also addressed in this volume, take us to the connections between infrastructure and natural resource management because they include the use of water for infrastructural projects spanning power generation, transportation, agricultural production, and consumption.

A fourth and final payoff to highlight is more methodological than simply substantive. The subjects we cover in this volume can be found in both East Asia and Europe. Because the motivation to look for such subjects came out of intensive study of early modern Japan, we have been able to avoid the more common selection practices that follow criteria that highlight the particularities of the most successful early modern European states. The results of such familiar exercises have often told us how some countries are not like European ones without explaining directly what they in fact were like. By choosing common concerns such as infrastructural construction, natural resource management, and the clusters of activities concerning poverty policies and famine relief efforts, we are able to make comparisons in a more neutral way. In fact there is no reasonable measure of what is better or worse before we catalogue what in fact occurred across a range of cases.

At the same time, we do recognize that there are advantages to examining some case in more depth than others in order to have a sense of how public goods were created in the context of one particular country. The choice of Japan for this purpose has been made possible by the availability of rich sources and careful scholarship. The country's small size also affords the same advantages that looking at England offers. At the same time we have deliberately chosen to use as our two main cases beyond Japan a connected yet contrasting East Asian one, namely, China, and a European case, namely, Prussia, that in itself contrasts with the paradigmatic English fiscal state. This allows us in this final chapter to distinguish three spatial scales of variation—those within Europe, those within East Asia, and those variations most usefully arrayed across both East Asia and Europe.

If we take for the moment the paradigmatic English fiscal state as a point of departure, but consider those activities that don't fall neatly under the fiscal-military state rubric, we can begin by considering poor relief, the one case study addressing this country that we include in this book. While there is an act of Parliament establishing the Poor Law across England, the English fiscal state had little to do with its implementation. No taxes collected by the centralizing state busy building military and fiscal bureaucracies were used to fund poor relief. No state officials were involved in administering poor relief. English poor relief depended on members of the local elites serving in the unpaid status of justice of the peace or magistrate. Resources for funding poor relief were raised and used locally. While certainly a nonmarket good, poor relief has traits of a community-based activity organized and funded by local people for the benefit of locals, at the same time it can be considered an activity promoted by the state. To the extent that it was a state activity, it alerts us to the limitations of the fiscal state concept for addressing public finance issues. But the notion we employ in this volume of public goods as nonmarket goods allows English poor relief to be a public good because our formulation explicitly includes the varied acts of elites to provide goods and services by nonmarket means that create value for others and typically with some kind of social benefits that are positive externalities to the individual benefits derived from market transactions. While the presence of nonmilitary expenditures at more local levels that are missing from the main message of the fiscal-military state concept has already been noted by others (e.g., Innes 2009), locating such efforts in a public goods frame of reference has not been, to our knowledge, done.

If we turn to another of our three subject areas, English practices for infra-structure building are distinctive. Where water control projects in both China and Japan, as well as Prussia, were undertaken by different constellations of actors and market mechanisms played little to no role, the development of the English rivers was similar to the development of roads. For both, private investments played a crucial role in the increased funding of transportation networks in the seventeenth and eighteenth centuries. Dan Bogart has shown that turnpike trusts could cover costs by charging tolls and accessing needed capital by mortgaging future toll receipts (Bogart 2005, 2011). From a related but distinct perspective, Piet de Vries has suggested that English canal projects were joint ventures, that is, public-private partnerships combining the efforts of government and private entrepreneurs (de Vries 2013, 15). These institutional innovations are part of the broader financial market innovations that spanned both public and private finance in eighteenth-century Britain. Another institutionally distinctive political feature was the opportunities for competing interests to express their concerns and desires regarding river navigation improvements in Parliament, where a series of Inland Navigation Acts enabled private actors to pursue projects they anticipated would yield profits (Yamamoto 2018, 143–156).

Infrastructural public goods for transport in East Asia and Prussia were handled differently in England. Among the East Asian and European cases, public goods creation along rivers was also pursued to improve and protect agricultural interests as well. The relative dependence on river control projects for agricultural production was higher in East Asia than in our European cases because the irrigation needed for paddy rice cultivation presented a need for which there was no near equivalent in Europe. East Asian households engaged in small-holder agriculture were unable to mobilize the resources or mount the organizational efforts themselves to assure the scales of spatial coordination needed to manage water control operations, the spatial scale of these projects being far greater in many Chinese cases than in Japanese ones. Returning to the Prussian case of transportation infrastructure, Sascha Bütow's chapter on road construction in fifteenth- and sixteenth-century Brandenburg explains how important municipal initiatives were to creating a network of roads that connected cities to one another and along which commercial traffic could develop. The status of German cities and their finances were embedded in the relations that cities had to other territorial authorities, including princes and the Holy Roman Empire. The activities Bütow recounts emerged from a thirteenth-century foundation of urban public finances being independent from and more developed than those of territorial noble rulers (Ormrod and Barta 1995, 74–75, Hocquet 1995, 91–92).

We see German territorial rulers taking on a larger role in subsequent centuries regarding infrastructure, as Heinrich Kaak shows in his detailed case study; while he certainly notes that there was a longer tradition across Europe more generally of organizing river dikes to reclaim agricultural land and protect land already being cultivated, the financial and organizational scales of dike projects in Kaak's Prussian example demonstrate just how large the capacities and commitments to infrastructure were that a major German ruler could mount in the eighteenth century. Under Frederick I (r. 1701–1713) and Frederick II (r. 1740–1786), Prussia became a leading European power and the core of what would be the future unifying drive for Germany in 1871. Kaak's Prussian case study combines local dike associations and the king's major projects into a single framework of riverine infrastructure. While regional in scope the organization of riverine infrastructure spanned local and central government actors in ways that fit Elinor Ostrom's concept of a "nested hierarchy" of actors taking on components of managing a common pool resource, much as Chinese water control projects reflected this attribute, often on yet larger territorial scales.

In Britain, the fiscal state was not much involved in either poor relief or creating the transportation infrastructure of roads and navigable rivers, beyond passing legislation to mandate local efforts at mounting poor relief and to encourage private investment in infrastructural improvements. Government involvement in financing and organizing poverty policies and infrastructure projects occurred in both China and Prussia and involved activities not conventionally considered to be part of the fiscal state's activities.

Moving on to consider English material related to our third subject of forests, early modern England had both public and private forestlands. The public lands were those forests claimed by William the Conqueror (r. 1066–1087) who brought with him from Normandy forest law and forest courts, which were then used to define the Crown's control over almost one-third of the kingdom's land. Initially the Crown's principal interest in forests, which included fields, pasture, and villages as well as forests proper, was the use of the forests themselves as hunting preserves. Rulers recognized their royal forests to be subject to multiple uses and granted licenses for use of the forest lands. In the early modern era, the expanding Royal Navy's need for timber meant that the royal forests joined private estates, the colonies, and the Baltic region as sources for naval timber (Scott 2008, 339–347). Private forestland in England was controlled by lords who held title over specific woods but shared with their manorial tenants the use of other woods. These common woods were managed according to custom, which included the commoners' rights to access resources and use them for specific purposes. Different categories of people enjoyed different rights to timber and wood for house building and repair and for firewood (Scott 2008, 448–498). The multiple uses of forestlands in early modern England suggest the accommodation of diverse claims that cannot be reduced to simple public-private binary. This general observation is in line with what the Japanese, Prussian, and Chinese chapters of the volume also suggest regarding the presence of various ideas about the commons that were variously accommodated alongside other claims or challenged by alternative demands. The multiple claims placed by different people on a lord or ruler's forestlands or, in the Chinese case, lands simply labeled "public" (公) suggest more similar and complex ranges of challenges in defining the commons and the relation of the commons to other claims on forestland.

In Takashi Iida's Prussian case the king used his forests as the source of timber for ship building in foreign countries. This revenue-making operation encouraged Frederick II to begin afforestation projects to sustain the timber supply from which he derived profits. The Prussian rulers also had to negotiate the access of their subjects to these forests for both timber and firewood. Nineteenth-century Prussian rulers moved to end the access of their subjects to timber and firewood in order to sell more of the former and make the latter available at lower prices to people clearly poorer than those who had previously exercised claims on firewood gathered in forests. The evolution of claim making on forests used by the ruler for market-based commercial operations and by his subjects as public goods differed in Prussia and Japan. Takeshi Aoki shows that the late-nineteenth-century Meiji government recognized the Tokugawa-era peasant claims to forestland nominally held by lords because peasants in some areas provided the upkeep of the forests through replanting. This Japanese practice of peasant-based afforestation contrasts both with the Prussian case of tree planting under the ruler and with the practice to be considered later of commercial afforestation in some Chinese forests that supplied a long-distance timber trade.

Yoshiyuki Aihara's chapter on Qing forests as commons considers the situation in a variety of forestland legal cases, especially from three provinces south of the Yangtze River, where he finds examples of the tragedy of the commons because forests were depleted without replanting. Not surprisingly, given the Qing empire's large size, there were other forest management regimes in other parts of the empire. In the northeast, the Manchus retained forests on which lived a variety of indigenous groups who supplied the court with different forest animal pelts and other forest products as tribute (Bello 2015, 63–115). The Manchus also established more than a hundred hunting reserves, which featured large amounts of forestland. The Mulan Weichang in what is today northeast Hebei province near the city of Chengde was the largest reserve and site of the annual autumn hunt begun in the 1680s and continuing until 1820 (Menzies 1994, 55–64). Other forests in China produced timber for commercial sale, a practice of considerable importance already by the twelfth century (Miller 2015, 234–283). During the early modern era the demand for timber in China's most economically developed region of Jiangnan, an area centered on modern-day Shanghai after the mid-nineteenth century, stimulated the development of commercial trade from the southwest province of Guizhou more than one thousand kilometers away. The financing of afforestation was met by selling forest land as shares for which a secondary market existed to facilitate the circulation of capital over the two to three decades required for the timber-yielding trees to mature (Zhang 2017).

The subject of poverty and famine shows variations within both East Asia and Europe regarding the roles and relative importance of different social and political actors. For infrastructure, the English case seems quite different from both the Prussian and the East Asian ones; the main difference between Prussia and East Asian cases was the more prominent role of water control issues for agricultural production in Asia. Finally, for forestry management we can see diversity of forest use and management within each case study as well as among them. It makes clear that the different dimensions of comparison help us to distinguish among types of comparisons worth noting and the challenges of combining different types of contrasts into more general evaluations of similarities and differences found in public goods provision in the early modern era.

Establishing the levels and dimensions of generality that come out of using English, Western European, or Euro-American metrics of evaluation can be advanced through adopting a non-Western case as the reference point for evaluating several others. In this volume we have chosen early modern Japan. Japan enjoys features that make it similar to European countries—especially the spatial and demographic scales of the country and other features that make it related to China—in particular overlapping sets of values and some similar forms of agricultural production. We can therefore observe different sets of similarities and differences that early modern Japan has with its Chinese neighbor and with European countries that are more similar to Japan in size and some features of political organization.

To recap our use of early modern Japan, as a reference point: Variations within East Asia begin from a shared cultural base. The Japanese and Chinese share some Buddhist, as well as Confucian, beliefs and practices, which include certain views regarding nature and the aspirations of people to live in some sort of basic harmony with that natural world. They also faced similar challenges in organizing paddy rice cultivation, which meant coordination of water use among groups of agricultural households depending on a common source of water who organized access in ways that could be deemed fair and effective. In both spiritual and material realms therefore, Japanese and Chinese shared sensibilities and challenges that were distinct from those found within early modern Europe. Yet, the ways in which Japanese and Chinese actually organized water control varied considerably. At very local levels, groups or networks of households reached agreements regarding how to manage access to water for irrigating their fields. In both societies there was also the need to mount larger water control operations that required local leaders to mobilize resources and labor to repair dikes and dredge river channels. The differences in geographical and demographic size of the two countries meant that there were far more local water control groups in China that were in turn linked to other similar groups than was the case in Japan. More specifically, Japan has a large number of relatively short rivers flowing down mountains so that the technological and organizational challenges of water management differ from those in China.

In Japan the marked expansion of water control projects depended on new kinds of mobilization taking place beneath the domain level of government. The provision of some public goods in early modern Japan depended greatly on nonstate actors. In China officials and local elites played related but often distinct roles, with officials becoming involved in larger projects that required some kind of special financing and plans for mobilizing labor to implement the work needed. A combination of official and local elite activism to maintain, repair, and even expand water control projects characterized eighteenth-century Chinese nonmarket provision of collective or public goods. The increased efforts at a particular local level of Japanese society contrast with the increased activism exhibited by Chinese officials at multiple levels, often responding to calls from the court or from provincial-level leaders. In both countries the historical evidence suggests an increase in public goods of the kinds we have examined being produced during the early modern era, especially during the eighteenth century. But the constellation of mechanisms deployed to achieve these increases was certainly different.

Innocent of the facts, there is little reason to expect the differences in mechanisms for public good provision in Japan and China to involve greater bureaucratic involvement in China and less in Japan since Japan is a far smaller area to govern and thus far more amenable to centralized bureaucratic control than an empire the size of eighteenth-century China. The actual contrast of greater bureaucratic involvement in public good provision in China than in Japan must however be qualified since the viability of Chinese public goods provision depended crucially on the efforts of local elites whose embrace of a neo-Confucian social agenda, the formulation of which began in the twelfth century, made elite efforts largely complementary to those of officials. The limits to bureaucratic reach and penetration below the county level were substantial in eighteenth-century China, but the impact of the bureaucracy's agenda cannot be measured solely by the formal bureaucracy's extension into local societies since local elites were in many ways responsive to the priorities that officials were setting (Wong 1997, 105–126). The relevant temporal frame within which to situate Chinese and Japanese public goods provision also differs since the early modern Chinese practices are part of a centuries-old set of policy strategies themselves developing out of political principles and practices articulated and elaborated beginning in the centuries before imperial unification in the third century BCE.

The temporal and spatial differences between the Chinese and Japanese cases lead us to consider the temporal and spatial similarities that Japan shares with European countries. The founding of the Tokugawa shogunate in 1603 and its successful ending to an era of military competition within Japan and the development of its capacities to rule successfully for more than two and a half centuries make it a state comparable to those European states that also embarked on processes of consolidating rule over previously fragmented territories and established themselves as effective states. The tendency to make these comparisons follows from a larger recognition that in the late nineteenth century and early twentieth Japan proved to be the only non-Western country to have begun processes of industrialization and militarization that made it comparable to and ultimately a competitor with European countries and the United States. Historians of Japan developed desires to establish a longer period of transition from the early modern era to the modern era to parallel that seen in European history, an important part of a larger process of making Japanese history more familiar and thus credible to Western sensibilities. There are indeed parallels and similarities worth noting, whether we wish to focus on economic developments like rural industry or proto-industry, social changes including urbanization, or political transformations such as the formation of stronger governments. In all these respects Tokugawa Japan's similarities to Europe can be clearly seen. Considering the ways in which public goods provision was formulated and the very specific ways in which Japanese public goods provision considered in this book was significant for economic infrastructure, common people's material welfare, and popular access to natural resources helps us see ways in which Japan was also different from Europe in some significant ways.

Before considering Japan-Europe comparisons among the major topics of this volume, we should recall how Tokugawa Japan does not fit very well the model of a European fiscal-military state since the central government was not pursuing an agenda of war making. Military expenditures would only become increasingly important in the late nineteenth century and the first half of the twentieth, as the Meiji state transformed Japan into a challenger to Chinese hegemony in East Asia and then in the first four and a half decades of the twentieth century subsequent Japanese governments made the country into an imperial power seeking political and economic dominance over Northeast and Southeast Asia as well as China. During the early modern era of the Tokugawa, however, the state did not pursue a European fiscal state kind of agenda. The crucial level at which new kinds of initiative emerged in early modern Japan, especially from the late eighteenth century forward, to expand public goods provision was both at the village level and at a level above the village, which lacked any administrative identity and which was led by elites who were not employed by either the shogun or any of the families leading the various domains. In part such actions were compensatory for the reduced capacities of government. These new activities were welcomed by the political authorities in charge of different domains who saw them as promoting the economic potential and security of their subjects.

Comparing the Prussian cases (Prussia defined to include those territories under eighteenth-century Prussian kings) with Japanese cases suggests that rulers and government officials played more prominent roles there than in Japan. These contrasts follow in part from the different kinds of political authority enjoyed by Prussian municipalities and by Prussian nobilities enmeshed in a feudal system's social relations. What the Prussian and Japanese cases share is the creation of public goods well below the spatial scale of what would be the late-nineteenth-century states of Germany and Japan. Both the Japanese and Germans states of the late nineteenth century grew and became military powers as their industrial economies expanded to support their larger territorial aspirations. But those developments are more parallel to the fiscal-military state narrative that highlights early modern and modern British successes at war making than the early modern German and Japanese public goods provision addressing poverty, economic infrastructure, and forest management covered in this volume.

If we turn to issues of water management in contemporary Germany, we discover that the German water supply issues are actually parts of a far larger European Union policy arena that takes on a spatial scale of issues more akin to those faced in China or the United States for water management matters. Germany-Japan contrasts seem irrelevant. The message of these different temporal snapshots of early modern, modern, and contemporary situations alerts us to the ways in which similarities and differences among the public finance concerns within a country can change in both related and distinct ways. What makes each country's particular history potentially relevant has already been raised by

Masayuki Tanimoto in the opening chapter, where he suggests that early modern local and regional public finance practices can influence subsequent patterns of activity in modern times, as the persistence of early modern expectations of claims made on Meiji-era state forestry policies suggests. This case demonstrates how the definition of what become legitimate claims early in the Meiji era was negotiated on the basis of older understandings—acceptance of a new public finance regime depended in this case on people believing that regime would likely carry forward some version of older practices. This case poses a perspective on the move from early modern to modern quite different than those posed by theories based on Western experiences that predict forward historical movements in regions beyond Europe and North America simply to follow their lead on the fiscal-military state model.

Returning to the incompleteness of the early modern fiscal-military state model for tracking changes in all the public goods relevant to economic success in a broader Eurasian context, the afterword chapter by Patrick K. O'Brien in a volume on the global history of fiscal states sets up the significance of the state's fiscal capacities for taking advantage of trade and developing human capital and new knowledge. "In the prevailing medieval and early modern international order of geopolitical violence, conquest, imperialism, and mercantilism, as well as weakly enforced laws and rules for the protection of production and exchange located within and beyond the frontiers of empires, realms and republics, marked by divided sovereignties, the formation of well and consistently funded centralized states remains (in the view of most historians who study these centuries) something approximating to prerequisites for securing greater gains from trade and from domestic and foreign investment in the accumulation of physical and human capital and for the production and diffusion of useful and reliable knowledge" (O'Brien 2012, 444). Defining the early modern international order by "geopolitical violence, conquest, imperialism, and mercantilism" certainly captures conditions within the European world region and Europe's relations to several other world regions. But it hardly applies globally—China alone had a larger population than that of Europe and politically was only marginally involved in the geopolitical violence initiated by Europeans. Significantly, they rebuffed early modern European military advances, achieving what Tonio Andrade has recently called military parity (Andrade 2016). The Chinese thus were able to exercise a far larger role in determining the conditions under which eighteenth-century trade with Europeans took place than people in other parts of early modern Asia or than they themselves would enjoy after British iron ships arrived in China in the late 1830s. They benefited from trade despite not having the kind of fiscal state exemplified by the British case. How important fiscal capacities actually were for influencing investment into human capital or for producing and disseminating new knowledge is difficult to pin down and O'Brien offers little concrete evidence of causal connections.

If we consider eighteenth-century China as a world region comparable to Europe in spatial and demographic terms and consider its domestic relations (same spatial scale as relations among European polities) and its foreign relations with countries of Central, Northeast, and Southeast Asia, we see no mercantilism and relatively little violence. Only with some groups in Central/Inner Asia did Qing dynasty military activity play a long-lasting role more similar to the even longer-lasting persistence of military violence in Europe's conquest and imperialism of Africa, the Americas, and Asia. O'Brien lifts the fiscal state from its original connection with the military to make the fiscal state key to the development of modern economies and modern state policies to support industrial economies. "State formation was part and parcel of the process of long-run growth and could well be an important chapter in narratives designed to explain divergence between Eastern and Western economies, and possibly a key factor behind the observed sequence of leaders, followers, and convergence in any global history of modern industrialization" (O'Brien 2012, 444). Interested principally in explaining economic change, his interest in the fiscal state leads us to see what he calls the "formation of economically effective Eurasian states," with the criteria of effectiveness relating to economic growth rather than criteria anchored more narrowly and deeply in public finance and the ways in which public finance changed in different parts of the world between the early modern and modern eras.

O'Brien's interpretation of the fiscal state is one of several ways the term has been understood. Philip Harling and Peter Mandler, for instance, see a clear change from a fiscal-military state to a laissez-faire state in Britain between 1760 and 1850. They remark, "It was primarily the need to wage war on an unprecedented scale that fueled government growth up to the late 1810s" (Harling and Mandler 1993, 47). They further note that government expenditures declined after the defeat of Napoleon in 1815: "In the immediate postwar period, there was consequently a considerable deflation of government expenditure in absolute terms, reaching its nadir in 1834; relative to the population, spending shrank rapidly" (Harling and Mandler 1993, 60). While there was a contraction of central government expenditures, the development of nineteenth-century British public finance supplies a striking contrast to both the early modern fiscal state's expansion driven by military expenditures and Patrick K. O'Brien's reformulation as a state fostering modern economic growth. According to Martin Daunton, "The fiscal system should therefore be located in the context of voluntarism and the strength of civil society, the role of municipal culture, and the relative autonomy of professional bodies. The English fiscal system combined a diffuse pattern of delegation or subsidiarity in the collection and administration of the tax, with an attempt to preserve generalized legislation that removed discretionary power from the authorities" (Daunton 2010, 50). Daunton's characterization reminds us much more of eighteenth-century poor relief practices than it does of the fiscal-military state and O'Brien's focus on state support for economic growth. This contrast between fiscal capacities to affect economic growth and government expenditures to serve social purposes in turn represents two competing priorities of public finance present over the course of the twentieth century and still with us today.

If we return to the eighteenth-century Britain of John Brewer's "sinews of power," a phrase that captured the close connections between warfare and taxation, we can recall that the fiscal-military state became the robust actor nourished by revenues created by the East India Company's commercial capitalists accessing the Asian commodities and that the state developed the military muscle to assert its political will within Europe and beyond. But Brewer also noted that this state in fact shifted from its earlier domestic concerns to place priority upon central state relations with people and places abroad. As Joanna Innes's research suggests, prime targets of eighteenth-century domestic expenditures became social issues spawned by those new priorities, even as the familiar concerns of dearth, disease, poverty, and crime continued to haunt government leaders. These older issues were now linked to the social problems caused by war making, in particular the domestic transition challenges of military demobilization after the conclusion of a war, when crime rose and the ranks of the vagrants and poor swelled. Innes shows that central government funding to meet such problems was in fact far more limited than local efforts to mobilize resources, but suggests the symbolic significance of central state interventions when and where they occurred (Innes 2009). Thus, social expenditures in eighteenth-century Britain were themselves responses to some of the consequences of increased military expenditures preceding them.

The diminished nineteenth-century focus on war making removed the military origins of domestic social expenditures, and, as Harling and Mandler's research indicates, expenditures overall declined through 1850. As we move through the nineteenth century, several studies of other countries in Europe stress the expansion of state expenditures for social projects, such as education, rather than for promoting economic growth (Cardoso and Lains, 2010). Taking capital away from investment in production is often seen to reduce economic growth. At the same time, however, social spending on education can help create human capital, which in turn contributes to making higher levels of labor productivity possible. Peter Lindert has demonstrated that the growth of nineteenth-century government social spending, a process he calls "growing public," does not appear to have had adverse effects on relative rates of economic growth (Lindert 2004). His work suggests that social expenditures could therefore at worst not derail economic growth, and indeed, could even be considered to create as a perhaps unintended consequence improvements in human capital that O'Brien counts as part of what his fiscal state pursues to support economic growth.

Our presentation of materials on early modern provision of public goods other than military ones identifies forms of spending that also have mattered in the modern era. From a perspective based on Japanese history, one could say that the reduction of military spending in at least some countries of Europe in the early nineteenth century created conditions in which public goods creation sometimes took place at more local levels, as had been the case in early modern Japan. Central governments became more involved in social spending by the late nineteenth century in both European countries and Japan; in a sense they converged temporally along a similar path, but not simply through the Japanese emulation of Western practices, as is conventionally claimed. Nor, to be sure, were Europeans copying Japanese practices. Rather, both European and Japanese states were attending to some increasingly similar economic, political, and social challenges even as they also faced distinct economic opportunities, addressed different social relations and expectations, and made varied political choices. The chapters of this book supply a new and different vantage point from which to assess public goods provision and public finance beginning from practices of the early modern era beyond those highlighted by the fiscal state.

Looking at early modern examples of public goods creation in both East Asian and Western European settings has led us to identify ways in which a range of actors, especially at the local level, and both within and beyond formal government, created some of the public goods either essential to early modern economic activities or conceived as interventions compensating for the limitations of economic production and distribution. Since we consider public goods as simply non-market-produced goods depending on more than just some immediate personal connections between producer and consumer, we can see how government and nongovernment actors created goods that mattered to early modern economies—the creation of economic infrastructure, the management of natural resources, and the capacities to address poverty. Some final remarks on each follow.

For infrastructure, the importance of community groups is especially salient in our Japanese case study by Jun'ichi Kanzaka on Japanese civil engineering projects between the seventeenth and nineteenth centuries. In his case study, the overwhelming purpose of water control projects was to expand paddy agriculture and thus improve people's material welfare and assure their capacities to pay the high levels of taxation imposed by domain and shogun authorities. Households within village communities pursued their shared interest in developing water control investments with the support of their local governments. Kanzaka also notes how villages disagreed with one another over water use, illustrating the kinds of issues that Elinor Ostrom highlights in her analysis of common pool resources and in particular her concept of nested hierarchy of relations responsible for creating durable management of common pool resources.

Our Chinese case study, which, being in the capital region, may especially include state efforts, demonstrates a larger scale of bureaucratic organization and greater range of intended goals from infrastructure investment, including environmental protection, riverine commercial transport, agricultural productivity, and work relief for famine victims. In addition, the author Takehiko To also makes clear the temporal dimensions of the central government's effectiveness in promoting infrastructure expansion and maintenance; eighteenth-century successes could not be continued in the nineteenth century for environmental, economic, and political reasons. The specific array of priorities for infrastructure expressed in the capital region were certainly reflected more generally across the eighteenth-century empire, but the practicalities of raising capital and marshaling labor were not left in the hands of officials but also included both local elites and community groups, as the chapter on Chinese approaches to poverty and famine relief outlined. In both China and Japan such infrastructure activities involved community groups, elites, and government officials. In Chinese cases especially, official involvement occurred from the center, through the province, and down to the county. It is difficult to discern any sharp division between public and private goods in the conventional economic sense of the categories because both are present and, between them, we find the crucial role of organizing common pool resources. We have opted for expanding the "public" category to include a variety of nonmarket approaches that span being community based, elite led, and state managed. Such a taxonomy makes clearer the alternatives or complements to market-based activities. The same conclusion can be drawn from forest management, where we observe another set of ways that the conventional taxonomy of public and private goods can be usefully revised to include those goods usually not included in either.

In the contemporary world, we can distinguish between three ideal approaches to forestry management based on state control, entrepreneurial exploitation, and community-based decision making. In reality the three ideal logics are entwined in multiple ways—in some countries, like Nepal, governments have promoted community regulation of forest land, while in larger countries with forests subject to multiple objectives a far more complex set of policy practices has emerged over time, as can be observed in American government approaches to public and private forestlands in the Pacific Northwest (Edmonds 2002, Cashore and Howlett 2007). Turning to our German and Japanese case studies one last time, we see in the transitions from early modern times to policies of the late nineteenth century that German people's access to forestlands became increasingly limited even if not completely terminated at the same time as Japanese villagers' claims to forestland use were affirmed. When we add Yoshiyuki Aihara's study of Chinese forestland commons, we learn that a state's capacity to defend the commons could be limited, in the Chinese case by the scale of the empire. Aihara suggests that the subsequent twentieth-century evolution of policies toward forestlands as commons remained unresolved. Together these cases make an argument for recognizing that twentieth-century changes in forestland management could only be varied and complex, well beyond the simple contrast for the use of commons promoted by the paradigmatic English case of enclosures.

The kinds of forestland policies pursued in this book's case studies also form a modest counterpoint to one of the prominent themes in early modern global history as it has taken an environmental turn. The environmental historians' views of natural resource depletion in the early modern era in some ways echo our contemporary concerns. Arguments about and evidence of deforestation in China, Japan, and England point to resource constraints in the early modern world that make their situations more similar to our own than might otherwise seem plausible. At the same time, we have seen different early modern efforts to navigate the issues posed by forestland management that we might consider as we evaluate the diverse challenges and complexities confronted by policy makers today. In particular we have mentioned Japanese evidence of peasant afforestation and some Chinese and Prussian practices of tree planting to assure the maintenance of sources for the eighteenth-century commercial timber trade, alongside other policies demonstrating competition among alternative uses of forestlands and their products with resulting strains on the maintenance of forestlands in some cases.

A similar takeaway regarding the potential usefulness of considering early-modern-era practices for pondering contemporary challenges comes from looking one last time at issues of poverty and famine. Mitsuo Kinoshita stresses in his chapter the importance of micropolitics to understanding the particulars of addressing the issues of poverty and famine and the reasons for variation within a single country. To this observation we can add that variations among early modern countries can be associated with the distinct sets of political ideologies and institutions each had. Differences in political ideologies help account for the relative priority that governments assigned to addressing poverty and enacting famine relief. Nobel Prize laureate Amartya Sen famously has argued that famines are not simply caused by supply shortfalls but in fact can occur when there is food available—famine in such situations therefore results from the absence of entitlements that the poorest strata of society can claim on existing food supplies. He further suggests that the failure to recognize the entitlement of the poorest people to food is less likely in a democratic political system where a free press will expose state failures to protect subsistence (Sen 1981). Sen's argument highlights the linkage between a free press and unacceptability to people in general of living in society where the poor are starving. This truth works to explain popular expectations and state policies in democracies after World War II, but doesn't help us grapple with contrasts in poverty famine relief policies in early modern times.

Our Japanese, German, and English cases all point to the crucial roles of local actors, in the English case guided by directives coming from the central government and in the German case from a smaller-scale territorial state. The Chinese case in contrast highlights the existence of both a political ideology and state institutions that framed and motivated activity to address poverty and famine on more than local scales. While the chapter on China doesn't include any analysis of the micropolitics that Kinoshita uses to suggest the reason for contrasts among other case studies, it is certainly plausible to posit the importance of micropolitics within China as well. Certainly, the changes in central state capacities and proclivities to sustain infrastructure that Takehiko To observes based on his analysis of capital region water control fit with what Kenneth Pomeranz finds for the part of inland North China he studied and what Pierre-Etienne Will and I found for China's granary system (Pomeranz 1993, Will and Wong 1991). In all these cases the nineteenth-century diminishing of state capacities combined with a shift in central state priorities necessarily made the provision of public goods far more dependent on more local levels of decision making. That would of course change dramatically after 1949 when the party-state centralized and expanded state capacities but would also fail tragically to manage the famines resulting from the disasters of the Great Leap Forward (1958–1960).

Readers who have worked their way through all the individual chapters of this volume may well have some uncertainty about how to combine essays that treat different centuries, centered to be sure on the early modern era, but also reaching back into the late medieval and stretching into the modern era. There is of course a virtue in being able to place an early modern set of practices in a deeper historical perspective, as I tried to do earlier in this chapter regarding the two German case studies of part 3. Placing those two cases from the fifteenth and sixteenth century and eighteenth century in an even longer temporal frame allows us to reconstruct what many scholars have argued that early-modern-era political successes displayed, namely, the centralization of political power and the construction of larger bureaucratic capacities. This is a major theme in Victor Lieberman's critically acclaimed *Strange Parallels: Southeast Asia in Global Context, c. 800–1830* (Lieberman 2003, 2009). Brandenberg-Prussia is not one of Lieberman's case studies because he only considers histories of polities that exist in the world today. But the building of the early modern Prussian state meets the criteria of "strange parallels" through the end of Lieberman's period of coverage, circa 1830, but Prussia doesn't become a twentieth-century state. In other words, parallels at one moment of history don't predict continued similarities at a later date; only Lieberman's case selection guaranteed that outcome. At the same time we can note that early modern public goods practices in Prussia likely helped prepare this polity to take a leading role in constructing the modern German national state, a complex amalgam initially comprising twenty-five formerly autonomous states.

By broadening our conception of public finance from that used in contemporary times and for which a stark divide exists ideologically and institutionally from private finance, we offer a view of early modern practices addressing poverty and dearth, economic infrastructure, and natural resource management that embraces the efforts of political actors to act as economic agents by influencing the productive capacities of their economies and to address the limitations of their economies to provide adequately for all the people all of the time. These activities do not figure very visibly in our understanding of how public finance worked in the early modern era or in our more general understanding of the significance of public finance to the twin processes of modern state formation and economic development.

Regarding politics, the reasons relate to our persistent preoccupation with narratives of the fiscal-military state basic to the larger themes of modern state formation and from which concerns about economic development have spawned related ideas about the importance of public finance to economic development.

By looking at other ways early modern public finance mattered to economic life, we have built on the insights of scholars who have considered the ways in which the Japanese economy was supported by policies pursued in domains outside the control of the shogun's government. Such a vantage point encourages us to look at types of public finance that did not concern the competitive concerns of early modern European rulers. In the first instance we can conclude that there were in fact other important targets of public finance that affected economic possibilities and prosperity in early modern times. These targets, including poverty and dearth, economic infrastructure, and natural resource management, certainly have been studied by specialists for quite some time, but their research fails to fit comfortably within more general narratives of historical change.

This volume has focused on the early modern era to view ways in which governments and elites addressed subjects they deemed important to their economic prosperity and the material well-being of their poorer neighbors in two parts of East Asia and two parts of Europe. Each of these places became important sites of economic development at some point between the late eighteenth-century onset of industrialization and the present day. We have considered the ways in which government agents, especially those below the level of a central state according to the norms crystalized in the nineteenth century, often played crucial roles in creating public goods important to the growth potential of their respective societies and to addressing the problems of poverty and dangers of dearth. Our findings are no substitute for but rather a complement to the more common concern expressed for what centralizing early modern European states did to increase their fiscal capacities in order to garner resources to build military strength.

Even as multiple paths from early-modern-era public goods provision to modern-era public finance become more visible from the kinds of topics covered in this volume, we also recognize that what had been a largely European interstate geopolitical competition in early modern times was transformed by the late nineteenth century into a form of competition found in other world regions as well. Thus, Japan's geopolitical rise in East Asia entailed its state undertaking military mobilizations akin to those of an earlier century in Europe. These in turn depended on the state extracting more revenue and devoting more effort toward expanding the country's war-making potential. What differed between Japan's rise in East Asia compared to Britain's rise within Europe beginning some two centuries earlier was the kind of economy providing the state its much needed resources—eighteenth-century British economic success was founded upon its commercial capitalism and late-nineteenth-century Japan was building the world's first non-Western industrial capitalist economy. Those industrial capacities also mattered to Germany's geopolitical rise following its relatively late formation, within a European context, as a national state. Germany's pursuit of geopolitical gain was premised on its expanding industrial might affirmed by its becoming Europe's largest economy by the turn of the twentieth century. Germany was thus able to pursue geopolitical competition within Europe that had evolved out of a pattern present in Europe in early modern times, much as Japan was able to extend what had been a more specifically European geopolitical process to East Asia in the late nineteenth and early twentieth centuries.

At the other end of the modern era, our present moment in contemporary history, the modern-era priority on economic growth as the focus for understanding economic development and dynamics has required some reframing as we increasingly acknowledge limitations to continued economic growth and recognize the intimate relations between economy and environment. We have become more aware since the late twentieth century about issues that were early-modern-era concerns regarding poverty and dearth, economic infrastructure, and natural resource management. The issues of poverty and vulnerability to food shortages affect not only people living in areas lacking access to modern technologies and the abilities to improve agriculture or develop industries, but also people in well-developed societies where gaps between rich and poor have been growing in some places for much of the past several decades. Neither markets nor states, whether separately or together, seem adequate to meet the present-day challenges of conceiving food availability in ways that increase access to those in need of sustenance, thus making the examples of how related issues were confronted in other times and places possibly relevant to our construction of policy alternatives.

Another weakness of markets and states concerns the maintenance of economic infrastructure in mature economies and the inabilities to expand infrastructure where economies lack such facilities. The popularity of the concept of "public private partnerships" to characterize a mix of government and private sector efforts to fund and manage large-scale infrastructure projects points to contemporary realities more in line with early-modern-era practices than those of the modern era when states had been able to fund and manage public goods and services that included infrastructure. Finally, among our three topic areas, forest management today involves a public goods aspect that extends the range of issues understood in the early modern era due to the role that large forests can play in carbon capture, a process crucial to environmental sustainability threatened by forest destruction, the economic value of which for conversion of land into commercially productive prosperity motivates deforestation.[1] Responses to the negative environmental implications of deforestation are of course part of a contemporary awareness of the dangers posed by climate change, yet they also represent an awareness of the different groups of people who benefit from forests as a public good that transcends the dichotomy of public and private enshrined in the state/market binary.

We hope this volume has persuaded the patient reader who has taken in the pictures of Japanese, Chinese, Prussian, and (for one of our cases) British scenes of early-modern-era public goods provision addressing poverty and dearth, economic infrastructure, and forestry management to recognize important traits of public goods and public finance that help explain why that era was both connected to and different from the modern era covering the nineteenth and twentieth centuries, and yet resembles in other ways the world through which we make our way today.

NOTES

1. To compensate for the economic value of destroying forests, a multilevel effort reducing emissions from deforestation and forest degradation in developing countries (REDD+) was launched in 2008 by the United Nations. Among the contributors is the Norwegian government, which has made major investments to reduce greenhouse gas emissions caused by deforestation and forest degradation. The effort is under the Ministry of Climate and Environment and includes a component geared toward supporting civil society organizations contributing to the goals of REDD+. www.un-redd.org/; www. norad.no/en/front/funding/climate-and-forest-initiative-support-scheme/.

REFERENCES

Andrade, Tonio (2016). *The Gunpowder Age: China, Military Innovation, and the Rise of the West in World History*. Princeton University Press.

Bello, David (2015). *Across Mountain, Steppe, and Forest: Environment, Identity, and Empire in Qing China's Borderlands*. Cambridge University Press.

Bogart, Dan (2005). "Turnpike Trusts and the Transportation Revolution in 18th Century England." *Explorations in Economic History* 42:479–508.

——— (2011). "Did the Glorious Revolution Contribute to the Transport Revolution? Evidence from Investment in Roads and Rivers." *Economic History Review* 64 (4): 1073–1112.

Bonney, Richard (1999). "Introduction." In *The Rise of the Fiscal State in Europe, c. 1200–1815*, edited by Richard Bonney. Oxford University Press.

Brewer, John (1989). *The Sinews of Power: War, Money, and the English State, 1688–1783*. Alfred A. Knopf.

Cardoso, José Luís, and Pedro Lains, eds. (2010). *Paying for the Liberal State: The Rise of Public Finance in Nineteenth-Century Europe*. Cambridge University Press.

Cashore, Benjamin, and Michael Howlett (2007). "Punctuating Which Equilibrium? Understanding Thermostatic Policy Dynamics in Pacific Northwest Forestry." *American Journal of Political Science* 51 (3): 532–551.

Daunton, Martin (2010). "Creating Legitimacy: Administering Taxation in Britain, 1815–1914." In *Paying for the Liberal State: The Rise of Public Finance in Nineteenth-Century Europe*, edited by José Luís Cardoso and Pedro Lains, 27–56. Cambridge University Press.

De Vries, Piet (2013). "The Modern Public-Private Demarcation: History and Trends in PPP." In *The Routledge Companion to Public-Private Partnerships*, edited by Piet de Vries and Etienne B. Yehoue, 9–28. Routledge.

Edmonds, Eric (2002). "Government Initiated Community Resource Management and Local Resource Extraction from Nepal's Forests." *Journal of Development Economics* 68 (1): 89–115.

Harling, Philip, and Peter Mandler (1993). "From 'Fiscal-Military' State to Laissez-Faire State, 1760–1850." *Journal of British Studies* 32:44–70.

Hocquet, Jean-Claude (1995). "City-State and Market Economy." In *Economic Systems and State Finance*, edited by Richard Bonney, 81–100. Clarendon.

Innes, Joanna (2009). *Inferior Politics: Social Policies and Social Problems in Eighteenth-Century Britain*. Oxford University Press.

Janssens, Paul (2012). "Taxation in the Habsburg Low Countries and Belgium, 1579–1914." In *The Rise of Fiscal States: A Global History, 1500–1914*, edited by Bartolomé Yun-Casalilla and Patrick K. O'Brien, 67–92. Cambridge University Press.

Lieberman, Victor (2003, 2009). *Strange Parallels Southeast Asia in Global Context, c.800–1830*. 2 vols. Cambridge University Press.

Lindert, Peter (2004). *Growing Public: Social Spending and Economic Growth since the Eighteenth Century*. 2 vols. Cambridge University Press.

Menzies, Nicholas (1994). *Forest and Land Management in Imperial China*. Macmillan.

Miller, Ian (2015). *Roots and Branches: Woodland Institutions in South China, 800–1600*, PhD diss., Harvard University. Digital Access to Scholarship at Harvard.

O'Brien, Patrick K. (2012). "Afterword: Reflections on Fiscal Foundations and Contexts for the Formation of Economically Effective Eurasian States from the Rise of Venice to the Opium War." In *The Rise of Fiscal States: A Global History, 1500–1914*, edited by Bartolomé Yun-Casalilla and Patrick K. O'Brien, 442–453. Cambridge University Press.

Ormrod, W. M., and János Barta (1995), "The Feudal Structure and the Beginnings of State Finance." In *Economic Systems and State Finance*, edited by Richard Bonney, 53–79. Clarendon.

Pomeranz, Kenneth (1993). *From Core to Hinterland: State, Society, and Economy in Inland North China, 1900–1937*. University of California Press.

Rosenberg, Hans (1958). *Bureaucracy, Aristocracy and Autocracy: The Prussian Experience, 1660–1815*. Harvard University Press.

Scott, Anthony (2008). *The Evolution of Resource Property Rights*. Oxford University Press.

Sen, Amartya (1981). *Poverty and Famines: An Essay on Entitlement and Deprivation*. Oxford University Press.

Tilly, Charles, ed. (1975). *The Formation of National States in Western Europe*. Princeton University Press.

——— (1992). *Capital, Coercion, and European States, AD 990–1992*. Basil Blackwell.

Will, Pierre-Etienne, and R. Bin Wong, with James Lee and contributions by Jean Oi and Peter Perdue (1991). *Nourish the People: The State Civilian Granary System in China, 1650–1850*. University of Michigan Center for Chinese Studies.

Wong, R. Bin (1997). *China Transformed: Historical Change and the Limits of European Experience*. Cornell University Press.

Yamamoto, Koji (2018). *Taming Capitalism before Its Triumph*. Oxford University Press.

Yun-Casalilla, Bartolomé, and Patrick K. O'Brien, eds. (2012). *The Rise of Fiscal States: A Global History, 1500–1914*. Cambridge University Press.

Zhang, Meng (2017). *Timber Trade along the Yangtze River: Market, Institutions, and Environment, 1750–1911*. PhD diss., UCLA.

Yoshiyuki Aihara is Research Fellow in Tōyō Bunko (The Oriental Library), Tokyo. His publications include "The Distribution Mechanism of Timber in Southeastern Guizhou Qingshui-Jiang Valley during the Mid-Qing Period" (in Japanese, *Socio-Economic History* 72, no. 5 [2007]) and "Jingping Documents and Routine Memorials to the Ministry of Justice" in *Jinping Documents and Legal Culture Research,* edited by Q. Gao and G. Wang (in Chinese, China University of Political Science and Law Press, 2017).

Takeshi Aoki is Postdoctoral Researcher at Keio University, Tokyo. He specializes in Japanese economic history, especially the history of forestland management. His publications include "Management of the Forest Owned in Common and the Development of the Postwar Urgent Plan of the Disafforestation" (in Japanese, *Journal of Japanese History* 609 [2013]).

Kenichiro Aratake is Associate Professor at the Center for Northeast Asian Studies, Tohoku University, Japan. His publications include *Circulation of Night-Soil in Early Modern Japan* (in Japanese, Seibundō Shuppan, 2015) and *The Modern Local History of Northeast Japan* (edited, in Japanese, Iwata Shoin, 2016).

Sascha Bütow works as a Research Assistant at the Zentrum für Mittelalterausstellungen (ZMA) in Magdeburg, Germany. He is the author of *Straßen im Fluss* (Lukas, 2015) and coeditor of *Das Mittelalter endet gestern*

(Lukas, 2014). His research interests are medieval history, Brandenburg and comparative regional history, and history of transportation and infrastructure.

JONATHAN HEALEY is Associate Professor in social history at the University of Oxford. He has written a number of articles on early modern English social history, as well as *The First Century of Welfare* (Boydell, 2014).

TAKASHI IIDA is Professor of economic history at Keio University, Tokyo. He has worked on the rural history of Brandenburg-Prussia and published *Ruppiner Bauernleben, 1648–1806* (Lukas, 2010) and "The Practice of Timber Granting from Lords to Peasants" (*Agricultural History* 87 [2013]), among others.

HEINRICH KAAK is Assistant Professor in the regional history of Brandenburg at University of Potsdam, Germany. He is the author of publications on the history of Brandenburg and Berlin such as a microhistory of the village of Alt-Quilitz/ Neuhardenberg, *Eigenwillige Bauern* (Berliner Wissenschaftsverlag, 2010), and an investigation of the bottomland cultivation by the Order of Saint John, *Korporative Gutsherrschaft* (Berliner Wissenschaftsverlag, 2012).

JUNICHI KANZAKA is Professor at the Faculty of Economics, Soka University, Japan. His publications include "Villein Rents in Thirteenth-Century England" (*Economic History Review* 60, no. 4 [2002]) and "Manorialisation and Demographic Pressure in Medieval England" (*Journal of Historical Geography* 60 [2018]).

MITSUO KINOSHITA is Professor in Japanese history at Faculty of Letters, Nara University, Japan. His publications include *Poverty and Poor Relief in Early Modern Rural Japan* (in Japanese, Jinbun Shoin, 2017) and *The Frontiers of Japanese History*, vols. 1 and 2 (in Japanese, coedited with K. Aratake and M. Ōta, Hōsei Daigaku Shuppankyoku, 2015).

KAZUHO SAKAI is Lecturer in economic history at Department of History, University of Sacred Heart, Tokyo. He is the author of "Unifying Regional Society through Sharing a Common Fund" (in Japanese, *Socio-Economic History* 84, no. 2 [2018]).

MASAYUKI TANIMOTO is Professor in economic history at Graduate School of Economics, University of Tokyo. His publications include *The Role of Tradition in Japan's Industrialization* (edited, Oxford University Press, 2006) and "From Peasant Economy to Urban Agglomeration," in *Labour-Intensive Industrialization in Global History*, edited by G. Austin and K. Sugihara (Routledge, 2013).

TAKEHIKO TO is Professor in Chinese history at Faculty of Humanities and Social Sciences, Kumamoto University, Japan. His publications include *The History of Economic Policy in the Qing Dynasty* (in Japanese, Kyūkoshoin, 2011).

R. BIN WONG is Distinguished Professor of history at University of California, Los Angeles. His publications include *China Transformed* (Cornell University Press, 1997) and *Before and Beyond Divergence* (coauthored with Jean-Laurent Rosenthal, Harvard University Press, 2011).

INDEX

Abe, Takeo, 133
Acemoglu, Daron, 2
Age of Civil Wars (Japan), 13
agricultural productivity. *See* productivity
agriculture, in Tokugawa shogunate, 15
Aihara, Yoshiyuki, 236
Allemeyer, Marie Luisa, 173, 176, 177, 180
alms, (*kayu-segyō*), 83, 87
almshouses, 107
Alt-Ruppin forest management and use:
building codes, 242, 243; compartment vs.
selection cutting, 243, 244; conservation
and afforestation, 239, 243, 247, 308; and
farm-owning peasants, 241–43; forest
authorities/management, 240–42; forest
revenues, 241–42, 249; livestock pasturing
and litter gathering, 244–45, 247–48, 248*t.*;
overgrazing, 247–49; potato cultivation, 245,
249; wood gathering entitlements, 238, 241,
243–44, 246, 247
Alt-Ruppin forest management reforms: access
fees, 250; entitlement redemptions, 245–46,
245–49, 248*t.*; redemption of entitlements,
249–50, 251; resistance to reform, 236, 245,
246; revenue increasing strategies in, 241,
242; usufructuary peasants and eviction
threat, 121–22, 235, 241, 243, 246; wood
gathering rights redemption, 249–51
Alt-Ruppin social structure: cottagers (*Büdner*),
120, 240, 241*t.*; demesne lord's obligations, 238;

direct management of (royal forests), 236,
298; forests in, 239, 240; impact of Seven
Years' war on, 242; large peasants (*Bauern*),
240, 241*t.*; lodgers (*Einlieger*), 119–20, 239,
240, 241*t.*, 242, 244; settler colonies in, 240,
242; small peasants (*Kossäten*) in, 240, 241*t.*
annual tribute (Tokugawa land levy): *See also*
outsourcing domain finances: calculation of,
39, 42–43; and county magistrates, 49–50,
52, 53; and fiscal deficits (lord's), 57–58; and
markets, 15; Meiji reforms and, 29; rates,
15–19, 18*fig.*, 25–56; and reserve funds, 28;
social obligations arising from, 38; and
structural change, 24–26; village collection
of, 40, 41, 44–47, 54n7
Aoki, Takeshi, 236
Appleby, Andrew B., 112
Aratake, Kenichiro, 16
Aruga, Kizaemon, 34
Asao, Naohiro, 157, 158
Assing, Helmut, 188
assize judges, 104

Basic Law for the Federal Republic of
Germany, 216
Bauch, Martin, 223
Baumann, Max, 222
Becker, Hartmuth, 183
beggars/begging: England, 107; Japan, 82, 83, 87,
88, 95n1; Prussia, 124–25, 124*t.*, 127n25

319

CPSIA information can be obtained
at www.ICGtesting.com
Printed in the USA
LVHW040457011218
598855LV00005B/7